The Dissent
of the
Governed
Alienation and
Democracy in America

This is a volume of

Quantitative Studies in Social Relations

Consulting Editor: Peter H. Rossi, University of Massachusetts,
Amherst, Massachusetts

A complete list of titles in this series appears at the end of this volume.

THE
DISSENT
OF THE
GOVERNED

Alienation and Democracy in America

James D. Wright

Department of Sociology
University of Massachusetts
Amherst, Massachusetts

ACADEMIC PRESS   New York San Francisco London   1976
A Subsidiary of Harcourt Brace Jovanovich, Publishers

ACADEMIC PRESS, INC.
111 Fifth Avenue, New York, New York 10003

United Kingdom Edition published by
ACADEMIC PRESS, INC. (LONDON) LTD.
24/28 Oval Road, London NW1

Library of Congress Cataloging in Publication Data

Wright, James D.
     The dissent of the governed.

     (Quantitative studies in social relations)
     Bibliography: p.
     Includes index.
     1.   Political sociology.   2.   Alienation
(Social psychology)   3.   United States—Politics
and government—1945-   4.   United States—
Social conditions—1945-   I.   Title.
JA76.W7   1976   301.5'92   75-32037
ISBN 0—12—765050—4

Contents

Acknowledgments

There is no adequate expression of gratitude for time, advice, and assistance rendered freely on one's behalf. Let me merely note that the persons and organizations to be mentioned have all contributed immeasurably to the research reported in this book, for which I am deeply thankful.

The initial idea of the manuscript, and many of its specific components, originate with Richard F. Hamilton, whose patience and thorough criticism have exceeded all that could be reasonably expected, even from one's friends. David Elesh monitored the day-to-day proceedings of the research and prevented many stylistic and analytic excesses from ever reaching print. Peter Rossi likewise contributed many valuable suggestions and provided the necessary encouragement for moving the work into its final form. Certainly my life, and hopefully my book, have been enriched through my association with these men.

The manuscript has also been blessed by the critical advice of several people, among them Robert Alford, Warren Hagstrom, Peter Hall, Roberta McKown, Russell Middleton, Clark Roof, Randall Stokes, Curt Tausky, and Sonia Wright, and, more generally, my graduate student and faculty colleagues at Wisconsin and Massachusetts. It is painful to admit to the deficiencies that they have corrected, but, at the same time, I am grateful for the tact and grace with which their wisdom was dispensed.

Most of the data utilized in this book were supplied by the Inter-University Consortium for Political Research, to which all scholars in the social and political sciences owe an enormous debt. The Data and Program Library Service (University of Wisconsin) and the Survey Archive for the Social Sciences (University of Massachusetts) also aided in procuring and processing the surveys analyzed here. Additional materials were made available by the National Opinion Research Center, through the auspices of the Roper Public Opinion Research Center (Williams College). The comparative evidence cited in Chapter 5 was supplied by the Amsterdams Sociaalwetenschappelijk Data Archief. A special note of thanks is due Evert Brouwer,

Director of ASDA, for preparing these comparative materials. My indebtedness to the aforementioned organizations, while vast, does not extend to the conclusions or analysis reported here, for which I retain full responsibility.

The Madison Academic Computer Center (University of Wisconsin) and the University Computing Center (University of Massachusetts) gave freely of their computer time and expertise. Especially able assistance in this regard was provided by Terry Bolsover and Scott Schreiner. I should also like to thank the Social and Demographic Research Institute (University of Massachusetts) for having supplied secretarial help, additional computer consultation, and, most importantly, for creating an intellectual environment in which research of this sort is possible.

The wearisome tasks of typing this manuscript, proofreading it, checking the bibliography, and otherwise attending to critical details were competently performed by Marcia Alves, Sue Herman, Hazel Kirouac, Laura Martin, Diane Waldman, and Valerie Wood.

Financial support for this research has been provided by a Graduate Fellowship from the Ford Foundation and by Faculty Research Grants from the University of Massachusetts. The Third European Summer School for Training in Comparative Research provided an opportunity to discuss my results with scholars throughout the world. In addition to the funds themselves, I am also honored by the confidence that they represent.

Finally, I extend a special note of love and thanks to my wife and sons, who have tried mightily, with little success, to keep things in their proper perspective.

Credits

Owing to the nature of this book, it has been necessary to quote selected passages from several sources. The following authors and publishers have graciously extended their permission in this matter:

Abcarian, G., and S. M. Stanage, Alienation and the radical right, *Journal of Politics* 27:4 (November, 1965).

Aberbach, J. D., Alienation and political behavior, *American Political Science Review* 63:1 (March, 1969).

From Thomas R. Dye and L. Harmon Zeigler, *The irony of democracy: An uncommon introduction to American politics*, Third Edition © 1975 by Wadsworth Publishing Company, Inc., Belmont, Ca. 94002. Used with permission of the publisher, Duxbury Press.

Easton, D., *A systems analysis of political life* © 1965 by John Wiley & Sons, Inc. Used with permission of John Wiley & Sons, Inc.

Easton, D., and J. Dennis, *Children in the political system* © 1969 by the McGraw Hill Book Company. Used with permission of the McGraw Hill Book Company.

Easton, D., and J. Dennis, The child's acquisition of regime norms: Political efficacy, *American Political Science Review* 61:1 (March, 1967).

Form, W., and J. Huber, Income, race, and the ideology of political efficacy, *Journal of Politics* 33:3 (August, 1971).

Gamson, W. A., *Power and discontent* © 1968 by W. A. Gamson, published by Dorsey Press.

Horton, J. E., and W. E. Thompson, Powerlessness and political negativism: A study of defeated local referendums, *American Journal of Sociology* 67:5 (March, 1962) © by the University of Chicago Press.

Kornhauser, W., *The politics of mass society* © 1959 by the Free Press.

Lipset, S. M., *Political man: The social bases of politics* © 1960 by S. M. Lipset.

Mason, G., and D. Jaros, Alienation and support for demagogues, *Polity* 1:4 (Summer, 1969).

Miller, A. H., Political issues and trust in government: 1964–1970, *American Political Science Review* 68:3 (September, 1974).

Thompson, W. E., and J. E. Horton, Political alienation as a force in political action, *Social Forces* 38:3 (March, 1960).

Permission for more extended quotation has been granted by the following:

pp. 50–52 and elsewhere: Selections from Gabriel A. Almond and Sidney Verba, *The civic culture: Political attitudes and democracy in five nations* © 1963 by Princeton University Press; Little Brown and Company, Inc. © 1965, pp. 74–490. Reprinted by permission of Princeton University Press.

pp. 282–283 and elsewhere: Campbell, A., P. E. Converse, W. E. Miller, and D. E. Stokes, *The American voter* (© 1960 by John Wiley & Sons, Inc.), reprinted by permission of John Wiley & Sons, Inc.

p. 48: Rogin, M. P., *The intellectuals and McCarthy: The radical specter* © 1967 by the Massachusetts Institute of Technology.

Parts of this book have been published elsewhere and, although rewritten, also appear here by kind permission of the original publishers. My thanks for the use of the following:

From Richard F. Hamilton and James D. Wright, *New directions in political sociology* © 1975 by the Bobbs-Merrill Company, Inc., reprinted by permission of the publisher.

J. D. Wright, Does acquiescence bias the SRC Index of Political Efficacy? *Public Opinion Quarterly* 39:2 (Summer, 1975).

J. D. Wright, Political socialization research: the 'primacy' principle, *Social Forces* 54:1 (September, 1975).

J. D. Wright, Alienation and political negativism: New evidence from national surveys, *Sociology and Social Research* 60:2 (January, 1976).

Introduction: The Theory of Political Alienation

Sociological theories persist, occasionally because they accord with bodies of relevant evidence, but more often because they nurture imagery that seems plausible at face value. A case in point is what might be called the "theory of political alienation," the focal concern of this book.

The imagery of alienation that informs this theory includes the following major components: First, political alienation is a potentially dangerous, irrational, phobic, or pathological phenomenon that poses hazards for stable and effective democratic government. Second, this alienation is rooted in certain social processes endemic to modernization, such as urbanization, industrialization, bureaucratization—in short, massification. An important corollary, then, is that modern democratic societies are essentially fragile structures whose stability requires that "the reservoir of discontent—always present—is not activated (Mason and Jaros 1969:481)."

The potential hazards posed by political alienation can also be enumerated. First, the alienated are susceptible to extremist, particularly right-wing, ideological movements and programs. The intolerable conditions of the present lead to a longing for a more pleasant past and, thus, to candidates, leaders, or movements that promise the elusive "restoration." Coupled with their tendency to extremist politics is a pervasive negativism directed toward the existing political institutions. The alienated believe that all politicians are corrupt, that there are few important differences between what the established parties and candidates stand for, that politics are for all practical pur-

1

poses, a case of " 'them' trying to put 'this' over on 'us' (Thompson and Horton 1960:191)."

Thus, their alienation and negativism lead the discontented to withdraw from politics under normal circumstances; yet these same attributes increase their "availability to groups with dictatorial ambitions (Mannheim 1940: 87)." Lacking the political restraints implied in cohesive social communities, the alienated are readied for service in mass movements "bent on transformations of the world (Kornhauser 1959:61)." They form a natural constituency for demagogues and, therefore, may upset the stability of democratic government in the modern era.

Since there are social strains posed by industrialization and modernization that favor the development of alienation, and since its existence raises problems for democratic government, it follows that stable democracies must insure themselves against the growth of alienation or, alternatively, protect themselves against the consequences. A democracy, in turn, will be stable only if it discharges these tasks. The "theory of political alienation," then, can be subdivided into three major premises: (1) Political alienation leads to threatening and dangerous political behavior; therefore, (2) stable democracies develop structures that minimize alienation or prevent it from getting out of hand; finally (3) a stable democracy is ipso facto one in which political alienation is kept at a chronically low ebb. This, in barest outline, is the theory that we are examining.

Like many sociological theories, this is more a loose set of assumptions and concepts than a tight body of deductively organized sociological principles. Much of its logical "structure" must be imposed from without; there is no single text or theorist with which it may be accurately identified. Still, the theory of political alienation has played its role in many recent theoretical developments in political science and sociology and has figured prominently in scholarly explanations of most important political events to have occurred in the West in the last three decades.[1] Unfortunately, as we demonstrate in the text, systematic attention to its empirical claims has been inversely proportional to its popularity in the field.[2]

---

[1] One key source puts it as follows:

> Political alienation is a phenomenon of fundamental importance in political processes. Recent empirical research, employing a variety of measures, has found alienation to be significantly associated with a wide range of political behaviors, including revolutionary behavior, reformism, support for demagogues, non-voting, protest voting, participation in radical political movements, and vicarious use of the mass media. [I]t is now widely accepted that the magnitude and distribution of political alienation are significantly related to the stability, integration, and development of political systems. Alienation, then, appears to be a fundamental human political orientation [Schwartz 1973:ix].

[2] Those somewhat familiar with the literature on political alienation may initially wish to take issue with this statement. In most recent accounts, for example, there is a recurring assumption that massive amounts of empirical evidence exist to support the

Due to the "looseness" of the theory that informs it, the slippage between assumption and evidence has probably been as great in the study of political alienation as in any other subfield of political sociology. Typical instances of this would be the study of a defeated fluoridation referendum whose theoretical sustenance is drawn from commentaries on the Fascist experience in Western Europe, or the small local study concerned with local political issues, where conclusions are drawn about wholesale disruptions said to leave entire political systems reeling in their wake. (Specific examples of these and related "slippages" are provided in Chapter 3.) The net result, as we show later, has been a body of assertions—extremely interesting and important assertions at that—whose empirical merit remains largely unexplored.

The intention of this book is to redress the imbalance between evidence and assertion and thereby to come to some conclusions concerning the empirical plausibility of political alienation theory as a whole. At key junctures, however, the theory is sufficiently ambiguous to rule out a decisive test. There is, for example, not even a firm consensus as to how one best measures the alienation phenomenon. The supply of candidate indices in the literature is expansive, yet little effort has been spent in tracing the correlations among them.[3] This results in the further frustration of uncertain comparability from one study to the next. (The proliferation of essays "on the meaning of alienation," moreover, has had little discernible impact on this situation.)

On the other hand, some agreement has emerged on the following basic points: First, it is now universally conceded that alienation is a multi-dimensional concept (e.g., Seeman 1959). Alienation from self, work, friends, religion, and politics does not necessarily cohere in one tight, unitary package. Consensus on this point has required that the many dimensions of alienation be kept conceptually and empirically distinct, and this, in turn, has allowed for the development of a "theory of *political* alienation" which is analytically separate from the more generally conceived "theory of alienation." Let it be emphasized at the outset, then, that the former and *not* the latter theory is the concern of this book. A second point might also be emphasized here: we shall address only those aspects of the theory that are amenable to empirical examination. As we shall see later, this rules out a fair amount.[4]

---

various components of political alienation theory. In this respect, the Schwartz passage cited in the preceding footnote is characteristic. A more detailed and critical review of this literature (see Chap. 3), however, suggests only *two* empirical points that could reasonably be said to have been confirmed by methodologically persuasive research: First, alienation, however measured, decreases as social status increases, and, second, with regard to politics, the alienated participate less.

[3] The effort that has been expended along these lines, moreover, has led to little by way of firm conclusion (see Dean 1961; Dodder 1969; McDill 1961; Middleton 1963; and Simmons 1966.) These studies are critically reviewed by Schwartz (1973:6–7), who concludes that "the empirical investigations of the subject show very mixed results."

[4] The study of alienation has, from its inception, been infused with largely unresearchable philosophical undertones and themes, many of which can only be described as neo-

There is also an emerging consensus, best expressed by Gamson, that the phenomenon of political alienation is itself multi-dimensional: "Political alienation includes both an efficacy (or input) dimension and a trust (or output) dimension (1968:42)." Likewise, Seeman cautions us to distinguish "between two forms of alienation that are often blurred; namely, between powerlessness and distrust (1972:401)." Other contributors to this consensus include Finifter (1970), whose analysis also suggests two dimensions to the political alienation concept, perceived powerlessness or inefficacy and political normlessness (close to but not identical to Gamson's dimension of trust); and Olsen (1969), whose "two categories of political alienation," incapability and discontentment, are the equivalent of efficacy and trust. Thus, in addition to limiting the analysis to political alienation, we treat the efficacy and trust components separately.

Concerning the validity of these decisions, we are reinforced by several points. First, as we argue later, there is ample theoretical reason to treat the concept of political alienation independently of other forms, or, in other words, there is a definable theory of *political* alienation whose confirmation or refutation requires this strategy. Within this theory, there is sufficient cause for treating the efficacy and trust dimensions separately. Moreover, despite the panoply of conceptualizations and indices already mentioned, our measures of efficacy and trust are by far the most commonly encountered. (These indices, the well-known Survey Research Center (SRC) political alienation scales, are described in Chapter 4.) Finally, as a practical matter, these measures happen to be available in the surveys at our disposal.

One implication of the preceding comments needs now to be discussed, namely, that we are attracted to the measures of efficacy and trust not so much in their own right as because of their centrality in the literature. In other words, the "hard" evidence which does exist on the theory of political alienation is based primarily on measures identical to or very similar to those employed in this research. Their use here means that we have accepted the common wisdom concerning the "meaning and measurement" of political alienation and have acquiesced in the view that it is defined by the components of efficacy and trust. These choices maintain maximum comparability between this and the bulk of prior work and serve to locate this research *within* the tradition against which it eventually argues. This, in turn, absolves

Hegelian in intent and focus. One treatment, for example, defines alienation as "a structural deformation of sociality," links the concept to "the intentionality of role-taking," and then adds, "conjoined in this way, alienation and intentionality are noetic correlates which undergird and constitute roles and role-taking (Natanson, 1967:256–257)." These aspects of the theory of alienation, even when they have an overt political dimension, are assiduously avoided throughout the book.

us from having to decide how *best* to measure political alienation; the manner in which it is *usually* measured suffices.[5]

There is a second implication that also requires some comment, namely, that the concern of this book is political alienation as a *mass political phenomenon*, as a concept that may be more or less appropriate in describing the political orientations and behaviors of populations sufficiently numerous to appear in sizable numbers in representative samples of the politically eligible adult population of the United States. This implies, for example, that we shall have relatively little to say about the political alienation of campus rebels, militant blacks, or right-wing paramilitaries. There is little doubt that political alienation figures prominently in movements such as these, but, at the same time, none of them even approach the status of a mass political movement, in the strictly statistical sense of the term. As such, they fall outside the purview of the current concern. Readers who are interested in alienation as an explanation of such phenomena would be well served by volumes such as Flacks (1971), Keniston (1965), and especially Schwartz (1973).

Another troublesome source of ambiguity is that, at critical junctures, the theory is formulated such that it is virtually immune to empirical refutation. For example, where in the continuum from all to none does the alienation of the citizenry begin to produce observable effects? Or what are the political circumstances that transform apathy into mobilization? Attempts to answer such questions are infrequent, and, where they exist, they are distressingly nonspecific: "when alienation reaches an intolerable level," "when the circumstances are proper," "when the right leader presents himself." Seldom is there a clear statement of what a proper circumstance, right leader, or intolerable level would be. Thus, the theory protects itself against negative evidence by appealing to an indefinite future; that is, there always exists some hypothetical future in which the theory *will* be confirmed in all its worrisome detail.

These ambiguities have caused us to forgo the "logic of disconfirmation" in favor of the "logic of limiting cases" as our operant argumentative mode. In the classic version of scientific method, one begins with some hypothetical effect thought to be observable under certain necessary or initial conditions;

---

[5] In this respect, then, we claim a certain measure of "consensual validation" for the alienation indices employed in this research (see Chaps. 4 and 5). These indices, to some extent, *define* the body of literature with which we are concerned. On this basis, we have treated lightly the cogent methodological critiques of these indices now available in the literature (e.g., Asher, 1974; Balch, 1974) and, likewise, recent attempts to reconceptualize the political alienation phenomenon (e.g., Schwartz 1973). To borrow a phrase from Thomas Kuhn, the following research is best understood as "normal science" in the fullest sense of the term. In our opinion, there is relatively too much effort spent in the social sciences in "breaking new ground" and relatively too little spent in seeing whether anything will grow on ground that has already been broken.

then one "disconfirms" (or "fails to confirm") the theory by demonstrating first that the initial conditions hold and, second, that the hypothesized effect was not observed. One can say fairly that the theory of political alienation is a marvel of detail concerning hypothetical effects but somewhat lax in specifying conditions under which those effects should be expected. Thus, we are told *what* to look for, but not precisely where or when. As a practical solution to the problem, we have looked for effects whenever and wherever the data allow it; failing to observe them, we can thus note initial conditions under which those effects were *not* observed. Such an enumeration simply delineates the set of *potential* initial conditions under which the theory is less than fully plausible.

The "potential conditions" explored in this research are those of the social and political history of the United States from 1956 to 1970. Included in our consideration, then, are the "calm" Eisenhower years, the tail end of the "cold war," the election and subsequent assassination of John Kennedy, agitation for civil rights, including the "sit-down," "sit-in," and "civil disobedience" movements that it spawned, the radical rightist candidacy of Barry Goldwater, the rise and fall of Lyndon Johnson and Richard Nixon, the demagoguery of George Wallace and the so-called "white backlash" that created and sustained him, periods of economic growth and decay, the birth and death of the counterculture and the youth revolt, race riots, rising crime, turmoil on the campuses, rebellion in the streets, and, finally, the source of much of this—the war in Vietnam. This, we believe, represents a broad array of opportunities for alienation theory to make accurate predictions; in other words, we think it a fair test to ask that the theory make sense in the context of these political events. To subtract from its initial conditions the social and political history of the United States in the last two decades, in short, is to render the theory empirically empty and is functionally equivalent to its disconfirmation.

These several related characteristics of the theory of interest—its ambiguity at key points, its "looseness" and lack of deductive structure, its diffusion throughout a large body of conceptual and empirical materials in both sociology and political science, and the absence of a single theorist with whom it may be fully identified—have all required, in order to obtain an adequate grasp of the thesis and its components, that we discuss in some detail the flow of sociopolitical theorizing since World War II and locate the theory of political alienation within it. These are the primary concerns of the first three chapters. In these chapters, we review the major studies and theoretical statements bearing on the phenomenon of political alienation, discuss a rather imposing body of seemingly disparate writings that implicitly define the major elements of the theory, and distill those essential theoretical principles that bind it into a single conceptual unit.

In the main, we isolate four streams of sociopolitical thinking whose confluence produces the theory of political alienation: the theories of *democratic elitism*, the *mass society*, *social pluralism*, and *consensus*. From these varying perspectives, a theory about the relationship between alienation and democracy ultimately emerges; this theory, in turn, is our main concern for the remainder of the book.

Of the four, the theory of democratic elitism is perhaps the broadest and, in a sense, encompasses the other three. The essentials of this position are well known. In contrast to the optimism of the Founding Fathers, the masses in modern democratic societies are not, in general, capable of self-government; on the contrary, the true potential for democracy resides more with the elites than with the masses. Indeed, in this view, mass political participation is not necessarily positive or beneficial; democracy is better served when the electorate is, as Lipset has put it, "mainly passive." The reasons for this view are discussed in the first chapter.

Undergirding democratic elitism's view of the mass as potentially dangerous or disruptive is the theory of the mass society. In its boldest form, this a theory of history in which industrialization and related social processes are the major actors (Rogin 1967:10). Central to the theory is the view that industrialization and its correlates—modernization, bureaucratization, urbanization, and so on—alter the fundamental structure of society and social relationships, and that these social "dislocations" have various pathological or disruptive consequences, among them the creation of a "mass public" whose personalities and political beliefs may become sufficiently degenerated and vicious that the very foundation of democratic stability is threatened. Among the potentiating syndromes is alienation—from self, family, friends, and work, but above all alienation from political systems that cannot or will not correct the inequities of the mass society. The details of this theory and its relationship to democratic elitism complete the first chapter.

Now, the social and psychological debilitations to which mass man is prone, and his attendant political "vulnerability," pose a serious problem for modern democratic regimes. On the one hand, if there were no mass input into the political process, one could hardly consider the system "democratic." Yet mass participation may itself lead to antidemocratic results. Thus, the regime must strike a balance between the need for participation, on the one hand, and its hazards on the other, and, because of this, the very stability of democracies is theoretically problematic. This theoretical problem, however, immediately contrasts with a striking empirical fact: During the period in which most of this theory has been written, the more democratic regimes, worldwide, have been the most stable, and authoritarian regimes have been the least stable. From this, theorists have inferred that, in addition to the various strains inherent in the modern democracy, there must also exist some set of circumstances, conditions, mechanisms, or social processes that curb the immoderation of the masses and thereby provide for stable democracy. Accordingly, "the sources of mass moderation" are considered in the second chapter.

By and large, modern theory has provided two related answers to the problem of democratic stability: social pluralism and consensus. Of these, the first has been, historically, the more common and more important. In brief, the pluralist argument suggests that certain structural features of modern democratic societies—in particular, a socially diverse population and its organization into voluntary associations—promote political moderation, lead to stable and efficient democratic government, allow for a modicum of representation while limiting the potential hazards, and otherwise provide an antidote to the mass society. Yet a number of recent empirical and theoretical studies, reviewed in the second chapter, make us doubt that pluralism provides an accurate account of modern political life. Thus, we turn to alternative theoretical mechanisms, of which consensus theory is the leading contender.

Almond and Verba have posed the essential question of consensus thinking more clearly than any other: "Is there," they ask, "a democratic political culture—a pattern of political attitudes that fosters democratic stability, that in some sense 'fits' the democratic political system? (1965:337)." The answer, of course, is yes, but the assertion that consensus promotes stability raises an entire series of questions, such as: What must this consensus be about? How much of it must there be? Where does it come from? Who must partake of it? Our search of the literature for empirical guidelines to these and related specifics occupies the major portion of the second and third chapters.

Concerning the first of these questions—What must consensus be about?—our review reveals little agreement and less specificity. Among political scientists, this consensus may be known as "diffuse support" or "internalization of regime norms." Among sociologists, legitimacy and "generalized support" are more popular. "Trust in elites," "deference to authority," "the democratic myths," and "public confidence" are also commonly encountered. However labeled, the terms are seldom defined with sufficient clarity to suggest an operationalization. McCloskey, we think, best summarizes this tradition: "Writers who hold consensus to be necessary to a free society have commonly failed to define it precisely or to specify what it must include (1969: 268)."

The opacity of the theorists on this point poses something of an analytic problem; that is, it is never very certain what one should be studying if one wants to study consensus. For our part, it has proven sufficient to approach the topic inferentially, in this case, by assuming that anyone who is alienated from a political system cannot, at the same time, be part of the consensus said to sustain it. Thus, we treat consensus as the empirical equivalent of an *absence* of political alienation, and, correlatively, consensus theory as the theory of political alienation in reverse.[6]

---

[6] In absolute terms, this is a rather unsatisfactory strategy, but one made necessary by the failure of consensus theorists to suggest a straightforward technique of operationalizing the "consensus" concept. As we note later in Chapter 3, most researchers who have tried to approach the notion of consensus empirically have made this same point, and there

It must, of course, be granted that, in the typical usage, the term "consensus" and its surrogates *seem* to connote more than an absence of political alienation and certainly much more than the attitudes of efficacy and trust to which we have already restricted our conception of alienation. For reasons detailed in the second and third chapters, however, we are not convinced that the distortion introduced by this identification is especially serious. Whatever else may be contained in the concept of consensus, it almost invariably implies, *at a minimum,* some notion of confidence in the political leadership or in one's ability to influence political decisions. What follows, then, may be taken as necessary, if not sufficient, for a critique of consensus thinking more broadly conceived.

How much consensus is necessary to assure the stability of democratic society? Here again, the texts provide only the slimmest of clues. The very term and certain common phraseologies (for example, the "democratic political *culture*" or "the attitudes of *the* democratic citizenry") seem to imply that everyone, or nearly everyone, must subscribe to the required beliefs. As stated, however, the thesis is manifestly implausible. Accordingly, we have again been led to the logic of limiting cases: Whatever the level of consensus in the United States—the archetypical "stable industrial democracy"—it should at least be *sufficient.* Empirical evidence for the United States, then, although it neither confirms nor disproves, does specify some upper and lower limits within which the plausibility of consensus theory lies.

A third major issue is where consensus comes from, and here the theorists are relatively specific and clear-cut. It is usually assumed (in most cases, *without* supporting evidence) that consensus is not likely to arise naturally in the course of political maturation; nor is it traded quid pro quo for political outputs. On the contrary, consensus is often seen as the mechanism that aids the system in weathering periodic crises of effectiveness. The implication is that the level of support ought not to respond, least of all dramatically, to fluctuations in the quality of the political product. This has resulted in a focus on *political socialization* as the main source of consensus: The necessary beliefs are instilled early in childhood, during a process of indoctrination into regime norms; these orientations then carry over into adult political life and insulate the system against harsh realities.

The final and most troublesome issue is precisely how political attitudes add to or detract from democratic stability. In many renditions (*The Civic Culture* being one prominent example), this relationship is taken as direct and immediately obvious. Here government is seen, metaphorically, as resting on a foundation of popular consensus and public support; any erosion of that

---

are obvious attempts in the theoretical literature on consensus to avoid (or at least postpone) the matter of operationalization altogether (e.g., Easton 1965:161–162). In truth, the use of terms like "consensus" or "generalized support" is largely intuitive. We are directed to these indices, in short, by the absence of an explicit alternative.

foundation, thus, immediately leads to instabilities in the political superstructure. Without some intervening mechanism, however, we find this to be a curious and unpersuasive position; thus, we prefer to assume that the relationship between attitudes and political stability is mediated by political *behavior*. That is, consensus is necessary for stability because its absence would presumably lead to political activity that in some way challenges the legitimacy of the regime. This assumption, then, completes the isomorphism between consensus and political alienation theories: Consensus is required because its alternative (namely, alienation) leads to dangerous and destabilizing political behaviors.

The consensus alternative to pluralism as a solution to the problem of stable democracy can, therefore, be summarized as follows: First, stable democracy requires a high level of consensus (a low level of alienation); second, the regime satisfies this requirement through a process of indoctrination which is essentially complete prior to entry into adult political life; and, finally, the first is true and the second necessary because the absence of consensus (the presence of alienation) may result in mass political behaviors directed against the established regime.

Chapter 3 discusses these propositions in more detail, draws out their apparent implications, and reviews available evidence bearing on their empirical merit. Unlike pluralism, our review concludes that it would not be possible to confirm or reject these principles on the basis of the literature at hand. Thus, the path is cleared for the original research reported in subsequent chapters.

Following a brief discussion (Chapter 4) of the metholological properties of the available alienation measures, Chapter 5 addresses the troublesome question of how much alienation there is in the United States. Unfortunately, it is not possible to give a very precise answer; the amount of alienation depends on the questions one asks and what one accepts as an alienated response. All that can be concluded with certainty is that something between all and none of the population of the United States is highly alienated from its political institutions. Since this range includes a level of discontent that would be consistent with consensus theory, however, we have felt the need to narrow it somewhat, and this, in turn, has resulted in a rather heavier reliance on the marginal distributions of our alienation measures than could be justified on any absolute grounds. Accordingly, the data of Chapter 5 are presented in explicit contrast to selected passages from the consensus texts.

More critical to the theory than the extent of alienation is its distribution in the society. Even majority levels of discontent might be consistent with the theory if the alienated were of a certain sort—if, for example, they were so geographically or socially dispersed as to make their alienation an impossible basis for political mobilization, or if they were uniformly drawn from recognizably "safe" social groups. Chapter 6, then, raises the question: Where in the society is political alienation located?

Chapter 7 analyzes the long-term upward trend of political alienation in the United States. The trend data pose a number of unique empirical possibilities. First, as is well-known, the traditional mode of explanation in the social sciences is that "changes in X are associated with changes in Y." Changes in anything, however, are seldom directly measured; rather, they are inferred from cross-sectional data gathered at a single point in time. Chapter 7 allows us to examine such correlational theories in light of actual changes in the dependent and independent variables.

More importantly, trend data bear on the view that consensus is formed early in life and remains relatively impervious to the encroachments of political "disappointments." Lacking direct data on the socialization of children, little can be said about the existence or operation of the indoctrination processes per se. What the trend analysis does allow is some specification of factors that modify, erode, or destroy the early childhood lessons, and this, in turn, bears directly on the plausibility of early socialization as a major stabilizing mechanism.

Chapters 8 and 9 present evidence on the hypothesized relationship between alienation and political behavior. We first consider certain elements of political consciousness—in particular, regressive ideologies and the sense of political negativism—that are said to be associated with political alienation and that "intervene" between alienation and its presumed political effects. These are the topics of Chapter 8. Chapter 9, in turn, raises the more direct question of whether the political behavior of the discontented differs in any discernible way from that of the more contented and nonalienated sectors of the population. We focus especially on political *withdrawal* and *mobilization*; these are the dispositions most often discussed in the theoretical and empirical literature. Some inferential evidence on "radicalism" and respect for the rules of democratic procedure is also presented.

Overall, the theory of political alienation fares rather poorly throughout the empirical analysis reported in Chapters 5–9. Evidence discussed in those chapters suggests that the theory has misrepresented the extent, nature, and causes of political alienation and has exaggerated its political "threat." Accordingly, Chapter 10, the concluding chapter, reviews the main aspects of the analysis that warrant these conclusions and then attempts a more plausible account of the relationship between democratic government and political discontent.

1

On the Hazards of Democratic Government

F EW have been so moved by the idea of democracy as Thomas Jefferson, principal architect of a system of democratic rule which he considered proof of "whether man can be trusted with self-government."

> We exist as standing proof that a government, so modelled as to rest continually on the will of the whole society, is a practicable government. . . . I am not among those who fear the people. They and not the rich are our dependence for continued freedom. . . . Sometimes it is said that man cannot be trusted with the government of himself. Can he, then, be trusted with the government of others? Or have we found angels in the form of kings to govern him? Let his history answer this question.[1]

Jefferson's faith in the "people," however, was not absolute. For example, his proposals for free, mass public education were to the end of alleviating the incompetence and ignorance of the masses, about which he continually wrote. In addition he did not hesitate to agree with his critics that there "are defects in our form of government." His confidence in the democratic experiment, however, was unshaken by such admissions, first because the alternative to democracy was monarchy, for which his derision was boundless, and second because he felt that democracy would create the conditions necessary for its own success. Give the people the responsibilities of self-government, Jefferson would say, and they will develop the skills needed to discharge them.

[1] The Jefferson passages quoted in this chapter are from Padover (1939).

12

Ask finally whether peace is best preserved by giving energy to the government, or information to the people. This last is the most certain and the most legitimate engine of government. Educate and inform the whole mass of people. Enable them to see that it is in their best interest to preserve peace and order, and they will preserve them. And it requires no very high degree of education to convince them of this.

There is no longer much enthusiasm for "participatory democracy," either in practice or as a political ideal. The phrase itself has recently been conscripted into the symbolism of the "New Left," yet even here one finds little but fear and distrust of what Jefferson would call "the democratic majority." Modern theorists have been soured by the history to which Jefferson refers—soured by worldwide repression and totalitarianism perpetrated in the name of the "masses," by Bolshevism and Fascism, and by numerous other antidemocratic upheavals. The lesson of recent political history has, thus, apparently been that "participatory democracy" is no sure guarantee of just and reasonable government, that, on the contrary, the masses in modern societies harbor many antidemocratic tendencies. Accordingly, Jefferson's image of the heroic granger, freed at last from the oppression of monarchs and solicitously concerned with the well-being of all, has been replaced by the hard-bitten, gun-toting status-panicked "silent majority" as the central symbol of "democratic man." The masses in modern democracies are said to have no particular commitment to the rules of democratic procedure, no special sensitivity to minority rights, and no notable competence in running the affairs of state. What good purpose is served, then, by entrusting power to them?

In this regard, the lessons of history have been enjoined with the lessons of modern social science, which has produced an imposing body of evidence to document the political deficiencies of the mass. Skimming briefly the postwar literature, one finds evidence that the mass is racially bigoted, anti-Semitic, disrespectful of the rights of minorities and intolerant of dissent, authoritarian, anomic, hostile to outgroups, politically simple-minded, demagogic, tough and punitive in foreign policy orientation, belligerent, irrational, and otherwise deficient in an entire range of matters far too numerous to list.[2] These indecencies, moreover, are apparently rooted in social circumstances and con-

---

[2] See, for example, Adorno et al. (1950), Berelson et al. (1954), Dye and Zeigler (1972: Ch. 5), Galtung (1964), Lipset (1963), Lipset and Raab (1970), Maccobby (1972), McCloskey (1964), Monsma (1971), Pettigrew et al. (1972), Prothro and Grigg (1960), Selznick and Steinberg (1969), Stouffer (1954), and so on. These are but a select few of perhaps several hundred studies that could be cited.

In the face of such a vast literature, one reopens the debate concerning mass political competence only with a certain trepidation. As Monsma has said, "It has become a commonplace among political scientists" that the "average citizen does not have the qualities the [classical democratic] model requires of him (1971:350)." Given that it is now a commonplace, one is tempted to conclude that the democratic incompetence of the mass has been proven beyond a reasonable doubt.

This, in our opinion, would not be an appropriate conclusion, at least not at this time.

ditions about which little can be done—in the structure of social class and class relationships, in the techniques of child-rearing and socialization, in the characteristics of work that come to predominate in industrial society, indeed, rooted in the very conditions of competition by which the modern capitalist society operates. Is there any realistic hope for democracy, in the classic sense, when the animating force of democratic government, "The People," exhibit tendencies such as these? What, in short, is a workable alternative—one that protects the ideals of democracy against the potential ravages of the mass?

This "workable alternative" has been supplied by modern theorists in the form of what is known as the "theory of democratic elitism." Summarizing briefly, the theory attempts to detail the best possible approximation to classical democratic ideals, given the aforementioned characteristics of the masses.[3] As such, the theory addresses the twin issues of *representation* and

---

One common subtheme in this literature, for example, is that the politically alienated and discontented masses pose a special threat to democratic institutions, and there is an assumption (as we noted in the introduction) that the evidence supporting this point is conclusive. A more detailed review of that literature, however, shows that this is not the case, and the evidence presented in this book consistently fails to confirm the common view. There is, certainly, no guarantee that there would be similar results from critical studies of other aspects of this literature, but our experience with the research reported here at least suggests it as a real possibility.

Along these lines, some characteristics of the larger literature can be mentioned. First, there is a tendency toward heavy mutual citation, the result being that the literature seems, on the surface, to be more imposing than it actually is. Second, some of the more commonly cited works, such as *The Authoritarian Personality*, are now recognized to be methodologically unsound (e.g., Campbell *et al.* 1960; Christie and Jahoda 1954). A third problem is that some of the "classical studies," for instance the famous Stouffer study (1954), have not stood up to recent efforts at replication (Davis 1974). Along these same lines, there is now persuasive evidence from a number of sources that many of the "antidemocratic" attitudes studied in the early literature have shown continual improvement in the decades since (e.g., Campbell 1971; Davis 1974; Greeley 1975; etc.). And, finally, as we discuss briefly in Chapter 10, there is some tendency for secondary accounts to misread and misrepresent the findings of many of these studies. A skeptical critic who approached the literature with these points in hand, we believe, would have ample reason to question its "commonplace" conclusions. (See Hamilton 1972, 1975, or Hamilton and Wright 1975a, for initial steps in this direction.)

[3] In this regard, the points made in the preceding footnote assume special significance. If the masses do, in fact, exhibit these antidemocratic and regressive political orientations, and if, moreover, efforts at amelioration are doomed to failure, then the prospects of humane government through popular participation are dim, and more workable, realistic alternatives are in order. The corollary is that, if the masses are *not* so politically backward, then the hope for participatory democracy is greater. The point here is that this is an *empirical* issue, one that can only be adjudicated on evidentiary grounds. In this, the often encountered "radical critiques" of democratic elitism—for example, that it takes the *status quo* for granted, that it condones the repression of the masses at the hands of the elite, that it is, in effect, a justificatory bourgeois ideology for the capitalist industrial state—are largely beside the point. Such fervent declarations, unaccompanied by evidence, are in themselves of little value.

restraint, or, in other words, how a system of government can guarantee that mass input into the decision-making process is sufficient to warrant the label "democracy" but, at the same time, protect that system from the potential political demiurges of the mass. Although central to most contemporary theories of democracy, the theory of democratic elitism is nowhere so consistently articulated as in the writings of S.M. Lipset; thus, his contribution forms the basis of our discussion.

THE THEORY OF DEMOCRATIC ELITISM

"Democracy," Lipset writes, "in the sense of a system of decision-making in which all members or citizens play an active role in the continuous process is inherently impossible (1962:32)." [4] There are, moreover, both structural and social psychological reasons for this. First, the tendency for any large and bureaucratically organized social system is to gravitate toward oligarchical rule, or what is known as "Michels' Iron Law of Oligarchy (Michels 1962)." Organizational elites who may at first be elected for short tenures gain natural advantages for future elections: They know what is going on in the organization, control the means of communication, and are skilled in the arts of politics. They quite naturally make use of these advantages to consolidate and solidify their position. Hence, the tendency is for a relatively permanent elite to emerge, protected by its own skills and advantages and also by what Michels called a "cult of gratitude" among the grass roots.[5]

In addition to the structural impediments to participatory democracy, themselves rather formidable, there is a second and somewhat more important question of whether or not the mass is even capable of democratic self-rule. As Jefferson himself often noted, functioning democratic government requires widespread acceptance of the rules of democratic procedure, especially agreement that the majority shall prevail but that the rights of the minority must everywhere be protected. Yet "acceptance of the norms of democracy requires a high level of sophistication and ego security" which, among the mass, is in chronically short supply. "The less sophisticated and stable an individual, the more likely he is to favor a simplified view of politics, to fail to understand the rationale underlying tolerance of those with whom he disagrees, and to find difficulty in grasping or tolerating a gradualist

---

[4] There are few democratic theorists, classical or modern, who would seriously contest Lipset's point. The "continuous process" of politics—the day-to-day decision making, the implementation and execution of specific policy decisions, the formulation of legislation, and so on—obviously requires skills and resources that are not widely distributed in the population. The only issue here is a matter of degree or emphasis, whether democracy is best served by *relatively* more or *relatively* less popular participation. Lipset and other theorists of democratic elitism, it is fair to say, argue on behalf of the latter.

[5] Lipset himself, of course, has provided the most detailed list of conditions under which the "iron law" is rendered inoperative. See Lipset, Trow, and Coleman (1956:Chap. 18).

image of political change (1963:108)." The required sophistication is a rare commodity, possessed infrequently by those very persons to whom the powers of democracy have been entrusted. Hence, *"realistically,* the distinctive and most valuable element of democracy in complex societies is the formation of a political elite in the competitive struggle for the votes of a mainly passive electorate (1962:33; see also 1967b:492)."

The passage just quoted contains, in cryptic form, all the major elements of democratic elitism; let us then unpack it and consider its constituent parts. First, there is the opening word, "realistically," which signifies the theory's claim to provide an empirically accurate account of politics in modern industrial democracies. The "brutal realism" of this point of view explicitly contrasts with the boundless optimism and plain wishful thinking of more classical democrats, of whom Jefferson is perhaps the prime example. Accordingly, there is little in the theory to excite the passions or to send one's blood surging through the veins. The theory, rather, is a calm and sober depiction of the dangers and possibilities of representative democracy, how the former can be avoided and the latter attained.

The next phrase, "the distinctive and most valuable element," however, suggests that more than simple empirical description is involved; the theory has unambiguous moral overtones of its own, in the sense that it embraces a particular vision of what is politically feasible and how it can best be realized. Hence, speaking of his own elitist theory of democracy, Lipset remarks, "This image of democracy. . .may be far from the ideal of the Greek city-state or of the small Swiss cantons, but in operation as a system it is far better than any other political system which has been devised to reduce the potential exploitation of man by man (1962:36)." Clearly, the political ideal envisioned by democratic elitists is tempered by a realistic appreciation of the strengths and weaknesses of alternative governmental forms.[6]

That the "distinctive and most valuable element of democracy" is "the formation of an elite" alerts us to the primary difference between classical and modern theories. In Jefferson's view, the "distinctive and most valuable element" of democracy was precisely its ability to *prevent* the formation of

---

[6] Lipset, for example, notes in many writings the contributions that monarchies have made to democratic stability:

> Notice that if we classify democratic states as stable or unstable according to the criteria of whether they have had the uninterrupted continuation of political democracy since World War One *and* whether there has been an absence in them during the past thirty years of a major political movement opposed to the democratic "rules of the game," . . . then we come up with the curious fact that ten out of twelve or thirteen stable democracies in the world . . . are monarchies [1967b:443; see also 1963:65ff].

The monarchy helps societies "to retain the loyalty of the aristocratic, traditionalist, and clerical sectors of the population (1963:66)"; moreover, the monarchy aids in the establishment of generalized deference to elites which Lipset elsewhere maintains is essential for civil liberties and minority rights (e.g., Lipset 1970:48; Lipset and Raab 1970:xvii).

elites—at least of permanent elites whose power would protect them from popular control.[7] No mindless democrat, Jefferson was aware that the day-to-day powers of government are necessarily delegated, but there was certainly nothing distinctive or valuable about this; it was merely a necessary inconvenience, possible abuses of which were to be zealously monitored and corrected. The distinctive and most valuable elements of Jefferson's democracy lie in quite the opposite direction: Democracy was to be nothing less than the agent of human liberation, the impetus for the advancement of enlightenment, science, and education. As for the elites, once democracy was put into practice, they would be reduced to "a few servants, performing a few plain duties."

Unalloyed faith in "the people" and thorough suspicion of political elites are largely missing in modern theories of democracy. In fact, in the modern theory, the entire relationship between elites and masses has been rethought. In the first place, the "democratic experiment" did not progress precisely along the lines that Jefferson envisioned. The placid agrarian society of the eighteenth century has been replaced by the turbulent industrial society of the twentieth. Jefferson's dream of free mass public education, once realized, likewise failed to produce all the intended effects. Democracy, by and large, has apparently *not* created the conditions necessary for its own success; rather, it has shown itself to be subject to manipulation by antidemocratic mass movements. The paramount problem of the modern democracy, in short, has been less one of controlling the elites and more a matter of containing the masses.

There arises, then, what has been called "the irony of democracy," which is that elites, more than masses, are the true defenders of the democratic faith. The elites (and the "talent pool" from which they are drawn, mainly the upper and upper middle classes), virtually alone among contenders, have the necessary ego control and sophistication, the required commitment to rules of the democratic game. Rogin characterizes the view as follows: "It is deference to elites rather than faith in the people that permits effective and democratic government. Behind [such] analysis is the hope that if only responsible elites could be left alone, if only political issues could be kept from the people, the elites would make wise decisions (1967:274)." One major dimension to the theory of democratic elitism, then, is the delineation of circumstances that permit elites to "make wise decisions," which protect and "insulate" them from the mass public.

[7] The theory of democratic elitism contains similar provisions, although they differ substantially from Jefferson's "fullest possible participation of all." In brief, the modern "solution" to elite domination lies in the concept of *competition among elites* and in conditions that make the competition fair and equitable. This point is discussed more fully later in the chapter. As before, the difference between classical and modern theory on this point is a matter of emphasis (see Footnote 4), whether masses or elites pose the *greatest* threat to democratic values.

There are, of course, any number of political mechanisms that safely isolate elites and masses; dictatorships, monarchies, and other forms of totalitarian rule come quickly to mind. Obviously, none of these is an appropriate solution to the problem of a modern democracy, which remains, at its base, fundamentally committed to "self-government" as a political ideal. Having stressed the necessity, inevitability, and even desirability of the formation of an elite, how then does the theory of democratic elitism resurrect this commitment? Stated simply, the theory substitutes the notion of *representation* for that of *participation* as the primary requirement of a democratic government. Or, as Bachrach has summarized it, modern theory forgoes the concept of a democratic political *process* in favor of democratic political results (1967: 3–6). Accordingly, a second major dimension of the theory is its focus on representational mechanisms that, at least in principle, guarantee some acceptable level of mass input into the policy-making process while simultaneously assuring that the result of that input is consistent with democratic ideals. In Lipset's rendition, this mechanism is contained in the "competitive struggle for the votes of a mainly passive electorate."

As is evident in the passage, the notion of competition is central to the theory's conception of democracy. The major democratizing mechanism is the wide or "pluralist" dispersion of power, which enables contesting parties to enter into fair competition for the sympathies and support of the mass. This competition, moreover, can exist at any number of levels: among candidates, parties, governmental elites, voluntary associations, and even among organized population subgroups. The ensuing competition for a democratic majority, in turn, assures that majority preferences will carry some weight in the policy process. It is important, however, that the arena of competition be restricted to responsible elites; for the most part, the *representational* needs of democracy are sufficiently met if elites are occasionally required to present themselves (or their policies) for public review. In this respect, the role of the mass becomes mainly one of ratifying predetermined elite decisions. If the majority finds those decisions totally intolerable or markedly at variance with its own political wishes, ratification can be withheld; in this manner, elites are held accountable to those ultimately affected by their decisions. At the same time, however, the elites retain primary control over initiation of debate, the recognition and formulation of policy problems, the narrowing of "acceptable" alternatives, and so on. Thus, the masses are relieved of the many difficult political obligations placed upon them in classical democratic theory, obligations which, in the modern view, they were probably incapable of discharging anyway. At the same time, their right to democratic representation is maintained.

Obviously, the key to the entire arrangement lies with the "mainly passive electorate." If the masses can be kept sufficiently disinterested in the day-to-day workings of politics, or alternatively, if their confidence and trust in the political leadership can be secured, then the system will function more or less in accord with democratic values. If, on the other hand, the masses are whipped into participatory frenzies by demagogues who challenge the legitimacy of the arrangement, then the system suffers accordingly and democratic values may be lost. Therefore, the continuous participation of the mass in the political process is not only unnecessary and impossible but may, in many instances, actually imperil democratic stability. For this reason, democratic concerns about the "fullest possible participation of all" are dismissed by Lipset as the arguments of "liberal rhetoricians." Correcting some earlier misconceptions, Lipset notes, "The belief that a very high level of participation is always good for democracy is not valid. . . . An increase in the level of participation may reflect the *decline* of social cohesion and the breakdown of the democratic process (1963:14)."

There are some related emphases contained in the theory that deserve at least a passing comment. For one, the theory gives clear preference to political behavior expressed through normal and usual channels and is, consequently, suspicious of any behavior that deviates from the routine.[8] Such deviations are more than inconveniences for the current incumbents; rather, they may, under certain conditions, assault the very *idea* of the democratic way. Likewise, there is relatively more emphasis placed in these texts on stability than on representation, mostly because the latter is almost automatically assured if the mechanisms function properly. A corollary here is a tendency to equate "stable" with "good" and, thus, to worry more about the possibilities of mass demagogic movements than whether or not scarce social and economic resources are being fairly distributed, whether or not the general welfare is being maximized, and so on. It would not be fair to say that the theorists ignore these issues altogether. Rather, they perceive the greater threat from appetitive masses than from nonresponsive elites.

There is a final emphasis that is somewhat unique to the modern theory of democracy, one that contrasts sharply with more classical views and one, moreover, that is especially relevant to the themes of this book: the emphasis on the need for mass confidence and trust in the political elites. In the classical view, of course, the people were expected to be profoundly suspicious of the elected leadership, to distrust their motives, and thereby to be constantly on guard against possible elite abuses of power. "And what country," Jefferson said, "can preserve its liberties, if its rulers are not warned from time to time, that this people preserve the spirit of resistance?" By and large, the modern theory of democracy inverts this emphasis. In the place of distrust and suspicion, modern theory argues the need for mass deference to elites, argues that the system can only function adequately if elites are left free to

---

[8] Jefferson himself, sadly, harbored no particular virtue on this score either, as witnessed by his reaction to Shay's Rebellion. "At first he was disturbed and worried; very little of his famous remark about watering the tree of liberty with the blood of patriots can be found in his early letters about the event. It was the work of 'mobs' and was 'absolutely unjustified' (Williams 1966:147)."

"allocate scarce resources" and "make authoritative decisions." These orientations toward the elite, which we discuss in the next chapter, are thought to be crucial in creating and sustaining the "mainly passive electorate" that Lipset and other theorists find essential for social and political stability.

In most versions of the theory, the political debilitations to which the mass is prone are found to be mainly rooted in the circumstances of social class. The lower and working classes in the modern industrial state, for example, are hobbled by a pervasive authoritarianism (Lipset 1963:Chap. 4). These classes lack the broadening educational experiences that widen perspectives and foster the necessary ego control and sophistication. Moreover, they are plagued by relative economic insecurity, located in unrewarded and unrewarding occupations, prone to the tortures of unemployment, and, therefore, covetous of hard-won gains. Accordingly, they become especially militant in protecting their fragile status against the ever-present "threat from below." Because of their cognitive simplicity, the lower and working classes are also likely to see politics as "black and white, good and evil." Accordingly, they are attracted to noncompromising, extremist solutions. These various orientations and characteristics, enjoined with other circumstances of the class, such as punitive child-rearing practices, little activity in voluntary associations, and so on, thus combine to forge a set of political values that may, under the appropriate circumstances, constitute a hazard to democratic government.[9]

Similarly untrustworthy are the lower or marginal middle classes—the small, independent businessmen and the lower white-collar employees. Historically, concern on this score arises from the alleged role of the marginal middle class in supporting European Fascist movements.[10] Central to this line of

[9] Lipset also notes, however, that working class political institutions, especially unions and political parties, have historically been democratic and progressive social forces, and, likewise, that these institutions may sometimes reverse the authoritarian tendencies of the class. See Lipset (1963a:121–126) and Lipset and Raab (1970:xvii).

The most recent and thorough review of literature bearing on the working class authoritarianism thesis is provided by Hamilton (1972: Chapter 11). This work surveys several dozen studies and concludes that the evidence is contradictory, and, where not contradictory, the differences associated with social class are small. Other challenges to the thesis include Hamilton (1968, 1975), Hamilton and Wright (1975a, b), Lipsitz (1965), Miller and Reissman (1961), and Wright (1972b).

[10] The role of the lower middle class in the rise of fascism is a key element in the "theory of the mass society," discussed in more detail later in this chapter. Lipset (1963a:Chap. 5) provides a detailed discussion of the relevant studies. Among the European mass society theorists, Geiger (1930), Lederer (1967:81), and Mannheim (1940:102) have reached this conclusion.

The historical evidence on the point is ambiguous. The most compelling evidence produced by Lipset, for example, is that suggesting that the rise of the Nazi party, in terms of a percentage of the vote, was accompanied by the "complete collapse" of the bourgeois liberal center parties (1963a:138–139). Inferences about the behavior of individuals (or of groups of individuals) on this basis, of course, are extremely hazardous.

Hamilton's (forthcoming) work on the NSDAP (Hitler's Nazi party) raises a

theorizing is the concept of *status anxiety* or *status panic*. Speaking of this class, C. Wright Mills remarked, "Their psychology can often be understood as the psychology of prestige striving (1951:240)." Yet, in periods of economic decay, the prestige and status claims of the lower middle class may be blocked, and, because of their economically marginal position, the class—either individually or collectively—may face impending downward mobility into the despised proletariat and a consequent loss of the coveted middle-class status. The small businessmen, moreover, are threatened by virtually every major institutional development in the modern capitalist state: by big business because it draws off the clientele, by big labor because it drives the price of labor up past what the independent businessman can afford, and, most importantly, by big government because, in addition to complicating the operation of small business, big government refuses to correct the inequities posed by big business and big labor. In response to the real or impending loss of status and the economic marginality that sustains it, the lower middle class may develop a syndrome of social and political alienation; once alienated, it is thought to be susceptible to fascistic appeals.[11]

Among the major population subgroups, then, this leaves the upper and upper middle class to bear the burden of political virtue and democratic tradition. Largely exempt from the vagaries of the economy, secure in their social and economic position, and beneficiaries of the best education the nation has to offer, these classes develop cosmopolitan outlooks, tolerance of minorities, political sophistication, and ego strength. These and related dispositions suit them for democratic political participation. That they are, in this and most other advanced industrial nations, by far the most actively involved in politics (e.g., Verba and Nie 1972) merely bespeaks the vigor of the modern democracy. These classes, in the modern theory, play no less a role than that of responsible managers for the entire democratic enterprise, and it is, therefore, upon their shoulders that the hope and promise of democracy must rest.

Realistic or otherwise, one must at least confess that this is an odd theory of democracy—one that warns of the potential hazards of popular participation, that suggests that such participation may, in fact, detract from democratic values, and that ultimately counsels that democracy is often better

---

serious question about the marginal middle class hypothesis. In terms of urban election districts, the greatest Nazi vote apparently came in the elegant upper and upper middle class sectors of the city. The "authoritarian" working class, as is well-known, showed relatively little attraction to the NSDAP, having voted socialist or communist throughout the Weimar period.

[11] Concerning specifically the marginal middle class in the United States, works advancing these conclusions include Kornhauser (1959:Chapter 11), Lipset and Raab (1970), Mills (1951), Trow (1958), and other mass society theorists discussed later in the text. Empirical evidence contradicting the position is provided by Hamilton (1966, 1975) and Nelson (1968) and, for the British case, Rallings (1974). See also Chapter 6.

served when entrusted to the hands of an elite few.[12] What, then, are its political and intellectual roots? How has it risen to its present position of prominence?

THE THEORY OF THE MASS SOCIETY

At the base of the theory of democratic elitism lies the theory of the mass society, which attempts to explain the social and psychological development of societies as they evolve from premodern to postmodern forms. A central claim is that industrialization brings about numerous major changes in the structure of modern society; among them are: Factory replaces family as the premier economic and productive unit; bureaucracy replaces guild as the organizing principle of work; urban areas replace traditional rural communities as the place of residence and the point of psychological contact; and rule-bound associations within secondary groups replace the primary ties of kin and friendship as the paramount experience of the social sphere.[13]

The psychology and orientations of the population are also altered by these structural changes. As ties to traditional society become severed, "mass man" is cut free from social restraints. No longer located in a nexus of integrating social institutions, the mass becomes isolated, atomized, and unattached—freed from the restraints that membership in tightly knit and cohesive social units implies. Lacking roots that come from firm attachment to primary groups, mass man is also prone to various identity crises. Thus, his central psychological characteristic is pervasive *anomie*; he is quite literally without the norms and expectations that formerly dictated his social behavior. Concomitant with anomie is an equally pervasive alienation or estrangement from the major institutions of the society—from self, from family, from work, but, most of all, alienation from political systems that cannot or will not correct these injustices.

The political dimensions of this argument are most important for our purposes. One significant aspect of the anomie and alienation of mass man is the belief that he is unable to take a direct hand in the events that affect him. His powerlessness, moreover, is alloyed with deep-seated negativism, particularly concerning things political; he considers the political world as the province of evil men. His powerlessness and negativism, then, lead him

---

[12] Its surface oddity, however, should not detract from the *empirical* issues that it raises (see Footnote 3). It may very well be that democratic elitism *is* the most practicable or realistic approximation to democratic ideals, given the capabilities and dispositions of the masses in modern industrial society. Whether or not this is so is solely a function of the evidence, most certainly not of arcane speculation in matters of normative political philosophy.

[13] The key theorists are discussed in the ensuing pages. For useful critiques of mass society theory, see Bell (1959:Chapter 1), Hamilton (1972:Chapter 2), Gusfield (1962), and Pinard (1968).

to withdraw from politics in normal times; he is usually apathetic, indeed, almost pathologically so. Yet, because he is "unrestrained" by the normative bonds of more integrated social groups, mass man is also open to the demagogue who promises to put an end to his political miseries. In addition to his normal political withdrawal, then, mass man is prone to occasional spasms of destabilizing political activity, especially when the circumstances are right and a clever leader presents himself. Lacking social restraints, unattached to the main institutions of the society, and prone to irrational political outbursts, mass man thus constitutes a threat to orderly democratic government.[14]

Like all such theories, the origin and development of the theory of the mass society can only be understood in terms of the social and political context of the times. As many have noted, this particular theory and, for that matter, most of what is known as "classical theory" in the social sciences, arose initially as a reaction to the French Revolution—a reaction expressed among such eminently conservative figures as Comte and Saint-Simon (e.g., Horowitz 1972; Nisbet 1966). Nisbet himself leaves little doubt as to the motivations of these early precursors of mass society theory: "What was conservatism against? The Revolution foremost, of course" and, more particularly, what the Revolution represented—"equalitarianism and centralized power based on the people" and certainly what was seen as their inevitable corollaries, "the debasement of culture, the consequence of its mass dissemination, the whole progressive-deterministic mentality (1966:13–14)." In a word, the theory of the mass society begins as a reaction to democracy, a European intellectual abhorrence of the very developments that Jefferson cherished, and it is this reaction that colors the entire sweep of its subsequent elaboration. Democracy, as a social and political system, was destroying the genteel and aristocratic society of the seventeenth and eighteenth century and replacing it with social developments that were neither wholly predictable nor obviously good. As Gustav LeBon, a century after the Revolution, aptly put it, "It is possible that the advent to power of the masses marks one of the last stages of Western civilization (1960:17)." LeBon's reasoning in the matter conveniently summarizes this early tradition:

> It cannot be gainsaid that civilization has been the work of a small minority of superior intelligences, constituting the culminating point of a pyramid, whose stages, widening in proportion to the decrease of mental power, represent the masses of a nation. The greatness of a civilization cannot assuredly depend upon the votes given by inferior elements boasting solely numerical strength [1960: 182].

Similar antidemocratic and aristocratic sentiments are found throughout the eighteenth and nineteenth century intellectual landscape, among the works

---

[14] These themes are elaborated in Kornhauser (1959), Aberbach (1969), Gerson (1965), Mason and Jaros (1969), and others whose work is discussed at length in later chapters.

of conservatives and reactionaries, such as LePlay, Burke, Durkheim, and others of similar persuasion.

There was, of course, little in the political history of nineteenth century Europe to dissuade the theorists of their views. Decade after decade found Europe wracked with violence and political revolt: the "peasant wars" in Ireland in the early part of the century, the revolution of 1848 so painstakingly chronicled by Marx, the Paris Commune of 1871, the abortive Russian Revolution of 1905 and the more successful effort in 1917. There were, in the period, revolutionary agitations in virtually every major city of Europe, most executed by or on putative behalf of "the masses." To the aristocrats of the intelligentsia, every battle joined and barricade mounted was, thus, a volley in the assault on civilization. "This is," as one commentator put it, "a remarkable century which opened with the Revolution and ended with the *Affaire!* Perhaps it will be called the century of rubbish." [15]

If the nineteenth century was indeed the century of rubbish, the twentieth could only be known as the century of horror. At its onset, world attention was focussed on the events in Russia and the eventual overthrow of the czarist regime. This focus, however, was somewhat averted by the outbreak of world war. The settlement of that war, in turn, and particularly the punitive terms of the Versailles treaty of 1919, set the stage for what must be considered the most overtly ruthless "mass political movement" in history, the rise of fascism in the West.[16]

The early Fascist successes—particularly Hitler's stunning rise to prominence in the 1930 German elections—greatly accelerated the development of mass society theory in its modern form. At no other time in history had the electoral manipulability of the masses been so credibly demonstrated; as such, anxious alarms about the future of democracy became the major intellectual themes of the period. The spanish liberal and philosopher, Jose

---

[15] The passage is attributed to Roger Martin du Gard, as quoted by Arendt (1951:1).

[16] As noted earlier (see Footnote 10), the precise role of the "mass public" in the various European Fascist regimes remains an open historical and empirical question. For example, even at the height of his powers in free elections, Hitler's National Socialists *never* won more than 44% of the popular vote, well short of an absolute electoral majority. In this respect, the specific electoral arrangements of the Weimar Republic contributed more to Hitler's actually coming to power than the preferences of the "democratic majority." The "class basis" of the Hitler appeal has, likewise, been somewhat exaggerated. As Hamilton and Wright note, "The Nazi vote is most simply characterized as Protestant and as varying inversely with city size (1975a:39)." It was not, by and large, the "alienated and anomic urban masses" that swept Hitler to power. It was the (presumably well-integrated) farmers and small town Protestants of the German countryside. Finally, as Hamilton and Wright also note, the role of the party activists, the Nazi cadres, has never been fully appreciated (1975a:40–41). These groups provided the intransigent and militant party base upon which the "mass effort" was built. (The Nazi experience in Germany is discussed in more detail later, see Chapters 8 and 9.)

Ortega y Gassett, opened his widely read *Revolt of the Masses* (published in 1930) with these nervous lines:

> There is one fact which, whether for good or ill, is of utmost importance in the public life of Europe at the present moment. This fact is the ascension of the masses to complete social power. As the masses, by definition, neither should nor can direct their own personal existence, and still less rule society in general, this fact means that actually Europe is suffering from the greatest crisis that can afflict peoples, nations, and civilizations [1957:11].

Similar views are expressed in Lederer's *State of the Masses*, first published in 1940. Expressing perhaps the quintessential mass society view on the prospects of democracy, Lederer remarks:

> The democratic way of allowing everyone freedom in what he thinks or does, politically, rested on the eighteenth century conviction that citizens are rational beings who know everything, who have clear judgment, and who—in accordance with human nature—are benevolent, tolerant, and want the common good. . . . Democracy did not realize that citizens are, so to speak, sheets of white paper on which anyone can write, . . . and it [democracy] refused to write anything on the sheet itself except the bill of rights [1967: 63].

Leading theorists across Europe soon echoed the thesis that industrial society was fast becoming mass society, and that mass society posed grave dangers to liberal, democratic institutions. Predictably, this thesis found most sympathetic enunciation among the German intellectuals or, rather, among those who did not themselves capitulate to fascism.[17] Like Lederer, they saw the decline of the traditional order, especially of the class structure, as atomizing society and creating mass man:

> One great unorganized, structureless mass of furious individuals who had nothing in common except their vague apprehension that the hopes of party members were doomed, that, consequently, the most respected, articulate and representative members of the community were fools and that all the powers that be were not so much evil as they were equally stupid and fraudulent [Arendt 1951:315].

Mannheim, among the more influential of these theorists in the United States, characterized the modern industrial society as a "negative democracy" in which groups come to power without the skills necessary for its intelligent use:

---

[17] "In the beginning many of the intellectuals were swept away by the enthusiasm of the moment. . . . It is amazing how quickly the learned professions, the artists, and to some extent even the church presented a united front against freedom of thinking (Lederer 1967:176–177; see also Arendt 1951:326ff)."

As long as democracy was a pseudo-democracy, in the sense that it granted political power at first only to a small propertied and educated group and only gradually to the proletariat, it led to the growth of rationality. . . . But since democracy became effective, i.e., since all classes played an active part in it, it has been increasingly transformed into what Max Scheler called a "democracy of emotions." As such it leads less to the expression of the interests of various social groups and more to sudden emotional eruptions among the masses [1940:45].

In Europe, of course, the net historical outcome of these "sudden emotional eruptions" was the raw brutality of Hilter's predatory regime, the murder of perhaps 6 million European Jews, and, ultimately, the Second World War. Thus, the survivors witnessed what to them was the most terrifying epoch in history. Their consuming need to understand and interpret this experience, to locate its causes in the very processes of modernization and industrialization, readily accounts for their attraction to mass society themes. The collapse of the German party structure, after all, could have only reflected the collapse of the traditional society upon which it had been erected; this alone bore ample testimony to the dangers of atomization and massification. There was, in addition, the sharp rise in turnout that accompanied Hitler's initial electoral successes, particularly in the election of 1930. From this highy visible evidence, theorists, such as Theodor Geiger and later Reinhard Bendix, concluded that the previously apathetic and alienated masses— the sullen nonparticipants in the traitorous Weimar republic—lay at the base of Hitler's support, readily mobilized in a time of crisis by the Nazi cadres. There was, understandably, little concern with methodological niceties and little debate about "ecological correlations." It was, so to speak, research on the run, a daily, living confirmation of intellectual fears that had steadily mounted since the French Revolution.

What is more difficult to understand is the appeal of mass society orientations to American social and political commentators in the immediate postwar era.[18] There had been, to be sure, an occasional instance of radicalism prior to the Great Depression, but the New Deal had seemingly "succeeded in giving American capitalism a reasonable and stable basis (Rogin 1967:9)." Economic and social disruptions, such as those of the late Weimar period in Germany, for example, were not apparent on the American scene. Indeed, the United States emerged from the war as a major political, economic, and military power, a key actor on the world stage. Despite the consensus and

[18] Mannheim, for example, feared that his principles would fall on unsympathetic ears in the United States. In the introduction to the English version of *Man and Society in an Age of Reconstruction*, he says, "To the Western countries the collapse of liberalism and democracy and the adoption of a totalitarian system seem to be the passing symptoms of a crisis which is confined to a few nations." And he found it necessary to warn, "Those who have had first-hand knowledge of the crisis . . . are united in the belief . . . that if this [totalitarianism] is an evil, it is an evil which sooner or later is bound to spread (1940:3)."

stability, however, the theory of the mass society soon swept American intellectual circles, and numerous sociologists, historians, psychologists, and philosophers began translating the thesis of Mannheim, Lederer, and others into an early 1950 American idiom.[19] What accounts for the appeal to American intellectuals of a theory based on political and social conditions largely absent in the United States?

Certainly, any number of potential factors might be cited, such as the preeminence of the Chicago school in American sociology, which was concurrently developing its own version of the mass society thesis,[20] or the migration of European intellectuals to American universities during and immediately following the war—among them Hans Gerth, Hans Speier, Hannah Arendt, and several transplants from the Frankfort school. These factors would have mattered little, however, were it not for the domestic political situation in postwar America—a situation totally dominated by the complex configuration of events and ideologies known as McCarthyism. The definitive treatment of the influence of McCarthyism on American intellectuals is Michael Rogin's *The Intellectuals and McCarthy* (1967), and we here borrow heavily from his analysis.

McCarthyism, according to Rogin, was seen as a classic instance of democracy gone awry. Elected by the traditionally progressive voters of Wisconsin and apparently sustained by popular opinion, McCarthy seemed to typify the

[19] See, for example, Selznick (1949, 1951), Nisbet (1953), Kornhauser (1959), Mills (1951, 1956), Fromm (1941, 1955), Viereck (1941, 1962), Hofstadter (1955) and so on.

Part of the effort, in this respect, necessarily involves the portrayal of calm as "inner turbulence," the denial of overt appearance, the depiction of apparent satisfaction as *Angst* residing just beneath the surface. As a result, many of the early American mass society renditions have a heavy overlay of Freudian imagery. See especially the Fromm works cited earlier. More recent examples would include Marcuse (1964), the work of Fromm's students (e.g., Maccobby 1972), and others now identified as "critical theorists" or, sometimes, as "the Freudian left." For an interesting but largely uncritical review essay on the subject, see Robinson (1969).

[20] Although physically located on Chicago's South Side, the dons of the Chicago school were firmly rooted in the small town and rural areas of the South and East. Mead, for example, the ostensible father figure of the Chicago school, was born in South Hadley, Massachusetts, the son of a professor of Biblical morality. Thomas was a product of rural Virginia; Burgess was from a small agricultural village in southern Ontario; Elsworth Faris was born in Salem County, Tennessee and later to do a stint as a Christian missionary to the Congo. Contrast between the urban decadence of Chicago and small town morality provided fertile ground for the development of mass society orientations, as witnessed in their studies of urbanism, deviance, and social disorganization. Although not expressly political, the dominance of the Chicago school created a receptive intellectual climate for the more politically attuned European mass society themes. (The best work available on the Chicago school is Faris [1967]. In his chapter on "urban behavior research," Faris mentions "nearly two dozen books" produced in "less than two decades" dealing with the sociology of the city. Of the works cited by Faris, not one deals expressly with the actual nature or operation of the urban political system. For a discussion of the apolitical focus of the Chicago school, see Mills [1943].)

excesses inherent in the Populist assumption that majority will is sovereign. The usual channels of debate were circumvented whenever McCarthy saw fit to air an issue in full public view; he "continually appealed to the mass of people for direct support over the heads of their elected leaders." His hostility to normal democratic procedures was legend, particularly his derision of the Senate, of which he was a member. Finally, American intellectuals were themselves often the target of his attacks. "All this," Rogin remarks, "suggested that popular democracy constituted a real threat to the making of responsible political decisions (1967:3)."

In the early 1950s, numerous studies of the McCarthy phenomenon appeared, in most cases fusing elements of mass society theorizing with classical pluralist theories.[21] On the one hand, McCarthy was seen as logical heir to the Progressive tradition, with its unique combination of fundamentalist orientations, economic liberalism, disdain for power, and traditional social conservatism. On the other hand, McCarthyism was seen as a manifestion of status anxieties and status politics, thus recalling the *Panik im Mittlestand* themes (Geiger 1930) that figured heavily in the European analysis of Hitlerism.[22] Underlying these explanations was a vision of men stripped by industrialization of their ties to traditional society and now "available" for demagogic movements. "Lacking a sense of community and alienated from the total society, individuals are vulnerable to mobilization by mass movements (Rogin 1967:15)." To American intellectuals, says Rogin, McCarthyism embodied "a nativist mystique which, glorifying the ordinary folk, threatened the civilized restraints of a complex society."

There was, in addition to McCarthyism, a second unique development present on the postwar American intellectual scene: the large-scale, mass social survey and, with it, the ability and resources to sample large populations and to ask directly about their preferences and predilections. Thus, the theorists and commentators were no longer forced to rely on ambiguous election returns or spurious newspaper accounts; the mass society themes could finally be examined directly. There soon appeared, accordingly, a spate

---

[21] The early literature is discussed in Polsby (1960) and Wrong (1954). A collection of sociological writings from the period is Bell (1964). The most recent review of the McCarthy studies is Lipset and Raab (1970: 209–247).

[22] For example, Lederer lists "the disappointed intellectuals, the university graduates with no prospects of an adequate job and the white collar workers" as the main elements of the "crowd" that propelled Mussolini to power in Italy (1967:81). Similarly, Mannheim lists "the lower middle class—the minor employees, petty officials, artisans, small business men, small peasants, and impoverished *rentiers*" as the key forces in Hitler's rise to power in Germany (1940:102).

Lederer comments:

> For while the workers had found their place in the society and their trade unions and cultural organizations had found ways of cooperating with their 'class enemies', the white collar workers were still undecided and constituted in a time of universal crisis a social dynamite which was the more dangerous because nobody knew how to handle it [1967:53].

of data-packed studies that seemingly confirmed, at long last, the key elements of the mass society view. There was, for example, the Berelson *Voting* study, which appeared in 1954, with its widely cited conclusion: "Our data . . . reveal that certain requirements commonly assumed for the successful operation of democracy are not met by the behavior of the 'average' citizen (1954:307)." This was accompanied, the same year, by Stouffer's *Communism, Conformity and Civil Liberties*, which documented that intolerance of dissent, disrespect for the rights of unpopular minorities, and so on were common, indeed majority, dispositions. These two works were accompanied, the following year, by Bell's collection of essays on *The New American Right*, in which radical rightist, anti-Communist, and McCarthyist tendencies were linked explicitly, by Lipset and others, to "the upward mobile ethnic population, and some of the downwardly mobile old American groups, . . . the *nouveaux riches* and insecure small businessmen, the traditionalist and authoritarian elements within the working class groups," and so on (Lipset 1963b:336). It was, in a word, a data-based recitation of the potential hazards of popular democracy.

Thus, rooted in the McCarthy experience, there soon emerged an American tradition of mass society theorizing that encompassed the ideological spectrum from Robert Nisbet to C. Wright Mills.[23] An early article by Selznick is characteristic: "Critics of egalitarianism have sometimes put forward the view that the mass, incompetent and vulgar, is unable by definition to uphold the standards which sustain a culture or to participate effectively in political decision-making (1951:320)."

The passage intimates a later rejection of the view, but none is forthcoming, rather: "This critique is not limited to anti-egalitarian ideologists. Even among those who favor the general process of democratization, and who lack

[23] Mills' contributions in this are often overlooked, because, critic that he was, he is seen as standing outside the mainstream intellectual traditions of his day. This interpretation forgets that *White Collar* was an uncritical translation and rearrangement of well-worn German mass society phrases. Their view of the new middle classes, for example, is the summarizing conclusion of the book:

> Since they [the new middle class] have no public position, their private positions as individuals determine in which direction each of them goes; but as individuals, they do not know where to go. So now they waver. They hesitate, confused and vacilating in their opinions, unfocused, and discontinuous in their actions. . . . On the political marketplace of American society, the new middle classes are up for sale; whoever seems respectable enough, strong enough, can probably have them [1951:353–354].

Commentators on Mills' *Power Elite* seldom remark on the close relationship that he noted between the power elite and "the mass society," despite the fact that the book contains a chapter with that title. In such societies, says Mills, men "lose their will for rationally considered decision and action because they do not possess the instruments for such decision and action; they lose their sense of political will because they see no way to realize it (1956:324)." Faced with such an apathetic mass, it is easy for the power elite to move in, to unify and coordinate their efforts; the public, denuded by massification, lacks the means of resistance.

any feelings of contempt for the non-elite, there is some acceptance for the notion that the mass is inherently unqualified (1951:321)." Later, this position is clarified: "It is not the quality of the individuals which is in point but their roles; it is not so much that the mass is unfit in any literal sense as that the nature of the system prevents the emergence of an effective social leadership (1951:321)." The essential characteristic of mass society, then, is that the leveling of cultural values to the lowest common denominator destroys the quality of political elites, and it is elite incompetence—specifically their inability to resist mass demands—that fosters totalitarian movements. The solution to the mass society is, thus, to protect elites from the leveling effects of mass participation; political activism is depicted as the tool of extremists: "It is the mass-oriented elite, Fascist and Communist alike, which is the advocate and engineer of activism (1951:329)."

Kornhauser's *Politics of Mass Society* closely follows the views already presented. In his second chapter, the "conditions of mass society" are discussed. Key features are the loss of community, alienation, and atomization of the mass, "democratization" of access to elites and the consequent degeneration of political leadership, and finally the "availability" of nonelites for conscription into totalitarian movements. Chapter 3 continues the discussion; the central proposition, again, is that mass society is "atomized" (1959:75). The crisis of liberal democracy, for Kornhauser, is a crisis of pluralism. Lacking strong "intermediate relationships" between elites and nonelites, the mass is readied for mass movements. "In the absence of intermediate relationships, participation in the larger society must be direct rather than filtered through intervening relationships." Consequently, elites lose "the basis for self-protection"; the quality of leadership declines; and the culmination is a "mass" that is unprotected by responsible elites. The resulting surge of mass behavior into the democratic arena destroys the foundation of political democracy and facilitates totalitarian movements.

By the end of the 1950s, the theory of the mass society had effectively penetrated the scholarly social and political literature; indeed, it was essentially indistinguishable from it. "The mass society thesis," according to one account, "is a basic assumption of most current social science texts (Schuler *et al.* 1960:196)." At the same time, however, there was little overt political disruption or even discontent of the sort that might have been expected were the mass society thesis an entirely adequate empirical account. McCarthyism itself had been thoroughly discredited as early as 1954, with McCarthy's censure by his Senate peers, and, by the end of the decade, had essentially disappeared as a significant force on the American political scene. In its place had come the calm consensus of the Eisenhower regime, signified especially by his landslide victory over Adlai Stevenson in the 1956 election. There was, in addition, the election of a Roman Catholic to the Presidency 4 years hence. Despite the apparent potential for mass politics and mass disruption, the

American political system was nonetheless running rather smoothly. How, then, could one account for this apparent contradiction?

The "solution," of course, comes in the theory of democratic elitism, whose modern development begins at approximately this time. The underlying logic of this development is roughly as follows: If, as mass society theory suggests, the modern industrial democracy naturally tends toward hazardous and unstable mass political movements, and if, in this modern industrial democracy, very little political behavior of the sort is empirically manifest, then there must exist other circumstances, conditions, or social processes whose happy consequence is to make democracy relatively "safe" after all. If the modern democratic citizen is, in fact, not the well-informed and politically sophisticated guardian of democratic virtues, as Jefferson's vision would have it, but, rather, lacks social restraint and is readily "swayed by the demagogue who cries conspiracy and promises an immediate solution (Horton and Thompson 1962:487)," and if, simultaneously, the apparently inevitable demagogic- and system-endangering consequence are absent, then there must be social and political mechanisms that sublimate the mass impulses, deactivate them, thwart their causes, and mollify their effects—in short, mechanisms to render the mass "mainly passive." As we shall see in the next chapter, the major portion of American sociopolitical theory since the end of the McCarthy era has been little but an extended commentary on the social and political conditions that facilitate this deactivation.

RECENT DEVELOPMENTS

The conclusion of democratic elitism, that democratic government is best served when mass political participation is modest, although rooted historically in the theory of the mass society, is supported by numerous more recent developments in the theoretical and empirical social science literature that bear some mention here. Chief among these is the continuing, and now rather extensive, documentation of backward and antidemocratic political preferences among the mass (see the sources cited in Footnote 2). A second and related theme, which has emerged from the public opinion literature, is that "the nature of belief systems in mass publics" (Converse 1964) offers little hope for the informed and intelligent political discussion envisioned by classical democrats (see also Converse et al. 1969; Edelman 1971; Lippman 1922:310). As Verba and associates summarize the current view, "most recent studies have demonstrated that the public has little information on most issues and that most people do not have thought-out, consistent, and firmly-held positions on most matters of public policy" (1967:318).[24] Here, too,

---

[24] Recent challenges to this view include Levine (1971–1972), Litwak et al. (1973), Luttbeg (1968), and Pierce and Rose (1974). The Verba et al. study is of special

the social class theme predominates: Most observers agree that, as class and education increase, the more prevalent "thought-out, consistent, and firmly-held" beliefs become. The implication, sometimes drawn quite explicitly,[25] is that democracy functions most justly and humanely when the "periphery" is excluded from participation.

Another variant focuses more on the requirements for effective leadership than on inherent mass deficiencies. This view holds that, no matter how competent the mass may or may not be, the very operation of government requires that mass influence be minimal. Elites must be free to "make authoritative decisions," to commit the society's scarce resources as best they see fit, without undue pressure from "public demands."

Almond and Verba provide a definitive statement of this position. They formulate the basic paradox of democracy as follows:

> Unless there is some control of elites by non-elites, it is hard to consider a political system democratic. On the other hand, non-elites cannot themselves rule. If a political system is to be effective, . . . there must be mechanisms whereby governmental officials are endowed with the power to make authoritative decisions [1965:341].

---

interest because the data therein reported do not support the common view. With respect to Vietnam, at least, they say, "Our first finding is that public opinion is relatively informed about it (1967:330)." Also of interest, they found considerable internal cohesion among the elements of public beliefs concerning the war, but these consistencies did not manifest themselves along the lines most often studied by public opinion researchers (1967:331). This finding is consistent with that reported by Luttbeg: "Although the *degree* of constraint within leaders' and citizens' belief systems is nearly equal, [the study] shows the *structuring* of their belief system to differ greatly (1968: 404)."

[25] One unambiguous recommendation in this respect, for example, is Galtung's "Foreign policy as a function of social position" (1964). Enumerating "conditions that would probably contribute to a stable, peace-oriented and effective public opinion in the field of foreign policy," Galtung lists, as his first desideratum, "the elimination of the periphery from influence on foreign policy, for instance, through a party structure that does not adequately reflect periphery foreign policy orientations (1964:277)." Actually, this turns out to be a rather bizarre recommendation, since the most recent studies suggest that peace orientations are strongest among the "periphery." Hamilton (1968) has shown that the greatest support for the bombing of Manchuria in 1952 and the invasion of North Vietnam in 1964 came from the higher status sectors of the population: the affluent, the well-educated, white collar workers, and the young. These findings have been replicated on nationally representative 1968 and 1970 data by Wright (1972a, b, c).

Dye and Zeigler (1972) provide a more recent example. Discussing measures that might be taken to "preserve freedom, human dignity, and the values of life, liberty, and property," these authors mention first: "Preserve fundamental constitutional principles designed to modify mass influence in government." Following is a short discussion of such constitutional guarantees and then the comment: "These arrangements, which make it difficult for majority preferences to become public policy, must be strengthened —not modified, 'reformed', or weakened (1972:367)."

Hence, the fundamental problem is the "maintenance of a proper balance between governmental power and governmental responsiveness." Regardless of mass competence, "non-elites cannot themselves rule"; mass participation may "strain the system." The adjudication of factional disputes, simultaneous consideration of contradictory demands, the seeking of compromise among competing groups—all these essential tasks are better left to an elite few who are skilled in the necessary manipulations.

A similar conclusion has been advanced in the literature on community power. Hawley (1963), for example, presents evidence that suggests that cities with centralized power structures will be more innovative and more effective in the delivery of services than cities with democratic power structures because "ability is greatest where power is most highly concentrated (1963:424)." Democratic political systems waste too much of their resources on contentious politicking and too little on getting the work done. Again, the implication is that government is best served when mass participation is sparse.[26]

Parsons's theory of power is yet another instance of the view that government is generally better served when left to elites. Parsons metaphorically links money in the economic sphere and power in the political sphere; like money, power is a medium of exchange. As economic ends are attained through concentration of capital, so are political goals met through concentration of power. Certainly, financial institutions would be immobilized by the need to obtain the consent of their investors before embarking on every venture; so too would government be immobilized by trying to secure public approval of all its projects and decisions. "[Political] effectiveness. . .necessitates the capacity to make decisions and commit resources, *independently of specific conditions prescribed in advance*. . . by some kind of prior agreement or contract (1961:52)." In Parsons's view, mass insistence on their own political determination is equivalent to a run on the bank and is destructive of political stability.

Dye and Zeigler have conveniently summarized "some of the reasons why mass democracy is neither feasible nor desirable (1972:365)." First, "It is impossible for a mass to govern. . . . Participatory democracy is a romantic fiction." As well it should be, "the masses are incompetent in the tasks of government. They have neither the time, intelligence, information, skills nor knowledge to direct the course of a nation. . . . Governing a nation is a task which is too important, too vital, too complex, and too difficult to be left to the masses." In addition, "The masses are anti-democratic and there-

---

[26] The evidence, however, does not support these contentions. Hawley *did* find that his measure of "centralization" was positively related to community innovativeness, but later re-analysis of Hawley's measure showed it to be, in reality, a measure of decentralization, just the opposite of what Hawley thought (Aiken, 1970:503). Recent papers by Aiken and Alford (1970a, b, c) have found community innovation to be highest in cities with decentralized power structures.

fore cannot be relied upon to govern democratically. Despite a superficial commitment to the symbols of democracy, the people are not attached to the ideals of individual liberty, toleration of diversity, freedoms of expression and of dissent, or equality of opportunity. . . . Masses are authoritarian, intolerant, anti-intellectual, nativistic, alienated, hateful, and violent. Mass politics is extremist, unstable, and unpredictable." Finally, "The masses are fatally vulnerable to tyranny." There is, moreover, little that can be done to improve these dreary circumstances: "The authoritarianism of the masses is unavoidable. . . . Efforts to re-educate or re-socialize the masses are futile. . . . Today, the masses in America . . . appear less capable of governing in a wise and humane fashion than the masses of Jefferson's time."

THE LESSON OF WATERGATE

There has, of course, been rather little "wise and humane" government in the United States in the last decade. Instead, the American people have suffered through the agonies of Vietnam and, more recently, the corruption and chicanery of the Nixon administration. Certainly Watergate, if nothing else, should convince us that political elites are sometimes less-than-perfect guardians of the public trust, that elite stewardship of democratic values is often less than zealous. After all, Watergate was nothing if not a direct, frontal assault on democratic traditions waged by one segment of the elite against another. One might, therefore, expect the democratic elitists to have reconsidered their position in light of these events or at least to have appended the apparently necessary qualifications. This, however, has not been the case. It is still too early to know what treatment Watergate will ultimately be accorded in the democratic elitism texts, but the initial indication is that the theorists see Watergate as a partial *confirmation* of their point of view.

This "initial indication" is provided in the most recent edition of Dye and Zeigler's *The Irony of Democracy*. As yet unpublished, excerpts from the new edition appear in the Winter (1974) volume of the *DEA News*, a house organ for the political science profession. According to these excerpts, Watergate is to be taken as "an excellent illustration of elite reaction to mass unrest, and the tendency of elites to resort to repression when threatened." From the available fragments, one infers that the phrase, "mass unrest," refers to Vietnam protest and other acts of public outrage directed against the Nixon administration—most of it, of course, well within the provisions of the Bill of Rights. The "reaction," in turn, apparently refers to steps taken by the Nixon administration to safeguard the republic against "threats" posed by this unrest. These would include, presumably, the infamous "enemies list," the conscription of the FBI, IRS, and, apparently, the CIA in the struggle against those "enemies," forcible entry into the Democratic National Committee headquarters, and so on. Watergate, it must be noted, is not to be seen as evidence of authoritarian character structures, as Nixon's panicky reaction to his own status insecurities, or as indicative of intolerance of out-groups, repression of dissent, or insufficient fealty to the rules of democratic procedure. There is the recognition that elites may sometimes "resort to repression," but cause is attributed to the masses who have broken, however fitfully, from their passive mold. Elites merely react; they respond to stimuli that are not of their own making; they do what they have to do. How far we have strayed from Jefferson's simple maxim, that "every government degenerates when entrusted to the rulers of the people alone."

2

The Sources of
Mass Moderation

Having enumerated the potential hazards of popular democracy, the theory of democratic elitism poses an initial paradox for itself. If, as the theory suggests, mass participation is often inimical to true democratic interests, and if successful democracy depends primarily on a deactivated or "mainly passive" electorate, then it would seemingly follow that instabilities will be greatest where participation is highest, or, what amounts to the same thing, that modern democracies will lead the list of the world's less stable states. World political history in the postwar era, however, does not show this to be the case. On the contrary, when one considers the less stable postwar governments—Algeria, Guatemala, Greece, Cuba, Vietnam, Korea—one is necessarily struck by the absence of democracies from this list. As we indicated in the previous chapter, however, the theorists are little troubled by this apparent anomaly. Instead, they have simply inferred that, in addition to its potential hazards, the modern democracy also contains social and political mechanisms that allow it to persist as a stable and viable governmental form. The lesson, in short, has not been that democracies are *necessarily* unstable; rather, they have the *potential* for instability but also structures and processes which, under normal circumstances, prevent that potential from being realized. In the present chapter, we consider the mechanisms of stability, the "sources of mass moderation," and the evidence customarily cited on their behalf.

It should be taken for granted at the outset that democracy itself is one such stabilizing mechanism, or, in other words, that certain political advant-

36

ages result from the extension of some modicum of power and participation to the mass. One advantage, certainly, is that popular participation may provide a check on the power and potential abuses of the elected elite.[1] In the classical theory, of course, this was to be the primary function of popular participation, but, in the modern theory, the "checking of elites" by the masses plays a rather minor role. As we have already seen, a key element of this theory is that elites, not masses, are the prime subscribers to democratic values, and, besides, the provisions for competition among elites, when functioning properly, virtually assure self-restraint. In fact, as we will discuss later in this chapter, these theorists are so confident of the good will and equanimity of those who rise to positions of power that even *actual* mass participation may be going farther than necessary; rather, the mere *threat* of such participation is seen, in some renditions, as sufficient to keep the elites "in line."

A second and somewhat more important benefit of democracy itself is that the extension of some political power to the masses (or, preferably, an *illusion* to that effect) aids in the development of what is known as the "democratic myth," which, in turn, performs important stabilizing functions. The key here is to assure widespread *belief* that the system is legitimate—that political participation is both a right and a duty, that popular participation determines public policy, that the majority rules, and so on. Through these beliefs, the system creates the impression that politics is a fair game in which all opinions are accorded equal treatment. This, in turn, defuses and delegitimizes attempts to seek redress outside the normal channels.

Now, it is presumably within the power of the regime to create and nurture these myths in any number of ways, but the most effective by far is to prove that they have some real basis in fact. "In a technical sense," as V.O. Key has said, "that belief may be a myth, an article of faith, yet its maintenance requires that it possess a degree of validity (1961:547)." The stabilities introduced by popular acceptance of the democratic myth, in short, are sufficient to warrant "enough" democracy to sustain it. Thus, limited democ-

---

[1] These concerns, it must be emphasized, are present in the modern, no less than in the classical theory of democracy. Lipset, for example, lists among his essential conditions of democracy that "if the conditions for perpetuating an active opposition do not exist, the authority of officials in power will steadily increase, and popular influence on policy will be at a minimum (1963a:28)." The difference between classical and modern views on this score is, once again, a matter of emphasis. In the classical theory, as we discuss in the text, the concern with elite abuses was paramount; in the modern theory, such issues are secondary concerns. The potential dangers of too much democracy receive detailed consideration in the modern texts; the potential dangers of too little democracy are seldom fully discussed.

In the Lipset view, for example, the main "condition for perpetuating an active opposition" is competition between contesting parties; in fact, the presence of competing parties is often employed as an operational definition of democratic government. For persuasive critiques of this definition, see Hamilton (1972: Chap. 1) and Wittman (1973).

racy or elitist democracy, rather than no democracy at all, is seen as the most practicable and workable political ideal. Limited democracy nourishes the necessary myths and, thus, protects against unruly populist and demagogic movements; it pays formal obeisance to cherished principles of self-government and self-determination. Yet, in so doing, the system may expose itself to the natural incompetence and immoderation of the mass. Thus, in addition to extending enough democracy to sustain the requisite myths and, in times of need, to restrain the political leadership, the system is next called upon to assure that the conditions for its intelligent use are also present. The people, in short, must not only believe that the system is democratic and open to their influence but must also acquiesce in the principles of conciliation and compromise that allow the system to function equitably.[2]

The practical consequences of Jefferson's theory of democracy were relatively straightforward: Democratic government is best served by the fullest possible participation of all. Modern theories are inevitably more complex since, as Almond and Verba remark, the modern democracy is called upon to pursue two somewhat contradictory goals, to strike "a delicate balance" between an active and a passive mass. After all, the ideal democratic citizen is supposed to be active and informed, but not overly so; self-interested, yet moderate in securing his interests; willing to "inform" elites of his policy wishes, yet remain deferential to them; cognizant of democratic rights and responsibilities, yet hesitant to exercise them; committed to the belief that popular participation should determine political policy, yet willing to turn power over to elites and allow them a free hand in its use, at least for specific periods of time agreed upon in advance—all of this, moreover, required of a mass thought to be appetitive and rapacious, plagued by economic insecurity and authoritarian character structures, and prone to status anxieties. What produces this type of citizen? How is the necessary moderation to be supplied?

THE PLURALIST THESIS

Until recently, the leading answer to the questions just posed has been pluralist theory, and most of the theorists considered so far would certainly

---

[2] This is yet another instance of the difference between classical and modern theories being one of emphasis and degree. As we mentioned in the first chapter, Jefferson himself often insisted that the success of the "democratic experiment" would depend on the receptivity of the people to the ideas of democratic process, compromise, open debate, moderation, and self-restraint. Following the views of the Enlightenment, however, Jefferson also believed that there were natural tendencies in these directions that would rise to the surface once the chains of oppression had been loosened. Modern theorists entertain mostly the opposite view—that the natural tendencies are toward immoderation and extremism, and, accordingly, that the system must provide mechanisms that restrain and sublimate these inclinations. This point is raised again at the end of this chapter and also in Chapter 10.

be included in the pluralist camp. Unlike the term "mass," which connotes sameness and homogeneity, the term "pluralism" connotes diversity and heterogeneity, and it is in the diversity of industrial life where pluralists first locate the sources of mass moderation.[3]

A central element in the pluralist view is that modern industrial societies are characterized by a plurality of institutions and that citizens have roles in most, if not all, of them. Hence, every citizen will have some familial attachment, some occupational commitment, perhaps a religious affiliation or identification with a racial, religious, or ethnic group, and certainly an age, a sex, and so on. Moreover, each of these roles will have particular political interests attached to it, and this, in turn, poses the possibility that the interests of one role may occasionally conflict with the interests of another. The resulting "cross-pressures," then, perform numerous moderating functions: Hostility in partisan conflict is reduced, because some legitimate and important interests may be jeopardized by passionate commitment to a single interest. The value of compromise is exemplified, because only through compromise will one's several competing interests be simultaneously guarded. Citizens are made aware of the contradictions among their various demands and, thus, become more moderate spokesmen. Finally, the essentials of democratic procedure will be appreciated, particularly the importance of minority rights.[4]

There is, however, cause for skepticism concerning these alleged palliative

[3] In this respect, the theory of the mass society is the "pathological inverse" of pluralism (Hamilton 1972: Ch. 2). Most mass society theorists, interestingly, accept pluralism as a normative ideal, as the ultimate solution to the problems of the mass society, but reject pluralism on empirical grounds. The debate between these theorists is whether the inherent tendencies of modernization and industrialization produce a more diverse or or less diverse population. For some evidence on this score, see Glenn (1967).

[4] See, for example Parsons, who urges that "there can never be any absolute commitment to a particular interest—ideological, religious, or otherwise—because this would lead to a burning of bridges which connect with elements necessary for an effective support-coalition, elements that would not go along with such a commitment (1967:77)."

Likewise, Lipset counsels, "Multiple and politically inconsistent affiliations, loyalties, and stimuli reduce the emotion and agressiveness involved in political choice. . . . The available evidence suggests that the chances for democracy are enhanced to the extent that groups and individuals have a number of cross-cutting, politically relevant affiliations (1963a:77)."

Kornhauser amply summarizes the view: "Where social pluralism is strong, liberty and democracy tend to be strong; and conversely, forces which weaken social pluralism also weaken liberty and democracy (1959:231)."

Other cross-pressure theorists include Berelson et al. (1954), Lazarsfeld et al. (1948), Lipset et al. (1954) Pool et al. (1965), and Segal (1969).

Lipset has offered an analogous argument concerning the role of political parties. "A stable democracy requires a situation in which all the major political parties include supporters from many segments of the population (1967b:457)." As when individuals are insufficiently cross-pressured, "A system in which the support of different parties corresponds too closely to basic social divisions cannot continue on a democratic basis, for it reflects a state of conflict so intense and clear-cut as to rule out compromise (1964:12–13)."

benefits. For example, the mere existence of a plurality of roles does not rule out some hierarchy of importance among them. Certainly, the number of communities and affiliations that provide psychological identification and political direction will be less than the total number of statistical categories into which persons can be sorted. Along these lines, one is reminded of Lederer's remark, that "modern society is split up into innumerable groups, and an individual belongs to several of them. Usually, he will avoid belonging to groups with conflicting interests (1967:24)." There are, moreover, reasons to suspect that the amount of cross-pressuring may *decrease* as industrialization proceeds. As societies industrialize, that is, there may be a tendency for the several dimensions of differentiation to become congruent (Treiman 1970), and this would imply some decline in the potential for cross-pressuring effects. Theories of modernization and industrialization have suggested that ascriptive bases of stratification (such as religion, race, sex, ethnicity) erode as the society moves to a more achievement-oriented basis. Religion and ethnicity, for example, are often said to cross-pressure social class influences (e.g., Lipset 1967b), yet, according to Parsons, these factors "have lost much of their force" in modern American society (1970). Other processes allegedly inherent in advanced industrialization—for example, the "democratization" of education, rampant upward mobility, religious secularization, and urbanization—would also seem to imply some decline in the social diversity that figures prominently in the pluralist account.[5]

   A more important issue is whether or not cross-pressures actually produce the moderation that is claimed for them. According to the theory, cross-pres-

[5] There are, to be sure, real questions as to whether or not any of these trends have occurred even in the United States. Numerous recent studies have questioned whether or not ethnicity has withered away as a factor in American sociopolitical life (Abramson, 1973; Glazer and Moynihan 1970; Greeley 1972a, 1972c, 1974; Hamilton 1972; Novak 1971; Parenti 1967; and others). Similarly, Greeley (1972b) has argued that the much discussed "secularization" of modern urban life is an exaggeration; rather, "The basic human religious needs and the basic religious functions have not changed very notably since the late Ice Age." Data on such matters as church attendance lend credence to Greeley's claims. The proportion attending church "regularly" or "often," for example, has held essentially constant (at about 60%) since 1952.
   The common depiction of the "democratization of education," especially higher education, has also been challenged. Hamilton and Wright (forthcoming) have shown that probably no more than a third of all eligible U.S. young adults attend an institution of higher learning, and, of these, only about half obtain a college degree. The third who do attend are drawn disproportionately from the children of high status families. The much heralded expansion of American higher education in the 1960s reflected (1) the entrance of the large "baby boom" generations into college; (2) an increase in the proportion of *upper middle class* children, especially daughters, who were attending college; and (3) some limited extension of "higher" education to the children of the working class, mostly in the form of junior and community colleges.
   Finally, Hamilton (1972: Chap. 3) has seriously questioned the view that the American labor force has been continuously expanding in the middle class occupational sectors. The apparent growth of the middle class has reflected, in large part, the increasing en-

sures teach the value of compromise, exemplify the importance of minority rights, and so on. The classic Columbia studies, however, demonstrated none of these effects. Rather, the major consequences of cross-pressuring is to reduce the stability of vote intentions and lower the probability that the individual would even vote. Rogin has summarized these studies: "In general, cross-pressured people are not moderate through involvement, but rather withdraw from politics because of conflict. Their multiple pressures lead not to rational moderation but rather to political withdrawal and confusion (1967:24)."

More recent studies have even questioned whether or not cross-pressures have *any* effects, either on moderation or withdrawal. Horan has analyzed the interplay of religion, occupation, income, and education and concludes that the evidence "for a national sample of adult males provides no support for the hypothesis that partisan cross-pressures *per se* affect non-voting (1971: 659)." Thus, he relegates the thesis to "that category of plausible theories whose empirical support has been cut out from under them." One would prefer not to attribute the stability of modern societies to forces whose existence must be held in doubt.

Lipset, a leading proponent of cross-pressures, provides another basis for skepticism. Despite the claimed dependency of modern democracies on "multiple and politically inconsistent affiliations," Lipset elsewhere maintains that "on a world scale, the principal generalization that can be made is that parties are primarily based either on the lower classes or the middle and upper classes. This generalization even holds true for the American parties, which have traditionally been considered an exception (1963a:230)." The principal tendency, in short, according to Lipset, is that political choice is rooted in the conditions of social class; the implication is that attachments that contradict class interest are likely to be subordinated.[6]

Data reported by the Survey Research Center in its 1972 election study provide additional information on this question. Respondents ($n = 2190$) were given a list of groups to which they might have some attachment (businessmen, liberals, Southerners, poor people, Catholics, Protestants, Jews, young

---

trance of the blue collar wives into the labor force at the clerical and sales levels. Taking male breadwinners only, Hamilton's data show a clear blue collar or working class majority for every census in this century, with only a modest decline in the size of that majority, amounting to about one percentage point per decade. (See also Levison 1974).

[6] In the U.S. case, Lipset's emphasis on social class as the primary determinant is somewhat misplaced; as Hamilton has shown, religion is more strongly associated with party identification than is social class (1972; Hamilton and Wright 1975a). This, however, is not an important point for our purposes and in no way dilutes the view being proposed in the text: Whether religion or social class constitutes the more important basis for politics and party affiliation, it is clear that some "social roles" will be vastly more salient politically than others and that the plausibility of "cross-pressures" theory is diminished accordingly.

people, whites, blacks, conservatives, women, middle class people, working-men, farmers, and old people) and then asked whether they "felt particularly close" to each of them. The total number of choices across these 16 potential attachments was 9334, an average of 4.35 choices per respondent, which indicates a considerable *potential* for cross-pressuring (although, even here, probably less than is implied in the standard pluralist account). The follow-up question, however, asked the respondent to pick from the list of 16 the one group he or she felt *closest* to. Only 39 of the respondents were unable to choose among the groups, and, for the rest, age and class categories accounted for more than three-quarters of all choices. This suggests that, despite the possibility of conflicting affiliations, roles are nonetheless arranged in a hierarchy of importance, with age and class affiliations by far the most important.

One final research finding worth mentioning in this context is reported in *Voting*. Respondents were asked how they intended to vote and then how their three best friends intended to vote; thus, the researchers were able to construct a measure of the "political homogeneity of the primary environment." Several aspects of the results warrant discussion. First, the level of homogeneity was high: Of the respondents, 72% ($n = 500$) said all three of their best friends were voting the same as themselves, and 86% thought at least two would. Approximately 75%, in short, felt exposed to no single cross-pressure from their three best friends. More important is the relationship of environmental homogeneity to age; as persons grew older, homogeneity increased. "Thus, political homogeneity of the primary environment, high to start with, becomes even higher with the passage of time (1954:97)."

Why might this be the case? One possibility is that persons sort among their friends, keeping those with whom they tend to agree and rejecting the rest. Clearly, any such "sorting" process would speak ill for the empirical plausibility of the cross-pressuring account. Another possibility is that interpersonal influence processes among friends render their politics more consistent over time. This would, however, suggest a rather permanent force operating to counter inconsistent attachments, again raising a serious question about the cross-pressure thesis.

There is, in short, ample theoretical and empirical reason to be skeptical of claims made for the moderating potential of social diversity and its attendant cross-pressures. There is more, however, to the pluralist's story; the proliferation of so-called "voluntary associations" is often cited as yet another major source of the required mass passivity.[7] As depicted in the pluralist thesis, these

[7] Correlatively, theorists of the mass society frequently cite the *decline* of voluntary associations as a major factor leading to the alienated and anomic mass. C. Wright Mills, for example, writing on the factors involved in the transformation of "publics" into "masses," notes that "one of the most important of the structural transformations involved is the decline of the voluntary association." Later, he reiterates, "Along with older institutions, voluntary associations have lost their grip on the individual (1956:306–307)."

voluntary associations perform many moderating and stabilizing functions. For one, they figure prominently in the "pluralist organization of power," which was mentioned briefly in the first chapter. Involved here is the view that the population is organized into associations and tends to work through them when seeking political change. This form of political organization is, in turn, felt to have numerous political advantages: First, it increases the level of political representation, since influence is increased when interests are aggregated; second, these associations compete among themselves for constituencies, thus producing additional cross-pressures; third, by having power dispersed among associations, domination by a single elite is forestalled; and, finally, requiring that interests and demands be articulated through the medium of voluntary associations means .that they will already be filtered through at least one level of "responsible" elite leadership before they emerge at the national political level.[8]

In addition to these various "structural" effects, voluntary associations have powerful direct effects on the political moderation of their members. Participation in such associations, for example, may vent political extremism and dissatisfaction at the associational level and leave the national government untouched. Second, voluntary associations are convenient arenas in which the essentials of democratic compromise are learned; seeing a miniature "system" in operation reinforces the lessons of political "give-and-take," which

[8] Our concern here, of course, is with voluntary associations as moderating mechanisms, not as representational mechanisms, but, on the latter score, the following deserve mention:

First, neither all nor even a substantial majority is organized into such associations (evidence on this point is discussed in the text). Indeed, if purely expressive organizations are omitted, the proportion belonging to a politically active association could scarcely be more than 25% (Hamilton 1972: Chap. 2). It would be an odd theory of democracy whose major representational mechanism is unavailable to the large majority.

Similarly, even among those who do belong, there is some question as to whether or not working through the organization is seen by them as a means of political influence. Data reported in the Civic Culture suggest that only about 5% of the population thought of working through some formal organization when asked what they could do to influence the national government (1965:160). More recently, the Survey Research Center asked in its 1968 study: "Suppose a law were being considered by the Congress in Washington that you considered very unjust or harmful. What do you think you could do about it?" In a probability sample of the nation's adults, about a third flatly stated "Nothing." More than half gave some sort of individualistic response (vote, write letters to a Congressman, etc.), and only about 6% mentioned some formal group political activity. Along these same lines, only about a quarter of the Civic Culture respondents felt that any organization to which they belonged was involved in political affairs (1965:251).

Other reservations might include: The organization is not always internally democratic, meaning that grass-roots opinion is not necessarily represented even after it is organized into the associational network; the organizations can (and often do) collude among themselves, to the detriment of their constituency; the means and ability required to organize an effective association are neither widespread nor necessarily democratically distributed in the population, meaning, again, that large segments are left out of the representing mechanism; and so on. See Hamilton (1972: Ch. 2) for a more thorough critique.

then carry over into national political life. Third, activity in such associations exposes the members to diverse points of view, thus fostering cosmopolitan orientations and sophisticated ego structures that are essential for commitment to democratic procedures. Fourth, such associations provide sources of identity and community and, thus, act as an antidote to the mass society. Fifth, the contribution made by associational activity to the necessary democratic myths should not be overlooked. Finally, pluralists often claim that citizens belong to more than one association, resulting in an additional source of cross- pressures and their accompanying benefits.[9]

Citizens only receive these many positive direct effects, however, if they actually belong to voluntary associations,[10] and the most recent, most representative, and most persuasive evidence gives little reason to be optimistic. On the basis of secondary analysis of nationally representative sample survey data, Hyman and Wright suggest that, at most, about three-fifths of the population belongs to at least one such association (1971:195).[11] When union membership (frequently not "voluntary") is excluded, the proportion drops to about two-fifths. Similar results are reported in the *Civic Culture* data (Almond and Verba 1965:246ff.). Thus, about half the adult population is automatically excluded from any direct moderating benefits.

The half that does belong, moreover, is not randomly distributed in the society; on the contrary, all researchers who have raised the question report that memberships increase with social class (Almond and Verba 1965; Curtis 1971; Hyman and Wright 1971; Komarovsky 1946; Smith and Freedman 1972; Wright and Hyman 1958). What this means is that those thought to

[9] Theorists articulating these views are far too numerous to list. Among the more recent and important are: Almond and Verba (1965), Kornhauser (1959), Lipset (1963a), Rose (1968), Smith and Freedman (1972), and Verba (1965).

[10] That is, will only receive the alleged moderating experiences and contacts. Obviously, nonmembers may sometimes benefit indirectly from activities of voluntary associations. Minimum wage laws, for example, benefit union and nonunion workers alike, even though the unions were instrumental in the passage of such legislation. A national program of federalized health care, if it ever comes to pass, would likewise be to the benefit of all, whether or not one belonged to associations lobbying for such a program. One can safely admit that, in these respects, voluntary associations may contribute greatly to the viability of democratic government, although even here one suspects that corporate and business interests are vastly overrepresented. The only point at issue in the text is whether or not voluntary associations contribute *directly* to mass moderation through the mechanisms outlined; the evidence is that they do not.

[11] Curtis has mentioned that, in spite of the importance of voluntary associations in pluralist theorizing, "thus far, only Wright and Hyman have presented detailed national survey data bearing on this question. They concluded that Americans are *not* a nation of joiners (1971:872)."

Despite the direction of the evidence, pluralists have not been dissuaded from their view. Rose's *Power Structure* is a case in point. He mentions, "There have been a few studies of membership in voluntary associations using polling techniques and national samples, but the results have been so different and the techniques of getting the data so questionable that these studies do not provide reliable information (1968:219–220)." Rose's main source for this comment is Wright and Hyman (1958). Summarizing

be most in need of moderation—the lower status sectors—are least likely to receive it, again diminishing faith in the pluralist view.

The evidence on multiple membership is even less encouraging. Hyman and Wright report that only 21% of the population belongs to two or more associations, 31% with union membership included. Multiple membership is also strongly correlated with social class. According to their data, the proportion of grade school drop-outs belonging to two or more organizations is around 10%; this figure increases to about 44% among the college educated. So, once again, those most in need of the moderating influences of associational activity are in the worst position to receive it.

If evidence on the *extent* of membership is not reassuring, evidence on the *effects* of memberships is less so. Verba (1965), himself a leading pluralist, has reported evidence bearing directly on the issue. Available for analysis were two measures of "political immoderation": first, the views of the respondent concerning his son or daughter marrying a member of the opposing political party; and, second, the tendency of the respondent to describe members of opposing parties in negative terms (e.g., as "selfish," "ignorant," etc.). The pluralist hypotheses are clear: Members of voluntary associations, particularly those with multiple affiliations, should be more moderate. The evidence, however, did not support the expectations. The percentage of U.S. respondents who described members of the opposition in negative terms varied from 12% of those with no voluntary associations, to 14% of those reporting one such affiliation, to 13% of those reporting two or more affiliations. On the question of marrying across party lines, 4% of the nonmembers, 3% of the single members, and 4% of the multiple members said they would be "displeased." Verba concludes:

> The data for the United States . . . do not support our hypothesis that organizational members become exposed to more heterogeneous political environments due to their organizational membership, [or] that the resulting

the findings in their later article, Hyman and Wright remark, "Voluntary association membership is not characteristic of the majority of Americans (a finding originally from data in the 1950's, now confirmed by data from the 1960's) [1971:205]." These results are based on approximately 20 separate surveys.

Of the several surveys summarized by Wright and Hyman in their 1958 article, Rose chooses to discuss only three. He emphasizes the different results reported from those three surveys and finds it particularly striking that one survey found a mere 36% belonging to at least one organization, whereas another found about 65% belonging. He does not mention that the first study excluded union membership, whereas the second did not, a point made clearly in the Wright and Hyman presentation. He concludes, "The very discrepancy between the figures should make us suspicious of all of them, and it cannot be concluded that the true figure is somewhere in between (1968:220)."

Having thus liberated himself from the restraining influence of the facts, Rose can then state later, without documentation or reference, that "while only a small proportion of the population is very *active* in the association, a very large proportion . . . are *members* of the associations" (1968:222). Clearly, it was his theory and not the evidence that led him to this conclusion.

cross-pressures lead to a reduction in the intensity of political conflict [1965: 495].

What is the reason for the negative findings? Verba himself suggests one possibility: Whereas pluralism assumes that multiple memberships will be "overlapping," that there will be some diversity in the clientele and political interests of the various organizations, it is more likely that they will be "cumulative"; that is, there will usually be a certain uniformity throughout one's various associations and, consequently, relative consistency in the political environment. The tendency to avoid dissonant situations, after all, is well-documented in social psychology, and there is little reason to expect that this tendency will not be present in an individual's choice of organizations. Finally, where memberships are cumulative, the expected effect on moderation would be negative: Such memberships introduce and aggregate persons of like minds and, thus, reinforce (not cross-pressure) political views; "an increase in the intensity of political competitiveness" might just as well be the result.

A second possibly spurious assumption is that the association or its leaders will have an interest in decreasing "political immoderation" among the grass roots. Yet, in many cases, "political immoderation" or "dissatisfaction" is the organization's paramount political resource, the one on whose account persons are drawn to, participate in, and seek change through the organization. This, in turn, means that the organization's main interests will usually lie, not in diffusing or sublimating discontent, but in nourishing and mobilizing it.[12]

In sum, even if everyone in the society belonged to a voluntary association, there are both theoretical and empirical reasons to doubt that the level of political immoderation would thereby be affected; moreover, the best evidence confirms that not nearly everyone belongs and that those who do belong are least in need of the alleged effects. It would appear, then, that pluralists need to look beyond both social cross-pressures and voluntary associations to locate the sources of the necessary mass moderation.[13]

One final set of pluralist mechanisms involves various features of the po-

---

[12] A similar argument has been made by Pinard (1968):
> Even if we assume that the various components of the intermediate structure [that is, the voluntary association structure] are taken as reference points, we must still raise a major criticism: it seems to us that the claim that primary and secondary groups exert restraining effects on their members implies a onesided view of the role of intermediate groups. . . . The intermediate structure may actually, under circumstances discussed below, exert *mobilizing*, rather than restraining effects [1968:684].

[13] These comments, of course, say essentially nothing about any restraints that voluntary associations may impose on the behavior of elites, nor about their effectiveness in presenting the policy preferences of their constituents to the political leadership. It may very well be, in these respects, that the voluntary associations perform important democratizing functions. There is, we believe, ample reason for skepticism on this score (see, for example, Hamilton 1975: Chap. 7), but this is not an issue that can be discussed in any depth here.

litical structure itself, in particular, the two-party system, which is thought to have numerous political benefits.[14] For instance, the two-party system guarantees that those in power are elected by at least a simple majority and, hence, that the party *not* in power must attempt to make inroads into that majority; this, in turn, means that both parties must appeal outside their natural constituency. Thus, the prospects for cross-pressures are increased as both parties strive to capture the votes of the center. Moreover, in order to compete, both parties must present the broadest possible programs, thereby foreclosing "extremist" movements within the party. Competition for an absolute majority also implies that issues will be discussed in the mildest, most conciliatory terms; "hard-line" party positions may alienate the critical center. The net effect is two parties as close to one another as possible; this has the further advantage of channeling all political conflict through a structure in which the parties are essentially indistinguishable. Political conflict, no matter how intense it is at its source, will, thus, necessarily be moderated before it emerges onto the national arena.

The history of the United States in the last decade, however, raises questions about the operation, even the existence, of these various two-party safeguards. The alleged "inhibitions," for example, did not prevent candidates who were said to be "ideologically extreme" from winning their respective party's nomination in either 1964 or 1972, nor did the system forestall the third-party effort of George Wallace in 1968. In three successive presidential elections, then, the mass public was presented with candidates of the sort that the system is supposed to protect us from—candidates with "extreme" views, making direct appeals to frustration and voter estrangement, urging that their candidacies be used as a forum for disgust with "politics as usual." Goldwater and McGovern, however, ran first and second for the worst electoral showing in modern times, and the Wallace candidacy, nation-wide, was

---

[14] As Jaros and Mason have brazenly summarized it:

> Citizens are viewed as having inherent tendencies to perform destabilizing political acts or to vote for extremist political figures. Somehow, we are told, these citizens are restrained from indulging these immoderate dispositions by the party system. In a sense, the argument continues, parties save the great unwashed from themselves; all democrats should be thankful that they do and appreciate them for this service [1969: 100].

Other "system features" in addition to the two-party system are often mentioned; constraints of space prevent a full review. Among the more important are: Appointment rather than election of administrators puts the actual levers of power beyond mass control; infrequent elections increase time in which elites are independent of popular review; nomination by convention rather than popular primary assures that the candidates are "filtered" through a "responsible" quasi-elite; complicated registration requirements, literacy tests, poll taxes, and so on assure that only the more responsible citizens get to vote; and systems of representation that award total victory to the majority rather than those that award parliamentary strength in proportion to popular support assure that "extremist" minority movements will be excluded from parliamentary assemblies. For a critique of these various "system safeguards," see Wright (1973b:23–26).

rejected by about 90% of the voters. On the basis of these elections, it would be difficult to argue that the system somehow protected the people from themselves; on the contrary, the people were "moderate" even when the system was not.[15]

In short, pluralism fails as a solution to the paradox of stable democracy.[16] If the citizens of advanced industrial societies such as the United States do require vast amounts of political moderation, it is unlikely that the various pluralist "mechanisms" alone are able to provide it. Claims made for the moderating potential of social cross-pressures, voluntary associations, and even the two-party system all lack a firm empirical base. Certainly, more thorough and systematic review will ultimately be needed to support these broad, sweeping conclusions; for now, it is sufficient merely to raise the strong suspicion that pluralism is not a compelling account of current political realities in the United States.[17]

The failure of pluralism to solve the "paradox" of stable democracy—if we may now speak brashly—poses a pair of analytic possibilities. The first, to

---

[15] The point here, of course, is that the two-party system by itself is insufficient to guarantee that moderate candidates or platforms will prevail. This does not imply that this system makes no contribution whatsoever to democratic viability. Any electoral arrangement will necessarily have its strength and weaknesses: the two-party system, for example, guarantees a ruling majority, but with some loss of democratic representation; a multi-party system, on the other hand, maximizes the "fit" between party structure and mass political preferences but lends itself to manipulation by minority interests. We have already mentioned in the previous chapter the role of the Weimar political structure in facilitating Hitler's rise to power. Concerning the American case since 1964, this much is certain: The system did not prevent "extremist" candidates from appearing on the national ballot in three successive elections. In all three elections, the "extremist" was soundly trounced. Therefore, we conclude that the American two-party structure is not a major source of mass moderation or restraint.

[16] That is, it fails to provide an empirically grounded account of the sources of mass moderation. The term, "pluralist theory," refers to an exceedingly broad body of sociopolitical speculation, and we hasten to state that these conclusions do not apply to any aspect of the theory other than that under explicit consideration here.

[17] Major steps towards a definitive critique have been taken by Bachrach (1967), Hamilton (1972, 1975) and Rogin (1967), from whose ideas we have borrowed freely for our own discussion. The latter provides perhaps the best available summary of pluralist theorizing as it presently exists:

> Pluralist thinking has not produced scientific propositions so much as useful insight. And for this it deserves credit. At the same time, because of its underlying preoccupations, the pluralist vision is a distorted one. The fear of radicalism and the concern for stability, however, legitimate as values, have interfered with accurate perception. Thanks to its allegiance to modern America, pluralism analyzes efforts by masses to improve their condition as threats to stability. It turns all threats to stability into threats to constitutional democracy. This is a profoundly conservative endeavor. Torn between its half-expressed fears and its desire to face reality, pluralist theory is a peculiar mixture of analysis and prescription, insight and illusion, special pleading and dispassionate inquiry. Perhaps pluralism may best be judged not as the product of science but as a liberal American venture into conservative political theory [1967:282].

which we are initially inclined, is that the theorists have greatly underestimated the intelligence and capabilities of the mass, that the stability of modern democracies depends on nothing so much as a public fund of political decency, that, accordingly, the "threat" posed to democracy by "mass politics" has been greatly exaggerated in the standard accounts, and, finally, that the stock theoretical horrors are mainly the misplaced illusions and fears of intellectuals who have lost touch with common realities.[18] There is ample evidence, as Greeley has argued, that "the American people are a tough, resilient, resourceful, sophisticated, and generous people, consistently underestimated by both left and right wing elites (1975:2)," that they are liberal and progressive concerning economics and the welfare state (Hamilton 1972), and that they are "educable" in matters of race, civil liberties, and civil rights (Campbell 1971; Davis 1974). We have also learned from American political history in the last decade that the people can recognize demagogues who appear on the scene and have the ability and intelligence to defeat them, in this case, with very little help from the "system." Finally, there is a persistent suspicion and a considerable amount of overt evidence that the greatest threats to democratic values in recent years have arisen not from the masses, but at the hands of presumably "responsible" elites. There is, in short, sufficient contrary evidence to raise a serious question about the fundamental assumption of democratic elitism—that the vassals, not the sovereign, require the greatest restraints.[19]

[18] Indeed, it often appears that the fantasies of the texts are their major distinguishing features. Consider, for example, the following representative entries: "Policy controversies have to be kept from escalating to controversies over total ways of life or among irreconcilable groups (Verba 1965:469)," or "In this way, the amount of citizen activity at any one point in time is not so great as to strain the system (Almond and Verba 1965:352)," or "How can society face continuous conflict and still maintain social cohesion and the legitimacy of state authority (Lipset 1963a:2)," or "Modern democratic systems possess a distinct vulnerability to mass politics because they invite the whole population, most of which has been historically quiescent, to engage in politics (Kornhauser 1959:227)" or "Demands have the capacity to impose strains on a system by driving its essential variables towards their critical limits (Easton, 1965:57)." One would scarcely recognize that the passages are meant to describe political systems like the United States, where calm prevails nearly as far as the eye can see in every direction. The persistant imagery that informs these texts is that the modern democratic government is a dangerously fragile creature whose frail equilibrium is constantly assaulted by "strain," "continuous conflict," "irreconcilable groups," and "critical limits." What on-going empirically observable political system are these alarums meant to describe? Is this, as it claims to be, a "realistic" depiction of the political process in *any* modern democracy? Or would we better conclude (as mentioned in the text) that the intellectuals who write these theories have only a passing familiarity with extant political realities? To anticipate the findings presented in later chapters, there is very little persuasive evidence to support these portrayals. (On the circumstances that insulate the intellectual class from the conditions of life in the mass, see Hamilton 1975: Chap. 8.)

[19] There is relatively little to be gained from romanticizing the political abilities of the mass public, just as there is little to be gained from fantasizing about largely imaginary

A second analytic possibility, of course, might acknowledge the failure of pluralism as a solution to the paradox of democracy but claim that theoretical mechanisms other than pluralism supply the required moderation. This possibility turns our attention to the leading alternative contender in the modern tradition, namely, the theory of political consensus.

CONSENSUS AND THE THEORY OF POLITICAL ALIENATION

Consensus theory shifts focus from the structure of society to the attitudinal attributes of individuals as the explanation for democratic stability. The crucial sustaining mechanism, then, is no longer the organization of society, but rather *beliefs* about its organization. According to this thesis, political beliefs, if strongly held and of the appropriate nature, can compensate for pluralist inadequacies. Almond and Verba, for instance, claim that:

> The tension between power and responsiveness can be managed to some extent by the structure of partisan conflict. But our main interest is in the relationship between this tension and political culture, particularly the civic culture. Can the set of attitudes held by citizens help to maintain the delicate balance between the contradictory demands placed on a democratic system? [1965:343]

Certainly, this view shares the pluralist depiction of governments as essentially fragile; however, the central stabilizing mechanism is not "the structure of partisan conflict," but rather a "set of attitudes held by citizens." What, then, are the characteristics of these stabilizing beliefs?

In general, any social institution persists because insufficient numbers oppose it. Attitudes or beliefs about the government that guarantee its stability, then, are necessarily beliefs that restrain citizens from active opposition. Such beliefs may be of three general kinds: first, that the government should not be opposed; second, that it could not be opposed; and, finally, that it need not be opposed. Each of these beliefs presumably generates its own brand of stability.

Beliefs that the government should not be opposed—that such matters are not the concern of ordinary citizens and are better left to the elite—constitute stability through apathy. In this situation, stability is insured because there is widespread unconcern with governmental affairs. Beliefs that the government could not be opposed—that it is beyond popular influence—con-

---

hazards. The task here, as C. Wright Mills once put it, is to "get it straight," to document the facts of the case, and to live with whatever political lessons those facts contain. Thus, we have suspended any more detailed elaboration of these themes pending the presentation of evidence in Chapters 3–9. The exception is a brief outline of the alternative position at the end of this chapter, which serves as a useful guideline to the rest.

tribute to stability through despair. In this situation, citizens pose no immediate threat because they believe there is nothing to be done about real or imagined governmental excesses. Finally, beliefs that government need not be opposed—that it is run by capable persons who are only dedicated to the public good—constitute stability through legitimacy. Here, stability (and moderation) is insured because everyone believes that the government is run effectively and fairly, in the best interests of all.

Any of these beliefs or any combination of them could, in principle, constitute the basis for democratic stability, since all would apparently sustain the required mass passivity, but some are "better" than others. Beliefs that government is not the concern of ordinary citizens may result in an insufficient check on elite power. Moreover, the important "democratic myth" demands that the citizens believe that their role in government is an important one. So too with beliefs that the government cannot be opposed. Citizens must feel that government is at least minimally responsive to sustain the necessary myths. In addition, the stability offered by despair is bound to be short-lived. Finally, blind belief that the government need not be opposed may allow elite power to run unchecked.

The combination of these beliefs most often asserted as being especially appropriate for the stability of democratic regimes is first that *government can be opposed* and, second, that it *usually need not be*. The ideal democratic citizen believes both that he can influence the decisions of his government and that under normal circumstances, such influence is unnecessary. He must have a high estimation of his own *political efficacy* and also retain a high level of *confidence and trust* in the political system. He covets his right to place demands upon elites, yet chooses not to, except in the prescribed manner and appropriate circumstances. The retention of this right sustains the democratic myth and checks elite power, and his trust in the political leadership prevents immoderation and affords elites their necessary freedom.

Among the many proponents of these views, Almond and Verba's *Civic Culture* is perhaps the best known. As we have already mentioned, these theorists see the balance between effectiveness and responsiveness as "one of the most important and difficult tasks of a democracy." Pluralism is seen as a great aid in this, but their primary concern is with the "set of attitudes held by citizens" that can "help maintain the delicate balance." They continue:

> The tension between governmental power [read: effectiveness] and responsiveness has a parallel in the conflicting demands made upon the citizens of a democratic system. Certain things are demanded of the ordinary citizen if elites are to be responsive to him: the ordinary citizen must express his point of view in politics so that he will know what he wants; he must be involved in politics so that he will know and care whether or not elites are being responsive; and he must be influential so as to enforce responsive behavior by the elites. In other words, elite responsiveness requires that the ordinary citizen act according to the rationality-activist model of citizenship. But if the alternative pole of elite power is to be achieved, quite contradictory

attitudes and behavior are to be expected of the modern man. If elites are to be powerful and make authoritative decisions, then the involvement, activity, and influence of the ordinary man must be limited. The ordinary citizen must turn power over to the elites and let them rule. The need for elite power requires that the ordinary citizen be relatively passive, uninvolved, and deferential to elites. Thus the democratic citizen is called on to pursue contradictory goals; he must be active, yet passive; involved, yet not too involved; influential, yet deferential [1965:343–344].

Clearly, Almond and Verba fear both too little and too much democracy. So, again, how is a workable medium to be achieved?

The first desideratum—maximizing governmental responsiveness—is attained by what they call "the sense of subjective political competence," or what is now more commonly known simply as "political efficacy." They remark that, in England and the United States ("two relatively stable and successful democracies"), "a large proportion considers itself able to influence the decisions of local government, and a substantial, though not quite as large, proportion feels the same way about the national government (1965: 345)." In their less stable and less successful democracies (Italy, Germany, and Mexico), these beliefs are less popular. They mention that, even for Americans, such claims may be farfetched: "It is clearly an exaggeration when 40% of American respondents . . . say that there is some likelihood that an attempt of theirs to influence the national legislature would be successful (1965:345)." It matters little, however, whether or not citizens can in fact influence their government; it is the belief that one has this ability that is crucial for their thesis. They explain:

> The citizen's . . . role, as an active and influential enforcer of the responsiveness of elites, is maintained by his strong commitment to the norm of active citizenship, as well as by his perception that he can be an influential citizen. This may in part be a myth, for it involves a set of norms of participation and perceptions of ability to influence that are not quite matched by actual political behavior. Yet the very fact that citizens hold to this myth—that they see themselves as influential and as obligated to take an active role—creates a potentiality of citizen influence and activity. . . . A citizen within the civic culture has, then, a reserve of influence. He is not constantly involved in politics, he does not actively oversee the behavior of political decision-makers. But he does have the potential to act if there is need [1965: 346–347].

"But," they continue, "this maximizes only one of the contradictory goals of a democratic system." The citizens' subjective political competence must be matched by hesitance to employ this competence; otherwise, the political leadership would have difficulties in being effective. The ordinary citizen, then, must not only believe that he is capable of influencing decisions; he must also believe that such influence is largely unnecessary. He must be willing, in short, to turn power over to elites and allow them a relatively free hand in its use. And what attitude reinforces this essential behavior? "The sense of trust in the political elite—the belief that they are not alien and extractive forces, but part of the same political community—makes citizens willing to turn power over to them (1965:357)."

Lipset, one of the leading pluralists, also looms large among these consensus theorists. In his *Revolution and Counterrevolution*, for example, he links the periodic upcropping of antidemocratic demagogues in the United States to the strength of antielite values. The tradition of *vox populi* is seen as "making Americans more derisive and critical of their politicians and governmental bureaucrats (1970:48)"; this, in turn, is a source of disruption in the normal political process. American insistence on regular review—"elections are more frequent [in America] than in any other modern society"—is also linked to "the lesser respect for public authorities (1970:48)." These "excesses of populism," as Lipset terms them, can best be avoided by a widespread confidence in the political leadership. Almond and Verba summarize the essentials of Lipset's contributions: "Loyalty to a political system, if it is based purely on pragmatic considerations, represents, as Lipset has suggested, a rather unstable basis of loyalty, for it is too closely dependent on system performance (1965:354)." The authors continue, "If it is to remain stable in the long run, the system requires a form of political commitment based upon a more general attachment to the political system (1965:354)." An excessive concern with system performance, or an insufficient quantity of political trust, "endangers the balance between activity and passivity [and] tends to 'raise the stakes' of politics: to foster the sort of mass messianic movements that lead to democratic instability (1965:355)."

That vast reservoirs of political good will are necessary for stable democracy is also a theme in the theories of Talcott Parsons. Recall Parsons's metaphorical comparison between money and power: For him, power is a medium of exchange. Political trust, then, is to political power what belief in the worth of money is to economics. "Generalized support," as he says, "is a fundamental ingredient of power . . . an essential condition of the functioning of a two-party democratic system (1967:233–250)."

Like other theorists, David Easton is also suspicious of an activist electorate and sees numerous mechanisms by which the required mass passivity might be maintained. Some of these are "direct measures" or "structural regulations" and include most of the standard pluralist features: cross-pressures, voluntary associations, multiple memberships, and so on (1965:247–265). But, he says "No system could rely exclusively on direct measures . . . as devices to alleviate cleavage or to compensate for output failure (1965:267)." Instead, "reservoirs of diffuse support" must be created and maintained. "A major means for meeting stress is to accumulate a high level of political good will or diffuse support (1965:276)." This "reservoir of favorable attitudes or good will . . . helps members to accept or tolerate outputs to which they are opposed (1965:273)."

Easton also subscribes to the complementary view that a high level of personal political efficacy is essential for democratic health (Easton and Dennis 1967, 1969). Like Almond and Verba, Easton and Dennis see it as essential that the "efficacy norm" be widespread. Citizens expect that their voices will carry some weight, but, in a "modern, rationally organized mass society," "the political importance of the ordinary member [is] undermined (1967:38)." Such undermining of the essentials of democracy, of course, could, in principle, lead to waves of citizen discontent; hence, "But for the inculcation of this [efficacy] norm at an early and impressionable age, later adult political frustrations in modern mass societies might be less easily contained (1967:38)." These early-established feelings of efficacy "provide a reservoir of diffuse support upon which the system can automatically draw, both in normal times . . . and in special periods of stress, when popular participation may appear to be pure illusion or when political outputs fail to measure up to insistent demands (1967:38)."

The importance of political trust is also a theme in Gamson's *Power and Discontent* (1968). Following Parsons, trust is seen as the "creator of collective power." Like Almond and Verba, Gamson sees political effectiveness as depending on the freedom of authorities "to commit resources without the prior consent of those who will be called on ultimately to supply those resources (1968:43)." Hence, "Within certain limits, effectiveness depends on a blank check. The importance of trust becomes apparent: the loss of trust is the loss of system power, the loss of a generalized capacity for authorities to commit resources to attain collective goals (1968:43)."

Gamson's discussion provides some closure to this diffuse and terminologically confusing tradition. "These attitudes," he says, "fall roughly under the rubric of 'discontent.' Words such as distrust, alienation, dissatisfaction, disaffection, and their opposites such as confidence, support, allegiance, trust and satisfaction also identify the class of attitudes that concern us (1968: 39)." Clearly, the defining characteristic is faith in the political regime. Of the several options, then, we believe that "alienation" is the more descriptive and certainly the most common. Thus, we conceive of this attitudinal complex as a continuum that ranges from *political consensus* at one extreme to *political alienation* at the other. The theorists who we are presently concerned with, then, are defined by their insistence that consensus is essential for stable democracy, or, alternatively, that political alienation detracts from the viability of democratic regimes.

Following the lead of Almond and Verba, Gamson makes one further distinction which proves useful here. "Political alienation," he notes, "includes both an efficacy (or input) dimension and a trust (or output) dimension (1968:42)." In this sense, political alienation is the more general concept and subsumes the entire range of terms already discussed: "legitimacy," "system affect," "generalized support," "subjective political competence," "diffuse support," and "regime norms." Thus construed, the general theory at issue can be summarized in a single sentence: *one essential condition for demo-*

cratic stability is that both input and output alienation be relatively rare. Empirical assessment of arguments made in support of this contention occupy the remainder of this book.

Certainly, the criteria for inclusion circumscribe an immense category of theoretical, empirical, and conceptual contributions; indeed, the number of theorists who emphasize the importance of consensus, efficacy, trust, allegiance, and so on is so large that one's review of them is limited only by tolerance for repetitive formulations.[20] Characteristic enunciations would include Aberbach and Walker, who suggest that "the existence of distrustful citizens who are convinced that the government serves the interests of a few rather than the interests of all is a barrier to the realization of the democratic ideal. . . . Leaders in a democracy cannot be successful until they have gained the trust of its citizens (1970:1199)," or Coleman, who argues that "it may be useful. . .to conceive of loyalty to country as a kind of commodity foundation upon which large accounts of trust [are] drawn. The trust [is] necessary in order that the country's work get done (1963:76)." Similarly, Litt speaks of "the dangers of political deterioration through the withdrawal of interest and involvement by citizens who view the political process as a vast conspiracy run by and for politicians (1963:312)." Thompson and Horton warn of the "potentially explosive position of the alienated voter (1960:195)" and elaborate their concerns in a later article: The alienated may, they tell us, "turn politics into a 'phobic' sector by projecting into available political symbols the fears and suspicions growing out of the alienated conditions of their existence (Horton and Thompson 1962:493)." More recently, Miller has flatly asserted, "A democratic political system cannot survive for long without the support of a majority of its citizens (1974:951)." Clearly, Muller understates the case when he says, "The assumption that legitimacy beliefs constitute an important source of support for political systems is widely entertained (1970:392).[21]

Indeed, these theoretical sentiments are so common that Gamson has been moved to remark, "Probably few need convincing that political discontent is important (1968:42)." In truth, however, we do not think that the matter is quite so cut and dried. Certainly, the diffuse orientations expressed by these various writers have implications that must be drawn out and considered before final judgments may be passed. How many "distrustful citizens," for example, can the regime countenance before its stability is imperiled? How much consensus is needed to assure political calm? If the required amount is not

---

[20] Most of the major statements are reviewed in the next chapter.

[21] Compare this with the Schwartz passage quoted in Footnote 1 to the first chapter: "Alienation is a fundamental human political orientation." These views on the importance of trust and legitimacy constitute "domain assumptions" in modern sociopolitical theory, but, as we show in the next chapter, there has been relatively little serious effort to assess their empirical adequacy. Given their wide dispersal and acceptance, to do so would only be to "belabor the obvious."

supplied by political outputs themselves, then where does it come from and how is it sustained? And how, exactly, does the absence of consensus detract from democratic government? What is the nature of the "barrier" that the alienated and discontented masses are said to erect? Once the specifics themselves have been supplied, the troublesome question of empirical support remains. The following chapter, then, discusses the implications of consensus theory in more detail and reviews the existing studies that bear on them. The major question to be addressed is whether or not consensus theory is a more plausible account of the sources of democratic stability.

SOME TENTATIVE RESERVATIONS AND A PRELIMINARY ALTERNATIVE

Much of the effort in following chapters proves to be rather negative in character. For the most part, it consists of unsupported hypotheses, insignificant effects, and negative results. In documenting what "doesn't work," readers may rightfully wonder what does or, in other words, may want to know what alternative account is envisioned, or how the specific components of the argument "fit" into a more general critique. The remainder of this chapter, then, briefly sketches the main points of our critique and the major themes of a preliminary alternative. A fuller discussion of both is provided in Chapter 10.

Granted that there is a lot of evidence to be examined before any ultimate conclusions are in order, there are some surface implausibilities to consensus theory that need to be discussed. Consider first the question of political efficacy. According to the theorists, feelings of efficacy among the population provide a potential for political activism; this, in turn, is seen as checking possible abuses of power. Yet how much protection against elite usurpation can this fragile "potential" provide? If Almond and Verba understand that it is largely an empty threat (or, as they say, an "exaggeration"), can elites themselves be expected *not* to understand it? And if elites themselves understand it, then what is there in the theory that provides for elite restraints? The absence of more plausible safeguards, of course, reflects the rather insistent view that masses, and not elites, require the restraints, but our recent experiences with Johnson, Nixon, Mitchell, Haldeman, Erlichman, and others might justify some skepticism on this score. What restraints, after all, did the public's sense of political efficacy impose on their behavior? [22]

The importance of vast quantities of political trust also seems implausible.

[22] The obligatory rejoinder here, of course, is that, while the "public" and its alleged orientations obviously exercised very little restraining influence on the Nixon crew, the system did nonetheless bring them to justice and force them to account for their crimes. And this, the rejoinder continues, is really what democracy is all about—not day-to-day control or "oversight," but providing the mechanisms of subsequent accountability.

Whether one sees in Watergate signs of the vigor or the decay of American political institutions seems to be largely a matter of taste. From any perspective, it must at least

Certainly, elites would *prefer* to operate in an atmosphere of enthusiastic support, but is all this presumed "allegiance" somehow *necessary* for the stable functioning of the government? The political elite must enjoy the confidence of the financial community, because its active opposition would pose problems for any regime. The same is true of the military establishment. But why is the warm and enthusiastic trust of the entire society essential? It is reasonably easy to see how thorough disgust might pose problems for democratic stability, but there is a wide latitude between thorough disgust and unreasoning allegiance—mild disgust, cynical detachment, bemused unconcern, mere quiescence, and so on—any of which would seemingly provide for relatively unencumbered government. Why is enthusiastic support so necessary? Why is not anything short of complete disgust sufficient?

One possibility, of course, is that anything less than wild enthusiasm is likely to turn into thorough disgust in a political system that is grossly corrupt and ineffective. These are not, however, the political systems that the theory of political alienation is meant to describe. Rather, the thesis deals with advanced industrial democracies such as the United States, societies in which "the fundamental political problems . . . have been solved (Lipset 1963a:442)," systems that are "far better than any other political system which has been devised to reduce the potential exploitation of man by man (Lipset 1962:36.)"

Now, one would normally think, in political systems so recommendable as these, that the allegiance that results from political effectiveness would be enough to insure mass moderation. Indeed, one might even think of political

---

be confessed that the wheels of accountability ground rather slowly; it was, after all, more than two years after the actual Watergate burglary that Nixon was forced to remove himself from office. There were, in addition, some monumentally fortuitous circumstances that conspired ultimately to bring Nixon to justice. With a single prominent exception (namely, the *Washington Post*), the press was content to accept official White House accounts of the events, at least in the beginning. By the time the press "woke up" on the matter, Nixon had already been inaugurated to his second term. Had the press taken seriously its investigative and informing functions, the outcome of that election might well have been different. A second and, in our opinion, far more important "fortuituous circumstance" was Nixon's incredible act of taping his own complicity. Without this Nixon-supplied evidence, there is a real question as to whether or not he would ever have had to resign. One should not count upon such tactical stupidity in the future.

By way of comparison, it is useful to contrast Watergate with the scandal that drove Brandt from office in West Germany. In the United States, as we have already mentioned, the Watergate scandal dragged out over several years, during which period, according to most accounts, the ability of the system to "make authoritative decisions" declined substantially. In contrast, the entire Brandt scandal was "wrapped up" in a matter of months. The key difference between the two systems is that West Germany makes provisions for new elections in times of declining confidence, whereas the American system does not. This is one instance of the increased "stability" that comes from more, rather than less, democratic arrangements.

allegiance in simple exchange terms: Allegiance is the commodity that citizens exchange for governmental effectiveness. Yet the theorists insist that allegiance based merely upon system outputs is insufficient. As Easton says, "Except in the long run, *diffuse support is independent of the effects of daily outputs.* It consists of a reserve of support that enables a system to weather the many storms when outputs cannot be balanced off against inputs of demands (1965:273, italics added)."

We have already noted on several occasions that the modern theory of democracy inverts many of the classical emphases. There is, for example, the distrust of popular participation, the arguments for mass deference to elites, and the view that masses, rather than elites, pose the greatest threat to democratic stability. In each of these, the classical and modern theories are, so to speak, polar opposites. There is, however, one final inversion, more stark than any of the others, that is evident in the texts just discussed, and this is the view that the people are servants of the government, not the reverse. The arguments just considered, once stripped to the bare essentials, amount roughly to this: that the people have an obligation to the system regardless of its contribution to their lives and well-being, that they ought not to bother with matters of effectiveness or social justice in professing their allegiance to the regime, that such concerns only serve to endanger "delicate balances," "foster messianic movements," and otherwise upset the stability of democratic government. What evidence forms the basis of arguments such as these?

The plausibility of these lines of argumentation, it appears, ultimately depends on what is now a common theme: the natural immoderation, indeed stupidity, of the masses. If one assumes that the *normal* proclivity of the mass is toward dangerous and threatening behavior, that there are *inherent* tendencies that favor the immoderate and the destabilizing over the rational and the sane, then it follows that no amount of political effectiveness will, in its own right, placate the unruly, the rapacious, and the appetitive. Any attempt to win their confidence through the quality of political outputs is necessarily doomed; thus, mechanisms other than political effectiveness must be sought to insure the stability of the system. Since the masses have already been accused of nonreasoning and irrationality, what better mechanism is there than to assure that their allegiance to the system has precisely these same qualities, that it is so resolute and unwaivering that it will hold up even as effectiveness declines?

There is, in short, a strain of "the king can do no wrong" that runs through these texts, except that it is in the system, rather than the king, that theoretical faith resides. It is assumed that the system is organized so that any political decision is ipso facto just; the problem then becomes one of securing the allegiance of the intransigent and unworthy mass to what are necessarily just decisions. Thus, democratic regimes are urged, *not* to provide the mechanisms that would assure effective political participation, but to create and sustain an *illusion* of participatory potential, they are counseled, *not* to earn for themselves their public trust, but to *inculcate* that allegiance "at an early impressionable age" so that adult political frustrations may be "contained." The cornerstone of democracy, then, is not (as Jefferson would have said) a deepseated suspicion of those who are entrusted with power, but rather unreasoning confidence in their basic honesty and virtue. Modern democratic theory, thus, owes less to Jefferson than to Plato: "If anyone at all is to have the privilege of lying, the rulers of the State should be the persons, and in their dealings with either enemies or with their own citizens, they may be allowed to lie for the public good."

As a contrasting account of the conditions of effective democratic government, we eventually argue the following points: First, there is no persuasive evidence that political alienation and discontent among the mass public pose a serious threat to democratic stability, in contrast to the consensus claims. Second, since the major observable consequence of mass disaffection with government is a decline in political interest and withdrawal from political activity, mass alienation is more threatening to democratic *representation* than to democratic stability Third, the primary "problem" of the modern democracy is, therefore, not one of deactivating the masses, but of creating mechanisms that *facilitate* mass participation. Here as elsewhere, it is important to understand this as a relative matter, not one that can be accurately expressed in "either-or" terms. It is primarily a question of *emphasis*, whether relatively more or less stress should be placed on the hazards or the benefits of participatory democracy, whether, over the long run, the net effect of mass participation would be to the good or to the bad. If the latter is the case, then the modern theory of democracy is correct in its emphasis on the mechanisms of restraint; if the former, then that emphasis is misplaced, and more attention should be devoted to mechanisms of facilitation. We believe that mass participation is the only realistic available safeguard against the arrogance of power and the best guarantee that scarce economic and social resources will be equitably distributed to the betterment of the whole society. Such participation, of course, is no *perfect* guarantee, and this does not imply that the masses have monopolized the commodities of decency and justice or that they are incapable of mean and vicious politics. There *is* an implication, however, that their proportionate share of intelligence and good sense is far greater than is commonly supposed, or, to put it otherwise, that there are experiences and lessons found in the daily lives of common, ordinary people that promote an acceptable modicum of political rationality, experiences that adequately counterbalance any rapacious proclivities. Thus, while mass political participation is not *certain* to result everywhere in decent and humane government, neither is it certain *not* to; thus, over the long run, democratic government is better served when the masses are included in the political process than when they are not.

This challenge to the conventional wisdom is based upon our later discussion of a series of inappropriate assumptions contained in the "modern theory of democracy," assumptions that have seldom been put to an explicit empirical test. These, of course, are noted and elaborated more fully in later chapters, but may be summarized briefly here. First is what we later call the "social contract" assumption, that there is some direct and immediate link between "the consent of the governed" and the ability of the government to go about its business. Stated so baldly, there is little reason seriously to argue the point; if any such link exists at all, it is obviously an extremely tenuous one, far removed from the day-to-day goings on of modern political life. Despite this, "social contract" assumptions, in fact, provide much of the basis upon which consensus theory is built. A second suspicious assumption is what we call the "democratic misconception," which is the failure to realize that political power (and, with it, the ability to challenge the legitimacy of the system in a serious way) is *not* democratically distributed in any modern political system. Again, there are few who would openly contest this point. Yet it has some often unappreciated implications, the most important being that those who have very little political power (or influence, or resources, or money) will *not* be in any position to mount an effective political challenge, no matter what their attitudes or political dispositions might be. For these portions of the society, any speculation on the mechanisms of restraint is somewhat beside the point: They are largely incapable of doing anything that would require their being restrained. Finally, we raise a question about the assumption that forms the cornerstone of democratic elitism and its theoretical offshoots, the assumption of mass insatiability. As we have already discussed, the implicit concern of modern theory is that mass demands continually outstrip the ability of the system to deliver, and that the resulting gap between demand and performance is a recurrent source of political strain. There is, however, ample evidence that citizens expect very little from their government or, for that matter, from their lives, that they can be easily satisfied by rather modest levels of achievement, indeed, that they are preoccupied with matters considered far more pressing and serious than "issuing demands" to the political elite. There is even some compelling evidence that government and politics is seen in the mass as being largely outside of life's salient concerns. This point, finally, brings us full circle to a resurrection of classic Jeffersonian themes: Namely, it is precisely the perception of irrelevance that dampens participatory enthusiasm, and it is dampened enthusiasm that permits the elite to violate, even flaunt, its public trust. Unrestrained by an active and politically involved public, the elite is, thus, freed to embark on ventures such as Vietnam, to squander scarce resources on military equipment and similar pork barrel programs, to allow a steady deterioration of the environment on behalf of corporate interests, indeed, to develop the arrogant and denigrating opinion of the public that led to Watergate. Such policies and programs, moreover, unnecessarily detract from the overall quality of life in the society; they waste resources that might otherwise go for health, education, housing, transportation, and other things that would directly ameliorate the day-to-day existence of the population. Contrasting the conventional wisdom and our "preliminary alternative" in a single phrase, the question is whether, overall, "mass passivity" adds to or detracts from the viability of modern industrial democracy. Our argument for the latter, of course, has only been briefly sketched at this point; its elaboration and the marshalling of relevant evidence next command our attention.

3

The Current State of
Political Alienation Research

I N this chapter, we raise the question of whether or not consensus theory is any more viable than pluralism as a solution to the "paradox of stable democracy," whether or not, that is, the theory of political alienation makes accurate empirical claims. This requires, however, that there be some major claims that are amenable to empirical inquiry, and these have not been liberally supplied. Available instead are the global themes discussed previously and innumerable studies on the correlates and consequences of political alienation. To make matters worse, these studies originate in roughly equal proportion among sociologists, political scientists, and psychologists, may have as their theoretical framework Marx or the theory of the mass society or nearly anything in between, avoid common conceptualization or measurement of the alienation phenomenon, and tend to come to contradictory conclusions. In order, then, to get a better grasp on this tradition, to integrate its diverse and contradictory parts into some semblance of a theoretical whole, it proves useful to erect an orienting framework that encompasses the viewpoints and research at issue. This tactic lets us deal with the diverse body of literature and trace the relationships among its constituent parts. More importantly, the results bear on the adequacy of the entire package and are not restricted to this or that specific hypothesis. To be sure, specific hypotheses are often examined, and, where possible, their prior existence in the literature is noted. Our primary interest, however, lies not with these hypotheses but with the overarching orientation to which they each contribute.

The major themes of this orientation can be quickly summarized: First, in any stable industrialized democracy, political alienation is relatively low. Moreover, since there are strains inherent in the "modern mass society" that favor its development, there is little alienation only because there are indoctrination processes that assure that supportive norms and orientations are firmly set in political consciousness prior to entry into adult political life. This early indoctrination is, in turn, crucial for the regime: The consequent "reservoir of diffuse support" provides a cushion of allegiance upon which the system can rely when disappointments with political outputs mount. Finally, the prevalence and relative constancy of political consensus sustains democratic government because its absence—namely, political alienation—leads to various disruptive behaviors. The remainder of this chapter draws out the implications of these several related principles, notes their currency in the literature, and reviews the relevant evidence.

THE EXTENT AND DISTRIBUTION OF POLITICAL ALIENATION

The basic empirical claim of the theory of political alienation is an assertion about its extent, namely, that, in any stable democracy, alienation is "sufficiently low." Political efficacy must be sufficient to assure the democratic myths and check elite abuses; trust, to prevent spasms of "corrective" activity that might imperil the regime. The major obstacle to evaluating these claims, of course, is the ambiguity in the phrase "sufficient."

Certainly, the language of the theorists often implies that nearly everyone in the society must subscribe to the necessary beliefs. One formulation, cited earlier, suggests that the very *existence* of alienated citizens "is a barrier to the realization of the democratic ideal." And elsewhere, phrases, such as *"the democratic citizenry," "must be widespread," "a high level* of political good will," and so on, add to this impression. McCloskey, in a relatively rare effort to explore the issue empirically, settles on 75% as a criterion level—"falling as it does midway between a bare majority and unanimity"—but admits that this is more a matter of convenience than a conceptual contribution.

At the other extreme, it is possible that no level of alienation—no matter how high—would be sufficient to disprove the theory. None of these theorists would deny, for example, that the United States is stable. Thus, by definition, the level of consensus here is "high enough." In other words, the "necessary amount" of consensus can be defined by whatever level happens to exist in a stable democratic state. Thus, the texts vacillate between stylistic exaggeration and conceptual tautology; neither is adequate for empirical research.

The problem might be alleviated were the theorists clear as to what consensus must be about or how one would measure it, but there is little specification of this kind. In fact, there are often efforts to avoid it. Easton, for example, asserts that "the task of refining [these] concepts and theoretical propositions for direct empirical application—operationalizing them—is a vital yet separate enterprise, one that falls outside the macro-scopic analysis under way here. We are spared the need to pause to deal with the onerous and complex technical problems involved (1965:161–162)." Thus, the work is guarded against empirical refutation, since the charge of improper measurement is always open.[1]

One final problem is that, even in those few instances in which the question of extent has been raised empirically, the theorists have shown a curious indifference to their own data. Almond and Verba, for example, show approximately 75% of their respondents feeling they could do something about an unjust national law (1965:142), yet this leaves a fourth subscribing to the "wrong" belief. Now, an alienated quarter may or may not constitute a threat to democratic stability; certainly, this is an issue that needs some consideration, but none is forthcoming. Rather, they simply assert that subjective political competence is "widely distributed" and then discuss the attitudes of "the" democratic citizenry. Apparently an alienated minority of 25% warrants no systematic analysis. But why is this so? Nowhere is there a justification offered on behalf of this standard.[2] Similarly, Aberbach and Walker found 33% of the whites and 52% of the blacks in their Detroit sample scoring "low" in political trust but surmise that "in the minds of Detroit residents, there remains a generalized sense of trust in the federal and local governments (1970:1203–1204)." Taking all respondents equally, some 40% were classified.as "low" in political trust, another 20% as "medium" and the remaining 40% as "high." One might just as well conclude that there is a generalized sense of distrust, or, alternatively, that the sense of trust has been "generalized" to less than half.

[1] Virtually everyone who has tried to deal with consensus theory empirically has remarked on the ambiguity of the theorists:

All of these theorists thus assume the necessity of consensus on some principles but without giving the term any precise meaning (Protho and Grigg 1960:269).

We now might ask "what is this consensus about?" And here different writers would produce different answers. . . . [Some] stress the commitment of social members to *ultimate values* . . . others, however, stress commitments to social *norms*, . . . and, finally, there are writers who stress commitments to *beliefs* about how society is actually organized (Mann 1970:423–424).

Writers who hold consensus to be necessary to a free society have commonly failed to define it precisely or to specify what it must include. . . . Rarely have writers on consensus attempted to state what the fundamentals must include, how extensive the agreement must be, and *who* must agree (McCloskey 1969:268–69).

[2] This particular result is presented in comparative context: Respondents from the United States and Great Britain showed the highest "subjective competence"; those from Italy, Mexico, and Germany showed the least. Thus, following their argument, political competence is higher in stable than in unstable democracies. Certainly, however, there are too many uncontrolled sources of variation among these five countries (literacy, education, income distribution, and so on) to accept without question the authors' causal inference.

Those whose commitment to evidence exceeds their commitment to the theory have come to less sanguine conclusions. Prothro and Grigg find generalized consensus on "abstract democratic principles," but "when these broad principles are translated into more specific propositions, consensus breaks down completely (1960:286)." They conclude, "The attitudes of voters . . . offer no support for the hypothesis that democracy requires a large measure of consensus among the carriers of the creed (1960:291)." Unfortunately, their data are not to be trusted; the study is based on 244 interviews in Ann Arbor and Tallahassee, and their measures are confounded with an uncontrolled acquiescent response set bias.

McCloskey's analysis of these same issues is more compelling, since it is based on a nationally representative survey sample (n = 1484). This analysis (of responses to approximately 65 items tapping various dimensions of "rules of the game and democratic values," "faith in the political system," and on) suggested the following: "Our first and most obvious conclusion is that, contrary to the familiar claim, a democratic society can survive despite widespread popular misunderstanding and disagreement about basic democratic and constitutional values (1964:290)."

The most recent contribution to this growing body of negative evidence is Mann's (1970) secondary analysis of "a variety of findings from other writers' empirical investigations into value-commitment in Britain and the United States." Drawing on approximately 40 such prior studies—themselves of uneven quality, to be sure— Mann concludes, "Value consensus does not exist to any significant extent (1970:432)."

Lacking an a priori criterion, the best a researcher can hope to do is to establish where in the range from none to all the "true" level of alienation resides and to let others judge whether or not the observed level is consistent with consensus claims. Even restricting the search to the specific components of efficacy and trust, however, the literature is a marvel of disparate results:

• Aggar et al. (1961) report interviews with 779 Oregonians and find between 6% and 60% "high" in political cynicism, depending on which measure one uses and how strictly "high" is defined.

• Litt (1963b) reports, in his study of 478 middle-class Bostonians, that more than half were "high" in distrust and about a third were low in efficacy.

• Muller (1970) studied 296 students at the University of Iowa and found that 25% were "low on trust in government."

• Farris (1960) found "high political anomie" among 40% of his sample of 546 white Tuscaloosans.

• Form and Huber (1971) found "high political efficacy" to characterize less than a third of their 354 Muskegonites.

• St. Angelo and Dyson (1968) report that 44% of their Tallahassee adults scored low on political efficacy.

• Olsen's (1965) analysis of the 1958 Detroit Area Study found 30% of the whites and more than half of the blacks to have "high political aliena-tion."

• Janda's interviews in three suburban communities of Chicago (1965) found more than a third "high" in political distrust and about a fifth "low" in political efficacy.

And so it goes. Depending on sample, study, and item chosen, anywhere from 10% to 50% of the subjects embrace political beliefs thought to be detrimental to the very foundations of democratic government. Compound-ing the obvious problems of the studies just reviewed (small local samples, incomparable measures, arbitrary definitions, and so on) are results reported by Converse (1972), Cutler and Bengston (1974), House and Mason (1975), Miller (1974), and Wright (1975a) that suggest that the "true" level of dis-content in the society is not a constant but fluctuates over time.[3] There is no way to know, in short, even how much alienation there is in the society on the basis of studies now available, much less whether or not the level of dis-content is consistent with the consensus view. Coming to some conclusion on these troublesome issues is, therefore, the focus of Chapter 5.

More critical to consensus theory, we expect, than the amount of aliena-tion is its social distribution. We assume, in other words, that the alienation of certain groups—for example, the aged and infirm, the socially or geographi-cally isolated, the politically indifferent and withdrawn, and so on—would matter little to the regime. Certainly, the threat of discontent is heightened if the alienated share other social, attitudinal, or political characteristics that bind them together as a potent force. As Parsons has put it, "There is an immense variety of particular acts which are disruptive in that they interfere with the role performance of one or more other actors. So long, however, as they remain nearly randomly distributed, they may reduce the efficiency of the system . . . but still not constitute a threat to its stability (1951:30)."

Even these elementary points, let us mention, are often overlooked by the consensus theorists. The Civic Culture, for example, provides "very little analysis of the sources of cleavage and dissention within each polity (Rokkan 1964:677)." Among the factors omitted or treated lightly are "regional differ-ences, even in the very obvious cases of Italy and the United States; dif-ferences among denominations and between the religiously active and passive

---

[3] The five studies just referenced all draw on the 1952–1970 Survey Research Center (University of Michigan) biannual election study series, the same data that form the basis for our research. Our analysis of the trends is reported later in Chapter 7.

The publication of Miller's (1974) article has resulted in a minor flurry of rancorous debate—a "comment" by Citrin (1974) and the inevitable "rejoinder" by Miller, with additional contributions certain to follow. In truth, both formulations overlook significant aspects of the data. First, only the trend in trust is discussed, whereas, in many respects, the efficacy trend is by far the more interesting; second, the analysis covers only the years 1964–1970, whereas alienation trends prior to 1964 certainly merit attention. These and other, more substantive objections are discussed in Chapter 7.

. . . and differences between social classes." Similarly, Easton's influential *Systems Analysis of Political Life* omits class, social class, status, age, region, sex, race, and ethnicity, among others, from the topical index. Rather, the categories of analysis, here, as elsewhere in the consensus literature, are "system," "inputs," "outputs," "stress," and "members of the regime." There is a preference, in short, for vague generalities over the analytically incisive; the result, if we may say it, is a lot of diffuse talk about diffuse support.[4]

In part, the ambiguity of the theorists on the question of distribution is overcome by numerous articles "on the correlates of" alienation and political discontent. Even here, however, contradictory findings abound. A brief review of the relevant studies indicates the magnitude of the problem.

Social Class

The most commonly explored correlate of alienation is social class, as well it should be, since any understanding of the political consequences will depend on where in the class structure potential insurgency is most likely to arise. The "hazards" of working class politics, for example, would presumably be exacerbated by an intense political alienation within the group. Similarly, a highly alienated middle, upper middle, or upper class would each pose its own special threat to the stability of the regime.

Most researchers report that alienation is highest in the working and lower classes or that it declines as status increases (Agger *et al.* 1961; Eckhardt and Hendershot 1967; Farris 1960; Finifter 1970; Horton and Thompson 1962; Form and Huber 1971; Litt 1963b; Olsen 1965, 1969; Quinney 1964; Templeton 1966; Thompson and Horton 1960; and so on). Thus, the class–alienation relationship is among the best documented in this literature. Even here, however, there is apparently some need for caution.[5] First, small local

---

[4] There is, to be sure, an occasional recognition of these points in the consensus literature. Easton and Dennis (1969:62), for example, mention that "of course stressful negative sentiments need not necessarily destroy a system. The discontented members require the resources and the will to act on their feelings." Later, in the same passage, they speak of "the members in a system who count—those whom we may call the politically relevant or significant members" and then warn that support among this group is especially critical to the regime. Given the obvious importance of this qualification, one expects a followup delineation of "those who count"—who are they, why do they count, where in the society are they located, and so on—and then a careful distinction in the remainder between the attitudes required of this group versus the rest of the population. No such delineation, however, is forthcoming. Rather, the language immediately reverts to "diffuse support," "members of the regime," and so on. The point about "those who count" is ignored in the analysis.

[5] Schwartz (1973: Chap. 3) has provided the most persuasive critique of the "class = political alienation" findings; indeed, in his view, the failure of traditional SES perspectives to account for the incidence of alienation is what mandates his "revision" of "the prevailing strategy of explanation," in this case, the development of a "three-variable, psychological model (1973:xii)." The Schwartz volume, by any standard, represents the

samples again preponderate, and the national surveys included in the list are dated. Second, at least one study has found "virtually no relationship between indicators of social advantage such as education, occupation, and income, and political trust" (Aberbach and Walker 1970:1205), and there is another study whose evidence suggests that alienation *increases* with social status (Schwartz 1973:72). Finally, research reported by Aberbach (1967: 117) suggests that the strength of the relationship may have waned over time.

Age

Beyond the issue of social class, there is little consistency in the reported results. The correlation of alienation to age is a prominent example. On the assumptions that (1) consensus is a function of political socialization and (2) the lessons of the early years probably erode with age, some have argued that alienation should increase monotonically with age. Studies reporting this result include Agger *et al.* (1961), Dean (1961), Eckhardt and Hendershot (1967), Hughes (1967), Milbrath (1965), Olsen (1969), and Wright (1975b). Thus, the bulk of the evidence favors this hypothesis. On the other hand, studies of the "youth revolt" have often cited political alienation as a critical factor, suggesting that discontent is highest among the young and, perhaps, decreases with age (e.g., Flacks 1971; Keniston 1965; Lipset and Altbach 1966; Roszak 1968). Still others argue, rather persuasively, that "political alienation is associated generally with lack of institutionalized power" (Thompson and Horton 1960:192), that this "lack" is highest among both the very young and the very old, and, therefore, that the relationship between alienation and age is curvilinear. Studies reporting this result include Farris (1960), Phillips (1970), and Thompson and Horton (1960), but this probably understates the level of support since few of the other studies diverge from a linear correlational model. Finally, Litt (1963b), Olsen (1965), and Templeton (1966) have reported that age and alienation were *un*related in their samples.

---

most novel and innovative study of political alienation to have appeared in recent years. In terms of the *evidence* discussed in that volume, however, the infirmities of the tradition are more than apparent. One reviewer characterized the problem as follows: "Thirteen samples provide the empirical base. In no two is the same measure used (Dizard 1974:794)." The thirteen samples, moreover, while useful from a "special interest" point of view, do little to establish the generality of the results. Four of the samples are from communities in Philadelphia, one is from Newark, seven are student samples from colleges and universities in and around Philadelphia, and the last is a national sample of academic social scientists ($n = 108$). Like so much of the literature on political alienation, the findings reported by Schwartz can only be taken as interesting themes to pursue in future research, not as empirically demonstrated points.

Race

The common hypothesis that blacks are more alienated than whites is supported by Aberbach and Walker (1970), Form and Huber (1971), Olsen (1965), Ransford (1968), and Templeton (1966), among others. Sometimes, however, this association disappears when controlled for social class (e.g., Form and Huber 1971),[6] and sometimes it does not (e.g., Olsen 1965). None of the aforementioned studies employs a nationally representative sample. The leading national study (Aberbach 1967) did *not* corroborate these results: Blacks were *more* likely than whites to have confidence in the federal government, but less likely to have confidence in state and local governments (1967:119ff.). A similar finding is reported by Langton in his nationally representative study of high school seniors (1969:105). Finally, at least one national study reports that race and political trust are not significantly related (Stokes 1962). Here again, there is some compelling evidence that the race-alienation relationship has itself altered dramatically over time (Wright and Danigelis 1974).

Party Identification

Most studies that have inquired into the matter report that Democrats are more alienated than Republicans, even with social class controlled for (Olsen 1965; Olsen 1969; Finifter 1970; and so on). An exception is the national sample analyzed by Aberbach (1969), in which Republicans were slightly more alienated than Democrats, and also Agger et al. (1961), Schwartz (1973:73), and Templeton (1966), in which the two variables were not significantly related. Moreover, Aberbach suggests that the relationship may well reflect which party is in power: Those who identify with the "in" party will be less alienated than others. Aberbach's comparison between 1958 and 1964 supports this conclusion, but the correlations in both cases were weak and did not control for social class (1969:94).

Sex

Two studies have reported that alienation is highest among females (Campbell et al. 1960; Olsen 1969); one reports that alienation is highest among males (Olsen 1965); one reports no significant relationship (Templeton 1966); and one reports different results depending on the measure of alienation employed (Finifter 1970). Of these, only Campbell et al. and Finifter employ nationally representative samples.

[6] Among the poor in the Form–Huber sample, 35% of the blacks and 16% of the whites scored "high" on political efficacy; poor whites, rather than poor blacks, were the most highly alienated. Among the middle income respondents, however, the relationship was reversed (1971:669).

Community Size

The mass society hypothesis that alienation will be highest among the more "fractionated" and "disintegrated" urban areas is contradicted by all available studies (Boynton et al. 1968; Fischer 1973a, 1973b; Finifter 1970). The Fischer alienation measures, however, are not expressly political in content; the Boynton et al. study is based on 950 residents of Iowa; and the Finifter study, while reporting an insignificant zero-order correlation, also finds a weak positive relationship with education controlled for (1970:403).

Length of Residence

On the mass society assumption that community integration decreases the level of discontent, Litt (1963b) and Eckhardt and Hendershot (1967) hypothesize that length of residence and political alienation will be negatively related. Both report this result, but neither employ national samples. In the national sample analyzed by Finifter (1970), these variables were not significantly related.

Organizational Membership

Pluralist theory suggests that organizational affiliations decrease the level of discontent, a finding reported by Finifter (1970), Neal and Seeman (1964), and Phillips (1970). This relationship held up under statistical controls in the Phillips and Neal and Seeman studies, but similar controls reduced the association to statistical nonsignificance in Finifter's results. The fact that Phillips and Finifter use the same survey (secondary analysis of the U.S. portion of The Civic Culture data) further complicates matters.

Media Consumption

Despite the prominence of "media manipulation" in various left-critical mass society theories (e.g., Marcuse 1964; Mills 1951, 1956), relatively little attention has been paid to the question of whether media consumption increases or decreases the level of discontent. McLeod, Ward, and Tancil (1965–66) found no significant relationship among 180 residents of Madison, Wisconsin; their result is contradicted by the only other available study (Olsen 1969), which reports a significant negative relationship (the consumers, that is, were less alienated) among 154 residents of Ann Arbor, Michigan.

Numerous other correlates have been reported in the literature, such as: social mobility (Jackman 1972; Simpson 1970); religious affiliation, church attendance, and fundamentalism (Finifter 1970; Lenski 1961; Quinney 1964); marital status and family size (Fendrich and Axelson 1971; Finifter 1970); community power structure (Janda 1965); region (Finifter 1970); as well as an immense array of psychological and social-psychological correlates that will not be reviewed here.[7] Generally speaking, the same confusion is present. Small local samples, noncomparable measures, few statistical controls, virtually no multivariate analysis, and contradictory results are the major distinguishing traits of this research literature. With the possible exception of social class, the relationship of political alienation to any other "background" variable remains largely an open question. Chapter 6, then, attempts to add somewhat to the present state of knowledge, to understand better the location of discontent and, thereby, its importance as a political force in contemporary American society.

THE GENESIS OF POLITICAL DISCONTENT

Once we have decided on the extent of alienation and its distribution in the society, we turn to its ultimate sources and roots. Where do the necessary feelings of political good will come from? What accounts for the level of discontent at a given historical moment? What causes political alienation to rise or decline? A number of possible answers are suggested in the existing theoretical and empirical literature.

The pluralist and mass society contributions in these regards have already been mentioned briefly. In the mass society account, alienation is seen as the more or less inevitable consequence of the decline of community and social disintegration that follow from industrialization (e.g., Kornhauser 1959). Thus, it is often suggested that alienation will be most intense among those who live at the "cutting edge" of massification—the geographically and socially mobile, the urban dwellers, and those in the "peripheral" groups and social classes. Similarly, in pluralist theory, affiliations that counteract the loss of community necessarily forestall its consequences; thus, participation in voluntary associations, multiple memberships, and so on are thought to decrease the level of discontent.[8] The few studies bearing directly on each of these views have already been mentioned; in general, they do not present a very clear picture. Generating firmer conclusions on the empirical adequacy of these hypotheses is one goal of Chapter 6.

A more recent theme in the consensus literature is that supportive beliefs

---

[7] We have omitted any consideration of the psychological and social-psychological literature mainly because little of it bears directly on the theoretical concerns of this book. The exception is the studies of the political–attitudinal correlates of alienation, which are reviewed in later sections of this chapter. The most thorough treatment of political alienation in a psychological framework is Schwartz (1973). An annotated bibliography in the field is provided by Lystad (1969), especially pp. 82–89. See also her review article (1972), which focuses heavily on the social-psychological literature.

[8] See, for example, Almond and Verba (1965:Chap. 10), Gamson (1968:52), or Rose (1968:Chap. 7). As discussed in Chapter 2, pluralists typically cite voluntary associations as a major antidote to the political degenerations of the mass society.

arise during early political socialization; as such, they are rooted in what may be called "political personality," tend to assume the constancy of personality traits, and are, therefore, largely impervious to the encroachments of adult political "disappointments." Thus, the system assures its stability through indoctrination into "regime norms"; this indoctrination provides a "reservoir of diffuse support" upon which the system relies when the quality of outputs wanes.

Of the consensus theorists, Easton and Dennis (1967, 1969) have most consistently articulated this view. In their rendition, the major recurring "crisis" of democracy is that demands continually outstrip the ability of the regime to produce. There are numerous reasons for this. First, demands are potentially infinite, whereas resources clearly are not. The natural immoderation of the mass worsens matters. Moreover, the demands of one group will often contradict those of another, which means that, on any given issue, some demands go unmet. For these related reasons, then, the regime constantly faces a group of "losers" whose allegiance must, nevertheless, be secured in order for the system to persist.

Regimes, of course, have a number of mechanisms at their disposal that may "restrain" the losers from active opposition, but paramount among them is political socialization.[9] Socialization, moreover, has numerous beneficial effects. First, "input stress" can be alleviated if children are taught that it is only appropriate to raise certain demands in the political arena (Easton and Dennis 1969:55); likewise, "output stress" is minimized when children are taught that "it is good and necessary to comply with authoritative outputs (1969:54)." Far more important than either of these, however, is the creation of a "reservoir of diffuse support" for the regime whose level remains largely independent of day-to-day outputs. Thus, Easton, speculating on the circumstances that might "compel acceptance of less than members may think they are in all equity entitled to in the way of outputs," mentions first that "members may be willing to accept the validity of [such] an outcome because of their prevailing attachment to the regime as such (1965:272)." This "vast

---

[9] For example, "A system may carefully match its outputs to demands in the hopes of keeping its members more contented (Easton and Dennis 1969:4)." Yet, as Almond and Verba argue, loyalty based on "purely pragmatic considerations" is highly unstable (1965:354–355). Alternatively, "The system may persistently nourish a set of beliefs conducive to winning the confidence and trust of its *adult* members (Easton and Dennis 1969:4–5)." Easton and Dennis themselves, however, warn against this solution: "But for the inculcation of these norms at an early and impressionable age, later adult political frustrations . . . might be less easily contained (1967:38)." Finally, the system "may even as a last resort compel by force those members who refuse to commit themselves spontaneously (1969:5)." The instabilities of support built on repression are well-known. The lesson, in short, is that, in a very fundamental sense, regime persistence depends heavily on the creation of supportive beliefs during the formative years; the system must "shape their orientations and behavior patterns at the earliest feasible moment after birth (1969:5)."

store of political good will," as Easton elsewhere calls it, "forms a reservoir of favorable attitudes . . . that helps members to accept or tolerate outputs to which they are opposed or the effects of which they see as damaging to their wants (1965:273)."

What, then, are the components of the reservoir of diffuse support? Although these theorists are never especially clear on the matter, the attitudes of efficacy and trust are certainly meant to be included.[10] As they say, "Members of a democratic regime ought to regard those who occupy positions of political authority as responsive agents and the members themselves ought to be disposed to participate (Easton and Dennis 1967:26)." These and related orientations thus constitute that critical "reservoir of diffuse support upon which the system can automatically draw both in normal times . . . and in special periods of stress, when popular participation may appear to be pure illusion or when political outputs fail to measure up to insistent demands (1967:38)."

An important implication of this view, unhesitatingly drawn by the theorists themselves, is that the attitudes of support, once established in early socialization, are relatively independent of subsequent political experience.[11] The reservoir of diffuse support, that is, could scarcely fulfill its cushioning functions if it were only full in good times and drained when effectiveness diminished. Thus, "The peculiar characteristic of this attachment is that it is not conditional upon specific returns at any moment. . . . It is a sentiment usually already present in the mature members of the system (Easton 1965:

[10] Easton and Dennis distinguish between *types* of support and also between the various *objects* of support. For example, there is a difference between *diffuse* and *specific* support—the latter is conditional upon performance, the former is independent of performance; similarly, support may be directed to the authorities, the political community, or the regime (Easton 1965; Easton and Dennis 1969:58–60). Gamson, elaborating Easton, distinguishes between four objects of trust, namely, "the incumbent authorities, the political institutions of a regime, the public philosophy of a regime, and the political community (1968:50–51)." Finally, Citrin has urged for distinctions among "dissatisfaction with current government policy positions, dissatisfaction with the outcomes of ongoing events and policies, mistrust of incumbent officeholders, and rejection of the entire political system (1974:987)."

We find these conceptual exercises to be largely beside the point. It is unlikely that the mass public entertains any such niceties in their own political thinking, or that they distinguish between incumbents and the institutions that they represent in meting out punishment for real or imagined excesses. In other words, "It is possible to have a fair amount of consensus approving the main characteristics of the formal system but still have considerable potential for insurgency. The 'man on the street' may be saying, 'The system is OK, its just the guys running it.' When he undertakes insurgency against those 'guys,' however, the system is also likely to suffer some damage (Hamilton and Wright, 1975a:25)."

[11] "Relatively" must be emphasized. No one denies that repeated incompetence over several years might cause some decline in public support: "If members continually perceive that their demands are being met on a day-to-day basis, their loyalty to all objects can naturally be expected to increase (Easton 1965:275)," and the same can be said,

272)." Elsewhere, Easton and Dennis state: "The peculiar quality of this kind of attachment to an object is that it is not contingent on any *quid pro quo*; it is offered unconditionally. . . . By adulthood, a member may have acquired a deep-rooted attachment to the system that could withstand enormous pressures of dissatisfaction (1969:63)." [12]

A number of things must be true in order for the Easton–Dennis thesis to be plausible. First, there must be indoctrination processes in the early years that create the necessary reservoir of diffuse support. Second, these "early lessons" must carry over into adult political life and remain relatively impervious to subsequent "resocialization" experiences. Finally, there must be some evidence that these belief configurations do, in fact, serve as a source of "restraint" when demands are unmet. Each of these conditions is equally critical for the overall thesis, yet only the first has received systematic attention. Even here, the support is less than the theorists would have us believe.

Data reported in Easton and Dennis's own study of "the child's acquisition of regime norms" are particularly instructive. Their main themes have already been summarized: In brief, they conclude that an "inculcation" process does exist, that the necessary norms are incorporated at an "early and impressionable age," and, thus, that early socialization "has vital implications for the input of support for a democratic regime (1967:38)." Their data, however, would support markedly different conclusions equally well. Their Table Two, for example, shows that the proportion "high" in political efficacy increases from 16% among third graders to 54% among eighth graders, but, even among the latter, there was a sizable plurality of 46% whose "acquisition" was less than perfect. Later, breakdowns by the social stature of parents

---

we presume, for the reverse. Still, the necessary independence of support from daily outputs is urged insistently in the Easton–Dennis writings:

> Except in the long run, diffuse support is independent of the effects of daily outputs. It consists of a reserve of support that enables a system to weather the many storms when outputs cannot be balanced off against inputs of demands. It is a kind of support that a system does not have to buy with more or less direct benefits [Easton 1965:273].

And again,

> But regardless of the many names we have for the sentiments that define diffuse support, its one major characteristic is that since it is an attachment to a political object for its own sake, it constitutes a store of political good will. As such, it taps deep political sentiments and is not easily depleted through disappointments with outputs [Easton 1965:274].

[12] The authors of the *American Voter* have come to a similar conclusion:

> Variables of this sort [that is, political efficacy and the sense of civic duty] in contrast to measures of involvement in the current election, may be conceived as lying at a relatively deep level in any hierarchy of dispositions. That is, they represent highly generalized orientations towards the world of politics and could be expected to remain rather stable over a period of time. In this sense, they approach "personality status" [1960:516].

are provided (their Table Four). Among high SES eighth graders, subscription to the efficacy norm ran to 66%, leaving a third whose socialization had apparently failed them. No mention is made of this group. Among the middle SES eighth graders, those "high" in political efficacy constituted the slimmest of majorities—51%. Among the low SES group, only 41% had incorporated this crucial regime norm. Some children, it would appear, do acquire regime norms early in life; others clearly do not. Their data suggest a nearly equal standoff between the two groups, and, among the "dangerous" working and lower classes, "the child's acquisition of antiregime norms" would seemingly be more descriptive.[13]

Although Easton and Dennis do not mention it, their evidence intimates that the content of political socialization varies by social class. Consonant with the facts of life in the middle class milieu, upper SES children are apparently instructed from an early age that voting is important, participation useful, political activity likely to get results. In social environments in which participation is less common and powerlessness more readily apparent, children acquire mostly the opposite beliefs. Thus, socialization is the mechanism whereby class political ideologies are transmitted across generations; in any case, the Easton–Dennis data are consistent with this conclusion. If this be the case, then, how does political socialization "insulate" or "cushion" the regime, especially against potential insurgencies in the working and lower classes?

Other studies support our interpretation. Jaros, Hirsch, and Fleron (1968) studied "regime support" among fifth through twelfth grade children in Knox County, Kentucky—where, they mention, "there is a great deal of overt, antigovernment sentiment in the adult population" (1968:565). Childrens' attitudes, predictably, mirrored this political environment: "Our subjects' evaluations of political authority have a very prominent feature: they are dramatically less positive then those rendered by children in previously reported research." Similar findings arise in Lyons' (1970) study of fifth through twelfth graders from the central slums of Toledo and also Greenberg's (1970) study of third- through ninth-grade blacks in Pittsburgh and Philadelphia. Finally, Litt's (1963a) study of civics curricula in three Boston high schools

---

[13] This discussion should not be construed to imply that the children of the working class are being systematically trained for the impending "revolution." It does imply, however, that orientations said to be essential in sustaining stable democracy do not, for the most part, appear to be a part of the content of political socialization in the working and lower classes. More evidence on this point is discussed in the ensuing paragraphs. Another implication of the point should be drawn: If, as the evidence discussed later strongly suggests, the primary effect of the feelings of distrust and political powerlessness is to reduce the amount of political activity, this would mean that the lesser participation among lower and working class groups (e.g., Verba and Nie 1972) has roots reaching back into early childhood. This, in turn, has obvious implications for any efforts to mobilize these classes for political purposes. Such efforts are going to run up against what appears to be a rather "deep-set" tradition.

suggest a relatively greater emphasis in the upper middle-class school on participatory norms, feelings of political efficacy, and the sense of civic duty.

That attitudes of efficacy, trust, and the like are more elements of class political cultures than global orientations that sustain the democratic regime has been argued most persuasively by Form and Huber:

> Those who vote most often, those who have the highest sense of citizen duty, and those who feel most effective politically believe that politics and government function according to their conception of the democratic ideology which, incidentally, favors them. Those who vote less have a lower sense of citizen duty and political efficacy, and see politics and government as favoring other strata. Thus the different strata are not arranged along a continuum of increasing adherence to a single democratic ideology, but two major orientations may exist, one that supports the on-going system as functioning according to the theory, and another that is not only suspicious of the theory but is also dedicated to an alternative interpretation of it [1971:663].

Form and Huber, to be sure, link these differences to economic and life circumstances in the various strata, but the studies just reviewed suggest that their roots go deeper than this. It is readily apparent, in short, that "indoctrination" processes exist. The problem, particularly in the more "dangerous" and "disruptive" strata, is that the content of that indoctrination is the precise opposite of what theorists, such as Easton and Dennis, claim is "vital to the persistence of a democratic regime."

Even granting (in the face of considerable contrary evidence) that the required beliefs are widespread and firmly established by the end of adolescence, the question remains whether or not they "carry over" into adulthood and remain unaffected by subsequent political experiences. Certainly, this issue is critical for the Easton–Dennis thesis, since it is explicitly held that these attitudes *must* persist even as effectiveness wanes. This aspect of the theory, however, has never been empirically investigated: "Since any test would require longitudinal data which are presently unavailable, the entire question has been set aside (Searing *et al.* 1973:415)." There is no study that discusses the erosion or nonerosion of support as a function of adult "disappointments," nor is there any in which adult alienation is examined in light of major sociopolitical events.[14]

[14] The only exception is Miller's (1974) analysis of trends in political trust (see Footnote 3). According to Miller, disappointments with political outputs figure very prominently in this trend: "This study demonstrates that the widespread discontent prevalent in the United States today arises, in part, out of dissatisfaction with the policy alternatives that have been offered as solutions to contemporary problems (1974:970)."

Having reached this eminently reasonable conclusion, Miller fails to take the next step and to question the adequacy of hand-me-down consensus themes. His data, after all, are the most persuasive published thus far demonstrating that support is *not* "independent of the effects of daily outputs" and, moreover, that massive declines in the level of public allegiance *do* apparently leave the stability of the regime intact. Instead, he suggests that further erosions of trust would probably have the effect of "increasing

Lacking longitudinal data, our contribution to this issue is necessarily indirect. Trends in discontent among probability samples of U.S. adults in the period 1956–1970 are available for analysis. Thus, we can discern the general drift of alienation among a population in which childhood socialization has long since been completed. As we shall see in Chapter 7, where the results of this analysis are reported, the trend has been unmistakably upward: That is, many apparently forgot, unearned, or otherwise altered whatever feelings of allegiance had been instilled in them in their youth. This alone casts doubt on the Easton–Dennis "socialization" model, but, more importantly, the major factors implicated in this erosion appear to have been exactly those political "disappointments" that consensus is supposed to protect the system against—in this case, steady deterioration of the economy and withdrawal of popular support for the war in Vietnam. If the "reservoir of diffuse support" itself depends on the quality of the political product, then how can it sustain the regime through periods when quality declines?

Let us assume, finally, that socialization *was* broadly "successful" throughout the social structure and, in addition, that the lessons of early socialization *did* remain unaffected by later political experiences. Proof of the "diffuse support thesis" would still require that the orientations acquired during childhood exert "restraining" influences on adults.[15] This raises the issue of political consequences, to which we turn next.

THE POLITICAL CONSEQUENCES OF POLITICAL ALIENATON

Ultimately, the viability of consensus theory turns on the relationship between behavior and discontent. It could scarcely matter, one way or the other, how much alienation there is, where it comes from, or whether it is increasing or decreasing, if there were no proclivity to translate hostility into behaviors that directly challenge the regime. Clearly, governments do not collapse merely by wishing them away; their stability is threatened only by active op-

---

the difficulty for leaders to make binding political decisions, as well as raising the probability of the occurrence of radical political change (1974:971)." Such references to the indefinite future, as we have already discussed, essentially exempt consensus thinking from empirical refutation.

[15] Compare this with what Searing *et al.* (1973:415) call the "structuring principle," which asserts that "basic orientations acquired during childhood structure the later learning of specific issue beliefs." In order to examine this issue empirically, they inquired into whether or not the orientations most often studied in socialization research (party identification, efficacy, legitimacy beliefs, and 10 others) were correlated, among adult samples, with various issue positions. They conclude: "Many of the most common orientations studied in socialization research are generally unrelated to attitudes towards the outstanding political issues of the day (1973:424)."

position. Consensus theory rests on the principle that the discontented supply this active opposition.

What, then, are the disruptive behaviors to which political alienation leads? Recurrent celebrations of "mass passivity" and a "mainly passive electorate" suggest that voting itself represents some hazard; Lipset's comment— "that non-voting is now, at least in Western democracies, a reflection of the stability of the system (1963:185)"—seems to be especially clear on this point. The implication, however, that alienation poses a threat because it increases participation, is so totally inconsistent with the available literature that it serves no useful purpose to hold the theorists to it.[16] Indeed, one could more easily make the opposite case: that massive amounts of alienation are, in fact, *functional* for system stability since they would lower "inputs" and, therefore, system "strain." Since this directly contradicts the thrust of consensus theory, we assume that there are other behaviors rooted in discontent that more clearly assault the stability of the regime.

A number of hypotheses have been suggested in this regard. First, political alienation fosters "backward," "regressive," and radical rightist ideologies. Suspicion of government and a fond longing for the more tranquil past fuel the rightist flames. Correlatively, the discontented are consumed by a vicious, denunciatory negativism directed toward existing institutions. Negativism, in turn, leads to the political withdrawal already mentioned: Since all politicians are corrupt and political choice a matter of tweedledum and tweedledee, it makes very little difference who is elected. Hyper-charged by political abstinence, however, it is also thought that the alienated can be mobilized in certain social and political circumstances—especially by right-wing demagogues who consciously articulate their negativism and discontent. Ultimately, then, alienation threatens a democratic society because it creates a natural constituency for the rabble rouser who "proposes to clean the Augean stables and establish an entirely new order (Bendix 1953:697)." [17]

Common as they are, it is unfortunate that these themes are asserted more often than they are researched and, when researched, are often treated with

---

[16] Virtually every study conducted on the matter reports that the alienated participate less (Aberbach 1969; Agger et al. 1961; Agger and Ostrom 1956; Almond and Verba 1965:188ff; Campbell 1962; Campbell et. al. 1960; Dean 1960; Eckhardt and Hendershot 1967; Erbe 1964; Fraser 1970; Hamilton 1971; Hawkins et al. 1971; Janda 1965; Levin 1960: 63–64; Levin and Eden 1962; Litt 1963; Mason and Jaros 1969:488–489; McDill and Ridley 1962; Merriam and Gosnell 1924: Ch. 6; Milbrath 1965:79–80; Rosenberg 1954; Stokes 1962; Templeton 1966; Thompson and Horton, 1960; Verba and Nie 1972; and so on).

[17] This refers to the legendary Grecian stables of King Augeus, which held 3000 oxen and were uncleaned for 30 years—they were scoured in a single day by Hercules, who diverted a river through them. Bendix's metaphor is apt: The accumulated droppings of 3000 oxen, festering for three decades, nicely encapsulates the image that the alienated are said to entertain of the political system; likewise, Hercules' simplistic and radical "solution" is of the sort that should appeal to the politically discontented.

methodological indifference. No point in this scenario, save the tendency not to participate, is sustained by concrete evidence. This, in any case, is the conclusion we draw from our review of relevant studies.

Alienation and Political Ideology

Central to the political pathologies said to accompany alienation is an attraction to radical rightist policies and programs:

> The drastic reshuffling of social and occupational positions that has accompanied [modernization] has contributed greatly to a deep and lasting sense of displacement and dispossession among persons drawn to the right. Rightists, in a word, feel powerless and alienated in contemporary American society as it is now constituted. The cry that . . . people like themselves cannot influence anything of importance any more is one of the right's basic tenets [Rohter, 1969:226].

Little, however, is known about the veracity of this thesis—as almost everyone who has ventured into the area remarks. Aberbach, for example, mentions that "empirical studies done in the United States on support for extremist leaders and groups do not present a very clear picture" (1969:87). Likewise, Abcarian and Stanage state, "Studies explicitly employing alienation analysis of the radical right are virtually nonexistent (1965:795)." Hughes states, "Empirical research on alienation, authoritarianism, and ethnocentrism . . . has presented a somewhat occluded picture (1967:139)." Olsen (1965:202–203) has reviewed the ostensibly relevant studies and concludes, "None of them have explored the possibility that feelings of alienation may influence a person's opinions and attitudes concerning political issues." The rightist propensity of the politically alienated, says Wolfinger et al., is "one of the most popular—and untested—themes in modern social science (1964:275)."

In a meritorious effort to redress the imbalance, Wolfinger et al. conducted personal interviews and administered structured questionnaires to approximately 250 participants in the Christian Anti-Communist Crusade. College-educated respondents from the 1960 SRC survey comprised a rough "control group." [18] The results are: "It does not appear that the Crusaders are possessed by feelings of powerlessness. As [the evidence] shows, they have a slightly *higher* sense of political efficacy than do white Northerners who have attended college (1964:276)." On the other hand, Rohter's analysis of "169 rightists and 167 non-rightists living in the Pacific Northwest" suggested the opposite conclusion: "We found our Rightists to be significantly more alien-

---

[18] The "control group" was restricted to college-educated respondents because some 78% of the participants in the Crusade reported having attended college (1964:268). They were also disproportionately drawn from the business and professional occupations and tended to have higher incomes than the average. "The Crusaders," says Wolfinger, "are predominantly an upper status group (1964:267)."

ated politically than the non-Rightists, to feel that their elected public officials do not actually represent them, that local officials avoid or ignore
them, responding only to special issues (1969:227)." [19]

Consistent with Rohter's findings, Abcarian and Stanage report that "alienation is one of a probable complex of causal factors that account for right-
wing ideology and style (1965:792–793)." Their data, however, come from a
content analysis of radical rightist publications, not from rightists themselves.
These data suggest that the opinion leaders of the radical right *believe* that
the themes of alienation, powerlessness, and estrangement appeal to their
clientele, but whether or not this is, in fact, the case among rightists still
remains unclear.[20]

Similarly, Mason and Jaros present evidence that "seems to confirm the
suspicions of the mass-society theorists. The alienated . . . are more likely to
support extreme politically disruptive candidates (1969:496)." These data,
however, are based on a laboratory study of 847 residents of Lexington, Kentucky; these subjects made hypothetical choices among hypothetical candidates in a series of hypothetical elections. Even here, the relationship was
weak: The proportion "choosing" the "demagogue" ranged from 1% among
the least alienated to 12% among the most (tau$_c$ = .08).

Olsen's (1965) study of "alienation and political opinions" is also relevant
to our concerns. Since the sample size is small ($n = 624$), the universe restricted (data come from the 1958 Detroit Area Study), and the measure of
alienation not expressly political, the results are, at best, suggestive. Alienated
respondents were *more* favorable than the nonalienated respondents to increased governmental activism on domestic matters, but *less* favorable to foreign aid. Both findings were independent of social class (1965:206–207). On
racial issues, the patterns were not clear-cut. The alienated were *more* likely
to oppose the integration of schools, but only among those with a high school
education or better. Among high school drop-outs, the relationship was not

---

[19] On the specific dimension of political efficacy, however, the difference between the
rightists and nonrightists was not statistically significant (Rohter 1969:228). Thus,
Rohter draws a unique distinction between *powerlessness* and *political efficacy*, the
former being associated with radical rightism, the latter not. The rightists, then, compensate for their powerlessness by joining right-wing organizations; this, in turn, increases
their sense of efficacy. See Rohter (1969:228) for details.

[20] These authors have conveniently catalogued the unanswered questions still outstanding
in the area of alienation and the radical right:
  Studies explicitly employing alienation analysis of the radical right are virtually non-
  existent. There is an obvious need for case studies on right-wing extremism from
  this point of view in order to shed light on such as the following questions: why do
  only some highly alienated individuals associate with or support radical rightist
  groups? Or conversely, what are the conditions under which alienation does not lead
  to such association or support? What are the interrelationships among the specific
  measures of alienation, as applied to political commitments in general? What are the
  chief sources of alienation, speaking both individualistically and sociologistically? To
  what extent does right-wing extremism attract the non-alienated? [1965:795]

significant. Similarly, among the better educated, the alienated were *more* likely to oppose neighborhood integration; among the lesser educated, the relationship was equally strong but reversed. This suggests that alienation fosters "backward" political preferences mainly among the better-educated population, quite contrary to the mass society expectation. A similar finding is reported in Templeton's (1966) study of 239 residents of Berkeley, California. Among manual workers, the alienated were *more* likely to think that "Negroes have too little voice in community affairs"; among white collar workers, the pattern was reversed. On each of three related items tapping other attitudes toward blacks, however, the alienated were *less* favorably disposed, regardless of social class (1966:Table 6).

Alienation and Political Negativism

Along with the alleged preference for radical rightist ideologies, there is a pervasive negativism toward all things political. The alienated believe, so the account goes, that politicians are corrupt and immoral, that there are no important differences between parties or candidates. When they vote, it is "against" rather than "for." Thus, their participation—meager as it may be—is not an expression of self-interest rationally considered, but, rather, a negativistic attack on the repugnance of "politics as usual." Levin and Eden summarize the view: "Assuming[21] that politicians are corrupt, these citizens have concluded that voting is useless, reform impossible, and the so-called democratic process a hollow mockery of what it is supposed to be (1962:49)."

Little research exists on the negativism hypothesis. Often, the link between alienation and negativism is simply asserted in the course of explaining some other relationship that *is* examined; thus, negativism is said to intervene between alienation and apathy or political mobilization. Certainly, however, the strength of this association imposes limits on the credibility of other relationships said to depend upon it; hence, the lack of research becomes all the more distressing.

The Horton–Thompson studies are by far the most commonly cited in this regard (1962; Thompson and Horton 1960); indeed, they have become

---

[21] The Levin–Eden phrase characterizes a recurrent bias in this tradition, namely, that "negativism" is somehow an inappropriate, perhaps pernicious, *mis*perception of the political system. "Assume" denotes belief held in the absence of fact, something taken for granted, a supposition. This particular study was done in Boston, Massachusetts, where (according to one account)

> [T]he politics glows with a radiance like that of the tubercular patients who lived in the sanatorium of Thomas Mann's *The Magic Mountain*. The corruption, shenanigans, and ineptness of the city's political life have meshed into a continuous political process that has sickened and fascinated observers of its abortive efforts at self-government [Litt 1963b:314].

So what, in Boston—or for that matter, in the nation at large—is "assumptive" about these beliefs?

minor "classics" in the field. In neither case is the sample compelling: 207 and "nearly 400" voters in one and two "upstate New York communities," respectively. In addition, both studies contain the common methodological flaw of not maintaining any empirical distinction between alienation and negativism; rather, it is assumed that these are only different manifestations of the same underlying phenomenon and, therefore, to be indicated by the same measures. Thus, the footnote that describes their measures begins, "Negative (alienated) responses are . . . (1960:192)." In the 1962 offering, the concepts are again conflated: "In the university town, the most negatively politically conscious would be those persons who felt alienated . . . and who were critical of education (1962:490)." In the literature, interestingly, the Horton–Thompson articles are described as "detailed investigations" (Aberbach 1969:88) or "careful studies" (Mason and Jaros 1969:482).

Local referenda defeats—particularly on fluoridation issues—are also often cited on behalf of the negativism thesis. Such proposals are typically suggested and supported by "the establishment—by big science, big government, and big business. A vote against fluoridation, then, is a vote against science expertise, modernization, and the mass society" (Sapolsky 1969:242). Similar arguments are made for school bond issues (Thompson and Horton 1960), Metro government proposals (McDill and Ridley 1962), and so on.

One direct implication of this view is that, as turnout increases, the probability of passage decreases (Boskoff and Zeigler 1964:17; Pinard 1968:515). Stone, however, studied the correlation between turnout and passage for 18 referenda in a single community and found "little evidence to support the generalization that 'no' voting increases as turnout rises" (1965:216).

Specifically concerning fluoridation referenda, Sapolsky notes, "There are reasons to be skeptical about the alienation explanation (1969:243)." He argues that public discussion surrounding fluoridation was cast in difficult terms, with both sides claiming the weight of scientific evidence. The intelligent choice of vote, thus, required expertise in deciding among competing scientific arguments, which was least prevalent among those also likely to be the most alienated—the less-educated, lower status segments. With scientific opinion apparently divided, the voters could, thus, "postpone adoption, knowing that experimentation will continue elsewhere (Sapolsky 1969: 247)."[22]

Beyond the local referenda studies—whose relevance for national politics is not obvious—support for the negativism thesis is even sparser. No nationally representative study exists. Levin and Eden's surveys (Levin 1960, Levin and Eden 1962), of voters in Massachusetts "must be regarded as the most influential work on the subject in political science (Janda 1965:55)" but do not contain a measure of alienation. Templeton's study was mentioned earlier: "At first glance, alienated respondents did not seem to differ materially from

---

[22] Some limited empirical evidence in support of Sapolsky's hypothesis is provided by Arcus et al. (1975).

non-alienated respondents in terms of their national political behavior (1966: 254)."[23] Finally, Nettler reports that, among the alienated, "there is a strong proclivity for 'voting against' (1957:674)," but this conclusion is based on "37 known alienated individuals" residing somewhere on the Pacific coast.

Alienation and Political Participation

That "the alienated are quiescent under normal circumstances, but subject to mobilization into mass movements when the material or psychological circumstances are proper and the right leader presents himself (Aberbach 1969:87)" is another of the common themes in political alienation research.[24] Unfortunately, empirical attention has focused on withdrawal in normal circumstances, not on the mobilization that allegedly occurs when events rage out of control. Approximately three decades of research have established, beyond any reasonable doubt, that, in usual times, the alienated participate less.[25] Since this self-removal from politics could scarcely pose a threat to democratic regimes, the only "danger" lies in the mobilization of discontent by "extremist, demagogic, and/or authoritarian political leaders." And here, as one might expect, the evidence is scant.

Studies of Hitler's rise to power in Germany are most frequently cited on behalf of the mobilization hypothesis. It is well-known that Hitler's initial electoral successes were accompanied by large increases in turnout (Bendix 1953; O'Lessker 1968); on that basis, theorists have inferred that the major source of Hitler's vote was a massive outpouring of previous nonvoters in support of their Hercules who promised to clean the stables of the Weimar Republic. Lipset, however, rejects this explanation because "when changes in the rates of non-voting and of the Nazi vote are broken down by districts, we actually find a small *negative* rank-order correlation of –.2 between the percent increase in the Nazi vote and the increase in the proportion of the eligible electorate voting (1963a:150)." O'Lessker, on the other hand, using the

[23] Templeton cautions, however, that not much should be made of this cursory finding because "radically different stances towards the political process can produce reasonably similar results (1966:225)." Hence, the votes of the alienated—the actual behavior, the "bottom line"—may be virtually indistinguishable from the votes of nonalienated, but the motivations which underlie the vote may be radically different: The alienated vote "against," whereas everybody else votes "for"; the alienated vote to register a protest, whereas everybody else votes their self-interests; and so on. Whether or not the motivations of the alienated differ in any significant way from those of the rest of the population is taken up later in Chapter 8.

[24] See, for example, Bendix (1954), Horton and Thompson (1962), Kornhauser (1959:61), Mason and Jaros (1969), McDill and Ridley (1962), O'Lessker (1968), Selznick (1951), Thompson and Horton (1960), and others.

[25] The relevant studies are cited in Footnote 16. Even given the near unanimity of the findings, however, one might still raise a question about causal priority. It has been suggested, for example, that themes of powerlessness and political corruption might well serve as justificatory attitudes for the prior decision not to participate (e.g., Alford and Scoble 1968; Form and Huber 1971).

same data, finds support for Bendix's original position: "We have seen that an indispensable component of Hitler's success . . . was an influx of new voters into the political arena. . . . I conclude that a combination of former non-voters and traditional Rightists gave naziism its first great sucess (1968: 69, 63)." Finally, Schnaiberg (1969), in yet another reanalysis of these same data, again rejects the Bendix–O'Lessker conclusion because "although the increased turnout had a large positive net effect on the Nazi gain, it also had a substantial negative joint effect (1969:734)," indicating that a sizable proportion of the increased turnout, in fact, went to the non-Nazi parties.[26]

Correlations between political alienation and votes for or attitudinal sympathy with various demagogic candidates (e.g., McCarthy, Goldwater, Wallace) are also commonly cited as instances of mobilization. Such citations, however, confuse an important distinction between *preference* and *mobilization*. It is, of course, one thing to win the votes of those who are disposed to participate anyway (the question of preference) and quite another actually to mobilize the previously apathetic. In the former case, one need merely present a program more appealing than the opposition; in the latter case, a prior history of inactivity must be overcome. These studies, then, are more appropriately reviewed in the next section.

A major exception is Aberbach's (1969) analysis of the interrelationships among political alienation, Goldwater voting, and participation in the 1964 election. That election, Aberbach reasons, "was a blessing for science" because Goldwater's candidacy was the sort of political stimulus that should have triggered the latent participatory impulses. The main appeals were to gut emotion rather than reason ("in your heart, you know he's right"); the "solutions" were simplistic and demagogic ("extremism in the defense of liberty is no vice"). Of particular interest was explicit incorporation of the mobilization hypothesis into Goldwater's campaign strategy (see also Polsby 1966; Converse *et al.* 1965). Aberbach's nationally representative evidence, however, "goes against notions about the mobilization of the alienated nonvoter in certain electoral situations. . . . [T]here is no evidence . . . that Goldwater was able to mobilize substantial numbers of politically distrustful voters who were previously politically apathetic (1969:96)."[27]

---

[26] As discussed in the first chapter, the social factors involved in the rise of nazism remain largely an open empirical question. Given the inherent limitations of the available evidence, the Schnaiberg analysis must be taken as definitive. The Schnaiberg piece, incidentally, was written primarily as a methodological critique of the O'Lessker article, and little confidence can be placed in the latter's conclusions. For a more detailed critique of the available literature, see Hamilton (forthcoming). The most recent contribution to the topic is Shively (1972), who concludes: "From 1928 to the end of 1932, the Nazi party did not draw unusual support from among previous non-voters. The 1933 election might have been an exception, but the likelihood remains that the Nazi party was essentially not a party of new and marginal participants (1972:1216)."

[27] Despite the strong negative evidence, Aberbach is unwilling to reject the mobilization thesis on the basis of his results. Rather, he suggests that Goldwater's hostility to basic

Mason and Jaros have rendered judgment on the current status of the mobilization hypothesis. After noting that the politically alienated "are repeatedly shown to shun voting and other forms of 'normal' democratic political activity," they add, "There apparently are conditions, however, under which the alienated will participate in extraordinary political activity (1969:481)." What, then, *are* the conditions that "move them into the lists?" Given the prominence of the hypothesis, the answer is almost pathetic: "The precise nature of the conditions which stimulate this type of protest at the polls is not known (1969:482)."[28]

Alienation and Political Choice

Apart from the question of mobilization, it may be asked whether or not the politically alienated typically favor right-wing or demagogic candidates. The hypothesis that they do is a mere behavioral implication of themes already discussed. Here again, however, the available literature suggests no definite conclusion.

Sokol (1968) reports data for 453 middle class Bostonians that suggest greater pro-McCarthy sentiment among the politically inefficacious. Similarly, Parsons has linked McCarthy's successes to a "crises of a national solidarity," "negativism," a "crisis of confidence," and a "deflationary spiral" on the commodity of political trust (1964:228–232), but no evidence is presented. The Parsons–Sokol conclusions are contradicted by Aiken, Ferman, and Shepard's study of displaced automobile workers (presumably fertile ground for the growth of political pathologies.) In their sample of 305 former employees of the Packard Motor Company, political alienation and "approval of McCarthy's activities" were not significantly related (1968:123). Many of the implicit themes of the "alienation explanation" of McCarthyism are also disputed by Rogin (1967).

Evidence on the Goldwater vote is also inconclusive. According to Aber-

---

welfare state measures cost him the vote of the alienated working class and, thus, that "if a populist type candidate were to present himself to the electorate, this might be reversed" (1969:99). Accordingly, he argues that "survey data on Wallace voters in 1968" might provide a more compelling test of the mobilization thesis (see Chapter 9).

28 On the *psychological* factors that favor mobilization over apathy as a response to political alienation, see Schwartz (1973).

One problem with the "alienation = apathy" literature that should be mentioned here is that both political alienation and political withdrawal are correlated with a large number of common variables, for example, with age, race, SES, religion, and numerous others. There is relatively little effort, despite this, to assess whether the alienation–apathy link is genuine or, alternatively, the spurious reflection of common association with "test" variables such as those just enumerated. The most compelling discussion of the point is provided by Verba and Nie (1972), who argue, rather persuasively, that political alienation (in their case, political inefficacy) *interprets* the relationship between the background variables and political withdrawal.

bach's analysis, political *efficacy* was essentially unrelated to Goldwater voting (1969:93), but political *distrust* was strongly related and in the expected direction: The distrustful were much more likely to favor Goldwater (tau$_c$ = .39). Further complicating matters were significant interactions between these variables: Goldwater support was strongest among those high in efficacy but low on trust and was lowest among the opposite group (1969:96). None of these findings, however, was subjected to statistical controls; thus, this may only reflect the confounding influences of social class, region, party identification, or a number of other uncontrolled variables.

Finally, numerous recent essays have linked Wallace voting and support to both powerlessness and distrust. Krickus, speaking of the young workers among whom Wallace sentiment has been disproportionately strong, argues:

> George Wallace was the first national political figure to appreciate the depth of their despair and he provided them with a way of mobilizing their discontent and channeling it politically. While most white workers rejected Wallace, his appeal to them was a symptom of their estrangement from our mainstream institutions [1971:505–516].

Unfortunately, no evidence is presented in support of these conclusions. Likewise, Pettigrew and associates have argued that Wallace supporters "were deeply cynical about government, and politically alienated (1972:49)"; and Converse and his associates have argued that "people drawn to Wallace tended to feel that they had little capacity to influence government, and expressed distrust of the morality and efficiency of political leaders (1969: 1101)." Both of these conclusions are apparently based on empirical evidence, but, in both cases, the data were not presented in the research report.

Aberbach has summarized what is currently known about the voting preferences of the politically discontent: "If research and knowledge on the relationship between alienation and vote are somewhat confused and definitely incomplete on local elections, they are virtually non-existent on national elections" (1969:90).

Alienation and the "Rules of the Democratic Game"

One final deficiency often attributed to the alienated, again following from the other pathologies already discussed, is a readiness to abandon normal democratic procedures and "take to the streets" to seek redress of grievances. A "profound, even fanatical alienation," for example, is often proposed as the crucible in which the counter-culture was forged (Roszak 1968:1). Lipset and Altbach (1966), Flacks (1971), Keniston (1965), and Schwartz (1973), along with countless others, enunciate these same themes. Evidence supporting this thesis, however, is rare. Muller (1970) polled 296 students at the University of Iowa and found that trust in government and a desire to avoid disruptive political practices were positively related. There are, in addition, a number of student surveys reported in Schwartz (1973), but with mixed results. Among the students, for example, there was much "attitudinal, but not necessarily behavioral, alienation (1973:55)." There was some evidence, however, that students who participated in the October, 1969 moratorium in Washington ($n = 50$) were somewhat more politically alienated than those who did not ($n = 57$) (1973:57–62). Beyond this, the "evidence" typically consists of mutual citations to the flat assertions of fellow believers. One study reports data from a nationally representative survey that suggests that "the college educated young are perhaps the *least* politically alienated of any segment in the population (Wright 1975b)."

Political alienation is also often linked to race riots and other aspects of the black revolt. Paige (1971) studied riot participation among black males in Newark and concludes that alienation was a significant factor; similarly, "powerlessness" was strongly related to a "willingness to use violence" in Ransford's (1968) study of 312 black residents of Watts. The measures of alienation, however, were suspicious in both cases.[29] The most comprehensive account of racial strife remains *The Report of the National Advisory Commission on Civil Disorders* (1968), which did indeed conclude that "the frustrations of powerlessness" were a contributing factor. On the other hand, this fell far behind white racism, pervasive discrimination, segregation, police practices, unemployment and underemployment, inadequate housing, and inadequate education on the Commission's list of basic causes (1968:7–11).

Finally, Citrin (1974) has analyzed the relationship between political distrust and verbal approval of various unconventional political tactics[30] and reports that it is "weak and unsystematic." "Political cynicism," he concludes, "plays a minor role in producing activists or rebels" (1974:982).

SUMMARY

What, then, supports the common consensus claim that "democracy rests upon the trust that citizens extend to their government" or "when that trust is undermined, the whole system of government is threatened (Miller 1974:

---

[29] Paige's theoretical discussion, for example, follows Gamson's arguments concerning interactions between efficacy and trust (Gamson 1968:48); thus, he attempts to demonstrate that riot participation is highest among those high in efficacy and low on trust (what he calls the "dissidents"). His measure of trust, however, contains only one item; thus, it is prone to the hazards of single-item indicators. What is worse, no measure of political efficacy was included in the instrument. "Thus, a measure of political information was used to approximate the concept of efficacy (1971:814)."

Ransford's measure of powerlessness, on the other hand, is sounder methodologically but mixes both political and nonpolitical items (see Rotter, 1966).

[30] An example is: "How about taking part in protest meetings or marches that are permitted by local authorities? Would you approve of doing that, disapprove, or would it depend on the circumstances?" See Chapter 9 for our own analysis of these items.

1001)?" As we have already argued, the ultimate plausibility of such a thesis depends on the relationship between political alienation and behaviors that challenge the legitimacy of the regime. Despite the profusion of assertions concerning vicious ideologies, irrational negativism, frantic mobilization, and demagoguery, the evidence is, at least, ambiguous. Mason and Jaros summarize the current state of the art: "Certainly it is unjustified, on the basis of what is now known, to anticipate horrendously disruptive political outbursts even if alienation is widespread (1969:484)."

"Given the widely acknowledged importance of political trust in maintaining political stability," Aberbach and Walker tell us, "it is surprising that empirical research on the origins and consequences of trust is so scarce" (1970:1200). It is surprising, perhaps, but it is certainly ludicrous. There now exists a rather large and pervasive theoretical tradition whose viability rests on principles about which almost nothing is known. The available literature does not tell us how much alienation there is in the society or even how much there can be, where it comes from, what it correlates with, nor what it leads to. Whether or not consensus theory is a reasonable alternative to pluralism as a solution to the paradox of stable democracy, in short, is not a decision that can be made with the evidence currently in hand.

4

Measuring Political Alienation

W E have already mentioned ambiguities in the concept of consensus and the correlative difficulty in
dealing with consensus theory empirically. In the present chapter, the reliability and validity of the available measures of political alienation are discussed.
The major question is whether or not these indices have the methodological
vigor necessary to assess so grand and persuasive a theory.

Data for this and subsequent chapters are from the Survey Research Center's (University of Michigan) election studies of 1956, 1958, 1960, 1964,
1966, 1968, and 1970. Some additional information from the 1972 survey is
also analyzed. These surveys are based on probability samples of the non-
institutionalized, politically eligible adult population of the 48 contiguous
states; they are generally recognized as *the* quality surveys of the American
population, the class entries in the field.[1]

In the introduction, we noted current agreement that political alienation
is two-dimensional—encompassing the sense of competence or "political efficacy" on the one hand, the sense of confidence or "political trust" on the
other. These components are herein measured by the SRC "Index of Political
Efficacy" and "Index of Trust in Government," respectively.[2]

[1] Further details on SRC sampling procedures are given in the study codebooks and also
Kish (1965).

[2] Extensive methodological information on both scales already exists in the literature. See,
in particular, Robinson *et al.* (1968), and also Aberbach (1969), Asher (1974), Balch
(1974), Farris (1960), Finifter (1970), Fraser (1971), and others.

Of these several sources, Balch (1974) comes to the most pessimistic conclusion, suggesting that "research which has used the SRC efficacy scale . . . should be re-analyzed
. . . [and] until this is done, the findings of such research should be viewed with great

The index of political efficacy is a four-item, agree–disagree scale; the index of trust in government is a five-item, forced-choice scale. The nine items comprising these two measures are as follows:

Political efficacy

Now I'd like to read some of the kinds of things people tell us when we interview them and ask you whether you agree or disagree with them. I'll read them one at a time and you just tell me whether you agree or disagree.

1. People like me don't have any say about what the government does.
2. Voting is the only way that people like me can have any say about how the government runs things.
3. Sometimes politics and government seem so complicated that a person like me can't really understand what's going on.
4. I don't think public officials care much what people like me think.

Political trust

People have different ideas about the government in Washington. These ideas don't refer to Democrats or Republicans in particular but just to the government in general. We want to know how you feel about these ideas— for example:

1. Do you think that people in the government waste a lot of the money we pay in taxes, waste some of it, or don't waste very much of it?
2. How much of the time do you think you can trust the government to do what is right—just about always, most of the time, or only some of the time?
3. Would you say the government is pretty much run by a few big interests looking out for themselves, or that it is run for the benefit of all the people?
4. Do you feel that almost all the people running the government are smart people who know what they are doing, or do you think that quite a lot of them don't seem to know what they are doing?
5. Do you think that quite a few of the people running the government are a little crooked, not very many are, or do you think hardly any of them are crooked at all?

---

caution (1974:28)." The major part of this conclusion, however, is based upon relatively weak correlations between this scale and "theoretically relevant external variables"—in particular, political interest, political knowledge, political participation, propensity to engage in protest behavior, and political trust. This assumes that the theory is valid and the measures bad; yet, as we have already pointed out, there is no good reason—aside from frequent assertion—to expect that political alienation will be related to any of these variables. Balch's contribution, then, is probably more substantive than methodological, even though this possibility is not acknowledged.

Ultimately, the merit of these scales for our purposes rests on a single question: Does their content resemble what the theorists have in mind by phrases such as consensus, legitimacy, support, allegiance, and so on? An equivalent question which can be more readily answered is: Are these measures typically employed in research that is said to support the theory? Concerning the first, we believe that the answer is clearly yes, but it proves more convenient to document this in the following chapter. Concerning the second, the answer is also yes: The SRC measures are by far the most commonly encountered in the literature on political discontent—so common, in fact, that contributions, such as Gamson's, are written with explicit reference to them. With the exception of The Civic Culture and others employing the same data, all studies of political efficacy cited in the previous chapter use either the SRC index or a modified form of it; much the same holds true for studies of political trust. Irrespective of other methodological concerns, then, these indices enjoy a degree of consensual validity: They are well-established, widely recognized, and commonly employed. Since the theorists frequently cite these measures in support of their views, they are obligated to recognize them as valid when the results diverge from their expectations.

Our intent, however, is not only to evaluate and criticize the existing literature but also to contribute to it, and this requires that the available measures conform to recognized methodological standards.[3] Along these lines, several related questions may be asked: First, are they reliable? Are the scales unidimensional? Do their constituent items correlate highly with one another? Are the scales stable indices of the phenomena under consideration? Second, are

[3] This phrase, of course, assumes that there are "recognized methodological standards" in matters such as this, and this, by and large, is not the case. Reliability and validity measurement remains a very inexact science.

One implication of the relative lack of agreed-upon standards in the area is that the skeptical critic could quite easily take evidence, such as that discussed in this chapter, and conclude that the scales are methodologically insufficient for the substantive themes of this research. (See, for example, the Balch paper mentioned in the previous footnote.) One implication of this position, of course, would be that nothing certain is now known, one way or the other, about the correlates and consequences of political alienation as commonly measured. This, in turn, would counsel that all alarmist commentary on the "dangers" of alienation in "the modern mass society" be suspended until better research with better measures is conducted.

In many ways, this is a very attractive conclusion, although obviously not one to which we are ultimately led. There can be little doubt that the study of political alienation would be vastly improved if its implications were taken seriously. On the other hand, however, suspicious as these measures might appear to be on absolute methodological grounds, when compared with other attitudinal measures commonly employed in research of this sort, they are certainly no worse than average and, perhaps, somewhat better than average (see, for example, Footnote 7). We also believe, and present evidence to support the belief, that the substantive content of these nine items accords rather closely with the kinds of things the theorists have in mind when speaking of consensus, diffuse support, and so on (see the next chapter). In this respect, their formal methodological properties may be somewhat beside the point.

they *valid*, that is, do they actually measure what they purport to measure? In the case of agree–disagree items, a special case of invalidity is often considered: Does the scale merely tap some tendency to agree with statements, regardless of their content (the problem of *acquiescence*)?

There is no agreement concerning how reliability and validity are best conceptualized; therefore, there is none on how they can best be measured.[4] Nor is it clear how much unreliability or invalidity can be countenanced before the substance of the research is threatened. Rule-of-thumb standards predominate but can be misleading.[5] Methodological information conveyed in the ensuing pages, then, is primarily descriptive; it does not "test" the hypothesis that these scales are sufficient to warrant continued research. Readers are merely invited to take it into account in assessing the remainder.

RELIABILITY

Of the several measures of reliability that have been proposed, "probably none combines simplicity with amount of information contained as well as the inter-item correlation matrix" (Robinson *et al.* 1968:16). High inter-item correlations suggest that the scale is homogeneous (all items tap roughly the same content) and unidimensional. Similarly, the higher the inter-item correlation is, the more "stable" the resulting scale is. Accordingly, these matrices are shown in Table 4.1.[6] As a summary measure of reliability, the average correlation (γ) across all item pairs has been computed and equals .635 and .565 for the effcacy and trust items, respectively—about average or perhaps slightly better than average for attitudinal scales of this sort.[7]

[4] In the most recent and thorough review of these subjects, Bohrnstedt mentions at least four analytically separable approaches to reliability and at least three distinct concepts of validity and notes that "not all the important methods" have been discussed (1970:80). Likewise, Weigert speaks of the "confusion that surrounds the labels of reliability and validity," and adds, "Since the behavioral application of the concepts is scientifically ambiguous, their continued use may well be attributed to their rhetorical functions (1970: 116)."

[5] For example, a set of items is often said to form a Guttman scale when their coefficient of reproducibility exceeds .90. As Robinson *et al.* point out, however, this criterion can be met when the average correlation among items is less than .30 (1968:8, see also Schooler [1968], Mokken [1971].)

[6] Unless otherwise specified, all data reported in this chapter are from the 1968 survey. Identical analysis of 1970 data produced equivalent results. See Robinson *et al.* (1968) for methodological data prior to 1968.

All items have been dichotomized; missing data are omitted on an item-by-item basis. For all efficacy items, agreement is taken as the alienated response. For Trust Item 1, "waste a lot" is the alienated response; for Item 2, "only some of the time"; and for Item 5, "quite a few."

[7] Using *r* rather than gamma, average correlation among efficacy items is .33, and, for the trust items, it is .27 (see Table 4.8). As a convenient point of comparison, the average inter-item correlation (*r*) of the Srole anomia scale is .30 (Srole, 1956). This latter is perhaps the most widely employed scale in social research (Bonjean *et al.* 1967).

TABLE 4.1
Inter-item Correlation (Gamma) Matrices for the Nine Political
Alienation Items: 1968

	Efficacy			
Item	1	2	3	4
1. Have say?	1.00			
2. Vote only way?	.75	1.00		
3. Complicated?	.48	.55	1.00	
4. Care much?	.81	.65	.57	1.00

N = 1553

Gamma = .635

	Trust				
Item	1	2	3	4	5
1. Waste?	1.00				
2. Trust?	.56	1.00			
3. Run by Whom?	.61	.73	1.00		
4. Smart?	.44	.55	.49	1.00	
5. Crooked?	.69	.53	.68	.37	1.00

N = 1553

Gamma = .565

Possible subgroup variations in reliability were examined by computing identical matrices within racial and occupational groups. The average correlation among efficacy items was largely unaffected by these controls.[8] The

[8] Average correlations among subgroups was as follows:

	Efficacy	Trust
Blacks	.585	.464
Blue collar whites	.610	.591
White collar whites	.692	.556

Despite its strong correlation to other items in the scale, efficacy item two ("Voting is the only way that people like me can have any say about how the government runs things") is ambiguous in its content. More specifically, what is a respondent saying when he or she disagrees with this statement? In scaling the disagree response as efficacious, it is assumed that respondents mean: "No, there are many ways to influence the government," but they might equally well intend to say, "No there are *no* ways to influence the government, whether through voting or otherwise." While the correlation between this and the other items is apparently unaffected by its ambiguity, the trend data discussed in Chapter 7 are not. Of the nine measures available for analysis, only this one shows a net decline in "alienation" over the last decade and a half. In order to maximize

internal coherence of the trust items, however, was considerably lower for blacks. Given the importance of black political alienation for our substantive concerns, additional analysis is clearly warranted. Thus, the inter-item matrix for blacks only is shown in Table 4.2.

At least two hypotheses might account for the lower average correlation among blacks. First, the items may simply "work" poorly for black respondents, reflecting less linguistic sophistication, inattention to the interviewer, and so on. An alternative possibility is that some of the items have a unique meaning for blacks. One way to approach this issue is to ask about the relative contribution of each item to the overall average correlation: The average correlation of item one with the other four items, for example, is .49, and, similarly, .45 for item two, .58 for item three, .35 for item four, and .45 for item five. Clearly, item four is the most serious "offender," despite the fact that the lowest correlation reported is between items two and five.

The meaning of the fourth item clearly turns on the adjective, "smart." On the one hand, "smart" connotes intelligence, competence, or ability; it is this meaning, of course, that is assumed in scoring the "yes they are smart" response as the trustful one. On the other hand, "smart" also connotes shrewd, clever, conniving—that is, smart in the sense of having a superior hustle. To affirm that most of the people running the government "are smart people who know what they are doing," in short, is not necessarily a warm or enthusiastic endorsement; instead, it may imply exactly the opposite sentiment. The possibility that "smart" more often has this connotation among

TABLE 4.2
Inter-item Correlation Matrix for the Five Trust Items, Blacks
Only: 1968

| Item | Efficacy | | | | |
	1	2	3	4	5
1. Waste?	1.00				
2. Trust?	.48	1.00			
3. Run by?	.59	.71	1.00		
4. Smart?	.21	.46	.38	1.00	
5. Crooked?	.69	.14	.64	.34	1.00

N = 169

Gamma = .464

comparability with prior studies, we have chosen to retain the item, except for in Chapter 7, where it has been dropped. (Error introduced by keeping the item again favors the theory, since some people who may have intended to convey a sense of powerlessness by disagreeing with the item are scored as efficacious.) (On the ambiguity of the "voting" item, see also Balch 1974; Converse 1972; House and Mason 1975.)

blacks is sufficiently strong to attribute the lower inter-item correlation to it.[9]

Assuming this interpretation is correct, one may then ask what biases are introduced by retaining the standard five-item index to measure political alienation among blacks. Clearly, the effect is to *under*estimate the true level of black discontent, since some persons who intended to convey a basically negative sentiment would be scored as "trustful" by conventional scaling of the item. Since this errs in a conservative direction and favors the theory, it can be safely ignored.

ACQUIESCENCE[10]

According to many recent studies, some proportion of the population tends to agree to an item regardless of its content. For example, Jackman (1973) has shown that, in Selznick and Steinberg's (1969) study of anti-Semitism, approximately 15% agreed both that "Jews are more willing than others to use shady practices to get what they want" *and* that "Jews are just as honest as other businessmen." Similar "acquiescent response set biases" have been demonstrated for the *F*-scale measure of authoritarianism (Campbell *et al.* 1960), the Srole anomie scale (Carr 1971), and a number of other agree–disagree indices (Peabody 1961).

Acquiescence is less of a problem if items are "reversed"—if agreement to half indicates the presence of a trait and, to the other half, its absence. This has the convenient effect of assigning acquiescers to the mid-point of the scale, where their methodological havoc is minimized. Unfortunately, agreement to each of the efficacy items indicates the presence of powerlessness; thus, the "highly inefficacious" include an unknown proportion of those whose only measured trait is a tendency to agree.

What is worse, acquiescence may not be uniformly dispersed throughout the population; therefore, the resulting measurement error may well be correlated with other analysis variables. For example, part of the higher alienation of lower and working class respondents may only reflect their disproportionate acquiescent tendencies. Thus, response-set bias threatens not only the estimation of extent, but also distribution.

The 1968 survey contains information bearing on the severity of these

---

[9] Consistent with this interpretation, the average inter-item correlation among blacks increases from .464 (item four included) to .541 (item four excluded). Interestingly, a similar result is apparent for working class whites (.591 to .627) but *not* for middle class whites (.556 to .555), suggesting that the cynical interpretation of "smart" may be characteristic of the lower status population generally. It is also possible that the cynical usage is a function of region.

[10] The findings in this section appear elsewhere in our paper, "Does acquiescence bias the SRC 'Index of Political Efficacy?'" *Public Opinion Quarterly* 39 (Summer, 1975) and are reproduced here by permission of the publisher.

problems. In addition to the four standard items listed earlier, the 1968 survey includes the following four revised efficacy measures:[11]

1a. Would you say that people like you have quite a lot of say about what the government does, or that you don't have much say at all?

2a. Would you say that voting is the only way that people like you can have any say about the way the government runs things, or that there are lots of ways you can have a say?

3a. Would you say that politics and government are so complicated that people like you can't really understand what's going on, or that you can understand what's going on pretty well?

4a. Would you say that most public officials care quite a lot what people like you think, or that they don't care very much at all?

The revised items clearly represent an attempt to create an equivalent scale that suffers from fewer methodological defects. Both these and the original questions have been combined into simple summated indices;[12] their cross-

TABLE 4.3
Cross-tabulation of the Standard and Revised Political Efficacy Scales: 1968

Revised Scale	Standard Scale				
	1	2	3	4	5
1	30.4	19.6	9.1	4.4	2.6
2	41.0	36.8	24.7	15.3	8.2
3	21.6	29.6	37.5	29.6	22.7
4	5.3	12.0	21.5	32.0	38.7
5	1.8	2.0	7.3	18.7	27.8
%	100.1	100.0	100.1	100.0	100.0
N	283	291	275	295	194

Gamma = .54

[11] The four revised measures were included in the pre-election wave of the 1968 study; the standard agree–disagree items were the last four questions in the postelection wave. Net of nonequivalence, acquiescence, and real change due to the outcome of the election, the correlation between scales can be construed as a test–retest measure of reliability.

[12] The average correlation among the four revised items is .445, still reasonably high but less than the .635 figure reported for the standard scale. This initially suggests that part of the "homogeneity" of the standard index reflects a method effect independent of content—that is, acquiescence.

The resulting summated index of standard efficacy items is used throughout the remainder of the research. Persons agreeing to all four items are scored as least efficacious; persons disagreeing to all are scored as most efficacious; and others are arrayed in between depending on their responses. In all study years, respondents with missing data on three

tabulation is shown in Table 4.3. The correlation between them (gamma = .54) is perhaps somewhat lower than might have been expected, but several factors might account for this: first, substantive nonequivalence between the two scales; second, real change in efficacy beliefs due to the 1968 election; and, finally, differential measurement of the tendency to acquiesce. Table 4.4 bears on the first of these and shows the proportions giving the alienated response for each of the four item pairs.

All else being equal, substantively equivalent items should produce similar marginal distributions. By this standard, item pairs (2, 2a) and (4, 4a) can apparently be treated as equivalent, whereas (1, 1a) and (3, 3a) clearly cannot. Textual examination supports the nonequivalence hypothesis. Item three asks whether or not politics and government are *sometimes* too complicated to understand, whereas the revised version omits this qualifier. Part

TABLE 4.4
Proportion Alienated for the Revised and Standard Political
Efficacy Items: 1968

Item	Per Cent Alienated
1. People like me don't have any say...	41
1a. Would you say that people like you...	75
Percentage Difference	34
2. Voting is the only way...	57
2a. Would you say that voting is...	58
Percentage Difference	1
3. Sometimes politics and government...	71
3a. Would you say that government...	44
Percentage Difference	27
4. I don't think public officials care...	44
4a. Would you say that most public...	40
Percentage Difference	4

or all four items are dropped from the analysis; respondents with missing data on two or fewer items were kept and assigned a score according to the following schedule:

Number of "agree" responses:	4	3	2	1	0
			Efficacy score		
Number of items answered: 4	1	2	3	4	5
3	—	2	3	3	4
2	—	—	2	3	4
1	Respondent omitted				
0	Respondent omitted				

of the "lowness" of the correlation between the scales, then, simply reflects the fact that more people find politics occasionally confusing than always confusing. Similarly, item one asks whether or not the respondent has *any* say about what the government does, whereas, in the revised item, "any" is changed to "much." Unsurprisingly, more people affirm that they do not have much influence than that they have none whatsoever.[13]

In addition to their partial nonequivalence, the two versions may also be weakly correlated due to changes in feelings of powerlessness caused by the 1968 election. Obviously, the topic can only be approached inferentially, since our sole measure of change is precisely the difference between the two measures. A reasonable inference, however, is that Nixon voters would be disproportionately likely to increase in efficacy beliefs, and Humphrey and Wallace voters likely to decline, but the data support neither of these inferences. Classifying those scoring 1 or 2 as the highly inefficacious, powerlessness among Humphrey supporters rises about 5 percentage points between pre- and post-election waves ($n = 337$); among Nixon supporters, it increases about 2 points ($n = 384$); and among all others (mainly Wallace supporters), it actually declines about 3 points ($n = 240$). The absence of a significant or interpretable pattern suggests that the real change hypothesis should be abandoned.[14]

In analyzing the contribution of acquiescence to the overall "lowness" of association between the two scales, it proves useful to isolate the acquiescers

---

[13] As the old joke had it, "There's good news and bad news." The good news comes first: Prior studies have sometimes voiced concern that respondents may only pay half-hearted attention to questions, or that they may respond to key symbols but ignore specifics; accordingly, responses may only reflect vague orientations toward the general "theme" of the question, not careful and reasoned answers that would support detailed analysis. McCloskey, for example, comments on a set of dissaffection items similar to these: "It is impossible in the present context to determine the extent to which [these data] signify genuine frustration and political disillusionment and the extent to which they represent familiar and largely ritualistic responses (1969:280)." Respondents, however, were obviously paying close attention to the difference between "any say" and "much say" and the clear change in meaning that results when qualifiers, such as "sometimes," are dropped. This would suggest responses, for the most part, can be taken at face value.

The bad news, of course, is the unmistakable indication that the marginal distributions of these items are sensitive to changes in wording and format, and, consequently, that these marginals could probably be manipulated to show either massive or nonexistent levels of political discontent. The following chapter should be evaluated with this point in mind.

[14] A lesson that follows here is that these attitudes are probably not mere proxies for political partisanship; that is, they do not rise and fall with the fortunes of one's candidate. Rather, their political content apparently lies "deeper" than this; as such, they are more suited to the theoretical purposes of this book.

Quite independently of our own research, Asher (1974) has raised these exact same questions about the same 1968 SRC survey and, surprisingly, comes to exactly the same conclusions. See, in particular, his section on "Question wording as a cause of low reliability" (pp. 46–48) and "Genuine attitude change as a cause of spuriously low reliability" (pp. 48–52).

in Table 4.3. Since their common trait is a tendency to agree to items regardless of content, one must presume that they are located among the 283 respondents in column one. Also located there, of course, are those who are genuinely skeptical of their ability to influence and who indicated this by scoring low on the revised index as well. For our purposes, then, the acquiescers are those who agreed to all four original items but gave alienated responses to two or less of the revised items—81 persons from a sample of 1337, or just over 6%.[15] Taking those who scored 1 or 2 on the standard index as the highly inefficacious, the proportion thus classified is 43%. Correcting this for acquiescence (that is, allowing no acquiescer, as defined earlier, to be included among the highly inefficacious) reduces the estimates to 41%. Since this is a relatively minor overestimation (and one, moreover, that is probably offset by *under*estimation due to other factors[16]), we find no compelling reason to worry about acquiscence when we later discuss the question of extent.

The tendency to acquiesce, according to most prior studies, reflects a certain "cognitive style" that is itself inversely associated with education; consonant with this, the proportion of acquiescers among the high school dropouts is 9.7% ($n = 545$); among high school graduates, it is 4.8% ($n = 412$); and, among those with some college or more, it is 2.1% ($n = 380$). The difference between most and least educated is statistically significant ($p < .001$, one-tailed test) but reassuringly slight.

How seriously is the relationship between education and efficacy affected by acquiescence? According to the data in Table 4.5, not very much.[17] Ignoring acquiescence, the correlation (gamma) between education and efficacy

---

[15] Even this figure probably overstates the amount of acquiescence, since persons who agreed to items in their original form may have had sound substantive reasons to disagree with them in their revised form. For the purposes of this analysis, however, all 81 respondents are treated in the same way.

[16] Three such factors might be mentioned. First, demand characteristics might depress socially undesirable statements of alienation. Second, the lead-in to the efficacy item does not specify a frame of reference, such as "the government in Washington"; some respondents may, therefore, answer with local or state government in mind. All studies, however, show that efficacy is higher at the local level than the national (e.g., Almond and Verba 1965:141). Finally, in every study year, some 10–20% of the original sample is not interviewed. Reasons for this vary from death to language difficulties, but the most common problem is outright refusal. (In the 1966 survey, for example, 61% of the noninterviews were due to this factor.) SRC studies of interview refusals show that the most common reason given is: "Respondent expressed anti-government, anti-administration, anti-business feelings."

[17] Variables in Table 4.5 are scaled as follows:

Efficacy:	1, 2 = low (see Footnote 10)
	3 = medium
	4, 5 = high
Education:	low = less than high school
	medium = high school graduates
	high = some college or more

TABLE 4.5
Education by Efficacy with Acquiescence Controlled and
Uncontrolled: 1968

	Acquiescence Uncontrolled			
		Efficacy		
Education	Low	Medium	High	N
Low	358[a]	104	87	549
Medium	142	104	167	413
High	75	70	235	380
N	575	278	489	1342

	Acquiescence Controlled			
		Efficacy		
Education	Low	Medium	High	N
Low	305	157	87	549
Medium	122	124	167	413
High	67	78	235	380
N	494	359	489	1342

a. All entries are raw frequencies.

is .56; allowing no acquiescer to be included among the highly inefficacious reduces the estimate to .53. Since there is no theory in social science, much less a theory of political alienation, for which a difference of this magnitude would matter, we have opted to ignore acquiescence in the remainder of the research.[18]

VALIDITY

Validity, according to the current standard, exists when a scale actually measures what it purports to measure. How one decides this is still a con-

[18] Why is the index of political efficacy relatively immune to acquiescent biases? A number of factors might be suggested:

First is the generally recognized superiority of the SRC field operation, in particular, their interviewing training. Amidst highly statistical accounts of "measurement error" and related methodological infirmities, it is often forgotten that the first category of quality control over one's data is assuring that interviewers ask the right questions in the right way.

Second, as Jackman (1973) has noted, acquiescence is most problematic when the questions themselves are ambiguous, poorly worded, or convoluted. The relatively straightforward wording of the efficacy questions probably facilitates "real" responses.

Finally, other sources of measurement error may operate to offset bias due to acquiescence. For example, "social desirability" biases may lead people to disagree with these "antidemocratic" statements in rough proportion to the tendency to acquiesce.

tested point (see Footnote 4). Campbell and Fiske (1970) suggest that validity exists when different measures of the same trait agree, and we find this to be a serviceable approximation for our purposes. The SRC surveys usually contain many questions other than the standard nine that relate to matters of powerlessness, efficacy, confidence, trust, and so on. The 1966 survey, for example, contains the following eight items in addition to the standard efficacy measures:

a. Suppose a regulation were being considered by [your local government] that you considered very unjust or harmful. What do you think you could do about that? [Respondents who replied "nothing" or "move away" are coded as low efficacy respondents.]
b. If you made an effort to change this regulation, how likely is it that you would succeed—very likely, somewhat likely, or not likely?
c. If such a case arose, how likely is it that you would actually try to do something about it—very likely, somewhat likely, or not very likely?
d. Have you ever done anything to try to influence a local decision? [Responses are coded "yes" and "no."]
e. Now, suppose a law were being considered by the Congress in Washington that you considered to be very unjust or harmful, what do you think you could do? [Respondents replying "nothing" are coded as the low efficacy respondents.]
f. If you made an effort to change this law, how likely is it that you would succeed—very likely, somewhat likely, or not very likely?
g. If such a case arose, how likely is it that you would actually try to do something about it—very likely, somewhat likely, or not very likely?
h. Have you ever done anything to try to influence an act of Congress? [Responses were coded "yes" and "no."]

These "alternative" efficacy measures, adapted from the Almond–Verba measures of "subjective political competence," clearly tap a wide range of efficacy belief components. Half refer to local government, half to the national government; all deal with the probability or utility of trying to influence government. A valid measure of political efficacy, we assume, would be strongly correlated with all eight. Table 4.6, then, reports the correlations (gamma) between the standard five-point efficacy scale and each of these items, first for the total, then for key subgroups. These correlations suggest that the validity of the efficacy index is adequate by current standards and largely invariant across education and race.

Five items from the 1968 survey may be used to examine the validity of the index of political trust:

a. Over the years, how much attention do you feel that the government pays to what people think when it decides what to do—a good deal, some, or not much?

TABLE 4.6

Correlations (gamma) between the Index of Political Efficacy and
Eight Alternative Efficacy Measures, by Education, by Race: 1966

Item		Total	Less than High High	High School	Some College	Whites	Non Whites
			Education			*Race*	
Local	a	.63	.49	.57	.69	.64	.53
	b	.43	.46	.31	.32	.42	.47
	c	.36	.27	.31	.36	.37	.27
	d	.42	.17	.34	.35	.40	.52
National	e	.63	.44	.60	.63	.63	.57
	f	.43	.40	.42	.27	.42	.53
	g	.38	.31	.35	.24	.39	.29
	h	.59	.55	.47	.46	.57	.70
	N	1289	571	413	301	1133	152
average gamma (local)		.46	.35	.38	.43	.46	.45
average gamma (national)		.51	.42	.46	.40	.50	.52

b. How much attention do you think most Congressmen pay to the people who elect them when they decide what to do in Congress—a good deal, some, or not much?

c. Do you think that the parties pretty much keep their promises or do they usually do what they want after the election is over?

d. Generally speaking, those we elect to Congress in Washington lose touch with the people pretty quickly—Agree–Disagree.

e. Parties are only interested in peoples' votes but not in their opinions—Agree–Disagree.

Both these and the original five trust items have been combined into simple summated scales[19] whose cross-classification is shown in Table 4.7. The cor-

[19] The average inter-item correlation for the five alternate trust items is .664, somewhat higher than the .565 figure reported for the five original items.

The summated scale of the five standard trust items is used in the remainder of the research. All items have been dichotomized (see Footnote 6) and persons assigned a score on the basis of the number of distrustful responses. Persons giving the distrustful response to all five items are scored as 1; those giving the distrustful response to none of the items are scored as 6; others are arranged according to the pattern of their response. Respondents answering only one or none of the five items are omitted in all

relation between them (gamma = .46) is again consonant with prevailing standards. Analysis within subgroups, however, produced results parallel to those found earlier for reliability: The correlation between standard and revised versions did not vary by education but was sharply lower among blacks than among whites.[20]

Analysis of the five standard items revealed at least one item whose meaning seemed ambiguous for blacks; a similar analysis of the five alternative items also suggests some ambiguity. More particularly, the five alternative items apparently tap two distinct dimensions of black political trust: trust in political parties versus trust in government generally. Items c and e of the revised version refer explicitly to political parties (average distrust among blacks = 52.2%); whereas the remaining items refer to national government (average distrust = 33.3%)—suggesting that, among blacks, trust in govern-

TABLE 4.7
Cross-tabulation of the Standard and Revised Political Trust
Scales: 1968

Low Trust		Standard Scale						High Trust
		1	2	3	4	5	6	
	1	26.7	19.6	10.8	6.3	2.3	1.8	
	2	36.6	24.4	16.5	8.8	4.3	3.7	
Revised	3	16.8	20.8	22.2	23.6	17.3	10.6	
Scale	4	13.9	22.0	28.8	27.2	32.3	20.6	
	5	3.0	11.3	15.1	22.7	24.3	28.9	
High Trust	6	3.0	1.8	6.6	11.5	19.3	34.4	
	Total	100.0	99.9	100.0	100.1	99.8	100.0	
	N	101	168	212	331	300	218	

Gamma = .46

study years; other respondents are assigned a score according to the following schedule:

Number of "distrustful" responses:		5	4	3	2	1	0
				Trust score			
Number of items answered:	5	1	2	3	4	5	6
	4	—	2	3	4	4	5
	3	—	—	2	3	4	5
	2	—	—	—	3	4	5
	1	Respondent omitted					
	0	Respondent omitted					

[20] Among subgroups, the correlation between scales was as follows: less than high school = .46; high school graduates = .41; some college or more = .50; whites = .48; nonwhites = .25.

ment and trust in parties are somewhat independent. This implies that a better measure of scale validity among blacks is the correlation between the original scale and a scale composed only of the three nonparty items. This correlation (gamma) equals .37—substantially higher than the original .25 but still less than the .48 found for whites.[21] Thus, however it is measured, scale validity is somewhat lower for blacks than whites. This means that we are less certain what the scale measures among blacks and, therefore, that the results reported for blacks must be assessed with special caution.

VALIDITY RECONSIDERED:
DO THE SCALES HAVE A DISTINCT POLITICAL CONTENT?

Prior studies of political efficacy and trust frequently report strong correlations with measures of personality traits. For example, a good predictor of political efficacy is often "personal efficacy" or "fate control" (e.g., Douvan and Walker 1956; Litt 1963); similarly, political trust is often highly correlated with a more general measure of "trust in people" (e.g., Aberbach 1967; Agger et al. 1961). On this basis, it is often asserted that these measures of political efficacy and trust have no unique political content; rather, they may only reflect (or serve as proxies for) more basic personality attributes.[22] As Fraser has put it, there is a clear possibility that "political [alienation] is not caused by political actors and objects at all, but is solely a function of essentially non-political feelings (1971:349)." [23]

Certainly, the utility of these measures for our purposes would be diminished were this the case. As we have already noted, our interests lie specifically with the theory of political alienation, not with alienation as a global personality characteristic. Thus, our ability to address the theory would be hampered were these measures only to reflect personality differences. Beyond

[21] Among whites, on the other hand, the correlation between original and three-item abbreviated scales is .48—it does not differ from the correlation with the full five-item alternative trust scale. In other words, the inclusions of "party items" in the alternative scale apparently counts for little or nothing among whites.

[22] There is a related question: Are the political alienation indices part of a global "sociocultural alienation" syndrome, or, again, do they have a distinct political content? Aside from the evidence discussed in the ensuing paragraphs, little can be done with the surveys at hand to explore this issue. There is, to our knowledge, only one thorough study of the topic, which concludes that political alienation is, in itself, a distinct empirical phenomenon (Schwartz, 1973: Ch. 2).

[23] To test this possibility, Fraser asked 83 undergraduates at the University of Kentucky to rate "the American system of government," "father," "the Nixon administration," "myself," "the American people," and "mother" on nine semantic differential scales. The relative independence of "personal" and "political" ratings led him to conclude: "It seems to me that these findings suggest that it is possible to proceed from an understanding that political cynicism is not simply a function of feelings about personal objects and seek its causes elsewhere. Political cynicism apparently does have political causes (1971:364)."

this, one's interpretation of the relationship between political alienation and any other variable obviously depends on the content of the alienation items. In Chapter 7, for example, we analyze trends in political alienation over the last decade and a half, and the possible explanations would clearly differ if the items only measured personality traits.[24]

Fortunately, the 1968 SRC survey contains information on the relationship between personal and political forms of efficacy and trust. More particularly, the survey contains the five-item "Index of Personal Competence" (Campbell *et al.* 1960), a commonly employed measure of personal efficacy, and also three items from the well-known "Trust in People" scale (Rosenberg 1956). These items are as follows:

Index of personal competence

1. Do you think it better to plan your life a good way ahead, or would you say that life is too much a matter of luck to plan ahead very far?
2. When you do make plans ahead do you usually get to carry out things the way you expected, or do things usually come up to make you change your plans?
3. Have you usually felt pretty sure your life would work out the way you want it to, or have there been times when you haven't been sure about it?
4. Some people feel they can run their lives pretty much the way they want to; others feel that the problems of life are sometimes too big for them. Which one are you most like?
5. In general, how satisfying do you find the way you are spending your life these days? Would you call it completely satisfying or not very satisfying?

Index of trust in people

1. Generally speaking, would you say that most people can be trusted or that you can't be too careful in dealing with people?
2. Would you say that most of the time people try to be helpful or that they are mostly just looking out for themselves?
3. Do you think most people would try to take advantage of you if they got the chance, or would they try to be fair?

The most meaningful test of independence (or lack of it) among the four personality and political traits is to inquire whether the items that comprise the scales cohere in any meaningful fashion, or, conversely, whether the sev-

---

[24] The very fact that there *are* trends in these items makes us initially suspicious of the "personality" hypotheses. If these orientations were ultimately rooted in personality traits, then the only conceivable explanation for trends would be massive changes in the personality profile of the population in the same period, and this seems to be fundamentally inconsistent with the concept of personality. See Wright (1975a) for an elaboration of these points.

eral items share so much variance that the designation of which items are measures of which traits is largely arbitrary. A useful manner of addressing this question is through factor analysis.

To summarize briefly, factor analysis reduces a large amount of data to a smaller amount. Generally, this means reducing a large list of indicators to a more conceptually parsimonious set of traits. This is done by forming linear combinations of the indicators in a fashion that maximizes the accounted-for variance according to some predetermined criterion. In the present case, one would hope that the 17 indicators could be parsimoniously reduced to four distinct traits, corresponding to the four hypothesized scales.

Now, it is true that *some* "four-factor" solution could be found to "account for" the variance in the 17 items, merely by continuing to factor until four factors had been extracted and then stopping. Since the number of factors required for the solution is itself of substantive importance in this case, however, some less predetermining criterion must be found. One such criterion is to stop factoring when the "eigenvalue" (the latent root of the factored matrix) reaches unity. The characteristics of an eigenvalue and the rationale for the criterion need not concern us. In the principal components factoring routine herein employed, the eigenvalue of the factored matrix reaches unity whenever the off-diagonal partialled correlation coefficients no longer significantly differ from zero. This results when the extracted factors account for all the significant common variation among the factored items; any variance that remains after the eigenvalue reaches unity is variance unique to each item.

The first step in the formal factoring procedure is to generate a matrix of Pearson r's for the 17 items (Table 4.8). This matrix was then factor analyzed, and a four-factor solution did prove sufficient. The matrix of raw or unrotated factor loadings for the four-factor solution is shown in Table 4.9.

These four factors account for 50% of the total variance among the items, or 100% of the common variance (this latter by definition). The remaining 50% is variance unique to each item, of which part is due to unique meaning and some other part to unreliability, measurement error, and so on. It should be mentioned that the last column of Table 4.9 is the percentage of item variance "explained" by the four factors. This number is equal to the squared loadings summed across rows.

To obtain a more interpretable picture of the data, the four factors were rotated according to the Varimax procedure. Varimax is an orthogonal technique that asks whether a strictly independent presentation of the factors renders them easily interpretable. The extent to which the four factors are not independent will be the degree to which the orthogonal rotation produces uninterpretable results. The results of this rotation are shown in Table 4.10; as can be seen, it reproduces the original four scales without ambiguity. These results, of course, overwhelmingly support the hypothesis of a distinct content for the nine political efficacy and trust items.

TABLE 4.8
Intercorrelations (r) among the Measures of Political Efficacy, Political Trust, Personal Efficacy, and Personal Trust: 1968[a]

	1	2	3	4	5	6	7	8
Personal Efficacy								
1								
2	342							
3	333	336						
4	300	253	330					
5	188	168	176	295				
Personal Trust								
6	220	199	250	271	171			
7	183	191	132	153	174	532		
8	166	162	165	143	163	496	567	
Political Trust								
9	040	034	017	-034	027	072	091	122
10	087	054	090	080	104	146	161	163
11	090	096	054	043	045	195	194	153
12	121	124	131	142	110	152	137	120
13	058	083	060	027	107	222	214	208
Political Efficacy								
14	-163	-105	-149	-191	-113	-204	-214	-154
15	-212	-140	-133	-221	-105	-204	-170	-170
16	-172	-138	-120	-204	-069	-187	-149	-071
17	-215	-144	-117	-197	-098	-236	-206	-195

a. Missing data are omitted on an item-by-item basis. Decimal points are omitted. All items scored as indicated in the text, save for the four political efficacy items, which, as the negative coefficients indicate, have been scored "backwards."

TABLE 4.8 (continued)

		9	10	11	12	13	14	15	16
Personal Efficacy	1								
	2								
	3								
	4								
	5								
Personal Trust	6								
	7								
	8								
Political Trust	9								
	10	308							
	11	324	389						
	12	189	275	220					
	13	301	253	313	166				
Political Efficacy	14	-104	-188	-187	-121	-137			
	15	000	-103	-054	-122	006	423		
	16	-018	-094	-126	-086	-068	214	275	
	17	-114	-252	-327	-220	-100	513	322	250

TABLE 4.9
Unrotated Factor Matrix for the 17 Alienation Items: 1968

Variable	Factor				
	1	2	3	4	5
1	-.483	-.359	.034	-.299	.453
2	-.434	-.330	-.094	-.367	.441
3	-.438	-.380	-.076	-.397	.500
4	-.475	-.436	.065	-.234	.474
5	-.362	-.218	-.142	-.244	.258
6	-.637	-.086	-.398	.261	.640
7	-.604	.005	-.455	.382	.718
8	-.563	.021	-.518	.335	.698
9	-.283	.579	-.024	-.260	.483
10	-.443	.485	.108	-.211	.487
11	-.459	.537	.086	-.139	.525
12	-.400	.228	.091	-.299	.304
13	-.400	.469	-.178	-.110	.424
14	.540	-.005	-.483	-.298	.614
15	.471	.236	-.418	-.337	.556
16	.391	.151	-.339	-.141	.310
17	.596	-.123	-.441	-.181	.598

TABLE 4.10
Rotated Factor Matrix for the 17 Alienation Items: 1968

Variable	Factor			
	1	2	3	4
1	.049	.641*	-.190	.066
2	.070	.653*	-.037	.092
3	.044	.701*	-.046	.067
4	-.039	.638*	-.246	.074
5	.077	.478*	-.005	.154
6	.103	.253	-.167	.733*
7	.112	.113	-.150	.818*
8	.121	.118	-.061	.816*
9	.691*	-.029	.060	.025
10	.677*	.065	-.152	.042
11	.697*	.000	-.168	.102
12	.481*	.244	-.116	-.010
13	.592*	.016	.031	.268
14	-.161	-.044	.759*	-.101
15	.082	-.131	.724*	-.131
16	-.020	-.170	.528*	-.041
17	-.324	-.080	.490	-.197

*Indicates a loading above .400.

SUMMARY

The forgoing analysis of efficacy and trust scales suggests the following conclusions: First, their reliability, homogeneity, and internal consistency are average or, perhaps, slightly better than average for attitudinal scales of this sort. Second, unlike many other agree–disagree scales, the index of political efficacy does not appear to be hobbled by insurmountable acquiescent response set biases. Third, the correlation between these measures and other items with which they should be strongly associated suggests that their validity is sufficient by current standards. Finally, factor analysis suggests that their content is empirically distinct from analogous personality measures. The major exception comes in the reliability and validity of the trust scale among blacks. Except for greater circumspection in discussing the black results, then, no other "adjustments" in the substance of the research are indicated.

All of this, of course, could be perfectly true, and the measures could still be insufficient to the theoretical task. Despite their formal methodological properties, that is, one might still maintain that the content of these scales is far removed from the conceptual domain of consensus theory. It proves useful, therefore, to contrast these nine items with selected passages from the consensus writings and, in that context, to note their apparent implications for the question of extent. These are the topics of the next chapter.

5

The Question of Extent[1]

$\mathbb{A}$ T the most basic, intuitive level, the theory of political alienation rests on a simple assertion of extent: In any stable democracy, alienation must be "sufficiently low." Our intention in the present chapter is to decide whether or not the evidence supports this simple claim.

How much political alienation is there in contemporary American society? How much can there be before the foundations of representative democracy are disturbed? The first of these questions is largely empirical, although it does not lend itself to a very precise answer: The best one can hope to do is to suggest some upper and lower limits within which the "true" level of alienation probably falls. The second question is more theoretical: Its answer depends not only on evidence, but also on the correlation between evidence and theoretical assertions. We deal with the first by discussing response frequencies to the nine alienation items, and with the second by noting the disjunction between those frequencies and selected passages from the consensus texts. Our conclusions can be quickly summarized: First, the level of political alienation in the United States probably falls somewhere between 25% and 75%; the "best guess" estimate is that about half the population is alienated from the existing political institutions. Second, it is unlikely that these estimates are consistent with consensus theory. The continued persis-

---

[1] Some of the material presented in this chapter appears in Richard F. Hamilton and James D. Wright, *New Directions in Political Sociology* (Indianapolis, Indiana: Bobbs–Merrill Publishing Company), 1975a: 23–31 and is reproduced here by permission of the coauthor and publisher.

111

TABLE 5.1
Percentage Distributions to the Nine Alienation Items: 1970 and
1972

Political Efficacy	1970	1972
N =	1507	2705

1. People like me don't have any say...

Agree	35.4	40.0
Disagree	63.6	58.8
Other[a]	1.0	1.2

2. Voting is the only way that people...

Agree	59.8	61.6
Disagree	38.8	37.2
Other	1.4	1.2

3. Sometimes politics and government...

Agree	73.0	73.3
Disagree	25.9	25.8
Other	1.1	0.9

4. I don't think public officials care...

Agree	47.1	48.8
Disagree	49.6	48.6
Other	3.3	2.6

Political Trust	1970	1972
N =	1507	2285[b]

1. ...waste a lot of the money we pay...

Not much	3.6	2.3
Some	26.3	30.0
A lot	68.6	65.7
Other	1.5	1.9

2. ...do you think you can trust...

Just about always	6.4	5.2
Most of the time	47.0	47.7
Some of the time/never[c]	44.2	44.8
Other	9.8	2.3

tence and stability of the "system," despite the alienation of half the population, thus suggests that consensus is less important to democratic regimes than we have been led to believe.

Table 5.1 contains the basic data for this analysis and shows the frequency

TABLE 5.1 (continued)

Political Trust	1970	1972
3. ...run by a few big interests...		
Few big interests	49.7	53.0
All the people	40.5	37.5
Other	4.6	9.4
4. ...know what they are doing...		
Yes, they know	51.3	54.7
No, they don't know	44.1	39.9
Other	4.6	5.4
5. ...are a little crooked...		
Quite a few	31.3	35.8
Not many	48.8	45.1
Hardly any	15.8	14.0
Other	4.1	5.0

    a.   Other = "don't know," "no answer," etc.
    b.   The political trust items were asked in the post-election
wave of the 1972 survey.   420 respondents from the first wave were
not re-interviewed.
    c.   "Never" is not one of the response options offered in the
question; nonetheless, in every study year, a small proportion
volunteer it.   These are included with "only some of the time" in
this and all subsequent analyses.

distribution of the nine alienation measures for the two most recent study years.

According to Almond and Verba, the sense of political competence is central to the set of attitudes that nurture democratic government. "Whether myth or reality, the extent to which individuals think they can influence the government and the ways in which they believe they can do so are important elements of the civic culture (1965:138–139)." Political efficacy, Easton and Dennis say, is "a fundamental norm of the American democratic regime. . . . Members of a democratic regime ought to regard those who occupy positions of political authority as responsive agents (1967:26)." According to the most recent data, however, nearly 40% of the U.S. population believe that "people like me don't have any say about what the government does," and about half agree that "public officials don't care much what people like me think." Showing little of their subjective political competence, about 75% sometimes find politics and government "too complicated to understand," and perhaps 40% find this *always* to be the case (see Table 4.4). Many "members of a democratic regime" apparently do *not* regard elites as responsive agents, do *not* consider that they have much impact on how the government runs things, and do *not* have a high estimation of their political abilities. The proportion explicitly denying these points ranges from 35% to 73%.

Consistent with their pluralist leanings, Almond and Verba also stress the importance of multiple channels of influence and cooperative citizen action. "From the point of view of the output of a democratic government, noncooperative and completely individualistic influence attempts could only lead to dysfunctional results. If the government is to be responsive to the demands of the ordinary man, these demands must be aggregated, and the aggregation of interests implies cooperation among men (1965:153)." In contrast, about three-fifths of the population affirm that "voting"—the quintessential "individualistic influence attempt"—"is the *only* way that people like me can have any say about how the government runs things." For the large majority, it appears, no other possible channel of influence is even considered.

Perhaps the most direct pronouncement along these lines comes from V.O. Key: "If a democracy is to exist, the belief must be widespread that public opinion, at least in the long run, affects the course of public action (1967: 547)." Despite equivocating phraseology, the thrust of this statement is clear enough: Most persons must believe that they can influence the government, otherwise democracy does not exist. The impression one gets from these data, however, is not one of a population happily subscribing to "regime norms" or warmly embracing "democratic myths." Across the four efficacy items, the average proportion professing contrary beliefs amounts to 54%. These beliefs, we might say, have not "spread" very "widely" after all. But where are the political ailments that accompany withdrawal of consent? Should we conclude that democracy no longer exists, that government is now losing its ability to perform effectively, that the regime totters on the brink of revolution? Or should we only conclude that the theorists have exaggerated matters beyond the point of credibility?

Concerning the importance of political trust, we have already cited Miller's contention that "a democratic political system cannot survive for long without the support of a majority of its citizens" and also Aberbach and Walker's belief that "the existence of distrustful citizens . . . is a barrier to the realization of the democratic ideal." Gamson summarizes this position: "The importance of trust becomes apparent: the loss of trust is the loss of system power, the loss of generalized capacity for authorities to commit resources to attain collective goals. . . . When [trust] is low and declining, authorities may find it difficult to meet existing commitments and to govern effectively (1968:43, 45–45)."[2]

---

[2] Theoretical nervousness in the face of "distrustful citizens" seems especially inappropriate in light of recent political events. Since the middle of the Johnson administration, for example, the phrase, "credibility gap," has been a part of the American political lexicon. This is a polite way of referring to a pattern of lies and deception on the part of the

The data again fit poorly with these descriptions. On the question, "How much of the time do you think you can trust the government?" only 1 respondent in 20 says, "Just about always." About half say "Most of the time," which is less than outright distrust but certainly not an enthusiastic endorsement. Some 45% respond, "Only some of the time," the most pessimistic assessment offered them by the question's wording. One would be hard pressed to find a "generalized sense of confidence" in these results. Rather, there is a rough standoff between the mildly and the clearly cynical—counter-posed against a tiny fraction of unconditional trust.

Almond and Verba's version is that "the sense of trust in the political elite—the belief that they are not alien and extractive forces, but part of the same political community—makes citizens willing to turn power over to them (1965:357)." In contrast, about two-thirds of the population affirm that government "wastes a lot" of the tax monies, and an additional fourth to a third affirm that it wastes at least "some." Only an insignificant proportion (less than 5%) say, "not much." Again, there is little to suggest widespread confidence in the effectiveness of the system or universal belief that elites are not "extractive." A third of the population even agrees that "quite a few" of the people running the government are a little crooked," and only a sixth can muster a flat denial. Two-fifths agree that "quite a lot" of the people running the government "don't seem to know what they are doing"; half believe that "government is pretty much run by a few big interests looking out for themselves." These citizens apparently harbor no great democratic illusions about government "of, by, and for the people." They show little of Lipset's "generalized deference to elites."

"Democracy," Arthur Miller tells us, "rests upon the trust that citizens extend to their government; when that trust is undermined, the whole system of government is threatened (1974:1001)." It would be difficult to summarize the lessons of consensus theory more succinctly. Despite its utter plausibility, the data seem to be largely inconsistent with this view. Those who believe that government can be trusted just about always, that hardly any of the elites are crooked, or that government does not waste much of the taxes constitute a small fraction of the American population. In contrast, majorities or large minorities deny the honesty, intelligence, competence, and trustworthiness of elites. Taking the most extreme responses across the five trust items shows the average level of distrust to be 47.7%. Averaging across all 18 data points of Table 5.1, the level of political alienation in the United States is 50.9%. At least a third, perhaps as many as two-thirds, and probably

---

Johnson and Nixon administrations. (To date, the Ford administration has been spared this evaluation.) In this context, "trust" becomes little more than gullibility, even ability to be manipulated, as such, one would normally think that the republic would be better served by healthy doses of that "eternal vigilance" of which Jefferson sometimes wrote.

about a half, in short, are not included in the "great consensus" that allegedly sustains and facilitates democratic government.[3] There has been no obvious diminution, however, in the ability of the system to govern, no overt decline in the supply of "authoritative decisions," no popular mass challenge to the legitimacy of existing institutions, in sum, no serious departure from what appears, on the surface at least, to be a stable condition.[4] This suggests that the theorists have greatly understated the extent of discontent in the United States and, by implication, have overstated its importance in assuring stable government.

As an aside, it can also be mentioned that these data do not come from private, unavailable sources. As of 1970, more than 140 major universities subscribed to the SRC data-dissemination service. Nor is any advanced methodological knowledge required to unearth the basic lessons; Table 5.1 was constructed from the marginals reported in the 1970 and 1972 codebooks. What we have here, then, is not theorizing in the absence of facts, but theorizing in wholesale disregard of facts that were both relevant and readily available.

That large segments of the U.S. population are alienated from the political system probably comes as no genuine surprise to anyone who has lived through political assassinations, the war in Vietnam, a deteriorating economy, the Johnson and Nixon administrations, and the other political disillusionments of recent history. Granted that the bulk of consensus theory was written prior to these events, there is a historical purpose to be served, then,

---

[3] Compare with Schwartz: "From our findings above, I believe that national studies would reveal that alienation is now also a majority position. America, I believe, has become an alienated polity (1973:237)."

[4] There are, to be sure, some qualifications that must be appended to this conclusion. As far as the stability and persistence of the system itself are concerned, there can be little serious doubt that they have remained intact despite the high level of alienation and discontent. With regard to the freedom of elected officials "to commit scarce resources to attain collective goals," the issue is not as clear-cut. During the late stages of the Watergate scandal, for example, it is reliably reported that decision making in the administrative bureaucracies was slowed considerably and, in some cases, halted altogether. This, however, seems to have been mainly due to uncertainty, from one day to the next, about who the President was going to be, and rather less a result of official hesitance on grounds that "popular consent" was insufficient to warrant going on with business. In the late summer and early fall of 1973, the Nixon administration faced two closely related, back-to-back crises: the "Mideast crisis" and the "energy crisis." At this point, to set the scene, the Senate Watergate committee had already done its damage, and the prosecution of key Nixon staffers had already begun. At this point, also, Nixon was doing very poorly in the polls. The response of his administration to the two crises is, therefore, quite instructive. Concerning the Mideast crisis, for example, part of the response included a "general alert" of U.S. troops. So far as is known, this order to alert was uniformly obeyed, and, had Nixon ordered it, there is very little reason to expect that the Chiefs of Staff would have refused to send troops into the area on the grounds that "declining confidence" delegitimized the command. The domestic political situation, while perhaps having had deleterious effects on morale and so on, placed very few limits

by asking whether the basic implication about extent was any more plausible when the theory was being written than at the present.

Table 5.2 displays the marginal distributions to the efficacy and trust items in 1956 and 1958, respectively.[5] These data were collected during the "quiet" Eisenhower years, well before the alienating experiences of the 1960s, during a period when the "absence of organized dissent" was taken to indicate a massive political somnambulism among the American population. Advanced industrial capitalism, it was claimed, had generated widespread political calm. Poverty was "nearly an afterthought," and even the "downtrodden" working class had become "integrated" into middle class status and consumption norms. Radicals, such as Herbert Marcuse, decried the bleak prospects of a "society without criticism" (1964:ix), and C. Wright Mills characterized the era as "a mood of acceptance and a relaxation of the political will (1955:22)." Barrington Moore expressed the fear that "as we reduce economic inequalities and privileges, we may also eliminate the sources of contrast and discontent that put drive into genuine political alternatives (1958:183)." Indeed, one commentator characterized the ongoing mode of analysis as follows: "The American people are so uniformly content that there simply does not exist a sufficient degree of popular disagreement to sustain a political debate between the parties (Reagan 1956:346)."[6] The era marked, as the phrase went, "the end of ideology."

Considering the events of the ensuing decade, the emphasis on the quietude of the era—and especially its projection as a long-term trend—seems mis-

---

on what Nixon was *actually* able to do in responding to the crisis. The one overt and obvious consequence of the lessened public confidence was the widespread suspicion that the entire crisis and subsequent "general alert" had simply been manufactured by Nixon to divert attention from his Watergate miseries. (On this score, see Footnote 2.)

There next arose the energy crisis. In the classical presidential manner, Nixon responded to this by going on national television with a plea for "public cooperation in this time of national crisis." Was the public response a surly and uncooperative disbelief? This was certainly not the case. Automobile speeds were quickly reduced, with the aid of very cooperative state legislators throughout the country. Thermostats were turned down, lights turned off, travel reduced, and firewood hoarded. (Poll evidence on the public response to the energy crisis is reviewed by Greeley, 1975.) In this respect at least, there is little persuasive evidence to suggest that the president's ability to initiate a policy or to secure public support of it was in any way diminished by rapid drainage of the "reservoir of diffuse support." As in the case of the Mideast crisis, however, there was again a common feeling that this was something of a manufactured "diversion" (Greeley 1975: 60a).

[5] The political trust items were not included in the 1956 survey; likewise, the political efficacy items were not asked in 1958. Comparing the data of Tables 5.1 and 5.2 previews the analysis of trends reported in Chapter 7.

[6] Reagan continues: "The other possibility is that all is not sweetness and light but that for a variety of reasons the existing disagreements are not being handled by the political system, are not being raised to the surface (1956:346)." Reagan, in what was obviously the "minority position" of the era, did find "the second of these two alternatives to hold the lion's share of the truth."

TABLE 5.2

Percentage Distributions to the Nine Efficacy and Trust Items, 1956 (N = 1762) and 1958 (N = 1822)

Political Efficacy	Agree	Disagree	Other[a]
1. People like me don't have any say....	27.9	70.7	1.4
2. Voting is the only way that people...	72.9	25.0	2.2
3. Sometimes politics and government...	62.8	35.6	.16
4. I don't think public officials care...	26.0	70.4	3.5

Political Trust

1. ...waste a lot of the money we pay...

Not much	10.0
Some	41.3
A lot	42.2
Other	6.5

2. ...do you think you can trust...

Just about always	15.5
Most of the time	55.6
Some of the time/never	22.8
Other	6.1

3. ...run by a few big interests[b] ...

Few big interests	26.2
All the people	58.8
Other	15.0

4. ...know what they are doing...

Yes, they know	56.0
No, they don't know	36.2
Other	7.7

5. ...are a little crooked...

Quite a few	23.4
Not many	42.6
Hardly any	25.6
Other	4.1

a. Other = "don't know," "no answer," etc.
b. This item was not asked of the 1958 sample. The data reported in the table for this item are from 1964 (N = 1571), the first year in which the item was used. The 1958 analogue to the item is: "Do you think that the high-up people in government give everyone a fair break whether they are big shots or just ordinary people (17.0%) or do you think that some of them pay more to what the big interests want (74.0%)? (Other: 8.9%).

placed; as Everett Ladd has said, "It now seems so curiously implausible (1969:xvi)." The interesting point, which is emphasized by Table 5.2, however, is that these perspectives were "curiously implausible" even during the period of their greatest persuasion: There were sizable pockets of disaffection even in the "quiet" Eisenhower years, pockets which many of the intellectuals of the period simply managed to overlook. In 1956, when the hypothesis of "uniform content" was first being seriously considered in academic journals, a fourth of the population agreed that "people like me don't have any say about what the government does" and that "public officials don't care much what people like me think." Similarly, nearly three-fourths found voting to be the only means of influence open to them, and more than three-fifths found politics too complicated to understand. In 1958, when the "end of ideology" hypothesis was sweeping through intellectual circles, two-fifths of the population believed that the government wasted a lot of their tax money, a mere sixth felt the government could be trusted "just about always," a third judged that "quite a few" of the people running the government "don't seem to know what they are doing," a fourth felt that "quite a few" of the politicians were crooks, and a rather spectacular three-fourths felt that government was more attentive to "what the big interests want" than to the interests of "ordinary people." One could not conclude from these data that discontent in the 1950s was rampant. Indeed, when compared with levels observed in the 1970s, it was not even particularly extensive— about a fourth in 1956 and 1958, compared to the more recent half. Nor could one reasonably conclude—however—as many theorists and commentators of the time concluded—that discontent was absent.[7] An alienated fourth, after all, is still an alienated fourth—a segment of discontent large enough to be found by nearly anyone with the inclination to look.

A final question that arises is whether the United States is unique among industrialized democracies of the West in its apparent ability to withstand the political alienation of much of its population. Outside the United States, survey data on political alienation is uneven but nonetheless sufficient to piece together a broad outline. In this case, the lesson appears to be that the

[7] More accurately, one could say that the theorists mistook the absence of organized dissent for a sign that no dissaffection was present. From a conventional "pluralist" point of view, this equation is understandable, since, in that theory, there are presumed mechanisms which are thought to bring discontent and disagreement to the fore and channel it politically. (See, for example, Arnold Rose: "For every way in which a dozen or more people in the community think the community should be changed there are one or more associations working in some manner for that change [1968:235].)" From this perspective, unorganized dissent is virtually a contradiction in terms. Left-wing critics such as Mills and Marcuse, being exempt from conventional modes of thinking, cannot be so lightly spared: They should have been able to note the presence of underlying disaffection and then to direct their considerable wisdom and eloquence against those who were failing to capitalize. As it was, the anxieties over "moods of acceptance" and the "society without criticism" resulted in a decade of political immobilism on the Left.

TABLE 5.3
Political Alienation in Canada: 1968 (N = 2767)

Political Efficacy	Agree	Disagree	Other
1. People like me don't have any say...	46.6	48.6	4.8
2. Voting is the only way...	76.5	20.1	3.4
3. Sometimes politics and government...	69.4	26.4	4.2
4. I don't think the government cares...	42.1	50.7	7.2

Political Trust

1. ...waste a lot of the money we pay...

A lot	43.1
Some	42.0
Not much	8.4
Other	5.6

2. ...do you think you can trust...

Always	8.2
Most of the time	49.7
Some of the time	37.0
Other	5.2

3. ...give everyone a fair break...

Yes	9.8
Pay more attention to big shots	83.4
Other	6.7

4. ...know what they are doing...

Yes, they know	47.6
No, they don't know	45.6
Other	6.8

5. ...are a little crooked...

Quite a few	23.9
Not many	37.0
Hardly any/none	29.4
Other	9.6

United States is *not* unique in this respect and that relatively high levels of political alienation exist in all "stable democracies" for which data are available.[8]

The most complete and comparable data exist for Canada. A 1968 elec-

[8] The surveys discussed in the following pages were made available to us as follows: The 1968 Canadian study was directed by John Meisel. Principal investigators for the 1972

TABLE 5.4
Political Alienation in West Germany: 1972 (N = 1584)

	Agree	Disagree	Other
Sometimes politics and government...	56.3	36.1	7.6
People like me do not have any say about what the government does...	55.2	36.5	8.3
Voting is the only way...	60.8	27.5	11.7
I do not think public officials care much...	45.6	40.5	13.9

tion survey there contained the same nine efficacy and trust items; marginals for them are shown in Table 5.3. With a few minor exceptions that scarcely warrant mention, the Canadian data are virtually indistinguishable from those for the United States. Large majorities agree that voting is their only means of influence, that politics and government are sometimes too complicated to understand, and that people high in government "pay more attention to what the big interests want." Two-fifths to a half agree that they have no say in what the government does, that public officials do not care what they think, that government wastes a lot of the tax money, and that quite a few of the people running the government "don't seem to know what they are doing." Finally, a fourth to a third think the government can be trusted "only some of the time" and that "quite a few" of those running the government are a little crooked. Averaged across the nine items, the level of political alienation in Canada runs to 52.0%.[9]

The four political efficacy items were also included in a 1972 survey of the

West German study were Manfred Berger, Wolfgang Gibowski, Max Kaase, Dieter Roth, Uwe Schleth, and Rudolf Wildenmann. The 1970 Dutch survey was prepared by Phillip Stouthard, Warren Miller, Felix Heunks, and Jerrold Rusk. The 1971 Dutch survey was directed by Robert Mokken. The 1972 Swiss survey was conducted by David Hentley and Henry Kerr. Our thanks go to the original researchers for allowing us the use of their data.

All surveys are distributed through the Inter-University Consortium for Political Research and were prepared for our analysis by the Amsterdams Sociaalwetenschappelijk Data Archief (Evert Brouwer, Director). We would also like to thank the Third European Summer School for Training in Comparative Research for making the analysis possible, and also Roberta McKown, who graciously assisted in the compilation of the comparative materials. None of the aforenamed is responsible, however, for our analysis and conclusions.

[9] In his Revolution and Counterrevolution, Lipset argues that Canadian attitudes towards elites are generally more positive and deferential than in the United States. "Sociologically oriented observers," he says, "have stressed the greater respect for political leaders in Canada than in the United States (1970: 46)." The data just discussed cast some doubt on Lipset's comparative claim. As far as we can tell, there are essentially no differences between the two nations on these matters.

TABLE 5.5
Political Alienation in the Netherlands: 1970 (N = 1838) and
1971 (N = 2495)

	1970		
Political Efficacy	Agree	Disagree	Other

1. Sometimes politics and the government seem so complicated that a person like me can't really understand what is going on.

	68.6	23.9	7.6

2. Voting is the only way that people like me can have any say about what the government does.

	57.9	29.4	12.7

3. Most of the time the members of the Second Chamber do not bear in mind enough the things the voters actually want.

	61.9	15.8	22.3

4. People like me don't have any influence over what the government does.

	58.0	34.9	7.1

5. I don't think MP's and ministers care much what people like me think.

	53.6	34.5	11.9

	1970		
Political Trust	Agree	Disagree	Other

1. In general, tax money is wisely spent in our country.

	31.4	38.3	30.3

2. Often the members of the Second Chamber don't know enough about the things they are talking about.

	34.7	36.7	28.6

3. There is too much wasting of money by the government.

	67.6	12.2	20.2

Federal Republic of Germany, which, like Canada, must rate among the more stable and successful postwar industrial democracies. Data are shown in Table 5.4. Following the common pattern, majorities or clear pluralities offer the alienated response on each of the four items. Well over half the

TABLE 5.5 (continued)

	1970		
Political Trust	Agree	Disagree	Other

4. MP's are paying too mucy attention to the interests of a few powerful groups instead of the general interest.

	57.8	18.9	23.3

	1971		
Political Efficacy	Agree	Disagree	Other

1. Members of the Chamber are not really concerned with the opinions of people like me.

	48.0	36.7	15.3

2. People like me have no influence at all on government policy.

	56.3	34.0	9.6

3. Parliamentary representatives are open to the opinion of people like me.

	40.2	47.4	12.4

West German population affirms that politics and government are sometimes too complicated to understand, that "people like me" have no effective voice in the running of government, and so on. Averaged across the four items, the level of political alienation in Germany runs to 54.5%.[10]

Election surveys from the Netherlands, in 1970 and 1971, contain useful, if not fully comparable, information. By any standard, Dutch society and government must stand among the most stable in the world; according to Goudsblom (1967:77), the last political assassination there occurred in 1672. Included in the two surveys are 12 reasonably similar efficacy and trust items; marginal frequencies are shown in Table 5.5. Again, the overall picture is very similar to that found in the United States, Canada, and West Germany; if anything, the sense of political powerlessness is perhaps somewhat *higher*

[10] There was a related question posed in a 1965 West German survey that merits a passing comment here. The question read: "Which of these sentences best expresses how you feel when you go to the polls?" Option one, "I have the feeling that thereby I am able to take part in a political decision," was chosen by 43%. The second possibility, "I do it simply because it is my duty as a citizen," was the plurality response, picking up 48%. There were, in addition, 7% who "do it only because it is the normal thing to do" and 2% who said, "I think that it is a waste of time." Here, as before, the majority rejects any suggestion that they are active participants in the policy process, even when they are voting.

in the Netherlands than elsewhere. Averaged across the 12 items, the level of political alienation in the Netherlands runs to 54.2%.

Some information is also available for Switzerland, which certainly numbers among the stable democratic states. A 1972 Swiss election study found two-fifths agreeing that "often it makes no sense to vote, for public authority does what it wants in any case." Three-fifths *dis*agreed that "people like me have many ways to influence politics," and the same proportion again found politics and government "too complicated to understand." Slightly more than 40% did "not believe that the government cares very much about what people like me think." Following the common pattern, nearly three-fifths (56.2%) affirmed that "the people who govern us give more attention to important persons" and just over a third flatly stated, "The government does what it wants, people like me cannot do anything about it."

The conclusions here seem fairly obvious: In all "advanced industrial democracies" for which data are available, something on the order of half the population rejects those beliefs which consensus theory claims to be essential for democratic stability. Perhaps the most interesting pattern is that at least a majority in all nations believe that government is more attentive to "big shots" and "special interests" than to the interests of "ordinary people." Granted that this proportion might be affected by changes in wording and format, wholesale confidence in and allegiance to elites is still obviously less than unanimous, yet all these societies apparently do quite well in spite of it. It would be difficult, we believe, to conclude that "the sense of trust in the political elite makes citizens willing to turn power over to them." Likewise, in all nations, two-fifths to a half affirm that "people like me don't have any say about what the government does." Many, in short, flatly deny that "public opinion affects the course of public action." It seems to us that only one of two conclusions is possible. Either the nations considered thus far are much less "stable" and "effective" than all outward appearances suggest, or else the role of attitudes such as efficacy and trust in promoting political viability is very limited.

How could this latter be the case? First, as we have already mentioned, political attitudes of any sort pose no serious challenge to the regime unless they are accompanied by the ability to mount an effective opposition. One possibility, then, is that the alienated, on the whole, lack this critical ability. In other words, there may be a correlation between real and perceived powerlessness. Alternatively, the alienated might share little beyond their alienation that could bind them together as a cohesive political force. If, for example, they were evenly dispersed among ideologies or split among the major parties, it is unlikely that they would respond, as a group, to any single political stimulus. Still another possibility is that the character of political alienation has been misrepresented in conventional accounts. It is usually assumed that political alienation is a diffuse and quasi-pathological reaction to "modernization and the mass society" and, therefore, that it leads to irrational political results. In contrast, political alienation may be a relatively specific and, indeed, largely accurate perception of the facts of political life. Once stripped of pathological and irrational connotations, the alarmist hypotheses are less compelling. Finally—this is more an implication of points already made—political alienation may simply be unrelated to any behavioral propensity, most of all to behaviors that might assault the legitimacy of the regime. All of these suspicions are somewhat supported by the analysis reported in the remaining chapters.

6

The Question of Distribution

$\mathbb{T}$HE evidence presented in Chapter 5 showed that approximately half the adult population of several exemplary "stable industrial democracies" can be considered alienated from the political institution. The major question to be raised in this chapter is how the alienated half is distributed in contemporary American society.

Since there are a number of issues addressed here, it proves useful to summarize them at the beginning. Our primary aim is to resolve the paradox noted in the preceding chapter, namely, that democratic societies can apparently function quite adequately even when half their citizens embrace beliefs said to detract from the viability of democratic government. Along these lines, two points should be mentioned: First, alienation is highest where the resources, ability, or inclination to mount an effective political challenge are lowest; second, despite the general tendencies, the relationship between political alienation and many "background" variables is weak. As we shall see, this means that alienation is not "of a piece" and, consequently, that the alienated will probably not react as a cohesive group to any single political issue, movement, or candidate.

The data discussed in Chapter 5 suggest that democratic societies can clearly persist despite the alienation of *some* of their citizens. A second purpose here is to specify this conclusion more precisely. The evidence will isolate some groups or·sectors of the society in which political discontent is especially high; continuing stability thus suggests that the alienation of these groups is largely irrelevant to the regime. Groups whose alienation is relatively low, conversely, cannot be so lightly dismissed. In other words, these data allow for an important addendum to the theory, namely, the

126

specification of groups whose positive support and allegiance apparently *is* "functional" for system stability.

A third issue is the adequacy of pluralist and mass society hypotheses about the sources of political alienation. Concerning pluralism, the data are not ideally suited to the task, but evidence on union membership, political party affiliation, and church activity is at least serviceable. On the other hand, there is extensive data on length of residence, community size, regional and social mobility, home ownership, and other dimensions of "societal integration" which bear on the mass society themes.

Finally, we hope to remove some of the confusion that currently exists in the literature concerning what, exactly, political alienation is correlated with.

There is relatively little in the following analysis that bears directly on major consensus claims, largely because consensus theorists seldom discuss the sources of cleavage in the society. Rather, they have often simply assumed that there is a widespread consensus encompassing nearly everybody. This assumption, in turn, seems to derive from an uncritical endorsement of perhaps the least persuasive of all classical democratic doctrines—that democracy rests ultimately upon the consent of the governed. Although seldom explicit, there is a "social contract" vision of democracy that runs very near the surface. Men and women of the distant past are apparently seen as having existed in some "natural," prepolitical state. Realizing the hazards of anarchy, government is, thus, created by the collective investiture of individual powers and a political elite formed to administer the affairs of state through the auspices of this mandate. Since government derives its power from the legitimacy that citizens extend to it, it may be dissolved when the people judge that it no longer serves their common purpose.

Stated thus, the social contract theory of democracy would find few contemporary defenders; it would be everywhere dismissed as quaint, if not naive. Is it not, however, implied in Almond and Verba's thesis that "the sense of trust in the political elite makes citizens willing to turn power over to them?" This formulation certainly suggests that citizens have some choice in the matter, that they might decide *not* to "turn over power" if they wished it. Or consider the passage from Gamson that was cited earlier: "The importance of trust becomes apparent: the loss of trust is the loss of system power, the loss of a generalized capacity for authorities to commit resources to attain collective goals." What can this passage mean, if not that government is somehow rendered impotent by the withdrawal of public trust? The best that can be said is that these theorists have fallen prey to an inappropriate metaphor; the worst that can be said is that this metaphor has clouded their vision of some obvious political truths.[1]

[1] One consequence of the metaphoric language is that it makes empirical inquiry very difficult. The Almond–Verba formulation, for example, suggests some specific occasion in which power was turned over to elites, but when and where was that? In a strictly empirical sense, of course, this "turning over" never happens. Or consider Gamson's

In support of his thesis, Gamson asks that we consider Johnson's Vietnam policy from 1964 to 1967 (1968:44ff.). According to Gamson, Johnson's 1964 landslide had given him a high "credit rating" of political trust and, therefore, "extraordinary latitude" in his conduct of the war. The discussion suggests that the size of the president's majority is directly related to his range of policy options.[2] Certainly, Johnson had extraordinary latitude, as any president would: He could escalate the war, negotiate a settlement, withdraw troops, deploy nuclear weapons, have Ho Chi Minh assassinated, or whatever else struck his fancy. The only "limits" to his options were set by available military technology and his own moral values; the level of public trust was beside the point. At least in part, Johnson's landslide victory over Goldwater was a specific mandate *not* to increase American involvement, but this obviously mattered little in his subsequent decisions.[3] Except for the 1964 election itself, the public was in no sense "consulted" about Vietnam in the entire period under consideration; had it been, there is a real question of whether it would have consented.[4]

---

phrase, "the loss of system power." What, exactly, does *that* mean? How would one decide whether or not a "system" had "lost power"? Such statements have no precise empirical referent; they are purely allegorical and, in that respect, are immune to empirical refutation.

[2] For example, "An overwhelming election victory in November, 1964, increased such latitude even further. At that point, the President had a virtually unlimited capacity to make commitments (Gamson 1968:44)."

[3] This signifies a problem in the "elitist" theory of democratic accountability. First, the outcomes of "competion for votes" are inherently ambiguous; they do not provide clear policy directives on specific political issues. The LBJ landslide is a case in point. On the one hand, it could be read as a "mandate" not to escalate the war, but it could also be read as a "mandate" not to abolish Social Security. A second problem, actually more an implication of the first, is that citizens consequently exercise little influence over the specific policies of the government, only some limited control over which candidate gets to choose which policies. "Accountability" for specific policy choices is thus postponed until the "next" election. In the case of second-term incumbents, however, this essentially amounts to no accountability at all. Moreover, faced with a sitting incumbent, the modern tendency has been for the out-party to essentially forfeit the election: Stevenson in 1956, Goldwater in 1964, and McGovern in 1972 would fit this pattern. Such "forfeitures" thus disrupt the mechanisms of accountability, even for incumbents not yet elected to their second term. Finally, in the extreme case, a sitting president who fears his up-coming "accountability" can avoid it by the simple expedient of not running for reelection, as LBJ did in 1968. This would be counted by the democratic elitists as an example of the "accountability" process at work; after all, LBJ *did* forgo his opportunity to run for a second term, which is the practical equivalent of being defeated at the polls. By opting not to run, however, LBJ also made it possible for the major issue that "drove him from office," namely Vietnam, to be ignored in the subsequent election. Both Humphrey and Nixon, neither being "accountable" for LBJ's Vietnam policy, could (and did) simply choose not to discuss the issue.

[4] As of late 1964, about 38% of the population felt that the United States had done the right thing by getting into Vietnam; about 24% felt that we should have stayed out of the fighting; and the remaining 38% were in various states of noninterest or confusion.

Johnson's policy, of course, was to continually escalate the war from his election in 1964 until March of 1968. "The consequence of such a choice," says Gamson, "was a heavy erosion of trust which reduced the President's freedom of action substantially (1968:44)." Here we have the social contract view in its purest form. As we shall see in the next chapter, public confidence did erode substantially during the Johnson administration. But in what conceivable way did this "reduce the President's freedom of action"? Johnson continued to escalate despite this erosion and despite well-articulated antiwar opinion. As trust diminished, according to Gamson, "the President became increasingly less free to take actions which would remove past errors and conceivably restore his credit rating (1968:44–45)." What was he "increasingly less free" to do? Was the president no longer *able* to order a halt to the bombing? Would the pilots have refused, unsure that the state of public confidence warranted this policy directive? Just what, exactly, did the lack of public trust prevent Johnson from doing? Judging from his behavior in the period, the answer is: nothing, except to seek re-election in 1968. There is, however, an immense difference between "not seeking re-election" and "unable to govern effectively." Certainly, the drain on public trust meant that anything Johnson said or did was immediately received with some suspicion, but it did not mean that he was hampered in his ability to act.

This is not to say that no erosion of confidence could ever possibly threaten a democratic regime.[5] In the case of Johnson's Vietnam policy, there emerged an active antiwar constituency able to mete out some "punishment" when Johnson ignored their policy preferences. The only visible effect of antiwar activism was to make it more difficult to embark on a Vietnam policy that everyone would find mutually satisfactory, certainly *not* to reduce the total number of policies that might have conceivably been initiated. (Repeated escalation despite an organized opposition is ample testimony to this fact.)

As for current policy preferences, about 9% favored an immediate withdrawal, 24% favored a cease-fire, and 31% favored an escalation, with the remaining 36% either not interested or unsure as to their preferences. These data were collected well after the Bay of Tonkin "incident" and hardly amount to an overwhelming public mandate to escalate the war. At this time, however, prowar sentiment was quite extensive among the better-educated upper middle class (see Hamilton, 1968); thus, if anything, it was upper middle class opinion, not mass opinion, that made possible Johnson's escalation.

[5] Even here, however, it is easy to exaggerate. It is probably true that no regime ever "went under" without some concomitant decline in popular support or citizen affection for it. It is equally true, as Crane Brinton remarks in his classic study of revolution, "that no government has ever fallen before attackers until it has lost control over its armed forces or lost the ability to use them effectively" (1965:89). This, certainly, would describe the history of the Third Republic in France, of czarist Russia, of the Weimar regime in prewar Germany; indeed, as Brinton continues, "This holds true from spears and arrows to machine guns and gas, from Hippias to Castro." This suggests another point, that one would probably learn more about the sources of democratic stability in the United States by studying what goes on at West Point or, for that matter, at the Harvard Business School, than by studying political alienation in the mass public.

More to the point, the political alienation of antiwar activists differed from that of the mass public in at least one essential respect: It was accompanied by a proclivity to act—to organize demonstrations, work for antiwar candidates, write letters, and so on. In Gamson's formulation, however, the effects of the erosion of confidence are direct and immediate: "The loss of trust is the loss of system power." There is no reference here to the intervention of behavior, no appreciation of the immense organizational effort necessary to sustain a viable opposition.[6] These are obvious points, to be sure, but they are often overlooked: If there is no attendant inclination to engage in behavior that challenges the regime, political alienation necessarily counts for little.

A close corollary to the "social contract" description is what might be called the "democratic fallacy." Since the form of government in question is democracy, and since, in a democracy, everyone's share of power is, by definition, more or less equal, then the disaffection of anyone poses an equivalent hazard. Accordingly there is neither reason nor need to delineate the correlates of discontent and their association with effective social power. Surely, however, the intense political alienation of aging widows counts for less than the political disaffection of the military or financial communities. What we should say, then, is that democratic regimes must enjoy the positive support of *some* of its members, that there must be a firm allegiance among *part* of the citizenry, not that these attitudes must be "widespread" or embraced by the entire population. This, then, raises the question of how political alienation is distributed in the society, which is the focal concern of the chapter.

Most of the analysis reported here is based upon the 1970 survey ($n = 1507$), primarily because it was the most recent survey available when the research began.[7] Typically, the tables present the proportions that are "highly

---

[6] Almond and Verba's rendition is another case in point. Like Gamson, they see these attitudes as directly affecting the ability of the government to function. They say, "The distribution in the society of such attitudes as the belief that the political system is legitimate, that it operates effectively, that it is amenable to the ordinary man's influence . . . —clearly, all these have important effects on the way the system operates (1965:42)." Just how, then, do these beliefs affect the operation of the system? They continue: "It is somewhat more difficult to pin down the precise relationship between these attitudes and the ways in which political democracies operate (1965:42)." Actually, it is not at all difficult to "pin down the precise relationship." If persons who do not share the optimistic attitudes subsequently engage in political behavior that challenges the government, then the attitudes (or lack of them) pose a threat; otherwise, they do not. What *is* difficult to pin down is how these attitudes by themselves could influence the government.

[7] The exceptions are, first, the data on religion and mass media attention, which are taken from the 1968 survey ($n = 1557$) and, second, the evidence on party identification, where all surveys from 1956 to 1970 are employed. Initial analysis on the more recent 1972 survey has indicated no major changes in the substantive conclusions of this chapter.

alienated" within various categories. Unless otherwise specifically noted, the "highly inefficacious" gave alienated responses to three or all four of the political efficacy items; the "highly distrustful" gave alienated responses to three or more of the five measures of political trust. These particular cut-off points were chosen because they best approximate the average levels indicated when the items are considered in their raw or unscaled forms.[8]

REGION AND RACE

Our analysis begins with region and race, not because they represent the most fundamental cleavages in the society, nor because their theoretical import surpasses all others, but because their correlation with other background variables introduces a potential element of spuriousness. Beyond this, both variables relate to the major concerns of the chapter. Blacks and white southerners, for example, constitute "subcultures" which are, in part, "marginal" to the mainstream of the society; thus, on the mass society account, their alienation should be somewhat higher. Second, there are a priori reasons to expect that both groups may have been unsatisfied with recent political developments. Finally, both variables appear regularly in the literature, although there is no agreement on their relationship with political alienation (see Chapter 3).

Political alienation clearly varies by region and race: Three-fifths of the blacks are highly alienated on both dimensions, compared to about a half of the white southerners and approximately two-fifths of the non-South whites (Table 6.1). The smallest of these differences (the 7 point difference between white southerners and blacks in political trust) is statistically significant at .06 (two-tailed test); all other differences are statistically significant at .001 or beyond.

Table 6.2 reports a regression analysis of efficacy and trust with city size, education, occupation, income, religion, region, and race, as independent

---

[8] The marginal distributions to the summated efficacy and trust scales are as follows: (1970).

	Efficacy %	(n = 1503) Σ%	Trust %	(n = 1496) Σ%
High alienation	19	19	11	11
2	23	42	17	28
3	26	68	20	48
4	18	87	22	70
5	12	99	18	88
Low alienation			11	99

variables.[9] All these variables are systematically correlated with region or race or both; thus the analysis asks whether the results of Table 6.1 are merely the reflection of these other factors. Region continues to have a statistically significant effect on both alienation variables. This contradicts the only other nationally representative study, which reported that the distinctiveness of the South disappeared when controlled for either education or income (Finifter 1970:402).[10] Race, however, retains its independent effect only on trust ($p = .049$); for efficacy, the racial effect disappears ($p = .213$).

[9] The coding of variables in the regression analysis was as follows (for dependent variables, the full five- and six-point efficacy and trust scales were employed):

City size: 1 = 50,000 +
            2 = 10,00–49,999
            3 = 2500–9999
            4 = less than 2500

Education: 1 = less than eighth grade
            2 = less than twelfth grade
            3 = high school graduate
            4 = some college
            5 = college graduate

Occupation: Ranges from 0 to 99 according to the 2-digit Duncan occupational prestige codes.

Income: 1 = less than 2000
            2 = 2000–2999
            3 = 3000–3999
            4 = 4000–4999
            5 = 5000–5999
            6 = 6000–7999
            7 = 8000–9999
            8 = 10,000–14,999
            9 = 15,000 +

Religion: 1 = Protestant
            0 = all others

Race: 0 = nonwhite
            1 = white

Region: 0 = non-South
            1 = South

Missing data were omitted from the analysis.

[10] What accounts for the divergence between Finifter's and our results? One possibility is regionally specific trends in the control variables. In 1960, when Finifter's data were collected, the South was well below the national average in education and income levels; the effect of "controlling" for these variables, then, is to lower the level of alienation against the national mean. In the subsequent decade, however, the rate of growth in education and income in the South exceeded that of the non-South (McKinney and Bourque 1971). In 1970, then, controlling the regional difference for education and income, relatively speaking, would neither raise nor lower alienation in the South against the national mean. As we shall see in the next chapter, the South–non-South difference in alienation has been fairly constant over the last 15 years (Table 7.2); this, in conjunction with differential rates of increase in education and income, renders our results and Finifter's consistent.

TABLE 6.1
Distribution of Efficacy and Trust by Region and Race: 1970

		Efficacy		Trust	
		Percent	Cumulative	Percent	Cumulative
Non-Whites[a]	1	31.3	31.3	16.3	16.3
	2	30.1	61.4	24.7	41.0
(N = 166)	3	25.9	87.3	19.9	60.9
	4	7.8	95.1	16.9	77.8
	5	4.8	99.9	12.0	89.8
	6			10.2	100.0
White South[b]	1	26.5	26.5	14.0	14.0
	2	21.4	47.9	17.2	31.2
(N = 430)	3	25.6	73.5	22.6	53.8
	4	15.6	89.1	23.5	77.3
	5	10.9	100.0	13.3	90.6
	6			9.5	100.1
Non-South Whites	1	13.8	13.8	9.3	9.3
	2	22.6	36.4	16.2	25.5
(N = 900)	3	26.5	62.9	17.9	43.4
	4	22.9	85.8	22.9	66.3
	5	14.2	100.0	21.1	87.4
	6			12.6	100.0

a. Non-whites are mostly blacks, but also include a small number of Puerto Ricans, American Indians, etc. Non-white and black are herein used as synonymous.
b. Includes: Alabama, Arkansas, Florida, Georgia, Louisiana, Mississippi, North and South Carolina, Texas, Virginia, West Virginia, Kentucky, Maryland, Oklahoma, Tennessee, and Washington, DC.

The racial findings are identical to those reported by Finifter (1970:399). Finifter's warning about these procedures, however, deserves to be repeated: "Since it is obviously more difficult for Negroes to attain the same achieved status, this type of statistical controlling procedure is in danger of being misleading." Table 6.2 suggests, if blacks enjoyed the equivalent education, occupation, and income of whites, then there would be no difference in their levels of political efficacy.

Some of the substantive implications of these data can be noted. First, that blacks and white southerners are the two more alienated subgroups suggests that it would be unwise to speak of "the alienated" as an internally homogeneous entity, or to expect "the alienated" to be mobilized together by a single demagogic candidate or program. In many respects, the interests, ideologies, and experiences of these two key "alienated subcultures" are diametrically opposed;[11] policies designed to appeal to the one group, then,

11 This, let us emphasize, is meant to be a relative claim. There is little doubt that hostility to blacks is higher in the South than elsewhere, but there is also considerable

TABLE 6.2
Efficacy and Trust Regressed on Education, Head's Occupation,
Family Income, Religious Affiliation, City Size, Region, and Race:
1970 (N = 1307)

	Efficacy			
$(R^2 = .245)$	β	σ	$r_{partial}$	p
City Size	.028	.066	-.012	.673
Education	.354	.033	.281	.000
Occupation	.004	.002	.076	.006
Income	.089	.017	.140	.000
Religion	.045	.071	.018	.525
Race	.132	.106	.035	.213
Region	-.201	.070	-.080	.004

	Trust			
$(R^2 = .245)$	β	σ	$r_{partial}$	p
City Size	-.207	.089	-.064	.021
Education	.111	.045	.068	.014
Occupation	.001	.002	.009	.756
Income	.050	.024	.058	.035
Religion	.128	.096	.037	.185
Race	.282	.143	.055	.049
Region	-.206	.094	-.061	.028

would probably elicit opposition from the other. Politically relevant internal differentiation *within* the ranks of "*the* alienated" is a persistent finding reported in this chapter.

Second, of the three groups being considered, the non-South whites are best "equipped" to organize a political opposition, but their alienation turns out to be the lowest. The relative objective powerlessness of blacks is well-known and requires no elaboration: They are least likely to vote or otherwise participate in politics (e.g., Verba and Nie 1972), least likely to be represented in legislative assemblies, least likely to participate in voluntary associations (but see Olsen 1970), and so on.[12] In the normal course of events,

---

prointegration sentiment in the South. Campbell (1971b) has presented nationally representative survey data bearing on these points. In 1964, about half the white southerners described themselves as in favor of segregation, as opposed to 10–20% professing this same orientation in other regions. Even in 1964, however, there was an entire half of the white South population who claimed to favor integration or "something in between." In the period from 1964 to 1970, the proportion of white southerners in favor of strict segregation declined to less than 30% (Campbell 1971b:153).

[12] Of the many studies of the race–participation relationship, Verba and Nie (1972:Chap. 10) have given the most detailed account. First, racial differences in participation disappear when social class is controlled for, or, in other words, at every level of SES,

their alienation is seldom considered in the political equation.[13] The same may be said, to a lesser extent, of southern whites. Compared to their northern counterparts, they are more geographically isolated from one another (that is, more rural), relatively less educated, and, historically at least, much less likely to have a viable system of competing parties to mobilize or channel their discontent. This, too, is a recurring theme of this book: The incidence of alienation is highest where the ability to act upon it is most restricted.

Finally, we should mention the "rationality" reflected in these results. In a crude way, the data speak to the correlation between real and perceived powerlessness. For better or worse, much civil rights legislation in the last two decades has been overtly or covertly directed against the white South; similarly, blacks have long received far less than their fair share of social benefits. The disproportionate alienation of both groups presumably reflects these facts.[14] This initially suggests that inefficacy and distrust may be more appropriately characterized as largely accurate perceptions of on-going political realities than as the diffuse and desultory orientations depicted in political alienation theory.

Because region and race are associated both with political alienation and with many other variables discussed in this chapter, there must be some strategy for taking these confounding correlations into account. Accordingly, the rest of this chapter is based primarily on non-South whites. There have been parallel analyses of blacks and southern whites; divergences are noted in the text, and evidence is presented in the footnotes.

SOCIAL CLASS

Table 6.3 shows the relationship between alienation and the four most commonly employed indices of socioeconomic status (white, non-South only).

---

blacks in fact participate *more* than whites. Olsen (1970) has reported a similar result. Second, among the politically active, blacks also participate more than whites, or, as Verba and Nie put it, "When blacks break through the barrier that separates the totally inactive from those who engage in at least some activity, they are likely to move to quite high levels of such activity (1972:155)." Finally, Verba and Nie also demonstrate that race consciousness among blacks raises the level of participation dramatically (1972:157–160).

[13] The rejoinder, of course, is that, because they are excluded from "normal" modes of participation, the blacks are forced outside the usual channels in seeking redress of grievances; in this respect, their disproportionate discontent may threaten the stability of the democratic regime. This, in our view, however, is an example of moving from a correlation to a cause in the wrong direction. If, as seems very likely, the blacks are more alienated precisely because the system has denied them full and equal access to its decision-making procedures, then it is the system itself, and not the alienation that it creates, that must bear the blame for subsequent instabilities.

[14] The trend data discussed in the next chapter are consistent with these views. Insofar as this is the case, it would suggest that the attitudes of powerlessness and distrust are

Consistent with virtually all prior studies, the data confirm the fact that discontent increases as social class declines.[15] This is particularly true of political efficacy, but much less true of political trust, where the correlations, although in the "right" direction, are weak.[16] All correlations shown in the table are statistically significant at .001 or beyond.[17]

Especially acute is the alienation of the less-educated, economically marginal, and of those who identify with the working class. Working class identifiers were about 15 percentage points more powerless ($p < .001$) and about 9 percentage points more distrustful ($p < .002$) than persons who identified with the middle class. Among white workers outside the South, approximately half are alienated from the political system.

The distribution by education is also of interest, particularly in light of Lipset's remark that "complaints about dehumanization and alienation are found more commonly among students, intellectuals, and other sectors of the educated middle class than among the working class" (1968:313). In fact, college graduates are perhaps the *least* alienated of any group in the society (see also Wright 1975b). Complaints about an inability to influence the

---

more firmly rooted in specific policy outputs than theorists such as Easton have led us to believe.

[15] Part of Schwartz's (1973) argument against the "social class = alienation" literature is that "almost all of the data in the studies . . . were collected before 1966. . . . This being so, we might well expect the relationship between SES and alienation . . . to disappear altogether in an era like the 1960's (1973:10–11)." The data shown in Table 6.3, drawn from a 1970 survey, directly contradict this expectation.

A later aspect of the argument focuses on a presumed decline in the "SES–alienation" relationship between 1956 and 1960 (1973: 11–12). This argument is supported by data from the 1956 and 1960 SRC surveys, which are used to show declining correlations between SES and alienation in 16 of 20 cases. Our own analysis of these data (reported in the next chapter), however, shows that the decline is due mainly to a rising sense of political efficacy among blacks during the period; among whites, the "SES–alienation" relationship is essentially constant from 1956 to 1970 (see Footnote 25 to Chapter 7 and also Wright 1973: Table 4.6).

[16] This turns out to be a rather common pattern in the data reported in this chapter: Trust is more weakly correlated than efficacy with almost any background variable of interest. We have no compelling interpretation of this, except to note that the correlation between the two measures is itself relatively weak (gamma = .29). One possible explanation, mentioned here for what it is worth, is that the political efficacy items explicitly mention "people *like me.*" Thus, respondents are invited to answer in reference to their politically salient social groupings, which might have the effect of raising the correlation between efficacy and those social groupings—age groups, social classes, or whatever. The trust items, on the other hand, contain no similar "directive."

[17] Omitting the occupational data (which would be hard to justify as an ordinal scale), the next smallest gamma in the table (.12) corresponds to $z = 3.56$, $p = .0002$.

Computing a Z-score for S (the numerator of gamma) is exceedingly tedious. In the remainder, we have taken gammas of .10 or higher as the minimum correlation worth discussing.

TABLE 6.3
Percent Highly Alienated by Education, Head's Occupation, Family
Income, and Subjective Social Class, Non-South Whites Only: 1970

Total	36.4	43.4	900
Education			
Less than 8th grade	75.7	48.7	78
More than 8th, less than 12th	53.2	52.0	223
High school graduate	33.3	36.3	333
Some college	20.1	45.9	124
College graduate	6.8	40.5	132
Gamma	.48	.12	
Occupation			
Professional, technical and kindred	15.0	40.9	160
Salaried managers, officials, proprietors	29.3	38.7	62
Self-employed managers, officials, proprietors	39.4	46.5	71
Clerical and sales	32.4	37.0	108
Craftsmen and foremen	44.5	43.9	164
Semi-skilled	45.7	44.1	127
Service workers	34.1	38.7	44
Unskilled	66.7	66.7	24
Farm	53.0	51.1	49
Other	44.6	46.8	92
Gamma	-.31	-.07	
Income			
Less than $3000	65.7	48.5	105
$3000 - $4999	52.6	51.0	110
$5000 - $9999	36.0	44.3	269
$10,000 or more	24.6	38.6	391
Gamma	.30	.15	
Subjective Social Class[a]			
Working class	44.6	48.1	452
Middle class	29.4	38.9	452
Gamma	.32	.14	

a. Working class includes those who responded "lower class,
average working class, working class, and upper working class;"
middle class includes "average middle class, middle class, upper
middle class, and upper class."

government were 11 times more frequent among those with less than eighth-grade education than among the college-educated middle class.[18]

[18] Part of the apparent "education" effect turns out to reflect only the lesser education of older and more alienated respondents. The joint effects of education and age are considered later in this chapter.

Of the specific occupational groups shown, two deserve special note. The first group consists of the service workers, whose disaffection is considerably less than that of other blue collar workers. Why service workers should be relatively unalienated is a matter of speculation. Service workers "service" mainly the upper middle class; thus, they may pick up the attitudes of the clientele more readily than those of their class cohorts. Also, a large proportion of the category is made up of "protective service" workers (policemen, sheriffs, and so on) whose special duty is to enforce elite decisions.

Second, among the "middle class" occupational groups, the highest incidence of alienation on either dimension is recorded by the self-employed. This initially suggests some support for the mass society view of the "old middle class," a topic to which we will return shortly.

Except for the service worker "divergence," other oft-hypothesized cleavages within the working class fail to materialize. Differences between skilled and semi-skilled workers are particularly slight; unskilled workers, on the other hand, show a somewhat larger incidence of disaffection. The small number of unskilled workers in the sample, however, cautions against making much of the divergence. Finally, the attitudes of farmers ($n = 49$) are indistinguishable from those of blue collar workers; as such, they are included with the working class in future tables.[19]

Paige (1971) has developed a typology of alienation which is useful in discussing these results. This typology derives from the four possible combinations of high and low measures of efficacy and trust: Those high on both measures are the "allegiants," whose efficacy means that they will be politically active, but whose trust means that their activity will not be directed toward radical change; those low on both measures are the "alienates," whose major predicted political response is "withdrawal from any active participation"; those low in efficacy but high in trust are the "subordinates," which "also suggests a passive adjustment"; and, finally, those high in efficacy but low in trust are the "dissidents," the potentially most "dangerous" group of all. "If the government is regarded as untrustworthy, and there is a feeling that something can and should be done about it, radical actions aimed at changing the system are likely to result (1971:812)."

Focusing first on education, the least-educated respondents tend to conform to Paige's "subordinate" pattern; the college-educated respondents, interestingly, show something of the opposite "dissident" pattern. The high school graduates, on the other hand, conform loosely to Paige's "allegiants." Among the occupational groups, the professional workers most closely approximate the "dissident" pattern, followed by the salaried managers. Taking Paige's typology seriously, the so-called "new middle class" emerges as the

[19] The subjective class identification of farmers is consistent with their placement in the working class. In the 1968 study, for example, 65% of the farmers ($n = 108$) identified with the working class. (The figure is for all farmers regardless of region.) This compares with 74% working class identification among blue collar workers and 34% working class identification among white collar workers.

potentially most "dangerous" group considered so far, the one most likely to embark upon "radical actions aimed at changing the system." Showing little of their "dissidence," however, about two-thirds of them voted for Nixon in 1972.[20]

As mentioned earlier, one group that figures prominently in mass society theory is the "marginal middle class"—the small, independent businessmen and marginal clerical and sales functionaries. According to the theory, this class suffers from various "strains" that make them threatening to democratic institutions; as C. Wright Mills noted, "Every basis upon which [their] prestige claims . . . have historically rested has been declining in firmness and stability (1951:249)." In response, the marginal middle class "develops a deep-rooted sense of alienation. Alienated, it is susceptible to the Fascistic appeal (Nelson 1968:184)."

Assessment of these claims requires a more complicated presentation than that of Table 6.3, since both the self-employed and the clerical and sales categories contain numerous respondents who are in no sense "marginal." Accordingly, Table 6.4 divides each of the middle class occupational categories into affluent and nonaffluent segments, with the cut-off line at a yearly family income of $10,000 (white non-South only).

Focusing first on the economically marginal segments of the "lower" middle class, the data support the mass society view. About half were highly alienated on both measures. Among the nonmarginal segment, discontent was less extensive. In the "upper" middle class occupations, however, income is unrelated to political disaffection. Between 10% and 20% were highly inefficacious; about two-fifths were highly distrustful, in each case regardless of income.[21]

[20] In the 1972 SRC survey, the proportion of white collar workers voting for Nixon was 63.8%. In the 1973 NORC General Social Survey, the equivalent figure was 64.4%. In both cases, the proportions were slightly higher for professional, technical, and managerial employees and slightly lower in the clerical and sales categories (data not shown).

These data suggest an error, or perhaps a mis-emphasis, in Paige's original typology. When accompanied by objective deprivation, as in the case of blacks, the "low trust, high efficacy" pattern might well lead to the dissidence Paige predicts. When accompanied by high levels of social "achievement," as in the case of the "new middle class," an entirely different response might be expected. Here, "vigilance" would seem to be the more appropriate phrase, the implication being that the group would be "on guard" against immoderate or "radical" candidates or movements and perhaps especially zealous in preventing any efforts at redistribution. McGovern's proposals for tax reform would fit this category, and the votes of the upper white collar employees strongly suggest that they were quite anxious to see him defeated.

[21] The noneffect of income in the upper middle class in part reflects the fact that many of the respondents in the low income group are younger persons at the start of careers that will, sooner or later, move them well into the affluent ranks (Hamilton 1975:Ch 3). About a third of them, for example, are under age 30, compared to about a fifth of the white non-South population generally. They are also disproportionately drawn from middle and upper middle class backgrounds. Their impending movement up in the society seems inevitable, which is reflected in their relatively low level of discontent (On this point, see also Hamilton 1972:338–341).

TABLE 6.4
Percent Highly Alienated among the Marginal and Non-marginal
Middle Classes, Non-South Whites Only: 1970

	Income			
Occupation	Less than $10,000	N	$10,000 or more	N
	Efficacy			
"Upper" Middle Class				
Professional, Technical	17.3	52	13.7	102
MOP-Salaried	22.2	9	19.6	51
"Lower" Middle Class				
MOP-Self-employed	50.0	20	33.3	48
Clerical and Sales	42.4	66	12.8	39
	Trust			
"Upper" Middle Class				
Professional, Technical	42.3	52	40.2	102
MOP-Salaried	33.3	9	39.2	51
"Lower" Middle Class				
MOP-Self-employed	50.0	20	41.7	48
Clerical and Sales	47.0	66	23.1	39

Taking the nonaffluent independents and clerical and sales respondents as the marginal middle class, some 44% of them feel powerless, and about 48% were highly distrustful ($n = 86$). The comparable figures for the nonmarginal middle class are 19% and 38%, respectively ($n = 301$). Both comparisons are statistically significant. The data thus support the view that the marginal middle class suffers from strains that increase its alienation from the political system. It should also be pointed out, however, that these strains are apparently no more severe than those suffered by manual workers. Among manual workers (farm included, service excluded, $n = 364$), 46% were highly distrustful and 48% were highly inefficacious. Thus, the working and marginal middle classes are indistinguishable in their level of political alienation.[22]

Except for generally higher alienation among all groups, patterns in the

[22] These data thus conform to Hamilton's (1972) view that the major cleavage in the class structure of the United States is *not* between blue and white collar workers, but rather between the upper and lower middle classes. According to Hamilton, working and lower middle class persons have similar levels of identification with the working class and with the Democratic party, have similar political attitudes and leanings, come from similar class backgrounds, have similar career lines, enjoy roughly equivalent incomes, and so on. Sharing the same backgrounds, living standards, and futures, it is to be expected that the two groups would show similar levels of disaffection.

white South are quite similar. The main divergence is among the white southern upper middle class, where distrust (but not inefficacy) was higher than expected.[23] Generally speaking, discontent was less strongly related to class among blacks: approximately three-fifths of all groups were highly alienated. The relatively small number of middle class blacks prevents a detailed analysis. Of some interest is the discovery that educated blacks were more efficacious, but no more distrustful, than the less educated.[24]

The finding that the alienated are disproportionately drawn from the working and marginal middle classes, and the contented mainly from the upper middle class, adds empirical weight to our earlier contention that real and perceived powerlessness are positively related. One would, after all, hardly expect it to be otherwise. Of all groups considered thus far, surely the white, non-South upper middle class is best able to effect genuine political change, but at the same time, they have little reason to do so. Given the social, political, and economic benefits which the system has provided for them, one would be very surprised to find them distrustful of its representatives or skeptical of their ability to work within the system. Having distributed an unequal share of political power and material rewards to approximately the same persons, the system thus guards admirably against potential insurgency among those best able to carry it out.

The sense of political competence in the upper middle class is not just a by-product of their social and economic well-being, although these latter factors, which provide the resources necessary for effective political action, obviously contribute no small part. Rather, their training and experiences throughout life make their nonalienation a reasonable and rational response.

[23] The data for southern whites are as follows:

| | | Percentage highly alienated | |
	Efficacy	Trust	n
Upper middle class	29.0	47.7	107
Lower middle class	55.4	50.0	56
Working class	55.6	56.1	214

[24] The data for blacks are as follows:

| | | Percentage highly alienated | |
	Efficacy	Trust	n
Less than eighth	74.6	73.2	71
Less than twelfth	66.0	52.4	103
High school	50.7	61.3	75
Some college	34.6	69.3	26
gamma =	.38	.07	

Paige's typology is useful when considering these data. Blacks with less than an eighth-grade education exhibit the "alienation" pattern; about three-fourths of the group were highly alienated on both measures. The pattern among the 8–12 years of education group

Here, it is useful to follow the class from youth to adulthood. From birth, they are located in a politically active and aware milieu; the positive "lessons" of prior generations are passed on to them. Thus, by the eighth grade, upper middle class children are already confident of their abilities to influence the government (Easton and Dennis 1967). Once they reach high school, the civics courses they encounter are more informative and provide a more accurate description of the realities of political life (Litt 1963a). After high school, of course, they are far more likely to enter college (e.g., Blau and Duncan 1967), and, thus, to acquire any political benefits imparted therein. Once in college, too, they are more actively involved in student politics than those from lower social backgrounds, and, thus, more likely to develop usable political skills (Braungart 1971). Once out of college, they are the most likely to enter politics (Matthews 1954) and, presumably, most likely to develop contacts with political figures at all levels. As a result of all this, as adults they are by far the most active political participants, however measured (e.g., Campbell et al 1960; Verba and Nie 1972). These experiences, in turn, provide the context for the political socialization of their own children, the active participants of succeeding generations. In this manner, upper middle class persons are, in essence, coached in the lessons of political power throughout their existence. It is little wonder that they see the system as a congeries of groups in equal competition for a share of the social resources, rather than as an unfair system which benefits only the rich and powerful (Form and Rytina 1969), or that they have relatively higher confidence in the political leadership and in their ability to influence the government.

Given their disproportionate share of political power and the ability to employ it, there is a very real sense in which the stability of democratic government requires the active "consent" of the upper middle class. They are, in a phrase, able to deal out "negative sanctions" when things are not going their way. There is very little mystery, however, in the "mechanisms" or "structures" that keep the upper middle class in line: First and foremost, they have the most to lose by any redistribution of scarce resources and therefore, the most to gain by the continuation of current arrangements.[25] Quite naturally, they "consent" to those arrangements and resist attacks upon

resembles Paige's "subordinates"; the better-educated blacks, finally, resemble Paige's "dissidents." This pattern is especially pronounced among college-educated blacks: Only 35% of this group were inefficacious, but over two-thirds were highly distrustful. The occupational data follow those reported for education: The working class blacks were highly alienated on both measures, while the lower middle class blacks exhibited Paige's "dissident" pattern. Surprisingly, the few black professionals and managers diverge from both patterns; they were quite inefficacious but relatively trustful, the pattern of responses that Paige labels as "subordinate" (data not shown).

25 On the opposition of the "responsible" upper middle class, especially the white Protestant segment, to basic "redistributive" welfare state measures, see Hamilton (1972: Chaps. 5 and 9).

them. In this one important sense, then, it is fair to say that consensus theory *does* contribute to an understanding of the sources of democratic stability. As a theory of *mass* politics, consensus theory apparently falls short; of the major population subgroups considered so far, only the attitudinal complex of the upper middle class is accurately depicted in the consensus account. In many respects, however, the upper middle class is the only group whose attitudes *need* to conform to the consensus theory for the stability of the system to be insured.[26] We return to this point throughout the remainder of our discussion.

AGE

The correlation between alienation and age interests us for a number of reasons. First, age, in conjunction with education, allows some assessment of the college-educated youth—one group whose "profound, even fanatical alienation" has figured prominently in much recent sociopolitical speculation. Similarly, the working class youth are also often said to be highly alienated; although they are likely to respond to it in a markedly different fashion. Krickus, for example, links the support of Wallace among younger workers directly to "their estrangement from our mainstream institutions (1971:505–506"; see also Parker 1972; Simon and Gagnon 1970). Third, there is the predictable confusion in the literature concerning the age–alienation relationship (see Chapter 3). Finally, the political "threat" posed by discontent is sharply affected by its relationship to age: Angry young workers, for example, might conceivably imperil the foundations of representative democracy; aging grandparents, however deeply alienated, probably would not.

Overall, political alienation increases with age (Table 6.5).[27] Neither rela-

---

[26] There are a few cases of the withdrawal of upper middle class support that are consistent with this interpretation. One prominent instance involves the war in Vietnam. As mentioned in Footnote 4, the upper middle classes, as of 1964, were disproportionately in favor of escalation. In the ensuing 4 years, there was a marked high status defection from that position in favor of more dovish or peace-oriented policies; outside the upper middle class, attitudes on the war were largely unchanged in the period (Wright 1972a, b). Domestic opposition to the war coincided exactly with the withdrawal of upper middle class support.

Likewise, the "instabilities" associated with the New Left were, for all practical purposes, the single-handed creation of students from upper middle class backgrounds. The high status origins of campus rebels are noted by almost all studies, (e.g., Finney 1971; Flacks 1967; Keniston 1967; Westby and Braungart 1966; etc.).

[27] Put more precisely, we should say that, in 1970, older persons were more alienated than younger persons. Whether the phenomenon of aging per se adds to the level of alienation is methodologically a separate issue. Cutler and Bengston (1974) have analyzed trends in political efficacy from 1952 to 1968 via cohort analysis. They suggest that the increases were roughly equivalent within all cohorts, casting doubt on a "generational" explanation. Likewise, "no maturation or aging effects were evident (1974:160)." Rather, the trends reflected a "period effect"—that is, they are attributable to social and

TABLE 6.5
Percent Highly Alienated by Age, White, Non-South Only: 1970[a]

Age	Efficacy	Trust	N
18-24	29.3	31.2	109
25-29	25.7	40.0	105
30-34	28.6	39.3	84
35-39	27.1	43.3	74
40-44	28.4	46.3	95
45-49	32.5	47.5	80
50-54	35.8	42.0	81
55-59	38.8	46.2	67
60-64	39.5	51.8	81
65 +	55.3	45.9	159
gamma	-.17	-.12	939

a.   The 1970 survey contains a supplementary sample of 18-21 year olds who would normally be included from the sampling frame by virtue of not being "politically eligible adults."   The 39 white, non-South respondents who fit this category are included in this table.

tionship shown in the table is especially pronounced; both are statistically significant. Contrary to Farris (1960), Phillips (1970), and Thompson and Horton (1960), no curvilinearity is apparent in the data. The relationship between alienation and efficacy is nearly flat up to age 65, with a sharp increase in powerlessness thereafter.[28] No similar pattern, however, is shown for politi-

political phenomena that are unique to the period. We expand this point in the following chapter. (On aging and powerlessness, see also Agnello 1973.)

Patterns in the white South were quite similar to those shown in Table 6.5. The correlation (gamma) of efficacy with age was —.24 ($n = 429$), and with trust, —.13. For blacks, the patterns were rather different. Younger blacks, following Paige's typology, exhibited the dissident pattern, middle aged blacks the subordinate pattern, and older blacks the alienated pattern (data not shown).

[28] The difference between our findings and Phillips's warrant some mention, since both are based on nationally representative data (Phillips's data come from the U.S. portion of the Civic Culture data). As mentioned in reviewing the "age–alienation" literature, the hypothesis of curvilinearity is based on the view that both young people and old people lack "institutionalized power," that both groups are, in some sense, "cut out" of the normal political process. In 1960, when Phillips's data were collected, this might well have been an accurate depiction of the current younger generation. The ensuing decade, however, witnessed the emergence of youth as an active and vocal political force; by 1970, every serious political contender on the scene had to deal with the "youth vote." (That this vote turned out to be far more conservative than anyone had imagined, especially in 1972, is beside the point at issue.) Thus, differences in the political position of youth as a group probably account for the divergence between Phillips's and our results. Another possible explanation for the divergence is that the average level of education among youth has increased substantially from 1960 to 1970, and, all else

cal trust. Finally, parallel to the social status results, age is more strongly associated with efficacy than with trust (see Footnote 16).

In most modern industrial nations, age and education are strongly correlated; thus, these variables are considered jointly in Table 6.6. There are several findings reported in the table that warrant careful consideration. First, the tendency for alienation to increase with age is modified by the level of education: Only among less-educated respondents does age seem to have a noticeable "alienating" effect, and, even here, the patterns are somewhat weak and occluded. Several factors might be hypothesized to account for this result. First, the "lessons" imparted in college may be so firm that they are exempt from the later "disconfirmations" of adult life experienced elsewhere in the society. Additional evidence in support of this possibility is presented in the next chapter. Similarly, the college educated may simply be spared the "loss of institutionalized power" which otherwise accompanies advancing age. They may, that is, stay active and interested in politics throughout life, thus escaping the "downturn" in participation experienced by lesser-educated older people.[29] This interpretation is consistent with evidence presented by Verba and Nie (1972: Ch. 9). A third and perhaps most likely possibility is that the patterns are linked to the various career lines experienced by the different educational groups. As Hamilton has shown, the normal pattern for the well-educated upper middle class involves steady increases in income throughout the career; this contrasts with the working and lower middle class pattern, where incomes typically peak in the ages 45–54 and decline thereafter (1972: 376–378). The "jump" in powerlessness among the less-educated older people, then, may coincide with declines in real income, consistent with evidence presented in Table 6.3.

A second finding which deserves some emphasis concerns the alienation of less-educated young people (for short, "working class youth"), whose discontent is decidedly unexceptional in these data. Taking the 18–29-year-old high school drop-outs, for example, half expressed feelings of powerlessness; and a third expressed feelings of political distrust. Overall, these figures are about average for whites outside the South—a bit higher than average, in one case, and somewhat lower than average in the other. Thus, the data contrast sharply with what, for lack of a better phrase, may be called the "Lordstown

---

being equal, this alone should lower their feelings of powerlessness somewhat (see Table 6.3).

[29] Here we are making the assumption that political participation itself has some effect on one's sense of political powerlessness. As discussed in Chapter 3, the more common argument reverses the causal ordering (but see the sources cited in Footnote 25 to that chapter). This is not likely to be an "either–or" matter: Some people will participate because they feel efficacious (for example, feel that it will make a difference); others will feel efficacious because they participate. There is some persuasive evidence, however, that the largest portion of nonparticipation is due to "structural impediments," rather than to attudinal "deficiencies" (Kelley et al. 1967).

TABLE 6.6
Percent Highly Alienated by Education and Age, White, Non-South Only: 1970[a]

Education	Age							
	18-29	N	30-44	N	45-59	N	60+	N
Efficacy								
Less than high school	47.7	23	51.5	62	55.8	86	63.8	141
High school graduate	33.3	99	29.6	98	31.8	91	42.9	56
Some college or more	15.2	92	10.9	92	7.8	51	14.0	43
Trust								
Less than high school	34.8	23	50.0	62	52.4	86	53.1	141
High school graduate	33.9	99	32.6	98	41.8	91	43.0	56
Some college or more	38.0	92	49.0	92	39.3	51	37.2	43

a. Includes the white, non-South youth supplement.

hypothesis," that working class youth are "angry," "bitter," "frustrated," and "resentful" over the lives and work that the "system" has accorded them, that they are prone to "rumblings of deep discontent and . . . hostile to and suspicious of management" (Gooding 1972), that they are "politically restive" and "cynical about government (Krickus 1971)." The "unfamiliar and unattractive alienation" of working class youth (Simon and Gagnon 1970: 48), in turn, is said to result in work stoppages and industrial revolt (Aronowitz, 1973: Chap. 1; Widick, 1972), in "flirtations with George Wallace" (Reissman 1972; Lipset and Raab 1969), or in other expressions of discontent with the society as they have come to know it.[30] The data presented here accord poorly with such depictions; overall, the political alienation of working class youth is somewhat less pronounced than that of older generations with equivalent educations.[31] This, in fact, is true of all youth, regardless of education. Despite the extended commentaries on "youth alienation" and the "youth revolt," older people turn out to be consistently more alienated.

This brings us to a third important finding, that the college-educated youth stand out mainly for the *low* levels of alienation which they express. A mere 15% of the college educated under 30 (compared with 36% of all whites outside the South) expressed feelings of powerlessness; likewise, their distrust was average or somewhat below average (38% highly distrustful, compared to 43% of the total for non-South whites). If the analysis is restricted to the under-25 college educated group the conclusions are identical; among that segment, 13% ($n = 46$) felt inefficacious, and 28% felt highly distrustful, both figures again well below average (data not shown). Additional analysis focusing only on the under-30 college graduates (that is, excluding the "some college" segment) indicated no essential modification of these results (Wright 1975b). These data thus suggest that the college-educated youth are among the *least* alienated of any population subgroup.

This evidence, to be sure, is not ideally suited for addressing the "youth revolt" hypothesis. The data mix under-30 Berkeley graduates with drop-outs from North Mankota State. If nothing else, however, the data caution admirably against generalizing from a minority group of student activists to the

[30] These comments are not meant to deny that *work* alienation and perhaps even political discontent played a part in the Lordstown experience. The problem lies in generalizing to working class youth as a whole. In the various Lordstown commentaries, there is usually an implication that the high turnover, absenteeism, wildcat strikes, and so on are "symptomatic" of frustrations and anxieties that are sweeping through the ranks of working class young people. Data, such as those being discussed in the text, caution against such generalizations. (On attitudes toward work among working class youth, see O'Toole *et al.* 1973:43–51; and Yankelovich, 1974:28–33.)

[31] Since "working class youth" usually implies more than simply low education, a second analysis was made with occupation, rather than education, as the defining factor. Among blue collar workers aged 29 or less ($n = 103$, data not shown), about a third scored high on both dimensions of alienation. Once again, these figures are somewhat *below* the averages for whites outside the South.

college-educated youth as a whole. Here we might mention that this survey was conducted in the fall of 1970, well-remembered as the year of Cambodia and Kent State. These events, one would assume, ought at least to have affected the optimism of the college youth, but the evidence presented here does not imply it. This suggests that the analytic focus implied by titles such as *Youth and Dissent* or *Youth and Social Change* is somewhat misdirected; the group of young people studied in these works is apparently so small that it has no discernible impact on large nationally representative samples.[32]

There is one final aspect of the evidence that warrants emphasis, which is that, of all groups represented in Table 6.6, the highest levels of powerlessness and distrust are registered by old people with less than a high school education. The political implications of this scarcely require comment. These persons are at or near retirement. Ill health and physical infirmity are more common here than anywhere else in the population. The tendency for men, particularly lower class men, to die earlier also means that the group is disproportionately widowed and female. Their major worries and concerns, one can safely assume, will involve tidying up the loose ends of whatever life remains to them; at this late stage, the appeal of "mass" political ventures will almost certainly have dimmed. All insults concerning "little old ladies in tennis shoes" aside, the prospect of a political "challenge" arising from this group is exceedingly remote.

THE PLURALIST VARIABLES:
PARTIES, UNIONS, AND RELIGION

According to the pluralist orthodoxy, participation in voluntary associations promotes societal integration, decreases political alienation, and otherwise "plays a major role in a democratic political culture (Almond and Verba 1965:265)." These associations need not be expressly political in nature, nor must they serve politically instrumental ends. The major "integrative" effects are due to the "communitarian" functions that they perform: They promote social contacts, provide sources of social identity, and generally lessen the "dissociation" endemic to modern industrial life.

The SRC surveys do not allow a direct and definitive assessment of these claims. The most relevant item asks whether respondents belong to a trade or labor union—but union membership is frequently not "voluntary" in any

[32] This is not to suggest, of course, that the group has no impact on national politics. This, obviously, is not the case (see Footnote 28). As before, our only point is that it is hazardous to make inferences about entire population subgroups on the basis of a relatively few highly visible cases—to assume that the experiences of students at Wisconsin and Berkeley characterize college youth as a whole, that the events at Lordstown are "symptomatic" of working class youth, or for that matter, that the "hard hats" on Wall Street speak for the urban working class.

literal sense and, relative to other voluntary associations, is disproportionately working class. There is also the question of church attendance, which should perform at least some "integrative" functions. Finally, one "surrogate" organization to which people might "belong" is a political party, but, in the United States, parties are not really "organizations" like they are in Europe; likewise, very few people belong to a political party in the sense of paying dues or carrying a membership card. These three variables exhaust the available evidence bearing on the pluralist thesis.

The correlation of political alienation with party identification is important for a number of reasons besides these just mentioned. One hypothesis (suggested by pluralist and mass society perspectives) is that party identifiers will be less alienated than self-proclaimed "independents." Independents lack affiliation to one highly important political "object" that might otherwise reduce their suspicions of democratic political institutions. The growing proportion of independents in recent years, concomitant with a general rise in political discontent (see Chapter 7), adds credence to this hypothesis.[33]

On the other hand, independents are—virtually by definition—relatively less organized and, thus, less likely to pose a serious "threat." According to most studies, they are also less informed about and less interested in all things political (e.g., Campbell et al. 1960, but see Dempsey 1975). Their disproportionate alienation would, therefore, be another instance of discontent being most pervasive just where it counts the very least.

A second issue is the possible concentration of alienation among either of the two major parties. Surely, the "threat" of alienation would be greater if the bulk of the persons alienated identified with a single party, simply because this would represent a potential basis for their mobilization. The corollary is that the hazards would be considerably less were they equally dispersed between the parties. This would imply that they would be split on any political issue or candidate for which party is a relevant consideration, that is most major issues and certainly all major candidates of recent political history.

Finally, it has been suggested (e.g., Aberbach 1969) that these attitudes are more proxies for partisan hostility than measures of "deep-seated" orientations towards the political system, implying that identifiers with the "in" party will be less alienated than the "outs." Respondents, that is, may be telling us more about their displeasure with current administrations than their disenchantment with the political system. Our theoretical concerns make this a serious issue; it is unlikely that a mere measure of partisan hostility would be adequate for our purposes.

Table 6.7 shows the relationship between political alienation and party

---

[33] The trend toward greater numbers of political Independents is analyzed by Burnham (1969), Dempsey (1975), and Glenn (1972). In the SRC surveys, the proportion of self-proclaimed Independents increases from 23% in 1952 ($n = 1718$) to 32% in 1972 ($n = 2478$). "Don't know," "No answer," "Other," etc. are omitted.

TABLE 6.7
Percent Highly Alienated by Union Membership, Religion, Church
Attendance, and Party Identification, by Social Class: 1968-1970
(white, non-South only)

	Working Class			Middle Class		
	Efficacy	Trust	N	Efficacy	Trust	N
Union Membership						
Member	40.9	42.5	186	29.4	39.2	51
Non-member	50.7	47.5	219	24.1	41.2	345
Religion						
Protestant	46.2	40.1	262	24.6	33.3	207
Catholic	47.1	33.3	102	29.6	27.8	108
Jew				52.0	52.0	25
Church Attendance						
Regular/Often	41.8	34.0	179	24.4	26.5	196
Seldom/Never	52.5	44.0	202	30.8	41.9	146
Party Identification						
Strong Democrat	45.3	44.2	86	25.6	41.9	43
Weak Democrat	47.1	51.9	104	22.5	36.6	71
Independent Democrat	50.0	41.7	36	17.2	32.8	58
Independent	58.0	50.0	50	23.7	31.6	38
Independent Republican	51.7	34.5	29	28.6	54.3	35
Weak Republican	36.8	41.2	68	29.5	45.5	88
Strong Republican	37.9	44.8	29	23.1	40.0	65

identification, religion and church attendance, and union membership.[34] Here, as in the remainder of the chapter, the data are presented with a control for social class and are for white, non-South respondents only.

Focusing first on the union variable, the data reveal that, in the middle class, unionization and alienation are unrelated. The relatively small number of unionized white collar workers in the sample cautions against overinterpretation of the results. Nonetheless, the group is often seen, in contemporary

[34] Party identification is measured by the following question:

Generally speaking, do you usually think of yourself as a Republican, a Democrat, an Independent, or what? Would you call yourself a strong (Republican or Democrat) or a not very strong (Republican or Democrat)? (If Independent) Do you think of yourself as closer to the Democratic or Republican party?

In the 1960 survey, this question was asked in both pre- and postelection waves; the correlation (gamma) between the two administrations was .84.

In order to maximize cases, a respondent was considered a "union member" if anyone in the respondent's family belonged to a union.

"Working class" are respondents whose family head is employed in a blue collar or farm occupation; "middle class" are respondents whose family head is employed in a white collar occupation.

"left-critical" circles, as the vanguard of what is known as the "new working class." White collar unionization, according to one account, "is a symptom of the increasing politicization of the white collar working class (Oppenheimer 1970:28)." The source continues, the group may "become the lever for revolutionary social change." According to these data, however, their dissaffection with the political system is essentially indistinguishable from that of their nonunionized class peers.[35]

In the working class, the pattern is somewhat different: Nonmembers are more alienated on both dimensions. Neither difference, however, is pronounced (only the efficacy difference is statistically significant, $p = .024$), and additional controls (e.g., for income) would probably reduce them even further. At best, the data suggest modest zero-order support for the pluralist thesis that "participation in . . . intermediate groups is likely to foster the development of a sense of political efficacy (Pinard 1968:683)." On the other hand, the data also indicate that, within the working class, organization and alienation are inversely associated; once again, those most able to do something about their discontent are also the least discontented.[36]

Contrary to Lenski (1961:173) but consistent with Finifter (1970:398), the data reveal no tendency for Catholics to be more alienated than Protestants, once social class is controlled. Jews, however, were markedly more alienated than either Protestants or Catholics of equivalent social standing; both comparisons between Jews and the combined Protestant and Catholic middle class are significant at the .01 level.

As predicted by the pluralist and mass society theories, church nonattenders are more alienated that attenders, regardless of social class. This replicates the only other national study investigating these effects (Finifter 1970: 398). The smallest difference (between middle class attenders and nonattenders on the efficacy measure) is significant at the .09 level; the remaining three comparisons are significant at .05 or beyond.[37]

---

[35] Debate on the political consciousness and revolutionary potential of the "new working class" rages in the left-critical journals. For representative entries, see Aronowitz (1971), Oppenheimer (1970, 1975), Stodder (1973), or Szymanski (1972). Hamilton (1975: Ch. 3) has presented nationally representative evidence on the "consciousness" of the salaried professionals, the key constituent group of the "new working class." The conclusions are: "The evidence indicates a remarkable steadfastness in their identification of themselves as middle class, a fact that does not suggest new or wavering loyalties. The examination of the political sentiments of the salaried professionals also does not suggest the presence of special progressive sentiments within the category (1975:121)."

[36] Among blacks and white southerners, essentially the same patterns are in evidence. For blacks, union members were more efficacious than nonmembers, but there were no differences for trust. Among white southerners, the only divergence of interest comes among the few ($n = 11$) *middle class* union members, who were much more alienated than middle class nonmembers. Among working class white southerners, union membership was unrelated to alienation (data not shown).

[37] In the predominantly Protestant white South, church attenders were also more efficacious than nonattenders; the results for trust, however, were not significant (data not shown).

(Continued on Page 152)

Of the religious results, only the greater alienation of middle class Jews warrants substantive emphasis. These data make it plain that the relationship between alienation and social class would be somewhat more pronounced if the high status, highly alienated Jews were omitted from consideration. As shown in the table, subscription to "regime norms" in the non-Jewish middle class runs to approximately 75%. Adding this to the other evidence considered thus far, we might note that it is the attitudes of the white, non-South, non-Jewish, middle-aged, upper middle class that are best described by consensus theory.

As of 1970, alienation and party identification were unrelated. Focusing first on the nonmanuals, we find a statistically insignificant tendency for Republicans to be more alienated than Democrats on both efficacy (p = .274)and trust (p = .224). Also insignificant are differences between middle class Independents and either Democrats or Republicans. (All comparisons are for collapsed party identification categories.) Among workers, the same conclusions hold true. Working class Democrats were somewhat more alienated than working class Republicans, in contrast to the middle class pattern, but neither difference is significant. In addition, working class Independents were more alienated than either Democrats or Republicans, but only the largest of these differences was statistically significant. In short, no important relationship between alienation and party identification emerges.

Predictably, things are different in the "one-party" South. Differences between working class Democrats and Republicans were again insubstantial, but the working class independents were considerably *less* trusting than their "attached" class peers (p = .006). In the middle class, a fairly clear pattern emerges: Middle class Republicans, particularly "strong" Republicans, were substantially *less* alienated on both dimensions.[38]

Among blacks, no clear patterns emerged on either variable. Of some interest, however, non-Protestant blacks (8.8% of the total black sample) were considerably *less* alienated on both dimensions. The data are as follows:

| | | Percentage highly alienated | |
	Efficacy	Trust	n
Protestants	63.3	62.0	237
Others	52.2	47.8	23

[38] The data for white southerners are as follows:

| | | Percentage highly alienated | |
	Efficacy	Trust	n
Middle class			
strong Democrat	28.0	52.0	25
weak Democrat	44.7	52.6	38
Independent Democrat	27.8	44.4	18

(Continued on Page 153)

Aberbach's "party in power" hypothesis is addressed in Table 6.8. Since the 1960 items were included in the pre-election wave, the 1956–1960 data represent a period of Republican control.[39] Consonant with the hypothesis, Democrats were slightly more alienated than Republicans during this time. All of these relationships, however, are weak; of six differences between Democrats and Republicans, only the largest is statistically significant ($p = .004$).

The 1964 and 1966 studies, on the other hand, represent a period of Democratic control; thus, there should be a reversal of the earlier relationship. Such a reversal is not shown for efficacy but is clearly apparent for trust: In contrast to 1958, Republicans in 1964 were markedly less trustful than Democrats, working class Republicans in particular.

Since the 1968 items were asked in the postelection wave, both 1968 and 1970 are again years of Republican control.[40] Thus, the relationship between party and alienation should revert to the pre-1964 pattern. Again, we find that this is not the case. Despite the Republican ascendancy, Republicans were still slightly less trustful than Democrats in 1968; the differences, however, are not statistically significant. For efficacy, as in all prior years, there was an insignificant tendency for Democrats to be more alienated.

Whether these data offer even modest support for the "party in power" hypothesis thus depends on whether or not the greater distrust of 1964–1966 Republicans can be attributed mainly to Democratic control. Other aspects of the data, however, make it seem unlikely that Johnson's administration itself was responsible for this "divergence." The proportion of workers identi-

Independent	55.6	55.6	27
Independent Republican	39.1	52.2	23
weak Republican	41.2	47.1	17
strong Republican	13.3	20.0	15
Working class			
strong Democrat	68.2	54.5	44
weak Democrat	50.0	48.3	58
Independent Democrat	57.9	63.2	19
Independent	58.8	70.6	34
Independent Republican	33.3	66.7	21
weak Republican	61.5	46.2	26
strong Republican	50.0	40.0	10

[39] In cases in which one party controls the presidency and the other party controls the Congress (e.g., 1958–1960, and 1968–1970), there is some necessary ambiguity as to which party is, in fact, "in power." Given the historical trend toward greater presidential power at the expense of congressional power, at least through 1970, we have chosen to designate the party controlling the presidency as "the party in power."

[40] The 1968 data are especially ambiguous in this respect, since they were taken *after* Nixon's election victory but *before* his formal inauguration. Thus, it is not clear whether the 1968 data reflect Democratic or Republican control. It matters little, however, since all 1968 relationships, as well as the 1970 relationship, are statistically insignificant.

TABLE 6.8
Percent Highly Alienated by Class and Party; White, Non-South Only: 1956-1970

Efficacy

	1956[a]	N	1958[a]	N	1960[a]	N	1964	N
Working Class								
Democrats	34.0	250			28.7	251	38.1	223
Independents	26.4	174			21.7	161	36.4	118
Republicans	28.1	192			24.2	149	35.8	95
Difference[c]	+5.9				+4.5		+2.3	
Middle Class								
Democrats	17.1	117			17.4	109	21.3	136
Independents	15.6	115			5.3	94	14.1	99
Republicans	7.9	151			11.7	163	14.8	122
Difference	+9.2				+5.7		+6.5	

Trust

	1956	N	1958	N	1960	N	1964	N
Working Class								
Democrats			40.1	269			21.8	211
Independents			35.8	120			28.7	108
Republicans			26.9	145			46.9	81
Difference			+13.2				-25.1	
Middle Class								
Democrats			30.9	123			17.8	129
Independents			36.3	91			29.2	89
Republicans			26.3	156			26.1	115
Difference			+4.6				-8.3	

Efficacy

	1966[b]	N	1968	N	1970	N
Working Class						
Democrats	43.3	104	52.0	167	46.3	190
Independents	43.1	65	41.3	121	53.9	115
Republicans	49.2	63	47.5	101	37.1	97
Difference	-5.9		+4.5		+9.2	
Middle Class						
Democrats	29.3	99	34.0	106	23.7	114
Independents	26.0	96	27.2	110	22.1	131
Republicans	24.3	115	22.0	136	26.8	153
Difference	+5.0		+12.0		-3.1	

Trust

	1966	N	1968	N	1970	N
Working Class						
Democrats	14.1	92	36.1	166	48.4	190
Independents	43.6	54	43.6	119	43.5	115
Republicans	35.1	57	38.6	101	42.3	97
Difference	-25.1		-2.5		+6.1	
Middle Class						
Democrats	11.6	86	29.2	106	38.6	114
Independents	20.5	83	46.0	109	38.2	131
Republicans	27.4	95	31.6	136	43.1	153
Difference	-15.8		-2.4		-4.5	

a. Trust was not measured in 1956 or 1960; efficacy was not measured in 1958.

b. The 1966 trust measure includes only two items. Hence, comparisons between 1966 and other years should not be made.

c. "Difference" equals the Democratic proportion minus the Republican proportion.

fying themselves as Democratic ranges from 56% in 1956 to 66% in 1970; the middle class Democratic proportion is usually between 40% and 44% (two-party identifiers only). Yet in 1964, some 70% of the workers and 53% of the middle class chose the Democratic identification; both figures are the highest for the 1956–1970 period. This indicates that the defection of moderate Republicans in 1964 occurred not only in vote, but also in partisan identification. The remaining Republicans, in turn, were presumably those who were not "turned off" by the Goldwater candidacy, that is, those most suspicious of *any* moderate-to-centrist federal administration. In short, self-selection rather than partisan hostility probably accounts for the 1964–1966 "reversal." This, coupled with generally insignificant relationships in all other years, leads us to reject the "party in power" hypothesis.

Substantively, the most interesting feature of these data is the clear and nearly equivalent dispersion of alienated persons between parties and the attendent implication that the "group" will be split along party lines in its reaction to any given issue, movement, or candidate. The importance of this fact has already been stressed. In most cases, it appears that the "response of the alienated" may very well be two distinct responses, one leaning to the right, the other to the left.[41] In this sense, of course, the two groups may simply negate each other's potential political impact. As we shall see in Chapter 9, something of this very sort appears to have happened in the 1964 election and, to a lesser extent, also in 1968.

THE MASS SOCIETY VARIABLES:
COMMUNITY INTEGRATION, MASS MEDIA, AND MOBILITY

The major thrust of mass society thinking in the matter of political alienation has been well-summarized by Gusfield:

> In both its structural and psychological elements the theory of mass politics states that political alienation—the disattachment of a person from political institutions—is a function of the disintegrating influence of mass society on the ties of sentiment and loyalty to specific groups. . . . Without attachment to primary or intermediate structures, the individual has no bond to national

---

[41] This assumes, of course, that they do "respond." As we shall see later, their major characteristic is political indifference. In all but the most unusual circumstances, their "response" will be a nonresponse; when they do respond, they will apparently be split along party lines. Their indifference and political fragmentation greatly lessen their potential "damage" to democratic institutions.

It is hazardous to infer political ideologies from partisan identification; the alienated Democrats, certainly, could constitute the right-wing of the Democratic party. If this were the case, then the prospects for mobilization of the alienated as a group would obviously be greater than we have admitted so far. A more direct examination of alienation and ideology is undertaken in Chapter 8 and suggests no substantive changes in these conclusions.

political institutions which commands his loyalty to its political norms [1962:21–22].

In an earlier chapter, we discussed an alternative possible conception: that the attitudes of efficacy and trust are more elements of class political cultures than global responses to the "disintegrating influence of mass society." In the case of "integration" into one's community, these two positions lead to divergent predictions. In the mass society account, greater community integration should imply less alienation; the well-integrated are presumably spared the "dislocation" and "disattachments" that foster political discontent. In the class culture view, on the contrary, the relationship between integration and alienation should vary according to the nature of the community one is "integrated" into. Persons who are highly integrated into working class communities, that is, would presumably come to share the outlooks and orientations of those communities, and this would imply *more* rather than less alienation. The reverse pattern, of course, would be expected for the middle class. Data on three "indicators" of community integration—city size, length of residence, and home ownership—allow a test of these competing hypotheses.[42] Evidence is presented in Table 6.9.

Although none of the differences is pronounced, their persistent direction favors the "class cultures" hypothesis over the mass society thesis. Focusing first on the patterns for the middle class, the better-integrated respondents are *less* alienated in five of six comparisons, the sole reversal being "city size by efficacy." Of the five nonreversed differences, only the largest is statistically significant ($p = .023$). On the other hand, there may be uncontrolled "suppressor" effects that weaken the results. Renters and short-term residents, for example, are on the whole younger than home-owners and long-term residents; on this basis, one would expect their alienation to be relatively low (Tables 6.5 and 6.6). Despite this, they are somewhat more alienated than the "more integrated" sectors of the middle class. Since integration into middle class communities should lead to less alienation in terms of both theories being considered, these results, modest as they are, allow for no clear choice between the two theories.

The crucial test, then, comes among the working class, and here the patterns are sharper and more consistent: As predicted by the "class cultures" hypothesis, highly "integrated" workers are *more*, rather than less, alienated. In the working class, the nonurbanites, long-term residents and home-owners show the highest incidence of political discontent—the reverse of the middle class pattern. Of the six possible comparisons, one is a reversal and is not

[42] Of the three available indicators, city size is perhaps the least compelling. As mentioned elsewhere, the mass society view that urbanites are more "disintegrated" and "anomic" is contradicted by most available studies (e.g., Fischer 1973a, b). In the case of city size, then, the "slippage" between concept and indicator is apt to be great. This, we assume, accounts for the "reversals" on city size reported in subsequent paragraphs.

TABLE 6.9
Percent Highly Alienated by City Size, Length of Residence, Home
Ownership, and Social, Regional, and Rural-Urban Mobility, by
Social Class (white, non-South only): 1970

	Working Class			Middle Class		
	Efficacy	Trust	N	Efficacy	Trust	N
City Size						
50,000 or more	47.7	35.6	90	21.9	43.7	146
Less than 50,000	45.6	48.5	318	26.4	38.5	254
Residence Length						
Less than 10 years	39.7	42.0	136	27.1	46.4	166
10 years or more	49.6	47.7	266	22.8	36.4	228
Home Ownership						
Own	47.7	49.5	287	23.5	38.4	268
Rent	37.9	37.9	103	27.9	46.2	104
Social Mobility						
Stable	48.0	44.7	318	18.1	38.7	155
Mobile	38.7	51.6	62	29.7	42.0	212
Regional Mobility						
Stable	43.7	41.5	350	24.6	41.0	301
Mobile	64.2	69.3	39	24.7	40.7	81
Rural-Urban Mobility						
Rural-Urban	50.6	39.6	81	29.3	45.5	99
Urban-Rural	40.7	35.6	54	21.8	36.4	55
Urban-Urban	45.0	42.5	80	21.6	41.9	134
Rural-Rural	45.6	51.5	188	26.6	39.4	98

significant (city size by efficacy); another is in the predicted direction but not significant (residence length by trust); and the rest are in the predicted direction and significant at .05 or beyond. Thus, the data, on balance, contradict the mass society view.

In the white South, only city size is significantly related to political alienation. For both middle class and working class white southerners, small town residents are *more* alienated than urbanites.[43] Among blacks, none of the in-

[43] The data for white southerners are as follows:

		Percentage highly alienated	
	Efficacy	Trust	n
Middle class			
50,000 and up	23.7	39.5	38
less than 50,000	42.4	51.2	125
Working class			
50,000 and up	44.1	47.1	34
less than 50,000	57.8	57.8	180

tegration measures is significantly associated with either measure of alienation.

Mobility across spaces and between classes is also often included among the many "disruptions" common to the modern mass society. The 1970 survey allows us to explore three forms of mobility: across regions, from rural to urban areas (and the reverse), and mobility in and out of the major social classes. The relevant data are shown in Table 6.9.[44]

Focusing first on regional mobility, the data show no effect among middle class respondents. Among workers, there is a strong and significant tendency for the geographically mobile to be more alienated.

Many of the 39 regionally mobile workers were raised in the South, where (as we have seen) a generally higher level of alienation prevails. Thus, the apparent mobility effect shown for workers may disappear when region of origin is considered. The data (not shown), however, suggest this is not the case. Among 24 nonsouthern-reared geographically mobile workers, 58% were highly alienated on the efficacy measure, 75% on the trust measure; both are well above the nonmobile group. (The comparable figures for the 15 southern-reared respondents are 73% and 60%, also higher than the nonmobile group.)

The data on rural–urban mobility may be more succinctly summarized: There are no clear, consistent, or statistically significant relationships.

Concerning social mobility, three distinct hypotheses have been entertained (Jackman 1972:463–465). One hypothesis, the cognitive dissonance hypothesis, suggests that "those who have been upwardly mobile will feel positively towards the system which has yielded their success, while downwardly mobile persons will feel negatively towards the socio-political structure in which they have fallen (1972:463)." The second hypothesis derives directly from mass society theory: Regardless of direction, the mobile will be more alienated than the nonmobile, because all mobility entails "dislocation" which leads to alienation. Finally, Jackman's "acculturation hypothesis" treats mobility as a "simple resocialization process unaccompanied by psychological rationalization or strain." The socially mobile person, that is, merely

---

[44] In Table 6.9, a working class respondent is socially mobile if he or she reports a father whose occupation was white collar; thus, the working class mobiles are the downwardly mobile. Likewise, the socially mobile middle class respondents are those reporting a father employed in blue collar or farm occupations.

To assess regional mobility, the population was divided into four regions: East, Midwest, South, and West, in each case following the standard SRC regional codes. A regionally mobile respondent now lives in a region different from the one in which he or she was born.

City size of origin is measured by a question that reads: "Were you brought up mostly on a farm, in a town, in a small city, or in a large city?" Those responding "farm" or "town" are assumed to have rural origins. Current city size is divided into rural and urban locations with the dividing line at 10,000 persons. Thus, the "rural–urban" group was raised on a farm or in a town and now lives in a city of 10,000 or more and so on.

"sheds the values of his origin status and begins to assume those of his new status group"—implying that the alienation of the mobile will lie midway between that of origin and destination statuses.

The data in Table 6.9 confirm this latter hypothesis. On both measures of alienation, the tendency is for mobiles to be between the levels of their origin and destination classes. The exception is that the downwardly mobile workers (that is, workers from middle class backgrounds) were less trustful than either their origin or destination classes, but the difference is not significant ($p = .138$). Thus, the data suggest no mobility effect per se on alienation from the political system.[45]

One final variable that has figured prominently in mass society theorizing, especially in left-wing variants, is the mass media—for Marcuse, the "agents of manipulation and indoctrination," for Mills, "instruments of psychic management." By broadcasting a smooth and optimistic vision of the society, the media are said to "narcotize" the masses, to reduce their discontent, to lessen their capacity for independent thought and criticism. Certainly, the image of American government portrayed in the mass media is far from negativistic. Frequently lacking direct access to information, the media often rely on official sources; this commonly leads to a more "wholesome" portrayal than might be justified were all the facts available.[46] Similarly, media editorials, particularly in the smaller and more rural areas, tend to be either innocuous

[45] Additional analysis, focusing on perceived rather than objective social mobility, revealed similar noneffects. In this case, origin status is measured by the respondent's assessment of "your family's social class when you were growing up," and present status is measured by class identification. The data for non-South whites are as follows:

	Working class			Middle class		
Class identification	Efficacy	Trust	n	Efficacy	Trust	n
Origin class						
working class	44.7	47.5	387	26.0	33.9	177
middle class	40.0	54.3	35	30.3	41.7	271

[46] An interesting case in point is press coverage of the "Attica massacre." In that event, inmates of New York's Attica prison seized several guards and issued a variety of demands, mostly concerning living conditions, guards' brutality, and so on. New York's Governor Rockefeller adopted a "get-tough" policy and decided that the prison was to be retaken by force. In the ensuing melee, several of the hostages were slain; in most of the nation's press (including the New York Times, the Newsday chain, the Washington Post, the Chicago Daily News, the UPI press service, and others), the official version of these slayings—that the hostages' throats had been cut and that some had even been castrated—was published as straight fact, without attribution, even though subsequent autopsies revealed that the hostages had died of shotgun wounds inflicted by the invading "peace" officers. The throat slittings and castrations, of course, were front-page material; the denials and corrections were relegated to the back pages (see Donovan 1971, for more details concerning the press coverage of the Attica uprising). The early coverage in the media of Watergate would be another case in point.

or laudatory.[47] Then, too, selective perception may minimize the effect of the critical material which does end up in print: The biggest consumers of the media, of course, are those with the highest education[48]—the same group that is the least politically alienated. Thus, these educated optimists may ignore the critical material which contradicts their point of view.

Evidence on the relationship between political alienation and mass media consumption is shown in Table 6.10. As always, data are presented with a control for social class and are for white, non-South respondents only. Since media usage is strongly correlated with education, education has also been controlled. Finally, data shown here are for 1968, because the 1970 survey does not contain the media attention questions.[49]

Overall, media consumers are markedly less alienated than nonconsumers, even with education and occupation controlled. Although there are some reversals and exceptions to this pattern (noted later), these correlations are among the strongest encountered thus far. The efficacy patterns are especially striking. Among middle class high school drop-outs ($n = 54$) and college-educated workers ($n = 49$), powerlessness and media consumption are unrelated: Alienation is high in both contexts, perhaps reflecting some "status discrep-

---

[47] Many of the editorials that appear in the daily newspaper are not written by the local editor but by centralized editorial "companies"—that is, by business concerns whose business it is to write and distribute editorials. One such concern is E. Hofer and Sons, an Oregon-based outfit which, according to one account, "each week mails out [editorial] material to 10,000 daily and weekly newspapers, material that is specifically designed to create favorable attitudes towards capitalism in the United States (Harwood 1971)." The account continues: "The Hofer service is supplied free of charge to the free American press. The company is able to do this, Lawrence Hofer explains, because it is underwritten by large industrial groups—oil, electric utilities, timber, shipping, railroads, pharmaceuticals—and by such private professonal groups as the American Medical Association." (For an interesting case study in "How the Media Support Local Government Authority," see Paletz et al. 1971.)

[48] In the data reported here, for instance, the proportion regularly reading a newspaper declines from 66% of those with some college education or more to 43% of those with less than a high school education. Magazine readership, of course, is even more strongly associated with social class. (The figures are for white, non-South only.)

[49] The media attention questions were as follows:

We're interested in this interview in finding out whether people paid much attention to the election campaign this year. Take newspapers, for instance—did you read about the campaign in any newspaper? (If yes) How much did you read newspaper articles about the election—regularly, often, from time to time, or just once in a great while? How about magazines . . . ? How about television?

It should be emphasized that the question specifically refers to media attention for political purposes and presumably does not measure attention for entertainment, relaxation, and so on.

In the table, those "high" in media attention responded "regularly" or "often" to the respective questions. The "print media' variable combines newspaper and magazine readership; those scored as "both" were high in both and so on. "NS" means that the correlation coefficient was less than .15.

TABLE 6.10

Percent Highly Alienated by Media Consumption, with Education and Social Class Controlled; White, Non-South: 1968

| | Education | | | | | | | | |
| | Less than 12 | | | High School Graduate | | | Some College or More | | |
Middle Class	Efficacy	Trust	N	Efficacy	Trust	N	Efficacy	Trust	N
Newspapers									
High	58.6	24.1	29	25.4	39.7	63	11.1	32.5	117
Low	64.0	48.0	25	34.6	25.0	52	23.0	32.8	61
Gamma	NS	-.49		-.22	+.33		-.41	NS	
Magazines									
High	66.7	33.3	9	14.8	25.9	27	11.2	27.5	80
Low	61.4	36.4	44	33.7	34.8	89	19.0	37.0	100
Gamma	NS	NS		-.49	-.21		-.30	-.22	
Television									
High	61.0	29.3	41	24.7	32.5	77	15.8	30.8	146
Low	61.6	53.8	13	38.5	33.3	39	15.2	42.2	33
Gamma	NS	-.48		-.31	NS		NS	-.25	
Print Media									
Neither	59.1	45.5	22	37.2	27.9	43	26.1	34.8	46
Only one	68.0	32.0	25	29.6	37.0	54	13.0	36.2	69
Both	50.0	16.7	6	11.1	33.3	18	9.5	27.0	63
Gamma	NS	+.35		+.33	NS		+.38	NS	
Working Class									
Newspapers									
High	56.8	39.2	74	27.8	41.7	72	29.4	35.3	34
Low	66.4	42.1	107	41.6	32.5	77	33.3	50.0	12
Gamma	-.20	NS		-.30	+.20		NS	-.29	

162

	Education								
	Less than 12			High School Graduate			Some College or More		
Working Class	Efficacy	Trust	N	Efficacy	Trust	N	Efficacy	Trust	N
Magazines									
High	50.0	50.0	12	25.0	42.9	28	26.3	31.6	19
Low	64.0	40.7	172	37.1	34.7	124	30.0	46.7	30
Gamma	-.28	+.19		-.28	+.17		NS	-.31	
Television									
High	62.3	40.6	138	34.2	39.6	111	25.0	40.0	40
Low	65.2	43.5	46	36.6	26.8	41	44.4	44.4	9
Gamma	NS	NS		NS	+.28		-.41	NS	
Print Media									
Neither	67.0	42.5	106	41.9	31.1	74	40.0	60.0	10
Only one	56.3	35.9	64	28.8	42.3	52	23.8	33.3	21
Both	54.5	54.5	11	26.1	43.5	23	33.3	33.3	15
Gamma	+.21	NS		+.26	-.20		NS	+.29	

ancy effect." Also, the effect of television is weak in all groups.[50] In all other cases, attention to the mass media is strongly associated with lower levels of inefficacy, producing gamma's that range from −.20 to −.49. The results for trust here, as virtually everywhere else in the chapter, are less distinct. Again, the obvious tendency is for the consumers to be more politically trusting, but the relationships are generally weaker and show more reversals.

Several hypotheses could account for these results. At face value, the data are consistent with the "narcotization" hypothesis: Those who are highly attentive to the mass media, especially the print media, are, on the whole, less alienated than those who have escaped "psychic manipulation." But "selective perception" is an equally plausible alternative account: The highly alienated, being by definition suspicious of government and, presumably, of other major social institutions, may simple avoid contact with the media—one symbol of the "despised" establishment. The direction of causality, in short, may run from alienation to media consumption, rather than the reverse. One final possibility is that, by being attentive to the media, the consumers are in a position to "pick up" politically relevant information; this information, in turn, increases their political effectiveness and, along with it, their estimation of their ability to influence political decisions. Lacking more detailed evidence, it is not now possible to choose among these several possibilities.

SUMMARY AND DISCUSSION

In 1970, the situation in the United States was as follows: First, perhaps half or more of the population did *not* embrace attitudes deemed necessary for a democratic political culture. The half not participating in the "great consensus," moreover, was drawn disproportionately from those very groups in which the political damage might have been maximized: from the "backward" and "recalcitrant" white southerners, from the "revolutionary" blacks, from the "authoritarian" working class, and from the "status panicked" marginal middle class, more generally, from the unintegrated, the unmoderated, and the unrestrained. This extent and concentration of discontent was joined by political turmoil of every conceivable sort: campus rebellion, rising crime, an uncertain economy, race riots, political assassinations, the war in Vietnam. Finally, there were bona fide presidential candidates, in both 1968 and 1972, who might have mobilized the frustration and the disenchantment with "politics as usual"—One was an "extremist" of the right who, in direct contest with two establishment centrists, managed to *lose* the votes of nine out

---

[50] The observation that the print media and not television appear to have the more pronounced effect contradicts the hypotheses proposed by Michael Robinson that "the greater the dependency upon television, the greater the personal confusion and political estrangement from government." (Quoted in a news story in the Montreal *Gazette*, June 15, 1975: "U.S. Malaise: Television News Followers Called More Confused, Cynical.")

of every ten citizens; the other was an "extremist" of the left who was crushed by a moderate Republican. The rather massive disjuncture between "initial conditions" and ultimate outcomes thus raises the question: How does a democratic society survive in the face of this much political alienation?

The evidence discussed in this chapter provides part, if not all, of the answer. First, the objective powerlessness of the alienated must be noted. The principal tendency revealed in these data is for those who have the least power also to *believe* that they have little power and to be most suspicious of those who do have power. On the whole, the alienated are drawn from social groups whose members characteristically participate little in politics, are inactive in political or other voluntary associations, and have little of the money, time, or resources that effective politicking requires. In this sense, their alienation matters little to the persistence, stability, or viability or the regime. It is unlikely, moreover, that they are either incensed or surprised by their powerlessness or by the corruption which they sense among the political elites; more probably, they are resigned to them as inevitable and inescapable features of their political existence. The "typical" politically alienated person, as far as we are able to tell, is aging, poorly educated, and working class, unlikely to attend church, inattentive to the mass media, probably not interested or involved in much of anything outside the family, work, and perhaps a close circle of friends. The common suggestion that political alienation represents a "threat" to democratic regimes seems farfetched in light of these results.

A second major conclusion is that, despite the general direction of association, the correlation between political alienation and virtually everything is decidedly weak. With the exception of education and mass media attention, most differences shown in the preceeding chapter are on the order of 10–15 percentage points. This means that the demagogue who wanted to "mobilize the politically alienated" would have to appeal mainly to blue collar workers, *but also* to a sizable proportion of white collar workers as well, mainly to blacks, *but also* to white southerners, mainly to the aged, *but also* to large numbers of the young and middle-aged, mainly to the poor and economically marginal, *but also* to a large group of affluent persons as well. Most importantly, the demagogue would have to be "acceptable" to Democrats, Republicans, and Independents in equal proportions. The unanimous support of the politically alienated, in short, would require a candidate or leader who was virtually all things to all people. It is unlikely that such a candidate could ever be found; if found, it is even less likely that he or she would be much of a "threat" to democratic institutions.[51]

[51] This and much of the preceding discussion assumes of course, that there will only be one demagogue present on the scene attempting to mobilize the discontent. A common historical pattern in unstable democracies, however, is the presence of multiple demagogues drawn from both ends of the political spectrum—usually a Fascist or proto-Fascist movement on the right, and a Communist or Marxist movement on the left.

These points, let us note, apply especially to the sense of political distrust, which is more weakly associated with all "background" variables than is the sense of political efficacy. Distrust is somewhat more common than inefficacy, especially among younger and higher status populations; in addition, it is more diffusely present in the social structure. It is important that this be kept in mind in subsequent chapters, for it helps to explain why the political consequences of the two components of alienation are sometimes quite different.

Overall, the pluralist and mass society theories of political alienation receive only limited support in these data. Consonant with the pluralist view, unionized blue collar workers were slightly less alienated than the nonunionized; similarly, church attenders were somewhat less alienated than nonattenders. None of these differences, however, was especially striking. At best, one could speak of modest directional support. Concerning the mass society theory, the following can be noted: First, alienation was generally more pronounced among the "less integrated" subcultures, especially blacks, white southerners, and Jews, although, in each case, one suspects that specific historical and political experiences, rather than "massification" per se, account for these results. Second, the higher alienation of the marginal middle class is consistent with mass society themes, although here too plausible alternative theories could be advanced.[52] Third, patterns by church attendance and media consumption are consistent with the theory. Finally, the data show extensive political alienation in this "modern mass society." Certainly, these data are *not* sufficient to sustain the "world-historical theory" that the mass society thesis claims to be, especially since few of the hypothesized "disruptions" are yet in evidence. Perhaps the best that could be said is that the theory offers some limited insights into the roots of alienation but seriously misrepresents its political effects. We return to this point, of course, in later chapters.

Most of our attention in this chapter has been directed toward defining who the alienated are; a corollary and, in many ways, more important issue is who they are *not*. In other words, which groups in the society are best described by the consensus account? Here, the principal conclusion must be that firm allegiance to the on-going arrangements most clearly characterizes the upper middle classes—more precisely, the white, non-South, non-Jewish,

---

When this pattern is accompanied by weak or fractionated parties in the "responsible center," instability is often the result. This, for example, would characterize the Weimar regime, the fall of the Fourth Republic in France, or the current situation in many Latin American "democracies," Guatemala and Argentina being perhaps the most visible cases. The prospects of a similar development in the United States are discussed later in Chapter 10.

[52] For example, it is probable that the alienation of the marginal middle class reflects much the same things as the alienation of the working class (see Footnote 22), not some special "vulnerability" to the mass society.

middle-aged, "well-integrated" upper middle class media consumers—the "responsible" paragons of democratic virtue. The political activity and competence of this group require no emphasis; of all groups that appear in significant numbers in sample surveys, this is clearly the one best able to translate its discontent into a serious political challenge. That it is also by far the least discontented explains, in large measure, why the "system" continues to operate as it always has. As Hamilton and Wright have put it, "With the manual workers and the lower middle classes ordinarily passive and inactive, playing no initiative role, the key to 'stability' is an accepting and approving upper middle class. When they give their consent and support, the entire mechanism will function more or less adequately (1975b:202)."

7

Trends in Political Alienation in the United States

A number of recent studies, most of them drawing on the SRC data, have confirmed that the level of political discontent in the United States has risen sharply in the last decade.[1] Our purpose in this chapter is to analyze these trends in more detail, to isolate their apparent causes, and to determine which theories and hypotheses accurately reflect these trends.

Table 7.1 shows the marginal distributions for each of the nine alienation items from 1956 to 1972.[2] The 1958 survey does not contain the four efficacy items; likewise, the 1956 and 1960 surveys contain no measures of political trust. The 1966 survey contains only two of the five trust items. Finally, the 1958 version of trust item three is not comparable with other study years (see Table 5.2). With a few exceptions to be discussed later, the alienation trend on all items is unmistakably upward. As a minor historical aside, one should note that these data disconfirm Robert Lane's (1965:893) prediction that "in the Age of Affluence, there will be a rapproachment between men and their

---

[1] The major studies include Converse (1972), Citrin (1974), Cutler and Bengston (1974), House and Mason (1975), Miller (1974), Reiter (1971), and Wright (1975a). Each of these studies draws on the SRC series. Duncan *et al.* (1973) have come to the same conclusion by analyzing alienation trends in the Detroit Area Studies.

[2] Owing to its late availability, the 1972 data are not analyzed in this chapter. The marginals shown in the table are taken from the 1972 codebook. For the most part, the 1970 and 1972 distributions are identical (cf. Citrin 1974).

168

TABLE 7.1
Trends in Political Alienation by Item: 1956-1972

Efficacy

	1956	1958	1960	1964	1966	1968	1970	1972	Change
Have any say?									
Agree	28.4		27.4	29.6	36.1	41.2	35.8	40.5	+12.1
Disagree	71.6		72.6	70.4	63.9	58.8	64.2	59.5	
N	1735		1911	1541	1215	1329	1492	2673	
Voting only way?									
Agree	74.4		74.3	74.0	72.0	57.5	60.0	62.3	-12.1
Disagree	25.6		25.7	26.0	28.0	42.5	39.4	37.7	
N	1721		1888	1546	1225	1321	1486	2671	
Complicated?									
Agree	63.9		58.8	67.9	72.2	71.2	73.8	73.9	+10.0
Disagree	36.1		41.2	32.1	27.8	28.8	26.2	26.1	
N	1732		1894	1534	1234	1334	1491	2681	
Don't care?									
Agree	27.0		25.0	36.9	37.8	43.7	48.7	50.1	+23.1
Disagree	73.0		75.0	63.1	62.2	56.3	51.3	49.9	
N	1700		1853	1525	1173	1310	1457	2634	

Trust

	1956	1958	1960	1964	1966	1968	1970	1972	Change
Waste a lot?									
Distrust		45.1		48.1		60.6	69.7	67.0	+21.9
Trust		54.9		51.9		39.4	30.3	33.0	
N		1702		1410		1307	1484	2241	

169

TABLE 7.1 (continued)

					Trust				
	1956	1958	1960	1964	1966	1968	1970	1972	Change
Trust Government?									
Distrust		24.2		22.3	32.1	37.2	45.3	45.8	+21.6
Trust		75.8		77.7	67.9	62.8	54.7	54.2	
N		1709		1421	1230	1308	1471	2232	
Few big interests?									
Distrust		80.4		27.8	38.5	43.6	55.1	58.6	+30.8[a]
Trust		19.6		72.2	61.5	56.4	44.9	41.4	
N		1676		1383	1103	1212	1360	2070	
Smart people?									
Distrust		38.7		30.9		39.2	46.2	42.2	+3.5
Trust		61.3		69.1		60.8	53.8	57.8	
N		1700		1333		1278	1437	2161	
Crooked?									
Distrust		25.5		30.1		26.4	32.7	37.7	+12.2
Trust		74.5		69.9		73.6	67.3	62.3	
N		1668		1380		1281	1445	2170	

a. Owing to the non-comparability of the 1958 item, this figure reflects the 1964–1972 trend.

government and a decline in political alienation." The widely heralded "end of ideology" was quite clearly a temporary phenomenon.

The most notable exception to the general pattern comes on the "voting is the only way" item, whose ambiguity was noted earlier in Chapter 4 (see also Converse 1972; House and Mason 1975). More specifically, there is a real question of what a respondent intends when he disagrees with the item. On the one hand, the respondent may mean: No, there are many ways to influence the government—the interpretation assumed in the conventional scaling. But the respondent might also mean: No, there are *no* ways to influence the government. Cross-tabulation of this with the preceeding item suggests that both interpretations are about equally common: About 41% of the respondents apparently believe they have no say whatsoever; an additional 24% believe that voting is the only way to have any say; and the remaining 35% believe in their ability to influence the government over and beyond merely voting. A second consideration is that the bulk of declining agreement with the item occurs between 1966 and 1968 and, thus, coincides with the emergence of youth protest and domestic agitation against the Vietnam war. Some respondents who disagree with the item, in short, apparently have mass meetings, demonstrations, marches, and the like in mind. On the face of it, it seems unwise to include this group as part of the "great consensus" that sustains democratic government. For these several reasons, then, we have omitted the "voting" item from the trend analysis and rescaled the remaining three efficacy items.[3]

Of the five trust items, only number 4 shows a pattern markedly different from the remainder. This reinforces our earlier suggestion (Chapter 4) that this item probably has an ambiguous content, especially among black and working class respondents. A more serious problem with the trust items is that only two of them were asked in 1966, and, of these two, only one was asked in comparable form in 1958. Complete and fully comparable information for all study years thus exists only for trust item Number 2; therefore, we have dropped all items but this one in the trend analysis that follows.[4]

[3] The correlation (gamma) between standard and revised efficacy scales is 1.00 (see Wright 1973b:271), which indicates that very little information is lost by omitting the ambiguous item. In the remainder of this chapter, the "highly inefficacious" agreed to all or all but one of the three remaining items. Missing data were assigned a scale position on the basis of information available, following the procedure outlined in Footnote 12 of Chapter 4.

[4] The correlation (gamma) between the single-item and five-item indices is .91. Despite the recognizable hazards attendant single-item measures, the comparability and scope of analysis facilitated by this decision is sufficient for its justification. That the item that is kept best expresses the overall meaning of the scale decreases our concern. Miller (1974) has performed an item-by-item analysis of the trust trend for years in which comparable information exists and finds no major discrepancies across items. In the analysis that follows, the "highly distrustful" responded "only some of the time" or "never" to the question on political trust. Missing data are omitted from the analysis.

TABLE 7.2
Trends in Political Alienation in the United States: 1956-1970

		Efficacy						
		1956	1958	1960	1964	1966	1968	1970
Total	%	34.5[a]			29.7	39.2	44.0	48.5	51.1
	N	1737			1902	1551	1252	1337	1499
Region and Race									
Non-South whites	%	29.5			25.8	35.0	39.2	45.1	46.0
	N	1167			1178	1005	791	843	900
Southern whites	%	38.2			34.7	47.0	49.8	51.9	55.9
	N	424			550	381	315	345	431
Blacks	%	64.6			39.7	47.9	57.5	59.7	66.1
	N	146			174	165	146	149	168

		Trust						
		1956	1958	1960	1964	1966	1968	1970
Total	%		24.2		22.3	32.1	37.2	45.3
	N		1709		1421	1229	1308	1471
Region and Race								
Non-South whites	%		21.9		21.5	31.6	35.3	42.3
	N		1115		920	784	821	886
Southern whites	%		27.5		24.3	35.3	42.0	46.7
	N		432		356	309	343	420
Blacks	%		31.5		22.6	27.9	36.1	57.6
	N		162		155	136	144	165

a. Cell entries proportions highly alienated.

Table 7.2 shows the 1956–1970 alienation trends for the revised efficacy and trust measures, first for the total population, then by region and race. According to these measures, the overall decline in feelings of political efficacy amounted to 16.6 percentage points, and, for trust, 21.1 percentage points. These trends are the focus of the remainder of the chapter.

GROSS TRENDS IN THE TOTAL POPULATION

Trends for the total population can be summarized as follows:

1. There was a slight and substantively uninteresting increase in feelings of efficacy from 1956 to 1960 (see also Cutler and Bengston 1974). As shown in Table 7.2, the bulk of this increase was concentrated among blacks. More de-

tailed analysis also uncovered a large *decline* in alienation among southern working class whites.[5] The early trust trends parallel the efficacy trends: Among blacks, distrust declined about 9 points from 1958 to 1964 ($p = .038$); among working class white southerners, a similar pattern was uncovered.[6] Thus, trends in black political alienation from 1956 to 1970 are our first concern, then working class alienation in the white South from 1956 to 1964.

2. In contrast to these early patterns, efficacy shows a clear decline for all groups from 1960 to 1964. The smallest of these trends (8 points for blacks)

[5] The data for white southerners are as follows:

	Percentage highly inefficacious				
	1956	n	1960	n	Change
Education					
less than eighth	78.7	80	60.8	102	− 17.9
less than twelfth	36.6	202	40.4	171	+ 3.8
high school graduate	31.9	47	27.3	143	− 4.6
some college	11.1	54	18.0	61	+ 3.7
college graduate	10.0	40	13.7	73	+ 3.7
Occupation					
white collar	17.0	147	23.0	204	+ 6.0
blue collar	46.6	148	38.8	183	− 7.8
farm	60.7	56	46.2	52	− 14.5
Class Identification					
working class	50.0	230	44.1	331	− 5.9
middle class	21.8	179	23.0	204	+ 1.2

[6] The data for white southerners are as follows:

	Percentage highly distrustful				
	1958	n	1964	n	Change
Education					
less than eighth	38.0	71	27.9	61	− 10.1
less than twelfth	31.7	126	31.6	98	− 0.1
high school graduate	25.4	130	20.0	99	− 5.2
some college	17.6	51	16.7	42	− 0.9
college graduate	16.0	50	21.4	42	+ 5.4
Occupation					
white collar	17.0	171	19.9	136	+ 2.9
blue collar	32.4	139	26.8	97	− 5.6
farm	47.4	38	26.5	34	− 20.9
Class Identification					
working class	29.7	219	24.6	175	− 5.1
middle class	23.4	205	22.8	162	− 0.6

As indicated, the 1958–1964 low status white southerner decline in political distrust was not nearly so pronounced as the comparable 1956–1960 decline in inefficacy (see Footnote 5). As such, less is made of this trend in the text.

is significant at .06; all others are significant at .05 or beyond. The 1960–1964 alienation increase is, thus, our third consideration.

3. Finally, sizable increases in alienation are shown for all groups in the period from 1964 to 1970. The smallest of these trends (9 point decline in efficacy among white southerners) is significant at .006. These trends are certainly the clearest and most pronounced of any shown in the table and, thus, command most of our attention.

The major theoretical issue to be addressed in discussing these trends is whether the attitudes of efficacy and trust are firmly "inculcated at any early and impressionable age," as consensus theory suggests, or, alternatively, whether the "reservoir of diffuse support" fills and drains roughly in accordance with the quality of political outputs. At the outset, it can be granted that this is not likely to be an "either–or" issue. There are certain to be *some* citizens whose early political indoctrination is so total and complete that no amount of corruption and inefficiency will diminish their allegiance to the system. These represent the ultimate "fall-back" cushion for the regime, the unwavering bedrock of the reservoir of diffuse support. In consensus theory, of course, the assumption is that all or most of the population in modern democratic societies fits this description, that, because of early socialization, the system is able to count on sufficient "diffuse support" to aid it in weathering periodic crises of effectiveness.[7] An alternative and initially more plausible possibility is that the attitudes of some citizens will have the characteristics just described and that others will not. The task thus becomes one of isolating the two groups, determining their relative sizes, noting their apparent determinants, and, in the latter case, providing an alternative to "early socialization" as an explanatory account.

Even at the relatively crude level of consideration thus far, the trends in political alienation over the last decade and a half raise a serious question about the importance of early socialization in sustaining "diffuse support." After all, the trends shown in Tables 7.1 and 7.2 occur among politically eligible adult populations among whom early socialization has long since been complete. Sizable portions of the adult population, in short, apparently forgot, unlearned, or altered the political lessons that had been imparted to them in their youth. Thus, the trends suggest that, at least for some large

[7] This depiction of consensus theory, to be sure, is somewhat overdrawn. See, for example, Easton and Dennis: "We do not hypothesize therefore that all members must learn to extend unrequited love for their system or its component objects. Rather we are only suggesting that for some kind of system to persist over time, . . . most of the politically relevant members must have learned to put in a minimal level of diffuse support for the various political objects, whatever their form (1969:64)." As mentioned earlier (Chapter 3, Footnote 4), the point about "politically relevant members" is not pursued in the subsequent analysis. Who are the "politically relevant members"? How many of them constitute "most"? And what is a "minimal level of diffuse support"? The analysis reported in this chapter is, in one sense, an attempt to provide some empirical answers to these questions.

segment of "the democratic citizenry," the "hold" of early socialization on adult attitudes is much less firm than theorists such as Easton and Dennis assert. This would, in turn, imply that the role of political socialization in nurturing regime persistence is perhaps less important than consensus theory suggests.

There are, of course, several possible explanations of the alienation trends that would be consistent with the socialization model, but two of the most plausible can be easily ruled out. The first might be called the "differential socialization" or "generational" hypothesis. The argument would be that younger cohorts have been progressively more "poorly" socialized than older cohorts and, therefore, that the younger cohorts enter adulthood with less positive feelings of support. The dying off of the older "better socialized" cohorts and their replacement by the younger, "poorly socialized" cohorts would, in turn, produce a "rise" in political alienation for the total population. Cutler and Bengston, however, have examined this hypothesis in some detail and have flatly rejected it. On the basis of cohort analysis of the SRC 1952, 1960, and 1968 surveys, they conclude, "While there are some generational differences in the overall level of political alienation expressed over the 1952 and 1968 period, these differences are small and appear to be the result of the different educational compositions of the different age groups rather than indicators of the existence of clearly identifiable generational groups (1974:174)." [8]

A second possibility might be that the "trends" are not true trends at all but, instead, reflect the growth of traditionally more alienated groups. It is well-known that the median educational level of the U.S. population has risen in the period under consideration as have average incomes, the proportion employed in white collar work, and the proportion upwardly mobile. Similarly, owing to the postwar "baby boom," the mean age of the population has decreased slightly. Thus, the 1970 population is relatively more affluent, better educated, more middle class, and younger. It is unlikely, however, that the alienation trends merely reflect these differences, since all these demographic trends would normally lead to less, rather than more, alienation. As we have just seen in Chapter 6, growth has been among groups where alienation is typically low. Thus, we conclude that alienation has increased despite, not because of, demographic changes in the American population (see also Converse 1972; House and Mason 1975).[9]

[8] A more refined analysis of these data, employing finer cohort distinctions and all available surveys, indicated no modification of the Cutler–Bengston conclusions (data are not shown).

[9] That the alienation trends are largely independent of these various sociodemographic trends bespeaks the hazards inherent in inferring causal connections from data gathered at a single point in time. Correlational "theories" of political alienation, such as might be suggested by the analysis of Chapter 6, are clearly inadequate as accounts of *actual changes* in the dependent variable. (These points are elaborated in Wright and Danigelis 1974.)

A somewhat more probably explanation than either generations or demography is that political alienation has political causes; attention thus turns to the major sociopolitical phenomena of the era—more particularly, to the New Frontier, the Civil Rights movement, the Great Society, the war in Vietnam. Each of these, we expect, will have had some impact on the popular image of government and political leadership, but this impact need not have been uniform across all groups. Likewise, each of these events was accompanied, crudely speaking, by increases in the objective influence of some persons, usually at the expense of others. The question raised in the following sections is whether these political events and experiences explain the alienation trends. If they do, of course, then the plausibility of early socialization as a source of diffuse support will be diminished.

BLACK POLITICAL ALIENATION: 1956–1970

Political alienation among blacks shows an early decline from 1956 to 1960 (or from 1958 to 1964, in the case of trust) and then regular increases thereafter.[10] Not surprisingly, the low point in black political discontent coincides with the birth and subsequent growth of the "sit-down" (later, "sit-in") movement—the most striking lesson to date in how blacks could best make their ·demands and conditions known.[11] National political events following the "sit-

---

[10] These trends are especially interesting in light of the literature on the race–alienation relationship, reviewed earlier in Chapter 3. To review briefly, prior studies have concluded, on the one hand, that blacks are more alienated than whites, and, on the other hand, that there is no significant difference. Studies coming to the "no difference" conclusion, as it turns out, used data collected between 1960 and 1967 (Stokes 1962 is the single exception), whereas studies concluding that blacks are more alienated used data collected before 1960 or after 1968. The trend data confirm the finding that black–white alienation differences were, in fact, least pronounced in the mid-1960s. "Confusion" in the literature, then, may only reflect the search for constants in a universe characterized by change (see Wright and Danigelis 1974 for further discussion).

Concerning the analysis of trends in black political alienation, it should be recalled that both alienation measures are less reliable for blacks than for whites. "Difference" scores, of course, are even less reliable than either of their constituent measures, which obviously compounds the problem. Finally, the black ns are invariably small. For these reasons, the analysis can only be taken as suggestive.

Note also that blacks are omitted from the remainder of the analysis.

[11] The possibility that the "early decline" reflects only black elation over the passing of the hesitant Eisenhower regime is ruled out by the fact that the 1960 efficacy items were included in the pre-election wave, prior to Kennedy's election.

The birth of the "sit–down" movement is conventionally dated February 1, 1960, the day on which five black students in Greensboro, North Carolina openly challenged Jim Crow by refusing to honor the "whites only" sign at a Woolworth soda pop counter. Spectacular growth followed from this inauspicious beginning: By May 1 of the same year, similar sit-downs were in progress in every state in the South except Mississippi and had won the approval and active support of vast segments of the nation. All this, of course, took place just months before the 1960 pre-election interview; pre-

down" movement confirmed its impact. Carl Rowan wrote in *Ebony* in October, 1960 that both national platforms contained "the boldest civil rights planks that either party ever put into its platform"; moreover, "in terms of civil rights, both Nixon and Kennedy are farther advanced than any man ever to run for President." The sit-down movement, in short, appeared responsible not only for the liberality of the platforms, but also for the enlightenment of the candidates themselves. As Rowan put it, "Even the most skeptical Negroes were willing to concede that something drastic had changed since 1956 (1960:40)"—and, on this point, the efficacy trend certainly supports him.

The optimism generated by integrated lunch counters and public facilities, however, was bound to be relatively short-lived; equality in housing, education, employment, and political rights was obviously going to be much more difficult to achieve (Killian 1968). What might have at first appeared to be genuine progress was soon denounced as mere tokenism. In a like vein, the liberal bloom of the New Frontier quickly faded: Kennedy's progressive civil rights planks somehow failed to translate into specific social legislation, and the ascension of Lyndon Johnson (and then Richard Nixon) to the presidency were especially bitter turns of fate.[12] Thus, after 1960, political efficacy among blacks regularly erodes, and, by 1970, political alienation among blacks was back to its pre-1960 level. An essentially identical pattern, with some "acceleration" from 1968 to 1970, is shown for political trust.

Table 7.3 shows the alienation trends by social status within the black population. The relatively few numbers of middle class blacks in the sample, coupled with the recognized methodological deficiencies of these items among blacks, suggest that these results should be treated with caution. Nonetheless, some interesting differences do emerge. First, the higher status blacks have a more pronounced reaction to the sit-down movement: Blacks employed in white collar occupations, for example, show a 1956–1960 decline in alienation of some 48 points, compared with a more modest 21 point decline among blue collar blacks. A similar, although much less pronounced, pattern is evident in the 1958–1964 trend in political trust. Second, the subsequent increases in alienation are much slower for higher status than for lower status

---

sumably, the events were fresh in everyone's mind. All told, it is unlikely that anything *but* this movement accounts for the dramatic increase in feelings of efficacy among blacks from 1956 to 1960; this point is presented in the text.

[12] According to one black writer, "Millions of blacks figured that their fate would be similar to that of the Jews in Germany" under a Johnson regime (Booker 1973:15). As stated, this is obviously a grotesque exaggeration, although LBJ's performance in the area of civil rights as senate majority leader might well have provided ample cause for skepticism. Whatever the initial fears, it is clear that Johnson was responsible for major civil rights progress in the early years of his administration, especially from 1964 to 1966. Once distracted by Vietnam, the record of his later years is less auspicious (the foreign policy "distractions" having culminated in his successor's policy of "benign neglect"). Trends in political alienation among blacks from 1966 to 1970 strongly suggest that the "lesson" of those distractions was not overlooked.

TABLE 7.3
Trends in Black Political Alienation, by Education and Occupation: 1956–1970

				Percent Highly Alienated				
	1956	N	1958	N	1960	N	1964	N
Efficacy								
Education								
Less than 8th	80.0	65			66.2	71	76.2	42
Less than 12th	54.2	59			23.5	51	49.3	67
High school graduate	60.0	10			10.7	28	39.4	33
Some college or more	30.0	10			29.2	24	9.1	22
Occupation								
Blue collar	68.2	110			47.6	107	51.1	92
White collar	66.7	15			18.5	27	19.2	26
Trust								
Education								
Less than 8th			34.8	69			28.5	42
Less than 12th			40.5	42			21.9	64
High school graduate			16.7	24			21.4	28
Some college or more			23.1	26			15.0	20
Occupation								
Blue collar			34.0	103			25.0	92
White collar			25.0	24			19.2	26

Percent Highly Alienated

	1966	N	1968	N	1970	N
Efficacy						
Education						
Less than 8th	80.0	35	77.8	45	83.0	47
Less than 12th	59.3	59	62.3	53	70.0	60
High school graduate	44.4	36	41.9	31	52.4	42
Some college or more	33.3	15	40.0	20	31.2	16
Occupation						
Blue collar	66.7	57	60.7	89	68.4	117
White collar	22.2	18	50.0	26	51.7	29
Trust						
Education						
Less than 8th	23.5	34	38.6	44	67.4	46
Less than 12th	35.3	51	42.0	50	46.7	60
High school graduate	17.1	35	42.0	30	60.0	40
Some college or more	37.5	16	30.0	20	62.5	16
Occupation						
Blue collar	26.3	57	39.3	89	58.1	117
White collar	22.2	18	30.8	26	65.5	29

blacks. Blue collar blacks attain their 1956 level of inefficacy by 1966; among white collar blacks, the 1970 level of inefficacy was still 15 points lower than the figure for 1956. Being closer to the "realities" of the modal black existence, it appears that lower status blacks (by far the large majority) were some what less impressed with the "lessons" of the sit-down movement and read the ensuing history more quickly.

One explanation for the status differences among blacks might focus on the role of the black media in interpreting and analyzing the meanings of the sit-down movement and subsequent political developments. A lengthy perusal of *Ebony* magazine [13] for the period in question reveals three sequential orientations: a somewhat critical period prior to 1960, followed by rampant optimism throughout the period of the Great Society, and, finally, a sharp critical orientation following the summer of 1967.[14] This, of course, is quite similar to the pattern shown for higher status blacks—the majority consumers of *Ebony, Jet, Sepia,* and so on. Trends in black alienation in terms of media attention are consistent with this interpretation.[15] Unfortunately, there are too few cases to control for status and media attention simultaneously.

[13] According to the publishers, circulation figures for *Ebony* magazine are not available. Some information on the readership of *Jet*, a closely related magazine, however, was graciously supplied. *Jet* claims a weekly circulation of 2,850,000 readers, the large majority of whom are black. Higher status blacks are disproportionate consumers: 92% of them are located in metropolitan areas, 58% have a high school education or better, and the median income is $8975 per year. At the same time that these data were collected, the income figure was about $875 *higher* than that for the nation as a whole. The occupations of *Jet* readers, likewise, were listed as "professional, technical, managerial, clerical, sales, business owners, craftsmen." Among blacks no less than whites, media consumption is strongly related to social status. (Our thanks go to Johnson Publishing Co. for making these figures available and to Mr. Gary Castaline for their compilation.)

[14] See, for example, the following *Ebony* articles: (1) Simeon Booker, "What Negroes can expect from Kennedy," (January, 1961); (2) Lerone Bennett, "What Negroes can expect from President Lyndon Johnson," (January, 1964); (3) Alex Poinsett, "The Ten Most Trusted Whites," (April, 1964); (4) *Ebony*, "Editorial," (November, 1964); (5) *Ebony*, "Letter Power," (May, 1967); (6) *Ebony*, "How long, O'Lord, how long?" (May, 1967).

[15] The data for blacks are as follows:

Media attention	Percentage highly alienated							
	1956	n	1960	n	1964	n	1968	n
Newspapers								
high	47.5	59	18.4	49	30.0	70	44.4	45
low	75.9	87	46.9	98	62.7	83	65.7	99
Magazines								
high	41.2	17	9.1	11	13.6	22	47.1	17
low	68.0	128	43.1	144	54.2	131	61.4	132

As is shown, the early decline was most pronounced among readers, and readers were

The only other aspect of the black trend that seems to warrant attention is the sharp upturn in political distrust from 1968 to 1970. As Table 7.3 shows, this acceleration was roughly uniform across all groups. Given the nearly unanimous Democratic leanings of blacks, one possibility is that this is mainly a partisan reaction to Nixon's 1968 victory, but, since the 1968 trust items were asked during the *post*election wave, an effect of this sort should be reflected in the 1966–1968 trends. A more probable explanation is that the conscious pandering of Nixon to a presumed "backlash" sentiment during his first two years in office decreased his trustworthiness among blacks tremendously.[16]

WORKING CLASS ALIENATION IN THE WHITE SOUTH: 1956–1964

Standard academic treatments of the working class and of the South might suggest that working class alienation in the white South would negatively reflect the patterns shown for blacks: Events that decrease the alienation of one should increase the alienation of the other and vice versa. Data presented in Footnotes 5 and 6, however, do not accord with these expectations: Although by no means as pronounced as the black trends, working class alienation in the white South also showed a clear decline from 1956 to 1960 (or 1958 to 1964). Conversely, it is among the middle class southern whites that alienation increases, although these trends are small and insignificant. These data raise two questions. First, why was there no massive increase in political alienation among white southerners, to reflect the black decline? Second, what accounts for the decline in alienation among working class southern whites?

---

much slower to respond in subsequent years. The patterns by magazine attention are especially striking. About half the magazine readers were highly alienated in 1956; this figure drops to a tenth in 1960 and stays at that low level throughout the Great Society period. Then, in 1968, the level of inefficacy among the group is back up to its previous 50% level.

[16] Here, a point made earlier can be emphasized. In the case of blacks, it is clear that attitudes of alienation respond to events in the immediate political environment, and, to that degree, the "socialization" hypothesis proves faulty. It is also clear, however, that among the blacks, sizable residues of "diffuse support" remain even in the dreariest of times. Consider, for example, the situation in 1970, which represents the high point of black alienation on both dimensions. Even then, an entire third of the black population did *not* express feelings of powerlessness, and slightly more than two-fifths were willing to affirm that the government in Washington could be trusted "most of the time." These proportions would apparently contain those blacks whose early socialization *did* proceed more or less as the theorists suggest. It may also be safely presumed that these "pockets" constitute some important source of support for the regime in periods of "crisis" or "output stress."

Whether or not the first of these questions is a puzzle at all depends on the assumption that white southerners were monolithically and resolutely opposed to the black cause. One question asked in both 1956 and 1960, however, casts some doubt on this assumption. The question reads, "If Negroes are not getting fair treatment in jobs and housing, the government should see to it that they do." In both years, approximately two-thirds of the white southerners *agreed* with this statement ($n = 257$ and $n = 336$, respectively). This figure, to be sure, is considerably lower than the level of agreement outside the South; likewise, the question makes no reference to the integration of schools, certainly the most volatile issue of the period. These data, however, do make it plain that the majority of white southerners were *not* unremittingly hostile on the race issue.

A more interesting aspect of this "jobs and housing" question was that, in both years, the working class white southerners were more likely than their middle class counterparts to give the *liberal* response, theories of working class "authoritarianism" notwithstanding. Neither difference is large; both are statistically significant.[17] One possible explanation for the decline in alienation among southern working class whites in the face of the new civil rights agitation, then, is that the large majority of them were relatively sympathetic.

Table 7.4 shows the white southern alienation trend by class and political ideology. Consistent with the points just raised, racial conservatives of all classes show net increases in alienation in the 1956–1960 period. The single exception is among the nonaffluent working class, which registered an insignificant decline. Similarly, racial liberals of all classes show net declines in alienation, with the sole exception of the upper middle class liberals who show a small increase. These patterns are more or less what one might expect, given the racial situation in the white South in this period. Those who were sympathetic to blacks showed increased confidence in their own ability to influence the government; those who were unsympathetic became more hostile. The significant fact is that the former were slightly *more* numerous than the latter, especially in the white southern working class. The overall level of racial moderation in the white South thus apparently accounts for the slight decline in regional alienation from 1956 to 1960 (or from 1958 to 1964), and

[17] The data for white southerners on the "jobs and housing" issue are as follows:

	Percentage Liberal	
	1956	*1960*
Total	66.3	67.1
n	257	336
Middle class	61.4	57.4
n	114	148
Working class	69.9	74.5
n	143	188
Significance level =	.07	.001

TABLE 7.4
Trends in Efficacy in the White South, by Class and Ideology:
1956-1960

	Liberals[a]			Conservatives		
	1956	1960	Change	1956	1960	Change
Upper Middle Class[b]	11.8[c]	20.7	+8.9	4.4	18.0	+13.6
N	34	53		23	39	
Lower Middle Class	22.2	9.4	-12.8	28.6	41.7	+13.1
N	36	32		21	24	
Upper Working Class	37.5	34.4	-3.1	25.0	76.9	+51.9
N	16	32		4	13	
Lower Working Class	48.8	28.7	-20.1	46.2	42.8	-3.4
N	84	108		39	35	

    a. Liberals and conservatives are divided according to res-
ponses to the "jobs and housing" question discussed in the text.
    b. The classes are divided into upper and lower segments on
the basis of income, with the cutting line at $6000. As always,
farm respondents are included in the working class.
    c. Cell entries are proportions highly inefficacious.

the differential distribution of racial moderation across classes also seems to account for the class-specific trends.[18]

EFFICACY TRENDS AMONG WHITES: 1960–1964

In contrast to the general decline in alienation from 1956 to 1960, political powerlessness shows clear increases for all groups from 1960 to 1964. The in-

[18] Similar, although much less pronounced, results are in evidence for the 1958–1964 decline in distrust among white southerners (see Footnote 6). Noncomparability between the 1958 and 1964 political attitude questions prevents us from saying anything about the attitudinal correlates of this trend. Again, dividing the white southerners into upper and lower middle and working classes, the following patterns were observed: The largest decline in alienation (7.5 points) again came among the nonaffluent workers followed by a 4-point decline among the affluent workers and slight and insignificant increases for both middle class groups. All these differences are slight and not significant, but they are consistent with the efficacy results.

    Again, we emphasize a point made earlier in Footnote 16, namely, that there is a fair amount of "diffuse support" left over after the trends are complete. The large increase in political alienation among white southern upper middle class conservatives from 1956 to 1960 is a case in point. The net effect of that trend was to reduce the level of "diffuse support" among the group from 95.6% to 82.0%—leaving a rather sizable "cushion" of support. This assumes, of course, that all of those who expressed no particular feelings of political powerlessness were firmly attached to the regime, and it is possible that many of them were simply suspending judgment, awaiting the outcome of policies and programs that were then just in the offing. Even taking the "undecided" into account, however, it is clear that sizable pockets of support remained.

crease amounts to about 9 points for whites outside the South, and about 12 points for southern whites. Further analysis showed no significant variation in this trend across the usual sociodemographic variables.

Certainly, the major political event of the 1960–1964 period was the transfer of federal power to the more liberal Kennedy administration in 1961.[19] Historically, this signified the temporary end of laissez faire republicanism and a return to a more activist New Deal conception of government. The first hypothesis to be entertained, then, is that conservatives contributed to the bulk of the efficacy decrease, reflecting their actual loss of influence in the Kennedy regime.[20]

Ideal data for testing this hypothesis are not available, since the wording and format of many of the SRC's political attitude items changed between the 1960 and 1964 surveys. There are, however, four items which tap the same substantive content and which are, thus, serviceable for our purposes.[21]

[19] Please recall that the 1960 efficacy items were asked prior to Kennedy's election. In the 1960 pre-election survey, respondents were asked, "Who do you think will be elected President in November?" The responses were: Kennedy, 33%; Nixon, 43%; Don't Know, 22%; Other, 2% ($n = 1954$). Thus, the 1960 efficacy data were collected during a period in which it was expected that Nixon would succeed Eisenhower to the presidency.

[20] Whether or not the *substance* of liberalism was present in the Kennedy administration remains an open historical question; his record on civil rights, labor legislation, and early U.S. involvement in Vietnam is certainly suspicious from the contemporary liberal point of view. There can be little doubt, however, that "Camelot" exuded the *image* of progress and enlightenment, as witnessed by the Kennedy slogans ("The New Frontier," "Let's Get America Moving Again") and early conscription of the Harvard professor brain trust. The prospects of a Kennedy victory horrified nationally prominent conservatives, such as David Lawrence, editor of *U.S. News and World Report*. In Lawrence's editorial of August 8, 1960, a vote for the Kennedy–Johnson ticket is equated with a vote for "state socialism (p. 104)"; in the September 12 editorial, Lawrence warns the nation against the "AFL-CIO and the radical groups" that were "sponsoring" Kennedy's candidacy. On October 17, we are told that "Nikita Kruschev would doubtless rejoice" over a Kennedy victory (p. 140), and so on. Lawrence's first editorial after Kennedy's victory is especially instructive. Unlike the more common "rally 'round the President" exhortations that are typical fare in postelection commentaries, Lawrence issues a blatant call for congressional obstructionism. The editorial, which was entitled "The Only Hope Now," ends on the following rear guard's note: "The only hope now is that the conservatives of both parties in Congress, supported by the conservative majority in the nation [which, of course, had just voted for state socialism!] will work together to save America from financial chaos and defeat in the 'Cold War' (p. 128)."

[21] The items, in both 1960 and 1964 format, are as follows:

1. Federal aid to education:

    1960: If the cities and towns around the country need help to build more schools, the government in Washington ought to give them the money they need. (Agree–Disagree; percentage liberal = 69)

    1964: Some people think that the government in Washington should help towns and cities provide education for grade and high school children. Others think that

Alienation trends across these items, controlled for region and social class, are shown in Table 7.5

Overall, the patterns conform rather closely to our hypothesis. First, prior to Kennedy's election, with a continuation of the "regime" via Nixon as a real possibility,[22] conservatives were generally *less* alienated than liberals. As might have been expected, the only consistent exception to this pattern is the school desegregation question; federal "activism" about this predates Kennedy's presidency. Excepting this item, the "conservatives less alienated" pattern is shown in 9 of the remaining 12 comparisons. That the sense of powerlessness was generally greater among liberals during the Eisenhower years is certainly not surprising, given their objective inability to influence governmental policy in that period.

In contrast to the 1960 pattern, the relationship between ideology and alienation was weak and inconsistent in 1964. All 1960 differences are greatly diminished or reversed. There is, in addition, very little doubt as to the source of these attenuations; there were large *increases* in alienation among conser-

---

this should be handled by the state and local communities. Which one do you favor? (percentage liberal = 40)

2. Federalized medicine:

   1960: The government ought to help people get doctors and hospital care at low cost. (percentage liberal = 75)

   1964: Some say that the government in Washington ought to help people get doctors and hospital care at low cost. Others say that the government should not get into this. What do you think? (percentage liberal = 64)

3. Federal aid to blacks:

   1960: If Negroes are not getting fair treatment in jobs and housing, the government should see to it that they do. (percentage liberal = 78)

   1964: Some people feel that if Negroes are not getting fair treatment in jobs and housing, the government should see to it that they do. Others feel this is not the government's business. How about you? (percentage liberal = 49)

4. Government-enforced school desegregation:

   1960: The government in Washington should stay out of the question of whether white and colored children go to the same school. (percentage liberal = 52)

   1964: Some people say that the government in Washington should see to it that white and Negro children be allowed to go to the same schools. Others claim this is not the government's business. How about you? (percentage liberal = 53)

The 1964 items invariably elicit a smaller liberal proportion. This apparently reflects the changes in wording and format rather than massive ideological realignment, as Goldwater's electoral fortunes suggest. It also implies that the 1960 and 1964 "liberals" are, in no real sense, fully comparable groups. Thus, the results can only be treated as suggestive.

[22] See Footnote 19.

TABLE 7.5

Trends in Efficacy by Political Ideology, Region, and Social Class: 1960-1964 (whites only)[a]

	Middle Class					Working Class				
	1960	N	1964	N	Change	1960	N	1964	N	Change
Non-South										
Federal Aid to Education										
Liberal	17.8	197	23.6	89	+5.8	32.3	303	42.8	140	+10.5
Conservative	3.8	130	16.7	192	+12.9	21.5	130	38.5	192	+17.0
Federal Aid to Blacks										
Liberal	15.6	246	17.0	135	+1.6	28.2	379	43.1	153	+14.9
Conservative	9.7	62	22.9	153	+13.2	21.8	101	40.7	182	+18.9
Federalized Medicine										
Liberal	13.2	174	29.4	143	+16.2	31.7	341	43.2	227	+11.5
Conservative	14.4	111	13.1	137	-1.3*	13.4	97	36.4	110	+23.0
School Desegregation										
Liberal	8.0	187	19.3	176	+11.3	23.6	271	37.1	175	+13.5
Conservative	13.7	124	22.9	118	+9.2*	29.9	184	44.4	162	+14.5
South										
Federal Aid to Education										
Liberal	27.5	91	26.7	30	-0.8	44.7	123	46.7	45	+2.0
Conservative	16.1	56	38.0	92	+21.9	25.0	52	43.3	67	+18.3
Federal Aid to Blacks										
Liberal	16.5	85	35.1	37	+18.6	30.0	140	61.0	41	+31.0
Conservative	27.4	62	33.3	84	+5.9*	53.2	47	40.0	70	-13.2*

	Middle Class					Working Class				
	1960	*N*	*1964*	*N*	*Change*	*1960*	*N*	*1964*	*N*	*Change*
South										
Federalized Medicine										
Liberal	34.2	82	36.5	52	+2.2	51.4	148	53.2	62	+1.8
Conservative	14.1	78	39.7	58	+25.6	3.0	33	31.0	42	+28.0
School Desegregation										
Liberal	27.9	68	20.0	45	-7.9	41.5	41	30.4	23	-11.1
Conservative	18.2	110	43.2	81	+25.0	42.9	147	50.0	44	+7.1

a. Cell entries are proportions highly alienated. Missing data are omitted on an item-by-item basis. (*) denotes a reversal of the basic pattern discussed in the text.

vatives from 1960 to 1964, especially in the white South.[23] In 16 relevant comparisons, this pattern is apparent in 12. These data thus support the hypothesis that political conservatives contributed disproportionately to the overall increase in alienation from 1960 to 1964—in response, one assumes, to the objective decline in conservative power that accompanied the Kennedy (and later Johnson) administrations.

POLITICAL ALIENATION IN THE UNITED STATES 1964–1970[24]

The final and most striking aspect of the trends is the large increase in alienation from 1964 to 1970. For efficacy, the increase amounts to about 12 points, for trust, about 23 points. As noted earlier, these increases were roughly uniform across regions and races. Additional analysis indicates that the trends were also invariant across social classes. The single notable exception to this pattern is among the college educated, whose alienation trends are examined later.[25] For now, it is sufficient to note the rather mas-

---

[23] These "large increases," as before, did not totally empty the "reservoir of diffuse support." The effect was only to lower the level somewhat. Take, as an example, the largest trend shown in Table 7.5, the increased alienation of working class white southerners with conservative responses to the "federalized medicine" question. Some two-thirds of them were still convinced of their ability to influence the government as of 1964.

[24] The findings reported in this section appear elsewhere in our paper, "Political socialization research: the 'primacy' principle," *Social Forces* 54 (September) and are reproduced here by permission of the publisher.

[25] The trends by occupation for non-South whites were as follows (farm omitted):

	Efficacy				
	1964	1966	1968	1970	Change
White collar	21.1	28.2	34.4	33.0	+11.9
Blue collar	40.4	49.4	52.1	55.7	+15.3
Difference	19.3	21.2	17.7	22.7	
			Trust		
White collar	15.7	33.4	32.4	37.1	+21.4
Blue collar	21.6	35.2	37.1	46.0	+24.4
Difference	5.9	1.8	4.7	8.9	

These data contradict the hypothesis advanced by Schwartz (1973:10–11), that the relationship between class and political alienation declined during the 1960s. That relationship, although never especially strong (least of all for political trust), has been essentially constant over the last decade (see Chapter 6, Footnote 15).

The trends in alienation by education were as follows, whites only (these trends are discussed in the text):

	Efficacy								Net
Education	1964	n	1966	n	1968	n	1970	n	change
Less than eighth	70.5	139	69.6	125	83.7	98	81.9	155	+11.4
Less than twelfth	51.4	436	58.3	326	64.6	350	64.7	348	+13.3

(Continued on Page 189)

sive withdrawal of consent among essentially all groups in the 1964–1970 period.

Concomitant with the alienation increases, there was a stark rise in "disappointments with political outputs" during this period. It is, to be sure, a rare occasion when systematic empirical research confirms the popular wisdom, but this is one such case. Data on two of the most significant issues—Vietnam and the economy—are shown in Table 7.6.[26]

High school	30.7	456	39.1	368	41.8	380	44.9	474	+14.2
Some college	20.7	184	17.2	163	31.0	187	31.4	185	+10.7
College graduate	16.0	163	12.6	119	19.7	173	18.6	167	+ 2.6
				Trust					
Less than eighth	27.4	125	36.9	122	46.2	93	50.7	142	+23.3
Less than twelfth	28.0	397	35.4	322	44.4	340	53.5	342	+25.5
High school	17.8	427	30.1	366	31.5	375	37.5	472	+19.7
Some college	19.3	161	29.6	159	38.7	186	41.0	183	+21.7
College graduate	19.9	151	33.0	121	29.4	170	37.6	165	+17.7

[26] The questions are as follows:

1. During the last few years, do you think our chances of staying out of war have been getting better, getting worse, or stayed the same? (1964)
   How about the chances of our country getting into a bigger war? Compared to a few years ago, do you think we are more likely, less likely, or have about the same chances to get into a bigger war? (1970)
2. Do you think we did the right thing by getting into the fighting in Vietnam, or should we have stayed out? (1964 and 1970)
3. Which of the following do you think we should do now in Vietnam—pull out of Vietnam entirely, keep our soldiers in Vietnam but try to end the fighting, or take a stronger stand even if it means invading North Vietnam? (1964 and 1970)
4. During the last few years, has your financial situation been getting better, getting worse, or has it stayed the same? (1964)
   Would you say that you and your family are better off or worse off financially than you were a year ago? (1970)
5. Now looking ahead and thinking about the next few years, do you expect your financial situation will stay about the way it is now, get better or get worse? (1964)
   Now looking ahead—Do you think that a year from now you people will be better off financially, or worse off, or just about the same as now? (1970)

In the table, *ns* for the 1970 study vary because questions were asked of random subsamples.

As before, it is clear that many of these items are not fully comparable in both their 1964 and 1970 formats, although, in all cases, the substance of both forms seems fairly close. Since these are the only items available for analysis, we have had little choice but to swallow the bitter pill of noncomparability, with the attendant hope that the results will again be taken mainly as suggestive.

In an earlier version of the analysis, racial questions were also included. Despite popular commentary on the "white backlash," the trend on all racial questions from 1964 to 1970 was toward a larger liberal percentage. One general question along these lines asked, "Are you in favor of desegregation, strict segregation, or something in between?" Those favoring desegregation increased by about 8 points, while the strict segregationists showed a 7 point decline (Wright 1973b:298). Interestingly, these racial trends were independent of the alienation trends (1973b:305), in contrast to the Scammon–Watten-

TABLE 7.6
Trends in Political Attitudes in the United States: 1964-1970

	Vietnam		
	1964	1970	Change
Are the chances of avoiding war:			
Getting better	30.4	25.1	-5.3
The same	47.7	32.6	-15.1
Getting worse	17.5	30.2	+12.7
Don't know, other	4.4	12.1	+7.7
N	1571	914	
Should we have gotten into Vietnam?			
Did the right thing	38.0	30.2	-7.8
Should have stayed out	24.3	49.4	+25.1
Don't know, other	37.7	20.4	-17.3
N	1450	1507	
Current Policy Preferences?			
Pull out	8.6	32.4	+23.8
Ceasefire	24.3	32.1	+7.8
Escalate	31.0	24.0	-7.0
Don't know, other	36.1	11.5	-24.6
N	1450	1507	

	The Economy		
	1964	1970	Change
Has your financial situation:			
Gotten better	45.3	30.7	-14.6
Stayed the same	39.4	33.7	-5.7
Gotten worse	14.6	33.2	+18.6
Don't know, other	0.7	2.4	+1.7
N	1450	1507	
How about the immediate future?			
Better	43.7	27.0	-16.7
Same	42.6	44.4	+1.8
Worse	8.7	15.2	+6.5
Don't know, other	5.0	13.3	+8.3
N	1571	914	

First, the evidence indicates a rising anxiety about the prospects of war and steady deterioration of public support for administration Vietnam policy. From 1964 to 1970, for example, the proportion feeling that the chances of avoiding a bigger war had gotten worse increased from 18% to 30%. Likewise, the proportion believing that our original involvement in Vietnam was

berg thesis that the "social issue" was the paramount point of political contention in the era.

a mistake doubled, and sentiment for an immediate pull-out more than tripled. (See Mueller 1971; Wright 1972a,b for analysis of the Vietnam trends.) Of some additional interest, the proportion choosing Vietnam as "the most important problem the government in Washington should try to take care of" increased from virtually nobody in 1964 to about half the population in 1970. The lesson here, in short, is that increasing numbers were becoming anxious about the prospects of a bigger war, were defecting from official Vietnam policy, and were rapidly moving Vietnam to the top of their political priorities. Vietnam, then, represents one clear area of "disappointment" which we would expect to have undergirded the alienation trend.

A second "disappointment" was the economy. The long-term increase in real purchasing power had ended, for all practical purposes, in 1966. In its place came serious inflation and the first balance of trade deficit in the twentieth century. Both of these, of course, were closely related to American involvement in Vietnam. Reflecting these developments, the proportion of the population feeling that their economic situation had been getting better declined some 15 points from 1964 to 1970; the proportion of feeling that things had gotten worse increased by 19 points. Optimism about the "next few years" also fell about 17 points. Thus, the economy was a second potential source of increased alienation.

Trends in political efficacy, controlled for attitudes toward Vietnam and the economy, are shown in Table 7.7. These data suggest that the attitude trends adequately account for the efficacy trend. Taking the "economic outlook for the future" question as exemplary, we note that about half the pessimists and a quarter of the optimists were highly inefficacious in both years; as the percentage change columns indicate, the efficacy trend essentially disappears when the attitude trends are controlled. This suggests that the 1964–1970 "movement" of the population into the "more alienated" categories—that is, those pessimistic about the economy and upset over Vietnam—was accompanied by a rather striking readjustment of alienated attitudes to reflect this movement. Thus, these data again demonstrate the sensitivity of feelings of powerlessness to the prevailing political realities. During a period in which public decisions at times consciously opposed mass political preferences (for example, Johnson's and Nixon's often expressed desire to "avoid the easy solution" in Vietnam), feelings of powerlessness increased accordingly. This would suggest, in contrast to consensus theory, that attitudes of "diffuse support," such as political efficacy, *are* tied, at least in part, to "day-to-day political outputs" and that, as the quality of those outputs declines, so too does the "reservoir" of political good will.[27]

[27] Let us emphasize one final time that this statement describes the general tendencies revealed in the data and says nothing about the level of diffuse support that remained. Among those who expected their financial situation to worsen "in the next few years," for example, there were still more than half (in 1970) who did *not* feel especially powerless politically, and still more than two-fifths who felt that the government could

TABLE 7.7
Trends in Efficacy by Socio-political Attitudes: 1964-1970

	War				
	1964	N	1970	N	Change
Big War					
Better	27.8	421	24.3	185	-3.5
Same	37.9	663	37.6	221	-0.3
Worse	38.2	254	40.4	203	+2.2
Don't know, other	44.2	52	56.0	75	+11.8
Vietnam Right					
Did right thing	25.6	516	28.4	429	+2.8
Should have stayed out	43.6	314	44.7	699	+1.1
Don't know, other	39.1	560	50.0	274	+10.9
Vietnam Now					
Pull out	44.4	108	41.7	417	-2.7
Ceasefire	28.1	313	37.4	430	+9.3
Escalate	28.6	433	40.9	350	+12.3
Don't know, other	42.5	536	45.8	155	+3.3

	Economy				
	1964	N	1970	N	Change
Financial Situation					
Better	27.4	632	29.7	209	+2.3
Same	40.6	549	40.6	234	0.0
Worse	43.5	200	38.7	230	-4.8
Don't know, other	55.6	9	54.6	11	-1.0
Finances Future					
Better	24.9	575	24.2	190	-0.7
Same	38.8	619	37.8	307	-1.0
Worse	53.1	128	45.8	107	-7.3
Don't know, other	54.4	69	41.3	80	-13.1

An exception to the general pattern concerns the question of current policy preferences in Vietnam. Despite their steadily declining numbers, persons favoring an escalation showed a marked increase in inefficacy during the period. A similar increase is shown for those preferring a cease-fire. Part of the apparent increase is no doubt due to the changing demographic composition of the "hawk" group from 1964 to 1970. In 1964, "hawks" were disproportionately drawn from the high status and less alienated populations (e.g., Hamilton 1968) but, by 1970, the "hawks" were more or less evenly dispersed

be trusted. There are some, clearly, whose support for the regime would probably never falter, no matter how seriously the situation deteriorated. As we have already mentioned, these no doubt constitute an important source of stability for the system.

throughout the status hierarchy (Verba *et al.* 1967; Wright 1972a,b). The defection of high status persons from the escalation option means that the 1970 "hawks" are relatively lower status and, therefore, more likely to feel inefficacious. Some of the alienation increase among both moderates and hawks, however, must also reflect a genuine sense of decline in their ability to influence Vietnam policy. Here it is useful to recall James Reston's remark that "everything in the Johnson strategy seems to be done in twos—something for the hawks, something for the doves." In an attempt to appease all factions simultaneously, of course, Johnson (and later Nixon) ended up pleasing no one, a fact to which these alienation trends certainly attest.

As indicated in Table 7.8 the 1964–1970 trend in political trust was un-

TABLE 7.8
Trends in Trust by Socio-political Attitudes: 1964–1970

	War				
	1964	*N*	*1970*	*N*	*Change*
Big War					
Better	18.9	402	35.0	186	+16.1
Same	28.9	603	45.0	222	+16.1
Worse	39.9	233	50.5	204	+10.6
Don't know, other	31.7	41	58.7	75	+27.0
Vietnam Right					
Did right thing	21.7	516	36.1	429	+14.4
Should have stayed out	37.6	314	53.9	641	+16.3
Don't know, other	28.1	448	46.7	274	+18.6
Vietnam Now					
Pull out	34.3	108	52.4	416	+18.1
Ceasefire	15.6	314	36.3	432	+20.7
Escalate	34.4	433	52.6	350	+18.2
Don't know, other	28.5	424	48.1	156	+19.6

	Economy				
	1964	*N*	*1970*	*N*	*Change*
Financial Situation					
Better	22.5	591	39.2	209	+16.7
Same	28.9	501	47.9	236	+19.0
Worse	42.3	182	49.1	230	+6.8
Don't know, other	20.0	5	33.3	12	+13.3
Finances Future					
Better	25.2	531	35.1	191	+9.9
Same	26.6	583	45.2	310	+18.6
Worse	36.3	113	58.9	107	+22.6
Don't know, other	50.0	52	53.2	79	+3.2

fortunately more occluded. In contrast to the efficacy pattern, the trust trend was essentially independent of all issues shown in the table. Taking the Vietnam policy preference question as exemplary, we can note that the relationship between Vietnam preference and trust was constant across the period: Both hawks and doves were markedly less trustful than moderates in both study years, but *increases* in distrust were constant across all three groups.[28] Similar conclusions hold true for the other four issues shown in the table. Thus, these data support our earlier suggestion (Chapter 6) that efficacy and trust are by no means equivalent or interchangeable indicators of the same underlying phenomenon. Powerlessness, as we have seen, appears to reflect the correlation between public policy and political preference: Where the correlation is high, powerlessness is low, and vice versa. Trust, on the other hand, may reflect the openness and competence whereby that correlation is attained. Groups whose policy preferences are being honored may still decline in political trust *if* the decision-making process is itself deceptive or corrupt. In short, even the winners of an unfair contest may object to the rules of the game. Vietnam policy, in the period under consideration, has something of this character. Escalations of the war effort were almost invariably preceded by assurances that no escalation was being planned.[29] In such a case, the ultimate policy might reflect the relatively greater influence of the "hawks," but confidence and political trust would be diminished among all groups. Lacking more detailed information, it is not possible to conclude definitely whether or not something of this sort accounts for the independence of trust trends from policy preference trends, but it is certainly a plausible explanation. In apparent response to what William Shannon has called "the worst one-two Presidential succession since the end of the Civil War," trust declines everywhere from 1964–1970.[30]

[28] In his analysis of these same data, Miller also notes the disproportionate distrust of both hawks and doves but *fails* to note the equivalence of the trust trend across all three groups. The 1970 distribution, in its own right, is easy enough to explain: The failure of the Johnson and Nixon administrations either to withdraw altogether or to escalate for a decisive military victory could reasonably be expected to alienate hawks and doves in roughly equal proportion. This is precisely the explanation Miller offers (1974:960). What this leaves unexplained, of course, is that *increases* in distrust were just as pronounced among the Vietnam moderates as among either hawks or doves. This again confirms the hazards one faces when inferring hypotheses about trends from cross-sectional data.

[29] This pattern of official deception was established early in the Johnson administration. In June of 1964, Johnson professed that "the United States seeks no wider war" yet two months later he ordered "the largest expansion in Washington's commitment in Vietnam since the U.S.'s first big build-up there in 1962 (*Time*, August 7, 1964:23)." Significantly, this "largest expansion" came one week *prior to* the Bay of Tonkin incident.

[30] Miller (1974) has attempted the most complete accounting of the 1964–1970 trust trend, although his contribution is flawed by confusing factors that account for distributions with factors that account for trends (see Footnote 28). He notes that distrust has always been more common among segregationists than among integrationists, but he does

One final aspect of the data that warrants mention is the relative *non*trend in political efficacy among college graduates in the 1964–1970 period. Evidence presented in Footnote 25 shows that, among college graduates, efficacy declines a mere 2.6 percentage points ($p = .28$), in contrast to the 12-point decline in the total. The college-educated trust trend, on the other hand, is quite similar to the trend shown for all other groups.[31] One possible explanation for this pattern might be that policy decisions during the period closely conformed to the preferences of the college graduates, but the data are inconsistent with this interpretation. On the contrary, "disappointments" rose *more* sharply among college graduates than among the population at large.[32] At the same time, there was no correlative decline in the group's sense of ability to influence government decisions. Perhaps we are here finally witnessing the "grand delusion," which theorists, such as Easton and Dennis, feel must characterize nearly the entire society, one prominent case in which attitudes of good will *are* impervious to the day-to-day encroachments of political reality. This would fit in with our earlier impression that consensus theory, like pluralism, best describes politics in the upper middle class.[33]

---

not control this difference for region (1974:957). Besides, as he also notes, the decline in trust was somewhat *more* pronounced among the latter (another instance in which correlational and trend explanations necessarily diverge). Another interesting finding is that persons with more extreme issue positions (measured by 1–7 scales) are also more distrustful, but this conclusion is based only on the 1970 data and is, thus, suspicious as an explanation of trends. The inability to perceive significant differences between parties was *not* related to distrust (see Chapter 8), although the "distance" between a respondent's issue position and his or her perception of the parties' positions was (1974: 965–968). We have quoted Miller's conclusions at length elsewhere; they are classics in the consensus tradition: Continued erosion of public trust would have the effect of "increasing the difficulty for leaders to make binding political decisions, as well as raising the probability of the occurence of radical political change (1974:971)."

[31] The implication of rising distrust and constant efficacy among college graduates is that more and more of them became "dissidents" during the period (see our discussion of Paige's "alienation typology," Chapter 6). According to Paige, the "dissident" pattern is associated with "radical actions aimed at changing the system." Very little "'dissidence," however, is apparent in their voting patterns for 1972: Presented with a left-wing (if not exactly "radical") alternative, about 62% of the college-educated rejected it in favor of the Republican incumbent. (Data are from the 1973 NORC General Social Survey, $n = 1504$). Here, as before, "vigilance," rather than "dissidence," seems to be the more appropriate characterization (see Chapter 6 Footnote 20).

[32] For example, the proportion of college graduates who believed that we should have stayed out of Vietnam rose 34 points from 1964 to 1970, in contrast to a 25-point rise in the total population. On the question concerning current financial situation, the college graduate decline in the proportion saying "better" was 23 points, compared to a 15-point decline in the total. Similar patterns are found on all other issues shown in Table 7.6 (Wright 1973b:313–314).

[33] The preceding discussion, in short, takes seriously the Easton–Dennis comment about "politically relevant members" (see Footnote 7). The potential role of "consensus" in restraining the college-educated upper middle class is discussed later in the chapter.

SUMMARY AND DISCUSSION

Evidence presented and discussed in this chapter has confirmed several prior findings (most of which are based on the same data) that the level of political alienation in the United States has increased sharply in the last decade. Our analysis further indicates that this trend has had political causes, that it represents the reaction of the mass public to the major sociopolitical phenomena of the era. In the remaining pages, we consider the implications of these data for consensus theory.

The first and theoretically most important implication is that attitudes of efficacy and trust are apparently *not* firmly established in early socialization, contrary to the suggestion of consensus theory. According to the theory, modern democracies face a fundamental dilemma. Given the constant scarcity of resources with respect to demands, the system perpetually harbors a group of "losers" whose allegiance to the regime is problematic. This "problem" is said to be solved, or at least alleviated, by early socialization: A reservoir of diffuse support is created; this reservoir is, in turn, thought to be independent of the day-to-day effects of political disappointment. Thus, the allegiance of the "losers" is guaranteed by their deep-seated attachment to the regime as such. Attitudes of efficacy and trust, that is, provide an attitudinal cushion upon which the system can rely when policy disappointments mount.

As the theorists themselves unhesitatingly note, the one essential characteristic of the reservoir that allows it to "protect the regime" in this fashion is its independence from political outputs (see Chapter 3). The analysis reported here, however, suggests that, on the whole, these attitudes lack this critical trait. Efficacy and trust, far from being independent of outputs, seem to be rather sensitive to them: Their level appears to rise and fall *precisely* in response to those "disappointments" against which the reservoir of diffuse support is supposed to protect the system. As such, it is difficult to see how these attitudes could, even in principle, fulfill their cushioning function, or, by implication, how political socialization in the mass contributes to the persistence of the regime. However well-inculcated these orientations may be in the early years, they can be quickly unlearned as they become discordant with the realities of adult political life.

This, of course, does not imply that there is no "unreasoning assent" shown in these data. In some sectors of the society, among college graduates in particular, the attachment to the regime has precisely these characteristics. In other parts of the social structure as well, there is undeniably a "cushion" of support which does not deflate no matter what the system's outputs are. Our quarrel with the "socialization" explanation, then, is not that it never happens; on the contrary, the data considered here belie any such claim. Rather, "it" apparently does not happen with anywhere near the frequency that the socialization texts suggest. Thus, we primarily object to the unwarranted, sweeping generalization. Socialization accounts for the nature of political attitudes, not among "members of the regime," but among *some* members, not in "the democratic citizenry," but in some empirically specifiable *part*. The next question to consider, then, is whether or not those "parts" are in themselves sufficient to guarantee the stability of the regime.

We have already discussed (in the preceding chapter) the importance to the regime of "diffuse support" in the upper and upper middle classes. So far as these classes contain the "politically relevant members," those "who count," then the stability of the regime could be said to depend, in a very real and immediate way, on their continuing allegiance and consent. In this respect, consensus theory might succeed as an account of democratic stability just as it fails as a depiction of political consciousness in the mass. Even here, however, we think there is some need for caution and more extensive, detailed research. The "unwavering assenters" in the upper middle class *may* constitute the bedrock of support for the on-going democratic regime. They may also be mere "compulsive conformers"—wedded to the status quo only because it exists and likely to "defect" in a time of genuine crisis, like the fervent Nazis who became equally fervent Communists on the day of the Soviet occupation of Berlin.[34] Thus, there is the possibility that they would "defend" an insurgent regime with equal vigor; this is perhaps especially true for a right-wing insurgency that would guarantee their position of privilege in the "new order." There is nothing in the data considered here that would rule out this possibility, although we hasten to add that there is, likewise, nothing to suggest that it is highly probable. On the contrary, these and similar data reported by Rytina and associates (Form and Huber 1969; Rytina *et al.* 1970) suggest that the upper middle class is firmly attached to the democratic ideology, believes that it is an accurate depiction of "how things work" in the United States, and, likewise, considers the current political arrangement to be "the best of all possible worlds." Thus, there is every indication that the upper middle class does provide a major locus of support for the democratic regime.

Assuming for the moment that their "diffuse support" does restrain the upper middle class from active opposition to the regime, the question may be raised about what restrains the rest of the society. Even to raise this question, however, exposes yet another of the implausible assumptions upon which consensus theory is erected—namely, that citizens, in some empirically real sense, do make demands upon their government, expect these demands to be satisfied, and are, in turn, disappointed and then driven to "corrective" mea-

---

[34] This, we expect, is especially probable for one key subgroup within the college-educated upper middle class, namely, the civil servants whose very employment can be a function of their "allegiance" to the regime. This group, presumably, would find it relatively easy to "support" any insurgency that appeared likely to "carry the day." Something of this sort appears to have characterized the German civil service during the Weimar regime. Although initially hesitant, the group easily "converted" once Hitler came to power (see Dahrendorf 1967:Ch. 15, especially pp. 246ff.).

sures when they are not satisfied. But what is the reality behind that arrow leading from the "people" to the "system" and labeled the "input of demands"? One such way to "input" a demand would be to write one's Congressman detailing a position on a policy issue. The 1968 SRC study asks, "Have you ever written to any public official giving them your opinion about something that should be done?" The proportion replying "yes" was about 19% (n = 1439). One might write a letter to the media expressing one's views and demanding action. The 1968 study also asks, "Have you ever written a letter to the editor of a newspaper or magazine giving any political opinions?" The proportion replying "yes" was just under 2% (n = 1441). One might actively work to elect candidates that shared one's special point of view. The 1968 study asks, "Did you do any work for one of the parties or candidates?" The proportion indicating that they had was about 5½% (n = 1432). One might choose to engage in informal persuasion designed to win supporters for one's chosen candidate. The 1968 study asks, "During the campaign did you talk to any people and try to show them why they should vote for one of the parties or candidates?" The proportion evidencing even this minimal "issuance of demands" was about 32% (n = 1430). One might belong to a political association that could articulate one's political interests. As Hamilton has recently argued, however, the proportion belonging to such an organization could scarcely be more than 25% (1972:34–36). There is little to be gained in belaboring the obvious: Aside from occasionally casting a vote, the immense majority engages in no other activity that even remotely resembles "issuing a demand." In other words, we could say that few lose because virtually nobody even plays. In the United States, the "game" of politics is essentially a spectator sport with no home team to root for and no opposition to jeer.[35] Theories that try to account for the allegiance of the "losers," then, suffer from the fallacy of explaining that which does not exist.

[35] To extend the analogy:

Overall, admission to the stadium is very expensive, but everyone is forced to buy a ticket. There is an assumption, moreover, that the price of admission is geared to one's ability to pay, although this, in fact, is false. There is little enthusiasm for either team, but since the price of admission has already been paid, almost everybody stays. Likewise, there is considerable confusion and misunderstanding about the rules of the game, but the players seem to understand them, and that is about all that really matters.

Little of genuine interest ever happens on the field itself. Every so often, both teams turn and face the stands, obviously anticipating a round of applause, which is politely given. Once the applause subsides, the captain of one team loudly proclaims victory and professes dedication to the "high principles" upon which the game is founded. Often, this is accompanied by outbreaks of fighting among the players of the other team. But play resumes almost immediately.

Late in the game, rumblings of discontent well up in the crowd. The spectacle on the field, some say, is not worth the price. They're changing the rules as the game proceeds, say others. The rules are unfair, shouts a third. The stands begin to empty. Far out in the right field bleachers, someone suggests that the spectators storm the field and get in on the game themselves, but this idea is greeted with little enthusiasm. There are, after all, more important things to do. The kids are home from school.

(Continued on Page 199)

The tendency to participate, of course, is not randomly distributed in the society; however measured, participation increases with social class (e.g., Verba and Nie 1972). In the upper middle class, then, it makes sense to speak of "players" and, therefore, of "losers" and to speculate on the circumstances that restrain the losers when their demands are not met. To emphasize this point, there is nothing thus far considered in this book that rules out consensus as a major source of upper middle class restraint. First, as we saw in Chapter 6, the reservoir of diffuse support is "vast" in the college-educated upper class: Even in 1970, approximately 80% of the college graduates affirmed their belief in their ability to influence the government. More importantly, this rather impressive subscription to "regime norms" was apparently unaffected by the "disconfirming" political events of the last decade. Among the upper middle class, in short, efficacy does have that one essential characteristic that allows it to "cushion" the system. Consensus theory, then, may not be false so much as misdirected: It falls short as a theory of *mass* politics, but it does apparently offer a viable account of that one group in the society whose mood and disposition might conceivably have an impact on stable democratic government.

The apparent irrelevance of the political attitudes of the majority, that is, of the *mass* public, emphasizes another important theoretical point. As we have seen, there was a rather impressive variation in the theory's independent variable from 1956 to 1970. Where, however, were the debilitating consequences that allegedly follow? Belief in one's ability to influence the government declined some 17 points in the period; trust in the government declined about 21 points. Surely, these declines should have been sufficient to trigger at least some of the hypothesized political consequences, but, on every occasion that the mass public was offered a "radical," "disruptive," or "demagogic" political choice at the national level, it was overwhelmingly rejected in favor of the moderate alternative. This would suggest considerable "slippage" in the link between alienation and behavior, a point to which we return in the following chapters.

Certainly, instances of instability and agitation were increasingly apparent in the period under consideration. Vietnam and race, together with an uncertain economy, represent the most notable examples. Likewise, it seems safe to assume that race rioters and Vietnam protestors were highly alienated from the political institutions. It is also clear that the vast majority of the politically alienated fit into neither of these categories. The protestors and dissenters were a numerically insignificant minority, whereas political alienation characterized half or more of the adult population. In our opinion, then, it would take a monumental leap of theoretical faith to assert that alienation was the *cause* of these various political disturbances. A more likely possibility, consistent with the analysis reported here, is that increasing alienation was

Supper is not yet cooked. Soon the stands are empty, but, on the field, play continues as always. Thank God, say the players, we have bravely weathered another attack.

the *effect*. Among those with the ability and inclination to act, political alienation might serve an important catalytic role, although even here alienation may be more a justificatory ideology than an independent causal force. Outside a small minority that is clearly defined by factors other than their distinct hostility to government, however, political alienation apparently counts for very little. In the mass, the politically disenchanted *respond* to events largely *not* of their own making.

Why has democratic government in the United States apparently been so unaffected by the massive decade-long withdrawal of support? One possibility, again suggested by the analysis of this chapter, is that the *character* of alienation differs from the common theoretical depiction. In the typical account, alienation is usually seen as an irrational or semi-pathological phenomenon, which is, therefore, expected to lead to equally irrational and pathological political results. As Easton and Dennis have unwittingly shown, however, many of the politically discontented, especially those from the lower social classes, have borne their alienation throughout most of their existence. Beyond that, the data reported in this chapter suggest that attitudes of efficacy (and, to a lesser extent, trust) are quite rationally adjusted to reflect on-going events in the larger society. As the federal government moves through cycles of responsiveness and nonresponsiveness, the level of powerlessness ebbs and flows accordingly. As governmental incompetence and lack of candor increase, so too does the level of political distrust. Thus, political alienation among blacks declines during the activism of the early 1960s and then increases as Johnson and Nixon retreat on equal rights; political alienation in the white South, in the early 1960s, declines among racial liberals and increases among racial conservatives; political conservatives profess increased powerlessness as the more liberal Kennedy regime comes into power; and, finally, political alienation increases sharply in response to Vietnam and a deteriorating economy. The one common feature of all these trends is their obvious sensitivity to changing realities. These data make it plain that alienation is much more a reasoned response to the politics of the day than an irrational "reaction" to modernization and the mass society. As such, it would initially seem unwise to expect that alienation will result in "dangerous" or otherwise disruptive political behaviors.

8

Alienation and Political Consciousness: Ideology and Negativism

The final element in an increasingly implausible theoretical scenario is that political consensus is necessary because it prevents behaviors that might otherwise challenge the legitimacy of the regime. For our purposes, it is convenient to consider this question in two parts: first, the relationship between political alienation and other attitudinal characteristics that allegedly facilitate "extreme" responses, especially negativism and political ideology, and second, the relationship between alienation and the "extreme" responses themselves. The former is our current concern.

We have already discussed the main political proclivities to which the alienated are supposedly prone. The theory of the mass society has provided most of these hypotheses. In response to the various "disruptions" of modern society and the attendant decline in societal cohesion, mass man becomes rootless, unattached, and politically alienated. He becomes suspicious of government and its representatives; indeed, he becomes hostile toward them. Politics is seen as the exclusive province of the stupid and corrupt; political contest is seen as a choice among lesser evils. Thus, when he votes at all, mass man votes *against* rather than for: His infrequent participation is not a positive expression of rational self-interest, but rather a negativistic attack on a system of politics that is morally repugnant. The motivations that underly his vote, in short, are qualitatively different. These various orientations—the tendency to vote against, the perception of normal politics as Tweedledum and Tweedledee, the inability to perceive important differences between established candidates and parties, the qualitatively different political motivations, and so on—constitute an all-pervasive "syndrome of negativism" which ultimately facilitates the potential mobilization of the alienated by radical demagogues. Negativism, in short, is often seen as intervening between alienation and its effects.

The precise direction these "effects" are likely to take is less clear. In neo-Marxist accounts, the direction is assumed to be toward left-wing policies aimed at radical change; in the more common mass society account, an opposite reaction is posited. In some treatments, it is said that the alienated are simply attracted to extremists, whether rightists or leftists (e.g., Kornhauser 1959:180). In the absence of compelling evidence bearing on the Marxist version,[1] we will focus on the mass society hypothesis that, for a variety of reasons, the politically alienated acquire right-wing ideological dispositions which accordingly increase their susceptibility to fascist or proto-fascist demagogues.[2]

Right-wing ideologies and pervasive negativism are, thus, two important elements of political consciousness which, in combination with the alienation that produces them, lead to potentially dangerous or disruptive political behaviors. The usual outcome, of course, is simple withdrawal: Believing that all politicians are corrupt and political choice vacuous, the alienated simple choose not to participate at all. Long periods of political abstinence, however, only increase the latent explosive potential: Hyper-charged by a history of inactivity, the politically alienated find occasional release in the extremist who promises the "quick and easy" solution to the miseries of their alienated ex-

---

[1] Although the concept of alienation in a sense originates with Marx, we have avoided any mention of Marx throughout this book, mainly because current conceptions of alienation, especially political alienation, and, therefore, the conception with which we are dealing, bears little resemblance to the concept as it arises in the Marxian theoretical corpus. In the current view, alienation is more a psychological or social-psychological state than an objective phenomenon of separation.

[2] Hypotheses to this effect have generally taken one of three forms. First is the "antigovernment" hypothesis: Resentful of federal "intrusions" into the private lives of citizens, the alienated reject "governmental solutions" and thus support policies that would weaken rather than strengthen the state; in modern times, this means that they are drawn to the right. Abcarian and Stanage (1965:789) favor this view.

A second common theme is the "restorativist" hypothesis: The alienated pine for the "old order" and thus support "restorativist" parties and programs. Speaking of the highly alienated working class youth, for example, Simon and Gagnon remark, "If he delights in the politics of George Wallace it is because these politics appear to him as a politics of restoration, restoration of an incomplete and somewhat mythic sense of the past (1970: 57)." See Rohter (1969: 226) for a similar exposition.

Finally, political alienation and anomie are often seen to be one component of a more general "syndrome of unenlightenment" which also includes anti-Semitism, hostility to outgroups, authoritarianism, and other "backward" and "regressive" political traits (e.g., Selznick and Steinberg 1969: 138ff.)

istence, in particular, the rabid rightist who will beat back the demands of blacks, Jews, students or any other convenient scapegoat and restore the entire society to some mythical and coveted prior state. In this respect, the alienated threaten the civilized constraints of the modern society and endanger the basis of stable democratic government.

Historically, this thesis has found its most persuasive example in the mass support for Hitler's National Socialist party (NSDAP) in prewar Germany. In this context, the thesis seems so immediately plausible and obvious that little is to be gained by subjecting it to careful empirical analysis. Unfortunately, the adequacy of this account of nazism is an open and, for all practical purposes, unanswerable question, since the detailed evidence necessary for its confirmation was never collected. Some of the more prominent attempts to infer conclusions on the basis of fragmentary historical evidence were reviewed in Chapter 3; as we saw, these data lend themselves to contradictory but equally plausible results. The major and inescapable hazard here has been the necessity of inferring individual characteristics from aggregated voting district data, a procedure which is fraught with well-documented peril.[3] Thus even the link between social class and Nazi support is empirically tenuous, and the link to political alienation and related matters obviously more so. The literature on the social bases of nazism, then, at best *suggests* some important hypotheses about potential mass political outbursts, but their confirmation must necessarily come from other sources.[4]

The utter plausibility and necessary ambiguity of the mass society account of nazism have had another unfortunate consequence: Subsequent compilations of negative evidence can be easily dismissed because the conditions under which it was collected invariably diverge from the social, political, and economic disruptions of Weimar Germany. Similar questions, of course, are seldom raised about supportive evidence. The drawing of bleak parallels between nazism and referenda voting are, therefore, common in the literature, whereas reasoned attempts to disprove the connection are not. This is related to the recurrent intellectual assumption that mass politics perpetually strives

---

[3] Robinson (1950) provides the earliest exposition of the "ecological fallacy." See also Goodman (1959) and Duncan and Davis (1953). A useful collection of papers discussing the issue in the specific context of political research is Dogan and Rokkan (1969).

[4] See Hamilton, *The Support for the National Socialists* (forthcoming), for an extended elaboration of these points. Due to war losses, actual voting records from the Hitler elections are fragmentary. The common theme that the lower middle class provided the bulk of the Nazi support has never been and can never be definitely examined, since neither survey data nor "pure" lower middle class voting districts can be found. As might be expected, the best records are available in the larger cities, but the Nazi support was disproportionately small town and rural. In the cities, as Hamilton shows, contrary to the usual view, the greatest Nazi voting was concentrated in the elegant upper and upper middle class areas, but conclusions about the behavior of individuals are difficult. The ability to generalize conclusively from the Nazi experience, in short, is inversely proportional to its importance.

toward the lowest common denominator: Thus, it is permissible to point to similarities between event X and the rise of fascism, but not to mention the divergences.[5] We have already noted the appeal of consensus theory to the indefinite future. The Fascist experience in Europe, likewise, is an appeal to an inadequately researched and ambiguous past.

The problem faced by researchers in attempting to explore these themes derives primarily from insufficient theoretical specification of the exact circumstances and conditions under which the hypothesized "disruptions" should occur. In some accounts, attention focuses on the "nature of the times." For example, Aberbach lists "economic dislocation, social shock caused by events like defeat in war and/or social confusion accompanied by demagogic attacks on the existing political system" as conditions which "can arouse the public susceptible to mass appeals (1969:87)." Other sources focus on the nature of the candidates and leaders themselves. Mason and Jaros, for example, suggest that "the presence of a figure who is associated with dramatic change is necessary, one who is totally dissociated from the alienating political establishment (1969:482)." Following these leads, we have chosen the year 1968 to bear the brunt of our analysis.

Given the materials at our disposal, the choice of 1968 is intuitively obvious.[6] Bitter divisiveness on Vietnam was certainly the most salient feature of the political landscape. In 1968, we were not flatly losing the war, but nor were we clearly winning it. Mass protest against American involvement and New Left violence on the campuses can be assumed to have added to the shock and social confusion. By 1968, the upward spiral of inflation had already begun; real purchasing power had been constant since 1966. As we saw

[5] A relatively rare effort to reject the "Weimar analogy" as applied to the contemporary United States appears in Draper (1972), but even here some "haunting similarities" (specifically, U.S. "defeat" in Vietnam and rising unemployment) are remarked.

[6] Despite our repeated comments about "appeals to the indefinite future," readers of an earlier version of this manuscript have pointed out that 1976 may prove a better choice still (and perhaps 1980 after that, or even 1984!) The 1976 election, after all, will closely follow the total collapse of American policy in Southeast Asia and will take place amidst a world economic crisis more severe than anything that has been witnessed since 1930. So once again, the conditions will be ripe for "mass political disruptions." (See, for example, Killian 1975, who has flatly predicted a "white national socialist America" by 1978 or 1980.)

Since history will never come to an end, these "appeals" can never be effectively countered. The Wallace experience (which we discuss in some detail in Chapter 9) is easily dismissed: The times were not quite right, the candidate was not sufficiently extremist, Nixon was an "acceptable" alternative to the latent Fascist sympathizers, and so on. All that can really be done is offer an alternative prediction, in this case, one based on some evidence, to wit: that there will *not* be a "white national socialist" America by 1980, that anything even approaching a Fascist or "extremist" candidate will be soundly trounced in 1976, and if either of these proves false (an almost infinitely remote possibility, in our view), at least that the "'politically alienated'" among the mass will have played no unique role in bringing them to fruition. (These points are elaborated later in Chapter 10.)

in the preceding chapter, the public had grown increasingly pessimistic about the course of the American economy, which provides some measure of their "economic dislocation." In addition, 1968 was preceded by the traumatic summer of 1967 with race riots in most major American cities. The rumbling of tanks and armored personnel carriers in the streets of Detroit could scarcely have been a pacifying vision. Finally, the political situation was not exactly calm as of 1968. One popular presidential contender had been assassinated. Both national party conventions were armed camps. The Democratic convention of 1968 was an especially visible symbol of all that had "gone wrong" in America. Add to all this a rising crime rate, permissiveness, drugs, public sex, and similar symbolic degradations of common values, and the result is a social and political situation which at least approximates the conditions specified in various mass society accounts.[7]

The appeal of 1968 for our purposes is greatly increased by the presence on the scene of a radical demagogic candidate to mobilize the discontent and channel it politically. First, Wallace provided public and "charismatic" articulation of the various negativistic orientations; tweedledum and tweedledee lay at the heart of his appeal. Speaking of national politicians, Wallace once remarked, "You can put them all in a sack and shake 'em up and it won't make any difference which comes out first 'cause they're all alike' (quoted in Sherrill 1968:352)." Second, there can be little doubt that Wallace was "associated with dramatic change" or that he was "totally dissociated" from the political establishment. His third party candidacy even spared his alienated supporters the embarrassment of pulling a party lever. Thus, both the candidate and the times themselves make 1968 an especially appropriate context in which to investigate the mass society themes.

ALIENATION AND IDEOLOGY

We have already come across compelling reasons to doubt the hypothesis that the politically alienated will be disproportionately drawn to extreme right-wing political programs. Their even dispersion between parties raises an initial suspicion. The distinct possibility that alienation is rooted more in class political cultures than in the disruptions of the mass society increases our doubts. Finally, the analysis of trends strongly suggests that ideological preferences and, more particularly, their relationship to actual public policy determines the level of alienation, rather than the reverse. Thus, during the

---

[7] How good an approximation 1968 provides is obviously an open question. From the available theoretical accounts, we conclude that the approximation is fairly good, but we are also quick to admit that the situation in 1968 in the United States was far short of the crises in late Weimar Germany (see Draper 1972). So we are forced once again into the "logic of limiting cases." The social and political circumstances surrounding the 1968 election, that is, may be taken as conditions under which the latent explosive potential of the alienated will apparently *not* be realized.

conservative reign of Eisenhower, liberals were more alienated than conservatives; as federal power changed hands, the relationship was attenuated or reversed. This suggests that ideology, rather than alienation, is the genuine independent variable.

A more direct test of the "alienation–ideology" hypothesis is afforded by a long series of political attitude items contained in the 1968 survey.[8] These

[8] The items are as follows:

1. Some people think the government in Washington should help towns and cities provide education for grade and high school children; others think this should be handled by the states and local communities. Have you been interested enough in this to favor one side over the other? If yes, which are you in favor of? (Code: "getting help from government" = 0; "handling it at the state and local level" = 1; all others = missing data.)

2. Some people are afraid the government in Washington is getting too powerful for the good of the country and the individual person. Others feel that the government is not getting too strong for the good of the country. Have you been interested enough in this to favor one side over the other? If yes, what are your feelings? (Code: "government is too strong" = 0; "not too strong" = 1; all others = missing data.)

3. Some say the government in Washington ought to help people get doctors and hospital care at low cost; others say the government should not get into this. Have you been interested? (Code: "help people get doctors" = 0; "stay out of this" = 1; all others = missing data.)

4. In general, some people feel that the government in Washington should see to it that every person has a job and a good standard of living. Others think the government should just let each person get ahead on his own. Have you been interested? (Code: "see to it" = 0; "let each person get ahead on his own" = 1; all others = missing data.)

5. Some people feel that if Negroes are not getting fair treatment in jobs, the government should see to it that they do. Others feel this is not the federal government's business. Have you been interested? (Code: "see to it" = 0; "not the government's business" = 1; all others = missing data.)

6. Some people say that the government in Washington should see to it that white and Negro children are allowed to go the same schools. Others claim that this is not the government's business. Have you been interested? (Code: "see to it" = 0; "not the government's business" = 1; all others = missing data.)

7. As you may know, Congress passed a bill that says that Negroes should have the right to go to any hotel or restaurant they can afford, just like anybody else. Some people feel that this is something the government in Washington should support. Others feel that the government should stay out of this matter. Have you been interested? (Code: "go to any hotel or restaurant" = 0; "stay out of this" = 1; all others = missing data.)

8. Which of these statements would you agree with: White people have a right to keep Negroes out of their neighborhoods if they want to (= 0). Negroes have a right to live wherever they can afford, just like anybody else (= 1).

9. Some people say that we should give aid to other countries if they need help, while others think each country should make its own way as best it can. Have you been interested? (Code: "give aid" = 0; "make its own way" = 1; all others = missing data.)

10. Some people think it is all right for our government to sit down and talk to the leaders of the communist countries and try to settle our differences, while others think we should refuse to have anything to do with them. Have you been interested? (Code: "sit down" = 0; "refuse" = 1; all others = missing data.)

11. Some people say that our farmers and businessmen should be able to do business

items tap opinion on a variety of issues and political principles: race, medi-care, guaranteed jobs, integration, foreign aid, relations with Communist countries, Vietnam, and so on. Factor analysis of 17 of these items produced four factors or "dimensions," of which three were both interpretable and theoretically meaningful. Summated scaling of the items involved gives us measures of three ideological components: classic "liberalism–conservatism," a dimension of "isolationism–internationalism," and, finally, a distinct "anti-communism" dimension.[9] The correlations between these three variables and the measures of alienation are shown in Table 8.1.

---

with communist countries as long as the goods are not used for military purposes; others say that our government should not allow Americans to trade with the communist countries. Have you been interested? (Code: "be allowed" = 0; "not allowed" = 1; all others = missing data.)

12. Do you think we did the right thing by getting into the fighting in Vietnam or should we have stayed out? (Code: "did right" = 0; "should have stayed out" = 1; all others = missing data.)

13. Which of the following do you think we should do now in Vietnam—pull out of Vietnam entirely (=0), keep our soldiers in Vietnam but try to end the fighting (=0), or take a stronger stand even if it means invading North Vietnam (= 1).

14. Would you say that in the past year or so the United States has done pretty well in dealing with foreign countries, or would you say that we haven't been doing as well as we should? (Code: "pretty well" = 1; "procon" = 2; "not too well"= 3; all others = missing data.)

15. Would you say that in the past year or so our position in the world has become stronger (= 1), less strong (= 3), or stayed about the same (= 2)?

16. How about the chances of our country getting into a bigger war? Compared to a few years ago, do you think we are more likely (=3), less likely (=1), or have about the same chances (=2) of getting into a bigger war?

17. The country would be better off if we just stayed home and did not concern our-selves with problems in other parts of the world. (Code: agree = 0; disagree = 1; all others = missing data.)

In order to reduce the sheer bulk of information, these 17 items were factor analyzed (principle components, Varimax rotation) to uncover the main ideological dimensions being measured (Wright 1973b:338ff.). Items 1–7 listed above represented the first and most important factor and clearly measure the standard "liberalism–conservatism" dimen-sion. Items 9, 12, and 17 emerged as the second factor and clearly represent an "isola-tionism–internationalism" dimension. Items 14 and 15 loaded highly on a third factor but lent themselves to no theoretically important interpretation. Thus, the factor was dropped. Finally, items 10 and 11, and 13 constituted a fourth "anti-communism" factor. The 4 factors reproduced 48.1% of the total item variance. (Items 8 and 16, by the way, loaded highly on no factor and were, therefore, also dropped.)

[9] The scaling was as follows:

"Liberalism–conservatism" ranges from 0 to 7, depending on the number of conserva-tive responses to the first 7 items shown in Footnote 8. Missing data were kept and assigned a scale value on the basis of available information, unless the respondent had answered two or fewer of the seven items, in which case he or she was dropped.

"Isolationism–internationalism" and the "anti–Communism" scales both range from

Overall, these data show some modest support for the "alienated more conservative" hypothesis. Of the six correlations, one is insignificant (efficacy by liberalism), one is pronounced (efficacy by isolationism), and the remaining four are moderate. All are in the predicted direction.

On the other hand, there are features of the data that seem to be clearly inconsistent with the mass society view. For example, the low trust group is clearly the most conservative, but less than half of them fell at the low end of the conservatism scale, with the majority about evenly divided between liberal and moderate categories. Likewise, the low trust group was by far the most anti-Communist, but about three-fifths of the group rejected the anti-Communist position. So, despite the general direction of association, there is clearly no monolithic tendency for the alienated to subscribe to a particular ideological predisposition. The closest one comes to a conservative ideological monolith is the 60–40 split among the least efficacious on the isolationism dimension. Thus, while it is clear that the alienated are generally more conservative, more isolationist, and more anti-Communist than the population as a whole, it is equally apparent that they are also sharply divided among themselves on each of these ideological dimensions.

This poses something of an analytic problem that will recur later, namely, whether data such as that reported in Table 8.1 should count for or against the hypothesis. On the one hand, the theory seems to predict the general tendencies revealed in the data; at the same time, it fails to account for the clear majority of the target group. We prefer, of course, to emphasize those aspects of the evidence that contradict the received account, such as the obvious dispersion of alienated persons among ideologies, rather than the moderate correlations shown in the table. We are reinforced in this by our belief that "statistically different from zero" is *not* sufficient to confirm hypotheses about wholesale political disruptions which leave entire political systems reeling in their wake. Thus, here as elsewhere in the analysis, we shall raise two related questions: first, a question about the general tendencies, and second, a question of whether or not the majority of alienated persons conform to the theoretical description.

In this context, the most striking feature of the data is the clear lack of ideological consensus among the politically discontented. In other words, they are about evenly divided on the major ideological issues of the day. The problems that this might pose for their common mobilization are reasonably obvious: A hard-line rightist demagogue, for example, would find proportionately more supporters among the alienated than among nonalienated,

---

1 to 4. Missing data were again kept if the respondent answered at least two of the three items in each case; otherwise they were dropped.

Most of the tables in this chapter employ a three-category alienation index. For efficacy, "low" = 1 or 2 on the full 5-point scale (see Chapter 4), "medium" = 3, and "high" = 4 or 5. For trust, "low" = 1, 2, or 3, "medium" = 4, and "high" = 5 or 6.

TABLE 8.1
Alienation by Ideology: 1968

	Efficacy				Trust		
	Low	Medium	High	Total	Low	Medium	High
Liberalism							
Low (5-7)	40.2	40.6	37.7	40.6	48.5	39.8	31.2
Medium (3-4)	22.9	18.8	27.7	23.3	24.8	21.4	24.5
High (0-2)	36.9	40.6	34.6	36.0	26.7	38.8	44.4
Total	100.0	100.0	100.0	100.0	100.0	100.0	100.1
N	555	276	483	1517	472	327	507
gamma	.003				.233		
Isolationism							
High (3-4)	60.2	45.3	26.8	48.5	55.0	44.1	35.9
Low (1-2)	39.8	54.7	73.2	51.5	45.0	55.9	64.1
Total	100.0	100.0	100.0	100.0	100.0	100.0	100.0
N	565	276	488	1526	478	322	512
gamma	.475				.272		
Anti-communism							
High (3-4)	37.5	33.8	29.1	34.1	40.3	33.8	27.3
Low (1-2)	62.5	66.2	70.9	65.9	59.7	66.2	72.7
Total	100.0	100.0	100.0	100.0	100.0	100.0	100.0
N	547	275	481	1509	471	322	501
gamma	.138				.206		

but even among the most alienated, he would apparently be opposed by 50–60%.[10] Given the degree of ideological dispersion, the possibility of their reacting as a group to any single political stimulus is necessarily remote. Thus, even their *potential* dangers to democratic political institutions are sharply diminished by these results.[11]

[10] This, of course, again assumes that there will only be one "extremist" on the scene trying to gain their affections (see Chapter 6, Footnote 51). Obviously, if both left extremists and right extremists were simultaneously active, each might expect some limited support from various elements within the ranks of "the" politically alienated. Yet even here, much caution is necessary. As we show in the next chapter, the disdain felt by "the" politically alienated for any sort of radical or unconventional political tactic is somewhat *more* pronounced than that felt by the nonalienated segment of the population. (On ideological "extremism," see also Footnote 11.)

[11] The possibility that the alienated are drawn to extreme positions of either the right or left was examined by taking respondents who scored only at the extreme ends (0 or 7) of the liberalism–conservatism scale. Data are as follows:

	Efficacy				
	(Low) 1	2	3	4	5 (High)
Extreme liberal	19.2	18.0	14.1	16.2	15.0
Extreme conservative	12.2	13.0	12.0	11.7	14.0
Total extreme	31.4	31.0	26.1	27.9	29.0
All other	68.6	69.0	73.9	72.1	71.0
Percentage	100.0	100.0	100.0	100.0	100.0
n	271	284	276	290	193

	Trust					
	(Low) 1	2	3	4	5	6 (High)
Extreme liberal	10.2	10.3	13.4	15.6	20.8	22.5
Extreme conservative	21.4	13.9	15.3	11.6	9.0	11.0
Total extreme	31.6	24.2	28.7	27.2	29.8	33.5
All other	69.4	75.8	71.3	72.8	70.2	66.5
Percentage	100.0	100.0	100.0	100.0	100.0	100.0
n	98	165	209	327	289	218

The data do not support the expectation. For efficacy, the proportion "extremist" declines from 31.4% among the least efficacious to 29.0% among the most efficacious; the difference has neither substantive nor statistical significance ($p = .219$). Similar results obtain for trust.

The possibility that the "alienation–ideology" link is stronger for some social groups than for others was also examined by computing correlations within racial, regional, and social class categories. The racial and regional controls uncovered nothing of substantive interest. A weak correlation between powerlessness and conservatism emerged only in the marginal middle class; in the working and upper middle classes, efficacy and conservatism were again unrelated. The distrustful, on the other hand, were significantly more conservative than the trustful in all class contexts, but the correlation was strongest in the upper middle class (gamma = .313) and weakest among workers (gamma = .226). This suggests that the combination of low trust and high status leads to especially conservative political preferences, which is consistent with evidence on the Goldwater vote discussed in the next chapter. (See Wright 1973b:347–349.)

ALIENATION AND NEGATIVISM[12]

In addition to the presumed attraction to "backward" ideologies, the resolute negativism of the alienated is also often said to increase their susceptibility to demagogic appeals. Available evidence allows us to explore four components of the negativism syndrome: the tendency to vote against, the alleged hostility to all politicians, the inability to perceive important differences between parties and candidates, and the hypothesis that the motivations which undergird the participation of the alienated are of a qualitatively different sort.

Four items from the 1960 survey[13] and one question from the 1964 survey bear directly on the "voting against" hypothesis. These items and their relationship with political alienation are shown in Table 8.2. Unlike the ideology results, there is no ambiguity in these data: They are flatly inconsistent with the negativism thesis.

The most directly relevant item asks whether the respondent's intended vote will be "for" his professed candidate or "against" the opposition. Approximately three-fourths of the most alienated respondents affirmed that they would be voting "for," as compared with 82% of the total population. An identical question asked of voters only in the postelection wave found nearly 90% of the most alienated respondents saying they had voted "for." Similarly, about 70% of the highly alienated respondents said that it was "a lot better" to have voted for their candidate, with a mere 9% confessing that it did not make much difference. Comparable figures for the total were 72% and 6%, respectively. Finally, the large majority of alienated voters (80%) said they cared "a great deal" about voting in the election. In 1960, then, immense majorities of alienated and unalienated alike became sufficiently attached to a candidate to vote "for" him rather than against his opponent, to feel that a vote for one's candidate was "a lot better" than a vote for the opponent, and to care a great deal about actually casting the vote. In all these regards, the politically alienated are essentially indistinguishable from the rest of the population.[14]

---

[12] The findings reported in this section appear elsewhere in our paper, "Alienation and political negativism: new evidence from national surveys," *Sociology and Social Research* 60:2 (January, 1976), and are reprinted here by permission of the publisher.

[13] Genuine issue differences between candidates were probably less pronounced in the 1960 presidential election than in any election since. The 1964 contest, on the other hand, is properly remembered as the "Choice, not an Echo" campaign. Thus, the two elections provide contrasting circumstances in which to investigate the "voting against" hypothesis. Please recall that the 1960 survey does not contain the political trust items.

[14] A methodological issue that can now be discussed is whether or not these and similar negativism measures are valid, whether or not, in short, the alienated are kept from expressing their "true" feelings by the demand characteristics of the interview situation. Two points are worth mentioning:
First, demand characteristics did *not* prevent clear majorities from affirming that

TABLE 8.2
Political Alienation and the Tendency to Vote Against

	Efficacy[a]			
	Low	Medium	High	Total

(1960) Would you say that you are voting mainly for (respondent's chosen candidate) or that you are voting mainly against (the opponent)? (Non-voters were asked: If you were going to vote, would you be voting mainly for...)

	Low	Medium	High	Total
For	75.5	84.2	83.5	81.8
Both	0.8	1.5	0.6	1.0
Against	23.7	14.3	15.9	17.2
Total	100.0	100.0	100.0	100.0
N	376	520	673	1569
gamma = -.14				

(1960) (Asked of voters only) When you voted for (respondent's candidate), did you feel that you were voting mainly for (your candidate) or against (the opponent)?

	Low	Medium	High	Total
For	87.7	87.5	85.6	86.7
Both	2.1	1.1	2.9	2.1
Against	10.3	11.4	11.5	11.2
Total	100.0	100.0	100.0	100.0
N	293	449	661	1403
gamma = +.06				

(1960) (Asked of voters only) When you voted for President in this election, did you feel that it was a lot better to vote for (your candidate), somewhat better, or that it didn't make much difference which one you voted for?

	Low	Medium	High	Total
A lot	70.5	77.4	68.5	71.8
Somewhat	20.5	18.8	24.7	21.9
Not much	9.0	3.8	6.8	6.3
Total	100.0	100.0	100.0	100.0
N	298	542	660	1410
gamma = +.07				

(1960) (Asked of voters only) Would you say that you cared a great deal whether or not you voted, cared somewhat, or didn't care too much this time?

	Low	Medium	High	Total
A lot	80.2	87.1	94.9	89.3
Somewhat	12.8	11.0	4.7	8.4
Not much	7.0	2.0	0.4	2.3
Total	100.0	100.1	100.0	100.0
N	298	456	665	1419
gamma = -.47				

TABLE 8.2 (continued)

	Low	Medium	High	Total
			Efficacy	

(1964) (Asked in the pre-election wave just after the item eliciting respondent's vote intention) Would you say that you are voting mainly <u>for</u> (your candidate) or that you are voting mainly <u>against</u> (the opposition)? (Non-voters were asked: If you were going to vote, would you be voting mainly <u>for</u>...)

	Low	Medium	High	Total
For	71.5	68.1	62.8	67.4
Both	1.1	3.0	4.8	2.9
Against	27.5	27.0	32.4	29.6
Total	100.1	100.1	100.0	99.9
N	473	404	459	1336
gamma = +.12				

			Trust	
For	65.0	64.3	69.7	67.4
Both	2.2	4.5	2.8	2.9
Against	32.8	31.2	27.5	29.6
Total	100.0	100.0	100.0	99.9
N	320	244	683	1274
gamma = -.09				

a. The efficacy and trust scales are collapsed into categories on the basis of criteria noted in footnote 8.

The one item from the 1964 election shows basically the same pattern: The tendency to vote "against" was unrelated either to efficacy or trust. As in 1960, about two-thirds of all groups, regardless of alienation, voted "for" their candidate rather than "against" the opponent. In neither year does one encounter evidence of the presumed negativism that infects the alienated "whenever and wherever they enter politics (Horton and Thompson 1962: 487)."

"voting is the only way that people like me can have a say" or that "sometimes politics and government seem so complicated that people like me can't really understand what's going on." Nor did they prevent large minorities from affirming that the government wastes a lot of tax money, that it is run by a few big interests, and that the people who run it can only be trusted "some of the time." It would be an odd "demand characteristic" that allowed people to express their alienation but somehow prevented them from expressing attitudes thought to be closely related to it.

Second, if the "negativism" to which the alienated are prone is so "soft" that it can be suppressed by an SRC interviewer, then how could it possibly pose a threat to stable democratic government? As the theory tells it, the alienated are literally champing at the bit to register their disgust. Why they would be prevented from doing so by the fact of their being interviewed is somewhat mysterious.

Additional analysis controlling for candidate preference uncovered nothing to alter this conclusion (Wright 1973b:365–367). Overall, there was a minor tendency for Nixon voters to have been voting "against" Kennedy (14.2%) more frequently than Kennedy voters voted "against" Nixon (7.5%), but alienation and the tendency to vote against were unrelated among supporters of either candidate. Likewise, voting "against" was somewhat more common in 1964 than in 1960 but again unrelated to alienation among both Johnson and Goldwater supporters. Additional controls for region, race, social class and political ideology failed to uncover a single group wherein the prediction was consistently supported. In sum, political alienation and the tendency to vote "against" are simply not related.

A second element in the negativism syndrome is pervasive hostility to all politicians. The 1972 survey contains information bearing on this hypothesis. Respondents were shown a "feeling thermometer" and then told that it is used to "get your feelings toward some possible candidates for president or vice-president." The interviewer then explained that "warm or favorable" feelings were to be indicated by a measure of 51° or more, unfavorable feelings by 49° or less, and so-so feelings to be placed at the 50° mark. In the 1972 survey, the respondent was then asked to evaluate 14 politicians. Of these, we have dropped 5 due to missing data (Lindsay, Jackson, Chisholm, Ashbrook, and McCloskey). For the remainder, responses were arbitrarily divided into "negative" and nonnegative evaluations, with 40° as the criterion. Table 8.3 presents the results of this analysis. Cell entries are percentage differences between alienated and unalienated respondents in the proportions rating each politician negatively. Data are presented with social class and political ideology controlled for.[15]

With some significant exceptions to be discussed later, the overall pattern does not support the negativism thesis. In all, 108 tests of the hypothesis are reported in the table (6 class-by-ideology groups by 9 politicians by 2 measures of alienation). Taking a percentage difference of ±10 as the minimum difference worth calling a difference, the alienated are *more* negativistic in 15 cases, *less* negativistic in another 15 cases, with no significant difference shown for the remaining 78 cases. Averaged across all 108 tests, the average percentage difference is −.02. The hostility that the alienated feel toward politicans, in short, is considerably less than "pervasive."

The data again reveal interesting differences between the inefficacious and the distrustful. In the 54 efficacy comparisons, the alienated were more negativistic only once, less negativistic in 9 comparisons, with essentially no difference shown in the remainder. The inefficacious, then, are marginally

---

[15] Social class and ideology are controlled for because both are related to these candidate assessments. Data are for nonfarm respondents only. Ideology is measured by a self-rated "liberalism–conservatism" scale. In order to maximize cell sizes, comparisons shown in the table are between the highly alienated as defined throughout this book and the remainder.

Percentage Differences between Low and High Alienation Groups in their Affective Assessment of Nine Politicians, Controlled for Political Ideology and Social Class: 1972

	Working Class			Middle Class			$\bar{X}^b$
	Liberal	Moderate	Conservative	Liberal	Moderate	Conservative	
				Efficacy			
Wallace	$-.02^a$	+.08	+.01	-.01	+.03	+.15	+.04
McGovern	+.05	+.15	+.16	+.07	+.12	+.15	+.12
Nixon	-.01	-.07	-.02	-.04	-.05	-.11	-.05
Muskie	-.07	-.05	-.03	+.08	-.01	-.09	-.03
Kennedy	+.08	-.08	+.08	-.02	+.18	+.12	+.06
Eagleton	+.08	-.09	-.02	+.07	-.02	+.09	+.02
Humphrey	+.02	-.05	+.03	.00	+.04	-.01	.00
Agnew	-.04	-.03	-.08	-.05	-.06	-.05	-.05
Shriver	+.02	-.07	-.02	+.05	+.09	+.16	+.04
$\bar{X}$	$+.01^c$	-.02	+.01	+.02	+.04	+.05	+.02
				Trust			
Wallace	-.12	+.01	+.01	-.02	.00	+.12	.00
McGovern	+.14	+.14	+.01	+.15	+.12	+.04	+.10
Nixon	-.17	-.13	-.05	-.26	-.17	-.12	-.15
Muskie	-.07	-.06	-.03	-.02	+.04	-.06	-.02
Kennedy	-.04	-.10	-.08	-.01	+.10	-.08	-.04
Eagleton	-.02	-.01	+.01	+.04	+.04	-.07	-.01
Humphrey	+.01	-.03	-.10	+.04	-.04	-.12	-.04
Agnew	-.26	-.18	-.08	-.18	-.21	-.05	-.16
Shriver	-.02	-.07	-.09	-.01	+.01	-.05	-.04
$\bar{X}$	-.06	-.05	-.06	-.05	-.01	-.04	-.04

a. For example, this cell shows that the difference between high and low alienation working class liberals in the proportion rating Wallace negativistically was two percentage points, with the high alienation group the most negative. (Thus, negative entries support the hypothesis; positive entries contradict it.)

b. Percentage differences summed across rows and divided by 6.

c. Percentage differences summed down columns and divided by 9.

less likely than the efficacious to be negativistic toward politicians. This same marginal distinctiveness is also apparent on the trust results, but the direction of the relationship is reversed: For trust, the data show 14 cases in which the alienated were more negativistic, 6 cases in which they were less negativistic, and no difference for the remaining 34 cases. Even for trust, the average difference in support of the hypothesis amounts to about 4 percentage points. If the concept of "all politicians" is adequately reflected by the nine chosen for this analysis, the alienated are not pervasively hostile toward them.

Interestingly, exception to the pattern comes on three of the four contenders for national office in 1972. Focusing first on the Democratic challenger, George McGovern, the data show that both the inefficacious and the distrustful were *less* likely to evaluate him negatively than their nonalienated counterparts; the differences are 12 and 10 points respectively. The corrollary is that the politically alienated were *more* negativistic in their ratings of Richard Nixon and Spiro Agnew, although here the differences for efficacy are not significant.

In the absence of other evidence, there is an initial temptation to suggest that the alienated are marginally hostile to incumbents and sympathetic to underdogs. On the other hand, and despite their incumbency status, it would be hard to argue that Nixon and Agnew were any more "symbolic" of the despised establishment than, say Hubert Humphrey, Edmund Muskie, or Sargent Shriver. Moreover, the obvious underdog status of George Wallace did little to increase his attractiveness to the alienated sectors, despite the common hypothesis that candidacies such as Wallace's should hold a "special" attraction for them (see Chapter 9). Another possibility, equally consistent with the evidence, is that the alienated in 1972 had a remarkably prescient vision of things to come, that theirs was a "true" consciousness whose wisdom was confirmed by subsequent events.[16]

In any case, the broad pattern of these data again fails to conform to the negativism hypothesis. If there is a tendency for the alienated to be "hostile" to politicians, it is by no means a diffuse hostility directed against all politicians in equal parts. In short, the alienated are not sufficiently distinct in this regard to justify the alarmist mass society views.

A third often mentioned element in the negativism syndrome concerns the alleged inability of the politically alienated to discern any difference between the establishment political parties. Most issue questions in the SRC surveys

---

[16] This suggests the possibility of treating the alienation variables as perceptual filters through which information about politics must pass. The "nonalienation" filter, it would appear, represents a rather formidable screen against undesirable information. At least, it would seem to nurture false optimism. The alienated, on the other hand, apparently do not suffer from such afflictions. Their basic skepticism concerning things political, far from the quasi-pathological state depicted in mass society accounts, would seem to be more realism than *Angst*. Their "alienation," we expect, will serve them well in the post-Watergate era.

are followed by an item asking which political party "comes closest to what you want" on the particular issue. In the 1968 survey, for example, the follow-up was appended to 12 questions.[17] In each case, one alternative was, "Or wouldn't there be any difference between them on this." There was an additional group who volunteered that "Wallace would do what I want." Persons responding in either of these ways constitute the "no difference" group; those responding either Democrats or Republicans constitute those who saw, on that issue, some difference between the parties. The correlations between this dichotomous variable and the trichotomous indices of efficacy and trust for the 12 issue areas are reported in Table 8.4. Negative correlations support the tweedledum and tweedledee thesis.

Taking a correlation of ±.10 as the minimum significant correlation, the hypothesis is supported in 6 out of 24 tests. The largest supportive correlation is −.22; this corresponds to a percentage difference of 14.5 points (data not shown). The average correlation across these 24 tests is a trivial −.04; for efficacy it is −.08; and for trust it is −.00. Generally speaking, in short, political

TABLE 8.4
Correlations (gamma) between Political Alienation and the Ability to Perceive Difference between the Political Parties: 1968

	Efficacy	Trust	N^a
1. Federal aid to education	-.22	-.01	965
2. Too much government power	-.16	+.07	897
3. Medicare	-.12	-.02	996
4. Guaranteed standard of living	-.10	+.03	1063
5. Jobs for blacks	-.04	-.01	1081
6. School integration	-.04	-.05	1087
7. Integrated public facilities	+.01	+.01	1090
8. Foreign aid	-.08	-.02	1072
9. Talk with Communists	+.11	-.02	1084
10. Trade with Communists	-.08	-.01	832
11. Escalate in Vietnam	-.11	+.01	1110
12. Bigger war likely	-.11	-.01	1172

a. N's vary because missing data were omitted on an item-by-item basis.

[17] The twelve questions are Items 1, 2, 3, 4, 5, 6, 7, 9, 10, 11, 13, and 16, as listed earlier in Footnote 8.

alienation and the inability to perceive differences between the parties are not significantly associated (see also Miller 1974). Replication of these procedures on nine items from the 1964 survey turned up similar results; with .10 as the minimum correlation of significance, the hypothesis was supported in 4 out of 18 tests (Wright 1973b:375–376). Additional controls, in both 1964 and 1968, for region, race, social class, and political ideology (data not shown) failed to isolate any group in which the hypothesis was consistently supported.[18]

The persistent nondifference between alienated and unalienated in the several issues considered thus far make us wonder whether or not the political motives of the discontented differ in any significant way from those of the rest of the population. In the typical account, the alienated vote only to register a protest, to say "NO" to the on-going arrangements; thus, their vote "does not represent an organized class conscious opposition, but a type of mass protest, a convergence of the individual assessments of the powerless who have projected into available symbols the fears and suspicions growing out of their alienated existence (Horton and Thompson 1962:485)."

Three decades of voting research have given a fair indication of the kinds of factors that "constrain" the votes of normal, nonalienated populations; party affiliation, political ideology, social class, region, sex, race, and age are by far the most important factors. A strong implication of the Horton–Thompson thesis is that variables such as these (which represent either political interests, political traditions, or factors related to them) have relatively less "hold" on the votes of the alienated than among nonalienated groups. That is, if the very *character* of voting among the discontented is qualitatively different, then the "usual" background factors should be proportionately less successful in predicting the alienated vote. On the other hand, if the alienated and nonalienated differ very little in political motivation, the group of variables just mentioned should have equal predictive capacity among all groups.

Table 8.5 summarizes the results of a series of regression analyses performed on the 1968 data. The dependent variables are dummy variables expressing Humphrey, Nixon, and Wallace voters, respectively. Independent variables are those already mentioned: party identification, the three indices of political ideology discussed earlier in the chapter, four measures of social class (education, occupation, income, and class identification), region, sex, race, and age.[19] Each equation was run separately within the six efficacy and

---

[18] The single exception was that alienated white southerners in 1968 were less likely to see differences between the parties than their nonalienated regional counterparts. (The average correlation of alienation and "seeing no difference" was −.155 among white southerners in 1968 as compared to +.01 among nonsoutherners.) This exception is discussed in Wright (1973b: 375–378).

[19] Coding employed in these regressions was as follows:

Region: 1 = South; 0 = non-South.

Political ideology was represented by the three dimensions of ideology developed and discussed in the text.   (Continued on Page 219)

TABLE 8.5

Multiple R^2 of the Regression of 1968 Vote on Selected Background Variables, with Political Alienation as Covariate: 1968

	Efficacy			Trust		
	Low	Medium	High	Low	Medium	High
Humphrey Vote						
R^2	.25	.32	.39	.29	.31	.30
N	570	278	486	479	333	511
Nixon Vote						
R^2	.26	.39	.32	.29	.33	.32
N	570	278	486	479	333	511
Wallace Vote						
R^2	.11	.15	.08	.15	.09	.00
N	570	278	486	479	333	511

trust categories (collapsed as in Footnote 8). Multiple R^2 for each of the six equations is reported as a summary measure of "constraint." The "differential motivations" hypothesis is supported when R^2 (the summed ability of the independent variables to explain variation in the dependent variable) increases as alienation declines.

Once again, the data fail to support the hypothesis. In six tests, the predicted pattern occurs only once (efficacy by Humphrey). In one case, the pattern is the exact reverse (trust by Wallace); in two cases, there is mild curvilinearity (efficacy by Nixon, efficacy by Wallace); and, in the remaining two cases, there is no pattern whatsoever. Comparisons of regression coefficients across alienation categories (data are not shown) revealed a slight tendency for region, race, and social class to be *better* predictors among the

---

Party identification was represented by dummy variables for Democratic and Republican identification, respectively.

Age is coded as number of years. Missing data were assigned to the mean.

Sex: 1 = male; 0 = female.

Race: 1 = nonwhite; 0 = white.

Education: 1 = less than eighth; 2 = less than twelfth; 3 = high school graduate; 4 = some college; 5 = college graduate.

Occupation: 1 = professional, technical, and so on; 2 = managers, officials, and so on; 3 = clerical and sales; 4 = skilled workers; 5 = semi-skilled workers; 6 = unskilled and service; 7 = farm.

Income: 1 = less than $2000; 2 = $2000–$2999; 3 = $3000–$3999; 4 = $4000–$4999; 5 = $5000–$5999; 6 = $6000–$7999; 7 = $8000–$9999; 8 = $10,000–$14,999; 9 = $15,000+.

Class identification: 1 = working class; 2 = middle class.

For all SES measures, missing data were assigned to the mean.

alienated, but the differences were not sufficiently large to support a substantive conclusion. The best that can be concluded on the basis of these data is that, when the alienated bother to vote at all, the factors that underlie their votes are essentially indistinguishable from those of the rest of the population.

SUMMARY AND DISCUSSION

At the heart of political alienation theory stands the supposition that "the politically alienated form the core of the disenchanted in a mass society. They are ripe for the appeals of demagogues who seek an undemocratic political and social order (Watson and Tarr 1964:507)." Hypothesized factors that facilitate this "appeal" include primarily an alleged common attraction to "backward," "reactionary," or "undemocratic" political ideologies and, in addition, a presumed bitter negativism directed toward the existing political institutions. Evidence presented here casts considerable doubt on both these linkages: In matters of political ideology, the alienated are marginally distinct from the rest of the population and, more importantly, deeply split among themselves; likewise, they are no more likely to vote "against," no more "hostile" to all politicians, no less able to discern policy differences between the major parties, and no less likely to vote according to party, ideology, or social class "interests" than are the "normal," nonalienated sectors. In sum, the politically alienated, as a group, lack the crucial potentiating traits that might otherwise facilitate the demagogic appeal.

The "negativism of the alienated," of course, is perhaps the most common theme in the political alienation literature; at first glance, then, the nonsupportive evidence presented here seems to subvert its own credibility. As we saw in our review of this literature in the third chapter, however, a convincing empirical demonstration of the "negativism–alienation" linkage has yet to be produced. The most frequently cited supportive studies are small, local, and typically contain no independent measure of negativism. In the many local referenda studies, the simple act of voting "no" is often used as the negativism indicator. No nationally representative study exists. The results presented in this chapter, then, do not contradict the unanimous findings of a well-defined and methodologically compelling research literature. Rather, they contradict a common assumption that has, for all practical purposes, never been empirically examined.

Several of the findings from the previous chapters help to explain the lack of a common ideology or a resolute negativism among the powerless and politically distrustful. First, the alienated are drawn from diverse and ideologically distinct groups: for example, blacks and southern whites, Democrats and Republicans, Protestants and Catholics, and so on. The generally weak correlation of political alienation with the usual background variables means that they lack those common social circumstances or political traditions which might otherwise culminate in a well-defined and cohesive group ideology. Second, the assumption that alienation leads to radical rightist political leanings depends on a conception of alienation that is not tenable in light of our results. The assumption, of course, is that alienation is fundamentally rooted in the disjuncture between an unholy present and the more pleasant past. Hungering anxiously for the prior existence, the alienated support political movements that promise the elusive "restoration." The many "disruptions" of the modern mass society, however, are likely to be episodic in nature, not permanent or enduring features of one's life. For example, moving off the farm into the "decadent" urban complexes normally happens once, if ever, in the course of a lifetime. Are we to expect that the new urbanite will spend the rest of his or her days hobbled by an icy state of anomie? On the contrary, new friends will be made, new sources of social cohesion will be found, new arrangements will be undertaken. Long-term political impacts are almost necessarily minimal. The mass society assumption that such "dislocations" might lead either to alienation or to uniquely regressive ideologies seems tenuous.

In contrast to the episodic character of "massification" stands the permanence of an objective lack of control, especially in the lower and working classes. Presumably, this fact of life promotes political viewpoints which are consistent with it; these viewpoints, in turn, are passed on from parents to children in the normal course of political conversation. Data bearing on the plausibility of this conception were reviewed in Chapter 3. They suggest that the roots of political powerlessness develop as early as the third grade. This being the case, it would appear that the typical politically alienated person will have had more than ample time to "adjust" his political consciousness accordingly. Such adjustments might take the form of a belief that this was the normal and inevitable state of affairs, that matters could scarcely be otherwise, that certainly no personal action would make things any different. An affirmation of one's powerlessness, then, is not necessarily a blanket condemnation of the on-going arrangements, not an empassioned plea for rectification, not a clear signal that "corrective" steps are about to be undertaken. It is a simple confirmation of an obvious political fact. What reason is there to expect that it will lead to irrational behavior?

Although it is perhaps rooted in early childhood training, political alienation is certainly not determined by it, as our analysis of trends makes clear. Among adult populations, alienation is quite responsive to major political events in the larger society; it ebbs and flows roughly in accordance with changing political realities. This suggests another important theoretical point, namely, that the politically alienated are *not* blind to the differences between parties or candidates but are especially sensitive to them, at least sensitive enough to adjust their beliefs when the course of events signals that the influence of their viewpoints has diminished. Their "hostility," then, is not directed against all things political in equal parts; they are "negative" toward politicians who ignore their political preferences. The selective offering and withdrawal of support, depending upon the responsiveness of the political leadership, seems more like the essence of participatory democracy than the "threat" that figures so prominently in the theoretical accounts. At the very least, the "irrationality" conception of alienation is very hard to square with these results.

In short, there is nothing inherent in the concept of alienation and nothing confirmed by prior studies requiring the politically discontented to subscribe to a common ideological view or to embrace a firm negativism. These are empirical possibilities which, as it happens, are inconsistent with the evidence we have discussed. The belief, for example, that all parties and politicians are corrupt does not necessarily imply that they differ in no other way, nor that one level or form of corruption might not be preferable to any other. One might just as easily vote "for" the lesser evil as "against" the greater evil; one might even care a great deal about casting such a vote. Likewise, the belief that one has little political power does not prevent one from intelligently deploying what little power one has. In other words, political alienation does not automatically strip one of all political interests nor strip away all traces of political intelligence. Thus, there is nothing to necessarily prevent the discontented from appreciating any real differences that do exist between the parties and candidates, from sifting among the differences to find which ones best enunciate one's own political interests, or from voting accordingly. All that alienation itself implies is a certain skepticism about whether one's vote really makes much of a difference. This model of the "alienated voter" lacks the drama of the mass society scenario but has the singular advantage of being consistent with persuasive evidence.

9

The Behavioral Consequences of Political Alienation: Participation, Mobilization, and Demagoguery

THE hypothesis that "the alienated are quiescent under ordinary circumstances, but subject to mobilization into mass movements (or at least support of extremist, demagogic, and/or authoritarian political leaders) when the material or psychological circumstances are proper and the right leader presents himself (Aberbach 1969:87)" is a central theme in the theory of political alienation, although compelling evidence supporting this proposition is rare. The major historical evidence comes from the Fascist experience in Germany, on which basis little can be definitively concluded. The "mobilization of the alienated" to defeat fluoridation or school bond referenda has been a second source of evidence, but the relationship between these referenda and the political disruptions of the "modern mass society" seems obscure, if not remote. The disproportionate tendency of the politically alienated to support demagogues, such as Joseph McCarthy, Barry Goldwater, or George Wallace, is also frequently cited, but these studies collapse an important distinction between *preference* and *mobilization*. The presumed "withdrawal" of the discontented in normal times, of course, is among the best-documented propositions in all of political sociology (see Chapter 3, Footnote 16), but their ability to be mobilized by radical demagogues remains an open empirical question.

The absence of conclusive studies is particularly unfortunate because the "mobilization" hypothesis contains the very heart of political alienation theory. Certainly, the political alienation of the mass would count for very little if its only certain outcome was disinterest and political withdrawal. Under this circumstance, alienation could only lessen "strain" on the system and would, thereby, constitute a source of "stability." The "dangers" of discontent depend upon the "availability" of the alienated to radical demagogues "bent upon the transformation of the world." It is not the more usual withdrawal that poses the political threat (How could it?) but rather the "waves of popular revulsion," the "extraordinary political activity," the "extreme behaviors" that predominate once the alienated are "activated" by appropriate leaders and circumstances.

As we mentioned in the previous chapter, the exact nature of the "leaders and circumstances" that facilitate mobilization has never been made very explicit. Sometimes these discussions are tautological. Kornhauser, for example, mentions that "the underlying disaffection of which apathy may be an expression readily leads to activism in times of crisis, as when people who have previously rejected politics turn out in large numbers to support demagogic attacks on the political system (1959:61)." Crisis, then, engenders mobilization, but a crisis is apparently defined as existing only when mobilization occurs. Mills is more straightforward: "The meaning of crisis has to be made clear before it can be hopefully asserted that political alienation will be replaced by alertness only in crisis (1951:330)." In the 25 pages that intervene between this passage and the end of the book, however, no "clarification" is offered. Rather, the effort is spent in showing why and how crises have been "sublimated" in American political life and why, consequently, the prospects for mass mobilization are dim. Borrowing Mills's phrase, we conclude that the "mobilization" hypothesis has been hopefully asserted, but the conditions necessary for its confirmation have not.

Lacking these critical specifications, it is doubtful that the mobilization thesis could ever be conclusively rejected. After all, who can say what mean instincts might come to the surface in the next turn of events? Here, as before, the best that we can do is to provide detailed evidence on some historical instances of "extremism" and "demagoguery" and, on that basis, to make inferences about the plausibility of political alienation theory. Such a strategy returns us to the "logic of limiting cases," which was discussed earlier. It allows us to enumerate some of the apparent "conditions" and "circumstances" which do *not* trigger the "latent participatory impulses." [1]

[1] The problem here, of course, is once again the appeal to an indefinite future. As mentioned earlier (Chapter 8, Footnote 6), there is no effective counterargument to such appeals. Evidence, such as that discussed in this chapter, can be easily dismissed, since it is drawn from a social and political context which has passed from the scene: It deals with "yesterday" and implies nothing certain about "tomorrow." It should be noted, however, that evidence from the Goldwater and Wallace elections is quite often cited

In this case, the conditions and circumstances are those surrounding the Goldwater and Wallace presidential candidacies of 1964 and 1968. Our examination of the thesis involves a judgment of whether or not the participation of the alienated was, in any sense, *increased* by either of these candidates. A corollary question is whether or not any observed participation increases actually favored the demagogic candidate. The mobilization hypothesis will be supported if there was an increase in participation among the "previously apathetic and alienated" in 1964 and 1968 *and* if the bulk of the increase went to Goldwater or Wallace.[2]

Justification for the use of the 1968 election in this manner was already presented in Chapter 8. Certainly, the political, social, and economic circumstances of that election should have favored a candidate such as Wallace or at least increased his appeal to the politically frustrated sectors. The conditions of 1964, on the other hand, were considerably less dismal, although Goldwater went out of his way to give an opposite impression. A typical campaign speech would run as follows: "There is a stir in the land. There is a mood of uneasiness. . . . Why do we see wave after wave of crime in our streets and in our homes? A flood of obscene literature? Corruption around our higher offices?"[3] Goldwater, to be sure, *was* the candidate of a major party, but the hesitancy of many nationally prominent Republicans to endorse his candidacy might have been taken as some measure of his "dissociation" from the ruling establishment. Liberals, the media, and even Republican moderates sensed that his nomination was a victory of extremism over responsible conservatism, and Goldwater's often quoted acceptance speech (". . . extremism in the defense of liberty. . .") did little to allay these

---

in support of various elements of political alienation theory (e.g., Aberbach 1969; Converse *et al.* 1969; Krickus 1971; Pettigrew *et al.* 1972; Simon and Gagnon 1970; etc.). This implies a correlative obligation to accept similar evidence even if it diverges from theoretical expectations.

[2] The addendum is necessary because evidence discussed in Chapters 6 and 8 raises the possibility that some of the political alienated might be "mobilized" in order to *defeat* ideologically extreme candidates. Mobilization of this sort, surely, should not be included among the potential hazards of political discontent. (This point is elaborated later in the chapter.)

[3] This speech is quoted in Kelley (1966:49). According to this source, a key element in the Goldwater strategy was "to portray Lyndon Johnson as a politician of dubious ethics, questionable associations, and brutal egoism," the sort of portrayal designed to win the "alienated" votes. The campaign sticker which read "LBJ—Lyndon Baker Jenkins" was no doubt formulated with these ends in mind. "Bobby" Baker, of course, was Senate majority Secretary under Johnson and a long-time LBJ confidant who was, at the time, under FBI investigation for various shady dealings, among them influence peddling out of LBJ's office. Walter Jenkins was another LBJ associate, dismissed from office in the midst of the 1964 campaign for alleged homosexual activities. This latter scandal led to another memorable Goldwater bumper sticker: "No wonder they turned the lights off at the White House."

fears.[4] Finally, the explicit incorporation of the "mobilization hypothesis" into Goldwater's strategy (Converse *et al.* 1965; Polsby 1966) makes the campaign especially interesting from our point of view: Goldwater, it will be recalled, justified his nomination and based his campaign on a presumed vast constituency of "hidden voters" who had "stayed at home" in the past because they were never offered a genuine alternative to "me-too" Republicanism.[5]

Some mention might be made of the different political "stimuli" presented by the Goldwater and Wallace candidacies. That both were widely identified as "extremists" is scarcely debatable; thus, the hypothesis is that both should have appealed to the alienated and discontented sectors. There were, however, some important differences in the brand of extremism being offered. Goldwater was something of a "classic reactionary"—suspicious of big government, punitive and belligerent in foreign policy outlook, and opposed to the "welfare state." As Aberbach has noted, this latter no doubt dampened his appeal among the politically alienated in the working and lower classes.[6] Wallace, on the other hand, represented the "Populist" option—economic "liberalism" coupled with a conservative *social* ideology best expressed in his hostility towards blacks, students, and other "dissident" groups. While certainly not exhausting the range of variation in types of extremism, these candidates cover two of the major possibilities. Thus, they represent two clearly different contexts in which to investigate the mobilization hypothesis.

[4] There is little genuine doubt that Goldwater's extremism was a major issue in the 1964 campaign. The *New York Times*, picking up a line from one of Johnson's campaign speeches, directly implied that Goldwater was a "raving, ranting demagogue (Kelley 1966:62)"—an assessment shared by most of the urban press (Thomson 1966). Moderate Republicans voiced similar concerns. For example, "Two days after the Goldwater nomination, former President Eisenhower declared himself unable to give active support for his party's nominee until Goldwater had explained his views on extremism, and the former President was joined in his decision to 'wait and see' by many other prominent Republicans (Kelley 1966:68–69)." We bother to mention these points only because readers of an earlier draft have raised a question about Goldwater's "extremism." It is true that many of the policies subsequently pursued by Goldwater's opponent seem, in retrospect, little different from what Goldwater himself might have done, especially as regards Vietnam. It is also true that Goldwater's refusal to support the Nixon administration at the depths of its Watergate "troubles" is commendable. These hindsights, however, should not be projected backward onto the 1964 campaign. At that time, the epithet, "extremist," was common currency in the realm.

[5] The best discussion of this aspect of Goldwater's strategy is Polsby (1966: 88–92). Polsby elaborates the "hidden vote hypothesis" as follows: "There is a well-known suspicion, voiced from time to time by imaginative writers, that conservative elements of the population are in fact alienated from politics and sit in the wings, frustrated, immobilized, and without party loyalties, until someone pursuing a Goldwater-like strategy gives them the 'choice' they are looking for (1966:90)." "This," Polsby continues, "is probably a canard." In a subsequent footnote, however, he also admits that "the study of right-wing ideologues and their supporters is more speculative than empirical." Evidence presented in this chapter is an attempt to reverse the imbalance.

[6] See Chapter 3, Footnote 27.

As we have already indicated, the analysis initially focuses on participation differences among the alienated between the "normal" elections of 1956 and 1960 and the "nonnormal" elections of 1964 and 1968. This reflects our belief that mobilization implies some rise in participation, rather than simply winning the votes of those who would have participated anyway. This latter question is taken up later in the chapter. In all, 10 measures of participation are available for each of the 4 study years. First is the simple measure of turn-out, whether or not the respondent voted. Five additional "behavioral" measures are also included: (1) "Did you go to any political meeting, rallies, dinners, or things like that?" (2) "Did you do any other work for one of the parties or candidates?" (3) "Do you belong to any political club or organization?" (4) "Did you give any money or buy any tickets to help a party or candidate this year?" (5) "Did you wear a campaign button or put a campaign sticker on your car?" There are three questions concerning attention to the campaign in newspapers, magazines, and television; these represent measures of vicarious participation in the campaign. Finally, there is one measure of "attitudinal" participation which asks whether the respondent was "very interested, somewhat interested, or not much interested in following the political campaign this year." Clearly, a wide range of participation components are represented by these 10 measures. Some would be fairly "ominous" (for example, increased turn-out or sharp upswings in rally attendance or donating money); others obviously would not be. Therefore, we have resisted the temptation to combine the items into a single "participation" scale. Also, to maximize detail, we have kept the full 5 point efficacy scale. (Political trust was not measured in either 1956 or 1960 and is, therefore, omitted from this analysis.) Table 9.1 displays the relationship between political efficacy and the 10 participation measures for all Presidential elections from 1956 to 1968.

Initially, the most striking aspect of these data is their unambiguous support for the less interesting "withdrawal" hypothesis. In 39 tests of the hypothesis, covering 4 elections and 10 measures of participation, the basic relationship does not suffer a single reversal: However measured, the alienated participate less.[7]

---

[7] Controlling the alienation–participation relationship for region, race, age, social class, and mass media attention diminishes, but does not eliminate, the effect (Wright 1973b: 390–392). Even net of these "contaminating" spurious correlations, the alienated participate less.

Correlation, of course, says nothing about causal direction. In the usual account, inefficacy is seen to be the cause of nonparticipation, but Alford and Scoble (1968) and Form and Rytina (1971) have suggested the reverse. First, persons who participate generally do have more influence than those who do not, simply because participation must have some effect. Participation, that is, increases power and, thereby, diminishes the feeling of powerlessness. Second, inefficacy might be a convenient justification for the prior decision not to participate. The belief that participation was useless, in short, would "rationalize" nonparticipation.

TABLE 9.1
Efficacy and Participation: 1956-1968

	1956	N	1960	N	1964	N	1968	N
Percent Voting								
1[a]	55.2	212	51.4	183	69.8	212	58.9	282
2	57.6	351	71.8	284	72.1	308	71.5	288
3	74.8	481	78.5	581	78.1	430	79.9	278
4	83.4	501	87.7	543	83.4	331	85.3	293
5	91.4	197	94.1	203	89.0	155	86.5	193
Total	73.3	1742	79.2	1794	78.0	1436	75.8	1334
Newspapers:	Percent Yes							
1	45.3	212	32.9	170	38.9	211	32.6	276
2	50.6	350	39.8	284	41.6	305	42.1	287
3	70.3	481	54.7	563	52.7	429	49.6	272
4	83.2	501	66.2	530	70.1	328	57.9	290
5	88.3	197	80.0	200	70.8	154	74.0	192
Total	69.0	1741	56.5	1747	54.2	1427	49.8	1317
Television:	Percent Yes							
1	61.1	211	64.7	184	74.1	212	71.3	279
2	63.4	350	68.2	283	68.2	308	74.5	290
3	73.3	480	77.4	575	75.5	432	74.5	278
4	83.8	501	80.6	540	82.2	331	80.6	293
5	83.7	196	82.8	203	82.6	155	81.5	194
Total	74.2	1738	76.2	1785	76.0	1483	76.2	1334
Magazines:	Percent Yes							
1	12.3	212	9.6	177	8.5	211	6.8	280
2	14.0	349	12.1	282	17.9	308	15.9	290
3	30.3	475	23.7	578	24.1	432	19.8	278
4	41.4	498	33.5	538	38.5	330	29.0	293
5	60.4	197	60.0	200	45.8	155	36.6	194
Total	31.4	1731	27.5	1775	26.1	1436	20.7	1335
Interested:	Percent Very							
1	10.0	211	13.6	199	20.2	238	24.1	282
2	19.1	351	18.6	311	30.6	327	34.6	289
3	26.2	478	37.4	623	38.8	472	40.3	278
4	42.2	500	48.2	571	50.1	351	46.4	293
5	48.2	193	61.4	210	54.9	164	57.6	191
Total	29.8	1733	37.7	1914	38.5	1552	39.5	1333
Give Money:	Percent Yes[b]							
1	1.0	212	1.1	181	2.8	211		
2	4.8	351	5.6	285	5.9	306		
3	8.3	481	7.6	581	7.4	433		
4	15.4	501	16.2	542	16.7	329		
5	18.8	197	28.6	203	19.4	155		
Total	9.9	1742	11.6	1792	9.8	1434		

TABLE 9.1 (continued)

	1956	N	1960	N	1964	N	1968	N
Attend Rallies:	**Percent**	**Yes**						
1	2.4	212	1.7	182	2.8	212	3.9	283
2	4.6	350	2.5	283	6.2	307	6.2	291
3	4.8	481	5.5	581	6.7	433	7.6	278
4	10.4	501	12.4	541	14.0	329	12.9	294
5	13.2	197	20.8	292	16.8	155	18.1	193
Total	7.0	1741	8.4	1789	8.8	1436	9.2	1339
Other Work:	**Percent**	**Yes**						
1	0.5	212	0.0	184	2.4	212	1.8	278
2	2.3	351	3.5	285	2.0	307	5.2	291
3	2.7	479	4.7	580	2.6	431	3.6	276
4	4.0	501	8.1	542	10.0	330	7.8	293
5	7.2	195	11.0	201	12.9	155	12.4	193
Total	3.2	1738	5.8	1792	5.2	1435	5.8	1331
Did You Belong:	**Percent**	**Yes**						
1	0.5	210	0.0	184	0.5	212	1.4	278
2	2.0	350	0.7	285	2.3	307	2.1	291
3	2.3	481	2.8	580	2.8	432	1.8	275
4	4.6	501	5.3	543	8.8	328	5.5	293
5	4.6	197	6.0	201	5.8	155	7.3	192
Total	2.9	1739	3.3	1793	4.9	1434	3.4	1329
Wear a Button:	**Percent**	**Yes**						
1	8.5	211	4.9	184	10.9	212	8.7	277
2	9.1	351	15.1	285	11.7	307	14.1	290
3	14.8	481	21.6	580	16.0	432	15.6	276
4	21.2	499	26.0	543	24.9	329	16.1	292
5	23.4	197	29.8	201	18.1	155	22.3	193
Total	15.7	1639	21.1	1793	16.6	1435	14.9	1328

a. *1 = low efficacy; 5 = high efficacy.*
b. *The format of the "donations" question was changed in 1968 and is therefore not included.*

Despite the clear tendencies, however, it should also be noted that a majority of even the most alienated respondents characteristically vote in presidential elections. These bare majorities, to be sure, are rather meager in comparison to the usual 90% turn-out among the most efficacious; nonetheless, global depictions, such as "the alienated manifest their sentiments in the only way possible—by refusing to participate in the political order (Eckhardt and Hendershot 1967:459)," actually only describe about half the target group.

A second striking feature of the data, bearing on points raised at the end of Chapter 7, is that, except for voting and following the campaign in the media, huge majorities, regardless of alienation, engage in no other form of political participation. If, as the leading account suggests, participation is important because "it communicates the citizens' needs and desires to the government (Verba and Nie 1972:5)," we can safely conclude that there is relatively little "communication" of this form in the United States.

The complexity of Table 9.1 makes it difficult to read from the perspective of the mobilization hypothesis; accordingly, it has been condensed and rearranged and appears in new form in Table 9.2. Owing to occasional (and, for

TABLE 9.2
Comparisons between the Political Participation of the Most and Least Alienated in 1964 and 1968 with the Average Participation in 1956 and 1960

Participation Measure	1956-1960 Average	1964 Change	1968 Change
Turnout			
Low	53.4	+16.4	+5.5
High	92.8	-3.8	-6.3
Newspapers			
Low	39.8	-.09	-7.2
High	84.1	-13.3	-10.1
Magazines			
Low	11.1	-2.6	-4.3
High	60.2	-14.4	-23.6
Television			
Low	62.8	+11.3	+8.5
High	83.2	-0.6	-1.8
Interest			
Low	11.7	+8.5	+12.4
High	55.1	-0.2	+2.5
Money			
Low	1.0	+1.8	
High	23.8	-4.4	
Rallies			
Low	2.0	+0.8	+1.9
High	17.0	-0.2	+1.1
Work for			
Low	0.3	+2.1	+1.5
High	9.1	+3.8	+3.3
Belong			
Low	0.2	+0.3	+1.2
High	5.3	+0.5	+2.0
Button			
Low	6.8	+4.1	+1.9
High	26.6	-8.5	-4.3

present purposes, uninteresting) differences in the level of participation in 1956 and 1960, we have taken an average "percentage participating" in those years as the basis for further comparisons. The 1956–1960 averages are reported in the first column. Column two reports the deviation of the comparable 1964 figure from the 1956–1960 average; column three reports the 1968 deviation. Plus signs indicate participation increases; minus signs indicate decreases. To represent the alienation variable, we have taken the most and least alienated groups (the 1s and 5s from Table 9.1). Thus, the first row of the table says that, among the least efficacious, the average 1956–1960 turn-out was 53.4%, that, in 1964, this figure increased by 16.4 percentage points, and that, in 1968, turn-out was 5.5 percentage points higher than the 1956–1960 average.

With some significant exceptions discussed later, the overall picture does not support the mobilization hypothesis. Taking a 10 point increase as the minimum supportive difference, the prediction is sustained in 3 of 19 tests, but even this is probably somewhat overly generous, given customary claims about "waves of popular revulsion" or "explosion of radical protest." If one took these formulations seriously and, therefore, insisted on a 20 or 25 point increase as the minimum supportive difference, the hypothesis would be sustained in none of the 19 tests. For the most part, the Wallace and Goldwater campaigns left the participation of the alienated pretty much unaffected.

The major exceptions are as follows: First, there was a clearly significant 16 point increase in turn-out among the alienated in 1964. This is by far the most "ominous" difference anywhere in the table and will be discussed more fully later. Also interesting are the 11 point increase in following the 1964 campaign on the television and the 8.5 point increase in "interest." Interestingly, the 1968 patterns closely resemble those for 1964: There were similar, although less pronounced, increases in turn-out, television watching, and interest in the Wallace campaign as well. The similarity between the two patterns is noteworthy, but they clearly do not pose much threat to democratic institutions. Some patterns that might signal a threat—for instance, a marked increase in rally attendance or in donations of time and money—simply do not appear in the results. In short, and excepting for the moment the obvious rise in turn-out in 1964, there is little evidence to suggest that the alienated were uniquely "available" to either Wallace or Goldwater.

Unfortunately, trends in political alienation from 1956 to 1968 make it difficult to place much confidence in these initial results. The 1956–1960 alienated, that is, are not strictly comparable to the inefficacious of 1964 or 1968 (see Chapter 7). Luckily, it is possible to identify the "previously apathetic and alienated" in each study year and, therefore, to replicate the analysis on data that are unaffected by the possible contamination of trends. In all their presidential studies, the SRC asks, "In the elections for President since you have been old enough to vote, would you say that you have voted in all of them, most of them, some of them, or none of them." Those who say "none of them" are the "previously apathetic," and, of that group, those who are also inefficacious are, therefore, the "previously apathetic *and* alienated." An independent test of the mobilization hypothesis is thus afforded by noting the response of this group to the 1964 and 1968 elections.

Table 9.3 reports the results of this replication. The table contains *only* those respondents who were low in political efficacy (the 1s and 2s from the 5 point scale) *and* who reported never having voted in a previous election. In all other respects, the table is the same as Table 9.2. Thus, the first row shows that, in 1956 and 1960, the average turn-out among the "previously apathetic and alienated" was 12.9%, that this figure rose by 13.7 percentage points in 1964, and by 4.2 percentage points in 1968. The lessons can be quickly summarized: The results diverge in no important respect from those obtained by our earlier procedure. As before, there is a sharp increase in turnout in 1964 and a much less pronounced increase in 1968. The clear increases in the proportion "very interested" are still apparent. Even the "television" results are similar across the two procedures. Finally, again paralleling the earlier results, no significant increases are shown in either year for the remaining participation measures. Neither of these techniques, of course, is an acceptable substitute for true panel data; that both produce nearly identical results, however, increases confidence in the conclusion. No matter how one operationalizes the concept, the Goldwater and Wallace candidacies

TABLE 9.3
Participation among the "Previously Apathetic and Alienated":
1956-1968

	1956-1960 Average	N	1964 Change	N	1968 Change	N
Turnout	12.9	245	+13.7	79	+4.2	81
Newspapers	33.9	237	-4.8	98	-17.7	80
Magazines	6.8	243	-3.0	79	-3.1	82
Television	56.4	246	+0.6	79	+9.0	81
% Very interested	5.8	354	+6.8	87	+8.8	82
Donations	0.4	244	+0.9	78		
Rallies	0.4	244	+0.9	78	+0.8	72
Work for?	0.0	246	0.0	78	+1.3	79
Belong	0.0	245	0.0	78	0.0	79
Button	4.1	246	+6.2	78	+2.2	79

left the participation of the "previously apathetic and alienated" largely untouched.

As already mentioned, the most pronounced and potentially most "disruptive" exception to the overall conclusion of "no effect" comes in the 16 point increase in alienated turn-out in 1964 (or the 14 point increase revealed by the second of our procedures). Irrespective of the remainder of the evidence, this pattern seems distressingly consistent with the mobilization hypothesis. On the other hand, we have already noted in previous chapters that "the" alienated are a relatively diverse group—evenly dispersed along the ideological spectrum, evenly split between the major parties, and so on. This raises the possibility that at least part of the apparent 1964 mobilization might have gone to Johnson rather than to his rightist opponent. Since the "mass uprising" of alienated citizens to *defeat* an extremist candidate would obviously not be counted as a "threat" to democratic institutions, this possibility warrants more extended consideration.

Because there are no panel data spanning the period from 1956–1960 to 1964, the actual vote distribution of the 1964 mobilization cannot be precisely determined. One plausible inference is that, if the bulk of that mobilization in fact favored Goldwater, then turn-out among alienated Goldwater supporters should have been considerably higher than turn-out among alienated Johnson supporters. The data, however, show only partial support for this thesis (Table 9.4). In the SRC question concerning the vote, respondents are first asked whether or not they voted, then whom they voted for. If they did not vote, they are asked which candidate they would have preferred. The total number voting for a candidate, divided by the total number preferring the candidate, is, thus, turn-out among the supporters of each candidate. Table 9.4 shows that about 80% of the alienated Goldwater supporters actually turned out for Goldwater, as compared to an average turn-out among the powerless of about 60% in 1956–1960. Certainly, *part* of the 1964 mobilization does appear to have gone to Goldwater. At the same time, however, turn-out among highly alienated Johnson supporters (about 70%) was *also* considerably higher than the 1956–1960 average. Given the well-docu-

TABLE 9.4
Turnout by Candidate Choice, by Political Efficacy: 1964

	Turnout					
	1956–1960 Average	N	Johnson	N	Goldwater	N
Efficacy						
Low	59.9	1030	70.2	353	80.4	143
Medium	76.8	1062	77.4	301	83.8	117
High	87.6	1444	81.7	323	91.8	160
Total	76.3	3536	76.2	977	85.7	420

mented tendency for Republicans to participate more than Democrats regardless of alienation (e.g., Verba and Nie 1972: Ch. 12), the most plausible conclusion to be drawn from these data is that the 1964 mobilization of the alienated probably benefited each candidate in nearly equal proportions.

Making some restrictive assumptions, it is possible to specify this conclusion more precisely. Assume first that if there had been no "mobilization of the alienated" in 1964, the same proportion of them would have voted as voted on the average in 1956–1960 (that is, 59.9%). On this basis, the "predicted" turn-out among the inefficacious in the 1964 sample would be 297 votes (.599 × [353 + 143] = 297). In fact, however, 363 of the 496 low efficacy respondents actually did vote—a net projected increase of 66 hypothetical votes due to "mobilization." Assume next that, in the absence of any "mobilization," the turn-out among alienated supporters of each candidate would have been the same.[8] On this basis, the "predicted" turn-out among low efficacy Johnson supporters would be 211 votes (.599 × 353), whereas the actual turn-out was 248 votes—a net increase to Johnson of 37 hypothetical votes, or 56% of the total 66 votes available from the 1964 "mobilization." Following the same procedure for Goldwater, turn-out among alienated supporters of Goldwater should have been 86 votes (.599 × 143), but was, in fact, 115 votes—a net increase to Goldwater of 29 of the 66 hypothetical votes due to "mobilization," or 44% of the total. Since the assumptions made earlier should, all else being equal, *exaggerate* Goldwater's share of the mobilization, we are again led to conclude that a large part, if not the majority, of the 1964 "mobilization of the alienated" probably worked toward Goldwater's defeat.[9]

The "allocation procedure" just outlined, of course, is somewhat arbitrary and rather inferential. A more direct method of determining the distribution of the 1964 "mobilization" is afforded by examining the votes of the "previously apathetic and alienated" group as defined earlier in Table 9.3. As

[8] The first assumption mentioned in the text is true by our definition of mobilization; the second is an assumption of convenience contradicted by fact. In this case, the fact is that Republicans always turn out in greater proportions than Democrats. The implication of this for our substantive conclusions is discussed in the following footnote.

[9] Since Republican turn-out always surpasses Democratic turn-out, the assumption of "equal turn-out in the absence of mobilization" is not empirically justified. "Correcting" our estimates to reflect this fact, however, only serves to *lower* Goldwater's estimated share of the 1964 mobilization, since the "predicted" turn-out in the absence of mobilization would be proportionately higher and, therefore, the projected net gain due to mobilization would be proportionately lower. (Recall that "net gain" is the actual vote less the "predicted" vote.) Any "corrections" along these lines, then, would only serve to strengthen the substantive conclusions.

There is a second assumption made throughout this analysis, namely, that the increased 1964 turn-out among low efficacy respondents was, in fact, a direct result of Goldwater's candidacy. If it was actually due to other factors (for example, secular trends toward increasing participation, demographic changes in the electorate, and so on), then the resulting support for the mobilization hypothesis is even less than what is indicated in the text.

shown earlier, the 1964 survey contained 79 respondents who were high in powerlessness (1 or 2 on the efficacy scale) and who claimed never to have voted in a previous presidential election. How did these 79 persons respond to the 1964 "offerings"? First of all, 58 of them (73.4%) also did not vote in 1964, which, on its own, says something about their "availability" to an extremist candidate. Of the 21 who did manage to cast a ballot in 1964, 19 (or about 90%) voted for Johnson.[10] In short, virtually all the mobilization of this group favored Johnson over the "extremist" alternative.

There is one final bit of evidence bearing on the distribution of the 1964 mobilization; this is the simple votes of the politically alienated in 1964 (see Table 9.7). Since this evidence says nothing about *participation* per se, we have suspended a full discussion until later in the chapter. For now, it is sufficient to note that, among the politically powerless who bothered to vote in 1964, about 70% voted for Johnson. (Different results obtain for trust, and these too are discussed in more detail later.) These and the related data presented earlier make it appear very unlikely that Goldwater benefited to any great degree from the "mobilization of the alienated" in 1964. Summing up the results as generously as possible, we conclude that there was a very minor "mobilization" of the politically discontented in 1964, restricted mainly to turn-out, and that somewhat less than half of this mobilization in fact favored the "demagogic" candidate. "Waves of popular revulsion" from the ruling "powers that be" are notably absent from these results.

[10] There were, in addition, 56 respondents who were not especially powerless (scoring medium or high on the efficacy scale) but who also never voted in previous elections. Concerning the "mobilization" of this group of "previously apathetic and *non*alienated" persons, 67.9% again chose not to vote in 1964, and, of the 18 who did vote, the large majority (72%) picked Johnson.

Replicating these procedures with trust as the measure of alienation produces similar results. There were only 31 "previously apathetic and distrustful" respondents in the 1964 survey, so little can be said about them. As before, the large majority (80.6%) did not vote in 1964. Of the 6 who voted, 2 picked Johnson and 4 chose Goldwater. Likewise, there were 102 "previously apathetic but trusting" respondents, of whom 67.6% remained apathetic in 1964. Of the 33 who voted, 30 voted for Johnson.

Interestingly, the largest Goldwater vote registered among any of the groups considered in this analysis was among those who were politically distrustful but *not* previously apathetic (*n* = 323). Of these, 19.5% did not vote in 1964, and, of the remainder, the majority (58%) voted for Goldwater. This reinforces a point made later in the chapter, that the alienated Goldwater votes were, by and large, *not* due to mobilization; rather, they were votes that would have been cast anyway.

As shown in Table 9.3, there were also 81 "previously apathetic and alienated" persons in the 1968 survey. The response of this group to the 1968 election follows the common pattern: 84% did not vote in 1968. Of the remaining 13 respondents, 4 said they voted for Wallace. Also paralleling the 1964 results, Wallace's best showing comes among those who felt powerless but who had *not* been previously apathetic (*n* = 453). Of this group, 26% did not vote in 1968, and, of the remainder, about 15% claimed to have voted for Wallace. This again suggests that the alienated Wallace voters were people who would have voted anyway, not prior nonparticipants suddenly mobilized by an extremist candidate.

Thus far, we have uncovered nothing that could not have been readily predicted from findings reported in Chapter 8. The general absence of a strong mobilization effect among the discontented may be explained, we presume, by the fact that they lack the hypothesized "intervening" negativistic traits. Having no apparent proclivities to cast a "protest" vote or to vote "against" or to object rancorously to the Tweedledum and Tweedledee of politics as usual, the moralistic pronouncements of both Wallace and Goldwater must have left them unimpressed. Likewise, their fairly even split between parties and ideological positions no doubt explains why both 1964 candidates apparently benefited in nearly equal proportion from the scant mobilization that did occur. As we have stressed elsewhere, the politically alienated lack the social and political cohesion that would allow their common mobilization by a single demagogic candidate.

On the other hand, these points also imply that we have not yet given the mobilization hypothesis its fairest possible test. Highly alienated liberals, after all, could certainly not have been expected to react favorably to the Goldwater candidacy, no matter what the depths of their despair were. Alienated conservatives, of course, might have done so. Similarly, both candidates obviously had a regionally specific appeal, so perhaps a more pronounced "reaction" might be found among the alienated white southerners. Accordingly, Table 9.5 shows the response of highly alienated conservatives and white southerners to the 1964 and 1968 elections.[11]

Focusing first on the alienated conservatives, their "reaction" was very similar to that of the alienated as a whole. There was again a sharp increase in turn-out in 1964 and a less pronounced increase in 1968. Clear upturns in "interest" are again apparent for both years. No other significant "mobilization" is found in these data.

As before, the most "ominous" finding is the 16 point increase in turn-out among alienated conservatives for the 1964 election. Following the allocation procedure discussed earlier, this increase produced an additional 35 hypothetical votes, of which 18 went to Johnson (Wright 1973b:408). Even among highly alienated conservatives, in short, there was apparently no common mobilization on Goldwater's behalf; perhaps as many as half the group found Goldwater too extreme even for their conservative tastes.[12]

---

[11] Given the absence of comparable indicators in the early studies, the liberalism scale developed in the previous chapter cannot be used in this analysis. Therefore, a new measure has been constructed, which sums responses to items 5 and 6 from the earlier scale (see Chapter 8, Footnote 8). A respondent is considered liberal if he or she gave liberal responses to both these questions, cosservative if he or she gave two conservative responses, and a "moderate" if the answers were mixed. This index of liberalism is used throughout the remainder of the chapter.

[12] Lacking detailed panel data, it is difficult to say exactly what this pattern represents. The best guess is that many of the "mobilized" anti-Goldwater conservatives were moderate Republicans (the so-called "responsible conservatives") seeking to "punish" the party for its extremist misdeed.

TABLE 9.5
Participation among Alienated Conservatives and White Southerners:
1956-1968

	1956-1960 Average	N	1964 Change	N	1968 Change	N
	Trends among Alienated Conservatives[a]					
Turnout	56.9	218	+16.1	196	+8.8	358
Newspapers	47.5	219	+0.4	192	-9.1	245
Television	71.8	216	+1.0	195	+4.7	247
Magazines	13.3	218	+5.3	194	-0.8	248
Interest	19.6	224	+9.0	220	+10.4	250
Money	6.9	217	-2.3	195		
Rallies	4.6	217	+1.0	195	-0.6	250
Work for	3.2	219	-0.6	195	+1.2	249
Belong	0.9	219	+0.6	195	+0.3	249
Button	8.7	219	+3.1	195	+2.2	248
	Trends among Alienated White Southerners[b]					
Turnout[a]	53.9	321	+10.3	159	+3.2	163
Newspapers	38.6	321	+14.9	147	-.06	163
Television	67.7	322	+13.4	159	+10.1	162
Magazines	12.8	319	+1.8	158	-2.3	162
Interest	20.0	330	+6.3	171	+10.1	163
Money	3.8	320	-0.6	159		
Rallies	4.1	320	-0.3	159	+0.8	163
Work for	2.2	322	-0.9	159	+1.0	158
Belong	0.9	321	-0.9	159	+1.0	158
Button	11.2	321	+5.8	159	+1.0	157

a. Only the low efficacy conservatives are included in the table. Thus, this row shows the trends in turnout among low efficacy conservatives from 1956 to 1968.
b. Only the low efficacy white Southerners are included in this table. Thus, this row shows the trends in turnout among low efficacy white Southerner from 1956 to 1968.

The patterns for alienated white southerners are slightly different but follow the same general lines that we have already discussed. The main divergence comes in increased attention to the 1964 campaign in the papers and television. Increased turn-out and "interest" are again apparent for both years. Excepting the media results, most of the alienated white southern increases are even *smaller* than those for the alienated in general, despite the conscious appeals which both candidates pitched to the South. The southern success of these "demagogues," then, was clearly not due to any "mobilization" effect. Rather, they won votes that would have been cast in any case. The non-response of alienated white southerners to the Wallace effort is particularly striking.

Although the clearly mixed reaction of the alienated *as a whole* to the

Goldwater and Wallace campaigns is consistent with points that we have made previously, the inability of these candidates to mobilize even the highly alienated conservatives and white southerners seems initially more problematic. Actually, however, there is very little of mystery in this: Neither had a remote chance of winning their elections. In all pre-election surveys, the SRC asks, "Who do you think will be elected President in November?" Only 8% of the 1964 sample said "Goldwater," and optimism about Wallace's chances were voiced by a mere 5%. Pre-election polls in both years, in fact unanimously predicted disaster for the "extremists."[13] What reason would the alienated voter have to get enthused about a candidate who was doomed to certain defeat, no matter how precisely that candidate articulated his ideological or regional interests? The alienated, by definition, consider political activity to be pretty much useless anyway, and no doubt even more so if frittered away on a sure loser.

Assuming that the "no-win" status of both candidates explains the nonresponse of even alienated conservatives and white southerners, an additional point should be made, namely, that considerations of probable success, while obviously important, never enter into the standard depictions. The participation of the alienated, rather, is seen as being symbolic: They vote to register a protest or to emphasize their disgust, not to elect a candidate. Thus, it is not the success but the symbol that is uppermost in their collective political minds. Therefore, two points must be noted. First, the fact that neither candidate stood a chance of being elected should not be construed as implying that our analysis is somehow inappropriate; according to the theory, this should not have mattered. Second, the theory is apparently wrong on this latter point.[14]

One final possibility is that "mobilization" by extremists will vary across social strata. The natural appeal of rightist demagogues to the alienated

[13] The "popular realism" indicated in these responses might be contrasted with intellectual alarms about the Goldwater and Wallace candidacies. Prior to both elections, the "literary-political" press, such as Commentary and the New Republic, was filled with anxious scenarios depicting the ultimate Goldwater or Wallace victory. Often, these scenarios were coupled with attempts to negate the accumulating evidence of public opinion polls, either by inappropriate citations to the 1948 Truman election or by some unsupported claim that those polled were not really "telling the truth." Actually, the outcome in both cases confirmed the common wisdom.

[14] One implication of this conclusion is that the politically alienated might well be mobilized by a possible winner, assuming that such a candidate could somehow overcome the ideological and organizational dispersion of the group. But what, in American electoral politics, makes for a potential winner? First and foremost, if the lessons of recent history are accurate, the candidate must avoid even the hint that he or she is an "extremist." Possible winners, virtually by definition, represent the political "center." They must have a "broad base of appeal," be "acceptable" to both business and labor, and otherwise strike a moderate and conciliatory stance. Obviously, there would be little damage done to democratic institutions by the unanimous mobilization of alienated citizens on behalf of such a candidate.

and unsophisticated masses is a persistent theme in both theoretical and popular accounts. Such candidates appeal to the sense of estrangement and promise to thwart the ever-present "threat from below." The lower strata, moreover, lack the attitudinal "safeguards" that minimize availability in the more "responsible" upper middle class. Using education as the measure of social status, evidence bearing on this possibility is shown in Table 9.6.

Focusing first on the high school drop-outs, those "persons of low socio-economic status [who] are presumably swayed by the demagogue who cries conspiracy" (Horton and Thompson 1962:486–487), the evidence shows that they were not particularly "swayed" by either Goldwater or Wallace, at least not in terms of their political participation. With one exception (watching television), mobilization among the less-educated alienated is, in every case, *less* than that shown for the alienated in general. Apparently, the political threat of the highly alienated low status groups has been exaggerated in current accounts: Wallace and Goldwater had almost no effect on the participation of the group.

Turning now to the alienated "some college or more" group, we find an even greater surprise: *It is among the college-educated alienated that the first clear indication of mobilization is found.* Turn-out among the alienated was generally up 16 points in 1964 and 5.5 points in 1968; among the college-educated group, the increases were 27 points in 1964 and 14 points in 1968. These figures are by far the most pronounced mobilization differences encountered so far. The same pattern is found on the political interest question; moreover, attendance at rallies and donations of money in 1964 were also both up 12–13 points among the college-educated alienated groups, and participation on all the other behavioral measures was also up by 5–6 points— these latter figures are in contrast to the 1 and 2 point increases shown for the alienated as a whole. These data make it plain that the participation increases registered by the alienated in both 1964 and 1968 were almost totally confined to the college-educated portion of the group.

Following the previous patterns, the increased 1964 turn-out is again the most striking aspect of these data. Among college-educated alienated persons, as we have already noted, the increase amounts to 27 percentage points. The common pattern, of course, has been for these increases to have gone to both Goldwater and Johnson in roughly equal proportion, and one might anticipate that this would have been the case for the "responsible" college-educated alienated as well. The evidence, however, does not sustain this expectation. Rather, *the bulk of the increased 1964 turn-out among the college-educated alienated seems to have favored Goldwater.*[15] This, of course, is a

---

[15] Following the allocation procedure discussed earlier, there were 51 highly inefficacious college-educated persons in the 1964 sample. Had the 1956–1960 turn-out for the group prevailed, 31 of them (60.8%) would have voted, in reality 45 of them actually did, producing 14 hypothetical additional votes due to mobilization. Had the 1956–1960 turn-out among low efficacy collegians prevailed among Johnson supporters in

TABLE 9.6
Participation among the Alienated by Education: 1956-1968

	1956-1960 Average	N	1964 Change	N	1968 Change	N
Turnout						
Low[a]	55.9	817	+9.2	341	+3.4	356
Medium	80.3	142	+1.8	123	-5.1	141
High	60.8	74	+27.4	51	+14.5	73
Newspapers						
Low	39.5	807	-3.7	338	-7.4	349
Medium	54.9	142	-10.2	123	-14.5	141
High	67.7	65	-4.9	51	-10.2	73
Television						
Low	61.1	817	+9.2	340	+12.3	354
Medium	77.1	140	-8.0	123	-10.4	141
High	82.6	69	-5.7	52	-0.2	74
Magazines						
Low	10.0	812	-1.5	340	-5.2	354
Medium	17.7	141	+1.8	123	-2.2	142
High	30.8	65	+6.5	51	+4.3	74
Interest						
Low	15.1	848	+4.5	367	+9.1	356
Medium	19.3	150	+15.2	130	+11.9	141
High	20.8	72	+30.0	61	+30.6	74
Money						
Low	2.4	819	0.0	338		
Medium	8.6	139	-3.5	122		
High	7.2	69	+12.0	52		
Rallies						
Low	2.6	816	-0.2	339	+0.8	357
Medium	4.3	140	-2.5	123	+1.3	142
High	5.8	69	+13.4	52	+6.2	75
Work for						
Low	1.1	819	-0.3	339	+0.9	353
Medium	4.9	142	-2.5	123	+0.1	141
High	4.3	69	+5.3	52	+3.7	75
Belong						
Low	0.9	816	-0.3	339	+0.5	353
Medium	1.4	142	+0.2	123	0.0	141
High	1.4	69	+6.3	52	+2.6	75
Button						
Low	8.1	819	+2.2	339	+0.1	352
Medium	19.3	141	-7.7	123	-4.1	140
High	13.0	69	+6.2	52	+7.0	75

    a. Low, medium, and high refer to education: low = less than high school; medium = high school graduate; high = some college or more. Only the low efficacy respondents are included in the table. Thus, this row shows the trends from 1956 to 1968 for the low efficacy high school drop-outs; the next row shows the trends in turnout for the low efficacy high school graduates, and so on.

clear departure from the expected result; as such, we will return to it later in the discussion.

With the few exceptions already mentioned, then, it can be safely concluded that Goldwater and Wallace had little noticeable impact on the level of participation among the politically discontented.[16] This, however, does not gainsay the fact that many of them do characteristically vote. An important corollary question to which we now turn is who the voting alienated tend to prefer.

Some important points should be mentioned at the outset. First, unaccompanied by a sizable mobilization, it would be easy to exaggerate the potential hazards posed by the disproportionate preference among the discontented for candidates like Goldwater and Wallace, assuming that such preferences even exist. Any immoderate leanings on their part, that is, must be assessed in light of their strong tendency to participate less. We have already suggested that perhaps half the adult population of the United States is alienated from politics, but only half of this group usually bothers to vote. Even unanimous support for a demagogue among the alienated would only add up to a quarter of the total possible vote. In a "winner take all" election, this would leave the extremist far short of the necessary majority; thus, an outright victory would require sizable support from other, nonalienated sectors. The potential for this "outside support" might very well exist. If it does, a theory of "mass politics" would need to take it into account. The "dangers" to democracy, that is, would not be confined to the alienated group but would necessarily encompass a portion of the nonalienated as well. Some possible sources of "nonalienated demagoguery" are isolated in the following analysis.

With these qualifications in mind, the relationship between political alien-

---

1964, Johnson would have received 15 of the total 45 votes, but, in fact, he received 20, a net increase of 5 votes, or 35.7% of the 14 votes available from mobilization. Correlatively, had the 1956–1960 low efficacy collegiate turn-out prevailed among Goldwater voters, he would have received 16 of the total 45 votes, but, in fact, he received 25, or 64.3% of the additional votes due to mobilization. Thus, the clear majority of the increased 1964 turn-out among the college alienated seems to have favored Goldwater. Among the high school drop-outs, comparatively, Johnson received 65% of the mobilization vote and Goldwater the remaining 35%—virtually the reverse of figures indicated for the college-educated group.

[16] One variant on the mobilization theme is that special combinations of efficacy and trust facilitate mobilization. As Gamson has put it, "a combination of a high sense of political efficacy and low political trust is the optimum combination for mobilization— a belief that influence is both possible and necessary" (1968:48; see also Fraser 1970; Hawkins et al. 1971; Paige 1971; Watts 1973). Lacking a measure of trust in the early years, this hypothesis cannot be tested by our earlier procedures. The basic prediction, however, was tested in the 1968 survey and was found wanting. Three measures of participation (turn-out, interest, and a summated "behavioral" index) were regressed on efficacy and trust, first as main effects and then in interaction. Following results reported by Fraser, Hawkins, and Watts, none of the interaction terms was significant (Wright 1973b:417–419).

TABLE 9.7
Political Alienation and Candidate Choice: 1964 and 1968[a]

	1964			1968			
	Johnson	Goldwater	N	Humphrey	Nixon	Wallace	N
			Efficacy				
Low	71.7	28.3	198	44.8	37.2	18.0	261
2	70.8	29.2	298	43.3	43.7	13.0	268
3	72.0	28.0	418	44.9	42.6	12.5	265
4	69.3	30.7	329	41.9	49.6	8.5	284
High	61.7	38.3	154	34.6	60.1	5.3	188
Total	69.9	30.1	1397	42.3	45.9	11.8	1266
			Trust				
Low	47.4	52.6	78	24.5	51.1	24.5	94
2	42.6	57.4	129	33.6	40.9	25.5	149
3	52.8	47.2	163	38.9	48.3	12.8	203
4	68.1	31.9	273	40.1	47.8	12.1	322
5	75.3	24.7	324	48.6	45.7	5.7	282
High	86.3	13.7	430	54.8	42.4	2.9	210
Total	69.9	30.1	1397	42.3	45.9	11.8	1266

a. Missing data are omitted. Rows sum to 100%. Preferences of voters and non-voters are treated equally.

ation and candidate preference is shown in Table 9.7. Although the evidence is mixed, the general patterns are consistent with the current account: The more alienated a respondent, the more likely he or she was to prefer Goldwater or Wallace. The major notable exception comes among the inefficacious, in 1964, who were somewhat *less* likely than the efficacious to have preferred Goldwater (gamma = +.07). The distrustful, on the other hand, were much more likely to have preferred Goldwater (gamma = −.47). In 1968, Wallace support was disproportionately high among both the inefficacious and the distrustful.

Focusing first on the Goldwater results, one question that arises is how to account for the divergence between efficacy and trust. Aberbach, whose analysis of these same data showed identical results, has suggested the following:

> One possibility, I think, is the nature of the Goldwater appeal. It was against a major governmental role in the society—opposed to a back-drop of social and economic security provided or supported by the government. This kind of appeal might ring true to those who distrust government, but the politically powerless would, if anything, tend to feel that they need this protection. [1969:99].

In light of this, some of the earlier efficacy–trust differences can be reviewed. First, as we saw in Chapter 6, social class is more strongly correlated with efficacy than with trust, which means that the distrustful are, on the average, higher status than the inefficacious. Likewise, Chapter 8 suggested that liberalism–conservatism is more strongly associated with trust than with efficacy; thus, the distrustful are not only higher status, but proportionately more conservative as well. Both these differences, let us mention, are consistent with Aberbach's suggestion.

Majority sentiment for Goldwater among the distrustful is certainly the most "dangerous" finding presented so far; as such, it warrants additional analysis. Accordingly, Table 9.8 shows the relationship between trust and

TABLE 9.8
Percent Preferring Goldwater by Trust, Region, Ideology, Party, Race, Age, and Social Class: 1964

	Trust							
	Low	N	Medium	N	High	N	Total	N
Region								
Non-South	48.8[a]	262	30.8	195	18.0	516	28.9	973
South	59.3	108	34.6	78	19.3	238	32.3	424
Ideology								
Liberal	34.0	97	21.8	110	11.4	352	17.4	559
Moderate	47.0	66	31.4	35	21.3	122	30.5	223
Conservative	66.1	180	43.9	107	27.9	226	44.6	513
Party Identification								
Democrat	28.7	157	8.6	139	6.1	444	11.4	740
Independent	52.8	91	33.3	57	15.1	152	30.0	300
Republican	82.5	120	75.3	73	58.1	148	70.4	341
Race								
White	55.5	344	35.5	245	21.2	656	33.5	1245
Non-white	3.9	26	0.0	28	0.0	98	0.7	152
Age								
18-35	52.1	94	27.5	80	15.1	252	25.6	426
36-59	52.5	181	29.3	133	18.5	367	29.7	681
60 +	51.1	94	43.3	60	24.6	134	37.2	288
Education								
Less than 12th	38.8	170	16.7	126	13.2	319	21.0	615
High school	58.5	106	38.0	61	20.9	268	32.6	445
Some college	69.6	92	52.0	75	23.9	163	43.0	330
Occupation								
Blue collar	43.2	162	16.4	110	14.0	349	22.0	621
White collar	65.2	118	49.0	104	21.7	267	38.0	489
Class Identification								
Working class	41.5	204	16.1	137	12.1	438	20.6	782
Middle class	66.0	147	46.3	121	26.8	295	41.2	563

a. Cell entries are the proportions favoring Goldwater.

Goldwater support, controlled for the usual background variables. Clearly, the tendency for the distrustful to have preferred Goldwater is not the spurious reflection of any of the variables shown in the table; the basic relationship is remarkably stable across all these controls. In 20 comparisons between most and least trusting, the evidence does not contain a single reversal. Even among those whose ideology or party affiliation should have led them away from Goldwater, there is still a pronounced effect for distrust.[17]

A second point, however, is that the politically distrustful are by no means the most "dangerous" group in the table, at least not with respect to Goldwater voting. Consider, for instance, the Republicans, whose Goldwater support, regardless of alienation, ran to 70%. Even among the most trusting Republicans, Goldwater support was higher than among the distrustful as a whole (58.1% as compared to 51.9%). Interestingly, Republican identification has also emerged as the single best predictor of membership in or support of other "extremist" movements and candidates, such as membership in radical rightist organizations (Wolfinger et al. 1964), support for the activities of Joseph Raymond McCarthy (Polsby 1960), and voting for George Wallace in the 1964 Presidential primaries (Rogin 1966). Judging from these studies and the evidence just presented, support for extremists is more likely to come from Republicans than from the politically discontented —a point to be kept in mind when one compiles the list of potential "disruptions."

Finally, the tendency for the distrustful to have given their majority support to Goldwater is not uniform across all distrustful groups. Majority preference for the extremist occurs among the distrustful in the South, among distrustful conservatives, Independents, and, especially, Republicans, and among the distrustful higher status respondents. The majority of even the *least* trusting nonsoutherners, Democrats, liberals, moderates, and lower status respondents rejected the Goldwater appeal. Taking a two-thirds majority as a first approximation of the nearly unanimous preference necessary for the votes of the distrustful to have a serious impact, we find only the distrustful conservatives, Republicans, and college-educated respondents reaching this level of support. White collar workers and middle class identifiers fall just a few points short. In the 1964 election, then, the "dangers" of political discontent were not evenly dispersed among the distrustful; rather, they were strongly concentrated in the higher strata. In the lower and working classes, large majorities of even the most alienated respondents refused the extremist alternative. We return to these points later in the discussion.

---

[17] The possibility that this represents "protest voting" among the distrustful is not supported by the evidence. Dividing the highly distrustful into those who voted "for" and those who voted "against" (see Table 8.2), we find 50.2% of the former ($n = 205$) and 48.6% of the latter ($n = 105$) to have preferred Goldwater. Thus, the "protest vote" of the distrustful was evenly split between the two candidates.

Turning now to the Wallace vote, the first and most obvious point to note is that, despite the general tendency for the alienated to have preferred Wallace in disproportionate numbers, immense majorities of even the most alienated rejected the Wallace candidacy. These majorities exceed 80% among the least efficacious and 75% among the least trusting. Here it is worth mentioning that Wallace was on the ballot in all 50 states. The use of his candidacy for "protest voting" or the registration of disgust would have been an exceedingly simple matter. Likewise, there would have been very little ambiguity in the "message" being sent. Having clearly opted *not* to exercise this once-in-a-lifetime opportunity, we may safely conclude that the "pull" of party, ideology, and political intelligence is still rather strong among three-quarters or more of the most discontented.

Wallace support, of course, was disproportionate in the South. A common theme is that white workers were also heavily drawn to his candidacy.[18] Accordingly, the relationship between Wallace support and political alienation, controlled for region and social class, is shown in Table 9.9.

First, the relationship between alienation and Wallace preference essentially disappears outside the South, particularly in the working class. Among white workers outside the South, alienation and Wallace support were not related, in contrast to the standard claims. Likewise, the Wallace appeal was uniform across social classes within the most alienated categories, or, in other words, the weak correlation of class and Wallace support disappears when controlled for region and alienation. Finally, taking only the most alienated blue collar workers in the South, (certainly a key group in Wallace's strategy), we note that a sizable 60% majority did *not* support Wallace. In other categories, the level of rejection is considerably higher. Among non-South blue collar workers, for example, some 90% rejected Wallace, regardless of alienation. These data make it plain that the Wallace vote was essentially a regional phenomenon, that, net of regional differences, the role of social class was insignificant, and that, net of region and social class, the role of alienation was minor. Given the potential for disruption posed by the Wallace effort, the evidence considered here supports our supposition that the "threat" of political alienation has been seriously exaggerated.

The obvious necessary appendage to this conclusion, of course, is: "insofar as normal electoral politics are concerned." There is an attendant and, in many ways, more important question to be asked about the likelihood of the

---

[18] See, for example, Lipset and Raab (1969) or Pettigrew *et al.* (1972). According to former, "the better educated, the more well-to-do, and those in middle class occupations were less likely to vote for Wallace than voters in the lower echelons" (1969:27). This conclusion, however, is based on a 4 percentage point difference between manual and nonmanual workers outside the South. The equivalent figure in the 1968 SRC survey was 1%. Controls for religion (no middle class Jews voted for Wallace) diminish even this trivial difference (Hamilton 1972:460–467). As the data discussed in the text make plain, the common theme of a special working class "vulnerability" to Wallace is a serious distortion.

TABLE 9.9
Alienation and Wallace Support by Region and Social Class: 1968
(whites only)

	Efficacy					
	Low	N	Medium	N	High	N
	Non-South					
White collar	8.9[a]	90	11.1	63	2.2	183
Blue collar	8.6	175	10.1	119	10.1	119
	South					
White collar	37.9	29	26.9	68	10.3	68
Blue collar	37.1	97	33.3	43	20.9	43

	Trust					
	Low	N	Medium	N	High	N
	Non-South					
White collar	11.1	108	6.9	87	0.7	141
Blue collar	12.2	139	9.5	84	6.8	148
	South					
White collar	39.1	46	16.7	36	2.4	42
Blue collar	43.0	71	28.9	45	18.8	48

a. Cell entries are the proportions preferring Wallace.

alienated abandoning normal democratic procedures altogether in favor of radical or disruptive tactics. Any clear tendencies along these lines would render the bulk of our previous analysis quaintly beside the point.

Behavioral possibilities for expressions of this sort are relatively infrequent. Despite the wholesale disruptions of the last decade—for example, race rioting or violent protest against the war—among representative American samples, there are only tiny minorities who have participated in any of these disruptions. The 1967 Verba–Nie sample, for example, found 8 cases out of 1495 who had taken part in the Vietnam-related demonstration or march (1972:282). In more recent surveys, this proportion would be somewhat higher, but still far short of the number of cases required to support detailed analysis.[19] Thus, the analysis of these *behaviors* in random probability sam-

[19] The trivial numbers involved in these actions, of course, do not belie their political significance. This, then, is a convenient opportunity to mention an important point

ples of the size we are working with is not possible. We are restricted, therefore, to examining *attitudes toward* various nonnormative or disruptive political tactics.

One question that is useful in this regard asks, "Suppose a law were being considered by the Congress in Washington that you considered very unjust or harmful. What do you think you could do about it?" Just what travesty the Congress might be contemplating is left to the respondent's imagination. Likewise, respondents are asked only what they *could* do about it, not what they would do. Thus, the question elicits a range of strategic possibilities, not a statement of behavioral intent. How, then, might Congress be opposed were it to pass a "very unjust or harmful" law? Table 9.10 shows the distribution of responses by political alienation.[20] Data are for 1968.

Focusing first on the population total, the following points should be noted. First, the majority of respondents would abandon any sort of group action in favor of the purely individualistic attempts at redress. In contrast to the pluralist view of how things work, cooperative group action is thought of by less than 10%. Second, next to the "dysfunctional" individual efforts, the most frequent response is "nothing." About a third offered this response. Adding this to the previous percentage, we find that about 90% of the electorate is effectively incapacitated by their perception of possible political strategies. This is an important point to keep in mind, when assessing the Almond–Verba claim that the sense of subjective political competence is what keeps the leadership responsive. According to these data, Congress could pass legislation that was widely seen as unjust or harmful and be effectively opposed in this action by less than a tenth of the population.

Breakdowns by alienation again reveal differences between the powerless

---

which we have ignored throughout this volume, namely, that a very small group of highly alienated persons—properly placed, organizationally sophisticated, and well-equipped—could wreak havoc with democratic institutions as we know them. Of the American population, 1% still represents more than 2 million people; the potential for insurgency among a "mere" 1% is enormous. The political alienation of race rioters, Vietnam protestors, New Left dissidents, or paramilitary reactionaries should obviously not be dismissed as politically irrelevant, and this, certainly, is not our intention. What we are trying to demonstrate is the analytic limitedness of these themes and perspectives when they are taken as a theory of *mass* politics, as categories or characterizations that describe entire segments of contemporary American society. It is to the sweep of these claims and their unwarranted generalization that we object.

[20] The coding of the responses is as follows: One class of response deals with "'working through informal groups." This includes such things as getting neighbors and friends to write letters, organizing meetings among neighbors and friends, talking to people, and so on. Another range of possibilities is "working through formal groups": through political parties, trade unions, voluntary associations, and so on. A third possibility is to work "as an individual": write letters, contact the media, consult a lawyer, and so on. Fourth, one might seek redress through the vote. Fifth, one might engage in some kind of protest or demonstration. Finally, one might believe that nothing can be done at all. The categories reported in the table reflect these various possibilities.

TABLE 9.10
"What could you do about an unjust law?" by Alienation: 1968

	Efficacy				Trust		
	Low	Medium	High	Total	Low	Medium	High
Work through formal groups	2.8	6.0	11.5	6.7	5.2	7.0	8.0
Work through informal groups	0.6	1.1	1.9	1.2	0.4	1.6	1.6
Work as an individual	36.5	65.3	74.3	56.7	54.5	55.4	59.6
Vote	3.3	3.7	2.5	3.1	4.1	1.9	2.8
Protest	0.4	0.0	0.6	0.4	0.3	0.6	0.4
Nothing	56.4	23.9	9.2	31.9	35.6	33.5	27.6
Total	100.0	100.0	100.0	100.0	100.1	100.0	100.0
N	539	268	479	1276	464	314	498

and the distrustful. Among the former group, "nothing" is the majority response, chosen by 56%. Apparently, the group takes its powerlessness quite seriously. "Working as an individual" was chosen by an additional third, with a smattering of respondents in each of the other categories. The results for trust, on the other hand, are virtually indistinguishable from the total. Among the alienated on both dimensions, any form of protest behavior occurs to less than 1%. Left to their own devices, then, it does not appear that the response of the alienated to a clear political injustice would be very threatening. Most would apparently do nothing at all; those who chose to act would overwhelmingly favor individualistic efforts over concerted group action; essentially none would "take to the streets" with their grievances.

A more informative and directly relevant set of questions is also included in the 1968 survey:

> There are many possible ways for people to show their disapproval or disagreement with governmental policies and actions. I am going to describe three such ways. We would like to know which ones you approve of as ways of showing dissatisfaction with the government, and which ones you disapprove of:
> 1. How about taking part in protest meetings or marches that are permitted by the local authorities? Would you approve of doing that, disapprove, or would it depend on the circumstances?
> 2. How about refusing to obey a law which one thinks is unjust, if the person feels so strongly about it that he is willing to go to jail rather than obey the law? Would you approve of a person doing that, disapprove, or would it depend on the circumstances?
> 3. Suppose all other methods have failed and the person decides to try to stop the government from going about its usual activities with sit-ins, mass meetings, demonstrations, and things like that. Would you approve of that, disapprove, or would it depend on the circumstances?

Again, it is important that the nature of these questions be appreciated. Respondents are not asked whether they would personally engage in these hypothetical behaviors, only whether they would approve or disapprove of their use. In addition, the nature of the "circumstances" under which they would be approved is not elicited; presumably, the respondent is free to consider *any* circumstances in which such tactics would be justified. Here again, these questions should not be seen as statements of behavioral intent, but rather as possible political tactics that might be approved when the circumstances are proper.

The relationship between political alienation and each of these three tactics is shown in Table 9.11. In the following discussion, we ignore the distinction between outright and conditional approval, since we assume that approval of these tactics would always depend on *some* circumstances. In the total population, then, about half said they would approve of protest meetings or marches that were permitted by the authorities; about two-fifths would approve of civil disobedience provided one were willing to pay the

TABLE 9.11
Approval of Radical Political Tactics by Alienation: 1968

	Efficacy						Trust					
	Low	2	3	4	High	Total	Low	2	3	4	5	High
Protest Meetings or Marches[a]												
Approve	10.7	16.9	18.1	25.8	27.1	19.7	16.5	10.9	16.1	21.9	21.8	25.2
Depends	24.6	24.4	32.1	25.4	28.7	26.8	24.7	32.0	23.6	21.5	29.7	31.2
Disapprove	64.8	58.7	49.8	48.8	44.2	53.5	58.8	57.1	60.3	56.6	48.5	43.6
N	244	254	265	287	188	1231	97	156	199	311	266	202
gamma	-.19						-.14					
Civil Disobedience												
Approve	9.7	15.3	14.6	14.8	19.6	14.7	10.6	15.0	14.3	17.7	12.9	14.8
Depends	26.6	23.0	23.8	23.2	23.3	23.7	26.6	26.8	30.6	19.7	22.7	20.8
Disapprove	63.7	61.7	61.5	62.0	57.1	61.5	62.8	58.2	55.1	62.6	64.4	64.4
N	226	261	260	284	189	1214	94	153	196	305	264	202
gamma	-.06						-.05					
Disruption of the Government												
Approve	6.9	8.4	9.4	7.3	8.1	8.1	9.5	5.8	5.6	7.6	9.5	10.4
Depends	16.9	15.1	19.3	19.4	18.4	17.9	15.8	14.1	18.4	18.9	19.5	18.1
Disapprove	76.2	76.5	71.3	73.3	73.5	74.0	74.7	80.1	76.0	73.5	71.0	71.5
N	231	251	254	288	185	1204	95	156	196	302	262	193
gamma	-.04						-.09					

a. Columns sum to 100%.

penalty; and more than a quarter went so far as to approve of disruptions that would prevent the government from going about its usual business. Without more extensive evidence on the propensity to employ these tactics, it is difficult to know how much of a "threat" these data represent. They do point to a lack of consensus on some of the basic rules of the democratic game.

The table also shows some moderate correlations between political alienation and approval of these tactics, but, in every case but one, the relationships are exceedingly weak and run in the *wrong* direction. The data, in other words, show a very slight tendency for the politically alienated to give *less* approval. This tendency is reasonably pronounced in two cases and insignificant in the remaining four. The best that can be concluded is that, if there is a "threat" posed by the approval of these tactics, it is certainly not one that is concentrated among the politically discontented.[21]

ALIENATION AND BEHAVIOR: SUMMARY AND DISCUSSION

The major empirical findings of the chapter can be quickly summarized. First, a clear and unambiguous characteristic of the political alienated is that they participate less. Second, this tendency was largely unaffected by the Goldwater and Wallace campaigns. The rather minor "mobilization" occasioned by those candidates was not unanimous in its direction; those favoring and opposing the demagogue were apparently mobilized in roughly equal proportion. The main exception comes among the college-educated alienated who were clearly mobilized at least by Goldwater and whose mobilization favored Goldwater. Although largely "unavailable" in terms of participation, there is some tendency for the politically alienated to prefer extremist candidates, but this tendency is not especially pronounced and masks the fact that large majorities of even the most alienated respondents in fact rejected the extremists. Again, major exception comes among the higher status alienated, especially in 1964, when Goldwater support ran to about two-thirds. Finally, the politically alienated harbor no special disrespect for the rules of democratic procedure, at least so far as we have been able to measure them. The only minor tendency that does emerge is that the alienated show slightly less support for nontraditional tactics. With the major exception of the college-

[21] Controls for region, political ideology, Vietnam attitudes, party identification, education, occupation, class identification, race, 1968 candidate preference, and age isolated no group wherein alienation and approval of these tactics was consistently associated in the expected direction (Wright 1973b:454–455). These controls presented 56 chances for the alienated to be more disposed than the unalienated to approval of these tactics; the correlation was negative in 43 of these cases. Even among groups in which approval of these tactics was high (e.g., Vietnam "doves," blacks, and so on), the most approving were also the least alienated.

educated alienated discussed later, the "threat" of political alienation does not appear in these results.

Concerning the tendency for the alienated to participate less, the data merely confirm a score of previous studies. As Rosenberg has put it, "in most cases, a precondition for political activity is the conviction that what one does will make a difference, will have an impact of some sort" (1954:354)—a conviction which the alienated, by definition, lack. The political implications of this, however, have seldom been fully explored. In many accounts, in fact, apathy is assumed to reflect some repressed and unwholesome instincts—a "latent" reservoir of discontent that may erupt at any moment, a bundle of potential responses waiting for the appropriate stimulus. There is very little that can be done to counter this line of argument, since the possibility always exists that some future demagogue will succeed where the others have failed. All that can be done is to formulate the results in negative terms, that is, to enumerate those apparent circumstances that leave the "reservoir of discontent" untapped. Thus, presidential candidates who profess no aversion to nuclear weapons, who prefer a militant and belligerent foreign policy, who are recognized as illiberal forces that will beat back the insistent demands of unruly blacks, students and other emerging groups, who advocate "extremism in the defense of liberty," who consciously appeal to the sense of estrangement and negativism, who urge that their candidacies be used as platforms for denunciation of politics as usual, who are hostile toward the political leadership, and who purposely design their slogans and strategies to appeal to the previously apathetic and alienated group—these candidacies, moreover, occurring in contexts of general economic stagnation, of bitter debate over the nation's foreign policy, during a showdown over the war in Vietnam, in the midst of racial riots and other turmoil, when public immorality is on the rise and the political situation is such that the party conventions must be militarily protected to insure that calm will prevail—these are the specific candidates and circumstances which did *not* mobilize the discontented.

Assuming that this enumeration contains most of the factors that are normally thought to "trigger" the latent repressed instincts, there is now a real question in our minds whether *any* set of conditions would be sufficient to turn the trick. Certainly, future claims in this regard must be treated with cautious skepticism. Such claims, we expect, will abound, most of all in the post-Watergate era and in the midst of world recession. Will a radical demagogue now emerge to exploit the new "crisis" situation? There is nothing in the recent political history of the United States to rule this out, but there is clear reason to doubt that he or she would be very successful or would conscript the growing body of politically alienated into the cause. The response of the alienated to such a demagogue, we expect, would follow rather closely along the lines of the Goldwater and Wallace patterns: Most of the discontented would still simply not participate, and the remainder would once again be split along party or ideological lines. Any "threat" to democratic government will have to come from other sources.

As mentioned, the usual tendency not to participate has been widely reported. In many cases, however, the report is coupled with some attempt to negate the apparent lesson. We read the evidence as follows: The politically alienated in the mass are unique only in their tendency to participate less. As such, their alienation is seldom even entered into the political equation. Therefore, they typically have no effect on the course of politics and government, one way or another. If we put it as simply as possible: Alienation + Inactivity = Nothing.

There are, to be sure, some qualifications to be appended. Demagogic candidates do seem to hold some residual attraction for the politically discontented, particularly when class, party, or ideological appeals are combined with appeals to frustration and estrangement. Thus, Goldwater was fairly successful among alienated upper middle class conservative Republicans but was not so successful elsewhere. The important point, of course, is that the alienated do not share a common party or ideological attachment; any "convergence" of appeals thus diminishes the alienated constituency enormously.

Party loyalties, in particular, prevent the "protest" vote of the alienated from being realized. In 1968, for example, between two-thirds and three-quarters of all Democrats preferred Humphrey, regardless of alienation; likewise, between 80% and 90% of all Republicans preferred Nixon, again regardless of alienation. In 1968, no less than any other year, party identification remained the primary vote constraint—among alienated and unalienated alike. As long as this continues to be true, it is clear that alienation per se will never have a decisive impact. To assume otherwise is to assert that party, ideology, background, and predisposition make no difference, that the alienated are driven, politically, by their alienation and nothing else. This, obviously, is seldom going to be the case. In other words, the category of "political alienation" contains some tough young workers, but it also contains some very untough aging grandmothers. It contains some hard-core reactionaries, but sizable numbers of liberals as well. It contains some whose negativism is total and diffuse, but others whose orientations are more moderate. The prospects of "the" politically alienated reacting as a group are exceedingly remote, no matter how deep their frustration, estrangement, or despair.

A related and equally implausible assumption is that alienation is a fundamentally irrational attitude that, therefore, leads to irrational behaviors. Both the correlates of and trends in political alienation suggest that this is not the case; rather, it appears that political alienation is little more than a simple statement of the realities of political milieu. This conclusion, to be sure, is present in the literature. Thompson and Horton, for example, suggest that alienation "reflects an accurate perception of the facts of life as they are lived in contemporary American communities (1960:192)." Later they note that the sense of powerlessness is "founded on social reality, social reality as lived and perceived by the alienated and projected onto the political world (Horton and Thompson 1962:493)." What *is* absent is any discussion of the political implications. If alienation is nothing more than an accurate perception of the political world, then on what grounds can one assume that it will lead to subsequent pathological behaviors? Consistent with this, we have found neither "danger" nor "irrationality" in the evidence considered here.

A final implausibility, related to the "irrationality" assumption, is that alienation is normally experienced as "the loss or absence of a previous or desirable relationship (Keniston 1965:454)." Such "losses," of course, will be most acute "where many persons have been socialized to the value of equality and find themselves living in circumstances of practiced inequality (Horton and Thompson 1962:486)." As our review of the relevant literature suggested, however, many politically alienated persons are *not* socialized to the value of equality; rather, many are taught from the earliest possible age that people like themselves have no political power and that those who do are not to be trusted. For them, alienation is not experienced as a "loss" simply because most of them never even thought they "had" what they are now "losing." Thus, they will not have experienced their alienation in a fashion that requires radical "corrective" measures.

On the other hand, trends in political alienation do suggest some formidable "losses" in the decade of the 1960s. As the decade progressed there were increasing numbers of the politically alienated whose early socialization might not have prepared them for the frustrations that they were encountering. The growing alienation among political conservatives from 1960 to 1964 is a case in point; they had certainly "lost" a previous "desirable relationship," namely, disproportionate influence on the federal government. Significantly, they were also the group most strongly attracted to Goldwater's candidacy. This suggests that subsequent research might profit from a careful distinction between the recently alienated and the always alienated, and, correlatively, that the search for "disruptive" consequences be focused on the former group.[22]

These points, of course, would seem to imply that the prospects for "disruption" should have been even greater in 1968 than they had been in 1964; after all, the proportion "recently alienated" increased dramatically during this period. Despite this, however, there was very little apparent mobilization due to the Wallace candidacy, and, nationwide, the proportion rejecting that option amounted to about 90%. Most of the explanation here is that Wallace had mounted a third party effort and, therefore, faced the difficult task of breaking the hold of party identification. A second problem is that his

[22] Such information would not be difficult to obtain. A possible sequence of questioning, for example, might be as follows:

How much of the time do you think you can trust the government in Washington to do what is right—just about always, most of the time, or only some of the time? (If "only some of the time") Have you always felt this way about the government in Washington, or was there a time when you felt you could trust the government more?
(If the latter) What made you change your mind? (If unclear) When was that?

main issue, namely race, was, in fact, unrelated to the alienation trends (see Chapter 7, Footnote 26). This means that the growing body of the recently alienated were split on the racial issue. Finally, the major source of increased alienation from 1964 to 1968 was growing disaffection with administration conduct of the war, and here all the trends were toward increasing support for the more dovish options. Thus, Wallace's position on the war was the exact opposite of that which might have appealed to the "recently alienated" group.

The above points also help explain why we have found support for the mass society claims to have been isolated primarily in the college-educated upper middle class. Among the college-educated alienated, as we saw, there was a pronounced mobilization effect, particularly in 1964, whose main beneficiary was Goldwater. Likewise, Goldwater support among the group ran to two-thirds. According to the Easton–Dennis research, the upper middle class *is* one group in the society "socialized to the value of equality," both as a normative ideal and as a matter of fact. Concomitantly, subscription to regime norms in the upper class is exceptionally high. The upper middle class alienated person, then, is proportionally more likely to experience his or her alienation as a "loss," and, moreover, the alienation will be at odds with the everyday ideology extant in the upper middle class milieu. Accordingly, hypotheses about potential "disruptions" have relatively greater credibility in reference to the alienated upper middle class. Their mobilization by and uncharacteristic support for the Goldwater candidacy is, thus, another example of the "hazards" posed by the withdrawal of upper middle class support.[23]

Political alienation, we are told, threatens the political constraints that make democratic government possible. This is a credible hypothesis, however, only if the alienated are disposed to activities that directly challenge the regime, and the evidence presented in this and the preceeding chapter strongly suggests that they are not. The theory of political alienation not only underestimates its extent and basic nature, but also greatly exaggerates its political effects. Along these lines, a passage from Thompson and Horton is instructive:

> Political alienation would be one thing if the alienated accept their lack of institutionalized civic power and express their feeling of alienation in political disinterest and nonparticipation; it would be quite another thing if, imbued with norms which hold that all citizens have and should exercise civic rights and responsibilities, the alienated systematically express their alienation in political action [1960:193].

[23] See also Chapter 6, Footnote 26. Although not especially prone to voting for Wallace in the 1968 Presidential election, upper middle class support for Wallace in the various Democratic primaries has been noted by several researchers (e.g., Kritz 1970; Conway 1968; Rogin 1966, 1969). The absence of this support in the general election, we assume, reflects the presence of a "safe," "respectable," and "trustworthy" conservative Republican alternative.

In this respect, the authors are accurate: What alienation "is" depends on its effects. On the basis of very little persuasive research, it is often concluded that alienation is, indeed, "quite another thing," but our data lead to a different conclusion. The unique distinguishing feature of the politically discontented in the mass public is that they participate less. The evidence reviewed here thus suggests that, whatever else political alienation might be, it most definitely is not a threat to democracy. If there is a compelling empirical case for the alternative, it has yet to be made.

10

Political Alienation
and Democratic Stability:
A Dissenting Opinion

A T the close of Chapter 3, the major empirical issue of this volume was posed, whether or not consensus theory is a viable alternative to pluralism as a solution to "the paradox of stable democracy." The ensuing six chapters have presented evidence bearing on the various facets of this question. The results of these investigations can be simply stated: Like pluralism, consensus theory fails as an empirical description of contemporary American political life.

In the following pages, we review the evidence and arguments which have led us to this conclusion. In the course of this review, we also note questions that still remain to be answered and discuss some revisions to the basic theory that seem necessary in light of the evidence presented in this book. Then we return to the "larger issues" that were first presented in Chapters 1 and 2—the character of "support" in democratic societies, the political competence of the mass, and the prospects for participatory democracy in the modern era.

AN OVERVIEW OF THE EVIDENCE

The critique of political alienation theory advanced here is based on the following empirical points: First, consensus on certain key particulars does not exist to any great degree. Second, the nature of political alienation has

257

been misrepresented in previous accounts. Third, the "linkage" between political alienation and many commonly hypothesized "disruptive behaviors" has not been empirically demonstrated. Each of these points is discussed later.

Concerning the first, it can be noted that about half the adult population of this and other stable western democracies reject important elements of the "democratic myth." Half, that is, are skeptical of their ability to influence political decisions, and half entertain some doubts about the intelligence, trustworthiness, and honesty of the political leadership. It is precisely the opposite beliefs, however, that are often said to make democracy possible. Despite this, the evidence presented here makes it plain that modern democracies can "persist"—indeed, manage to do quite well—even when there is widespread disagreement concerning the efficacy of citizen participation and the competence of political elites.

One implication that obviously should *not* be drawn from these results is that there are *no* "shared norms and values" extant in the American population. Widespread consensus on matters other than efficacy and trust might well exist. For example, almost everyone would probably agree that the rule of law is preferable to the rule of force, that violence is worth avoiding whenever possible, that honesty and justice are laudable virtues. Some disagreement *is* likely to arise in the application of these principles to concrete political situations, that is, when it is possible to avoid violence and when it is not, or what constitutes a just and honest policy. On the principles themselves, however, there may be wide agreement, and, if so, consensus theory would make a valuable and salient point. At the same time, however, there is some question as to whether or not any profound "mechanisms" are needed to create and enforce the elements of this consensus. They seem to be the kinds of things that would occur to most people in the normal course of maturation.

Conversely, there are other beliefs that probably would not "naturally occur" to many people. One of these is that they have some significant impact on the policy decisions of their government. At face value, such a belief would appear to be farfetched; it is something that is almost immediately contradicted by one's daily experience. As the theorists themselves recognize, it is simply not possible for this belief to be literally true. The theorists know this; the political leadership probably also knows it; and the people themselves know it, or, more precisely, about half of them do. As mentioned earlier, however, American democracy seems to survive anyway. At the very least, this suggests that there is something amiss in the received account.

Much the same could be said for political trust, another attitude that probably could not be sustained over any extended period without some evidentiary basis. There may well be an "advance" on the commodity of trust paid at the point of entry in adult political life, but it is unreasonable to assume that no return on the advance is expected. Rather, trust is probably offered on the condition that some demonstration of trustworthiness be forthcoming, and, otherwise, it is withdrawn. According to the theory, this would constitute an "unstable basis" for democracy. To emphasize this point, however, democracies apparently function even without large reservoirs of unconditional trust. How can this be the case?

Part of the answer lies in the implausible roles envisioned for the attitudes of efficacy and trust. Why, after all, is widespread "subjective political competence" said to be necessary? The answer is that this creates a potential for citizen activism which, in turn, checks and restrains the elite. But what restraint, really, does this potential provide? Elites are restrained, if at all, by their own sense of what is right and equitable, by the dictates of their political ideologies, and by their suspicion that if they are corrupt or inefficient, there is a chance that they will suffer defeat in the next election. In this respect, it is *elite* beliefs, not mass beliefs, which constitute the primary source of restraint. If *they* believe that they will be punished for misdeeds and wrongdoing, then they will be restrained. What the mass believes is, more or less, beside the point. The same holds true for the attitude of political trust. According to the theory, trust is essential because it makes citizens willing to "turn power over." As mentioned elsewhere, however, citizens really do not "turn power over" in any empirical sense. They are born into an on-going political system; they might not (but probably do) "go along" with its structural arrangements and adjust their lives accordingly—not in any overt, conscious way, but as part of the process of acclimatizing oneself to realities about which little can be done. It is, certainly, an empirical *possibility* that this "adjustment" would lead to vast quantities of trust and allegiance, but it is also possible that it would not. It is not clear that the operation of a modern democracy would be seriously affected, one way or the other. The evidence presented here strongly implies that democracies can "absorb" a fair quantity of *dis*trust and *in*competence without major adverse consequences.

In this, it may be useful to distinguish between attitudes that are *necessary* for the stable functioning of democracy and those that are *convenient* for incumbent regimes. The beliefs of efficacy and trust fall primarily into this latter category. For example, if citizens *do* believe that they have a voice in the running of the government, and that public policy is the expression of majority interests, then the blame for policy failures is shifted from the system or its representatives to the people themselves. If the people are responsible for what goes wrong, then the impetus to "change the system" is greatly diminished. This, to be sure, is no minor convenience, but it is not something that is absolutely critical for the persistence of the regime. One obvious alternative, for example, is to assure, as best one can, against policy failures in the first place. Concerning political trust, it can again be safely admitted that elites would *prefer* to operate in an environment of warm and enthusiastic confidence. This gives them a certain latitude that they might otherwise not enjoy. Here again, if it is widely believed that elites are responsible persons whose only dedication is to the common good, the blame for inefficiencies or outright failure must lie elsewhere. Can it be argued, however, that such confidence and trust *must* be present before the system can actually function—before garbarge can be collected or Social Security paid? Evidence presented here makes this claim seem dubious. The alternative to "unreasoning allegiance," after all, is "reasoned allegiance"—allegiance based upon the continued good conduct of public affairs. So here too, the alternative to "inculcating regime norms" is to assure that the government is indeed being run as fairly and effectively as possible.

There is a recurring assumption in the texts that no amount of political effectiveness would, on its own, be sufficient to restrain the mass. Mass demands, it is said, will perpetually outrun the ability of the system to deliver, hence the need for manipulating political consciousness at "an early and impressionable age." We will have more to say about the "assumption of mass insatiability" later in the chapter. For now, let us only note a paradox in this line of reasoning. As already mentioned, the theorists themselves understand that the attitudes of efficacy and trust will only have a marginal relation to political realities, and this is why they are commonly referred to as "exaggerations," or even "myths." Despite the overt fantasy of these beliefs, however, the theorists argue that the system, not only can, but *must* make citizens adhere to them. If citizens can and must be convinced of something that is recognized as *false* (namely, that they do have some important say in how the government runs things), then why should it be especially difficult to convince them of things that are obviously *true*, namely, that resources are necessarily limited, that everything cannot be done at once, and, therefore, that some modicum of restraint must be commonly exercised when "issuing demands" to the government? One might also ask which of these beliefs seems, on the surface, to provide a more stable and reasonable basis for democratic government, and which is more likely to contribute to "political disappointments." Surely, the myths themselves must add to the overall strain, once one realizes that the system really does not function according to the fairy tale description.

Although the sheer quantities of powerlessness and distrust present in American society cast doubt on political alienation theory, other aspects of the evidence strengthen the critique. First is the social distribution of discontent. As we have shown, alienation is most extensive just where, according to the theory, the potential for damage is thought to be greatest—among the blacks, white southerners, and the working and marginal middle classes. Excepting the blacks, these groups are commonly depicted as authoritarian, proto-fascist, anxious, and unstable. When they are calm and placid, the system enjoys a temporary respite, an "uneasy truce." Their alienation, likewise, is an "explosive potential." If this were taken seriously, one would have expected the American system to have long since collapsed. There has been, moreover, no lack of opportunities for these groups to express their discontent. They might well have risen up in unanimous support of Goldwater. Again, excepting the blacks, they were widely *expected* to succumb to the demagoguery of Wallace's appeal. Certainly, they might have, at any time in the past decade, "taken to the streets" with their grievances. By and large, however, they did not, least of all in a collective political action. This, then, suggests that the threat of a highly alienated lower, working, or marginal middle class has been exaggerated well beyond anything that can be supported with persuasive evidence.

How has the system withstood the alienation of these "peripheral" social classes? The answer to this question need not be mysterious: For the most part, these classes lack the political resources to engage in an effective challenge, even assuming (in the face of a strong contrary suspicion) that they would otherwise be inclined to do so. Consider the time and effort that would be involved just in electing an "insurgent" to a local or state office. Some acceptable candidate would first have to be located. An office would have to be opened and staffed, leaves of absence from work secured, mailing lists created, updated, and maintained. Monies would have to be found, canvassing undertaken, the legalities of appearing on the ballot attended to. All along, there would be the constant risk that it would all be for nothing, that the candidate would go down to defeat. Where in the society are these resources located? For the most part, they are *not* located in the lower, working, and marginal middle classes. It would take a rather immense amount of zeal to overcome the barriers just enumerated, far more than anything indicated in the data considered here. The effort required to mount an insurgency at the national level would be vastly more formidable. Thus, the alienation of these classes is probably "contained," first and foremost, by the strong positive correlation between real and perceived powerlessness.

It can be expected, therefore, that the alienated and peripheral classes in democratic societies will ordinarily play no *initiative* role in challenging the legitimacy of the regime. In that respect, they are relatively harmless. On the other hand, it may be asked whether they might not support insurgent movements that were initiated elsewhere in the society, but here the data seem fairly clear: They did *not* support the Goldwater "insurgency" in dangerous or disproportionate numbers; they did *not* support the Wallace insurgency; indeed, they seem to be somewhat hostile to the very concept of insurgency itself—that is, if their attitudes towards the tactics of insurgency can be taken as an indication. This, in turn, suggests that the very character of political alienation in the peripheral classes has been misrepresented, a point to which we return later.

One final disconfirming aspect of the evidence is the sharp increase in political alienation over the last 15 years. As mentioned in Chapter 7, there was considerable variation in the theory's independent variable during the period, but relatively little "system instability" resulted, at least little that could be empirically tied to a rising level of alienation *in the mass*. There was, to be sure, an increase in "disruptive outbursts" during this time, but the alienated masses were probably more the victims than the perpetrators. Certainly, they were not responsible for Vietnam and, therefore, not responsible for any "outbursts" that Vietnam might have occasioned. Likewise, it was not their policies which resulted in the oppression of blacks nor was the steady decay of the economy their doing. These policies were formulated and pursued by political elites, in some cases *against* the expressed policy preferences of the mass. In this respect, it is the political leadership itself—"the best and the brightest"—which has led to the discontent of half the population. In this same vein, one might also ask whether there was ever an occasion during the 1960s when the democratic regime itself was in danger of "going under." Probably, there was not. With the exception of black riots and New Left violence, both readily contained by the deployment of military force (this point will be more fully discussed later), most of the "disruption" of the 1960s was well within the boundaries of the Bill of Rights. Even at the nadir of the Johnson administration, there was no apparent decline in the supply of "authoritative decisions." Presidential directives were still issued and obeyed. Laws were still passed and enforced. Bureaucrats and civil servants still showed up for work; governmental checks were still cashed. Even during the worst of times, things proceeded more or less as they always had. One possible exception to this conclusion would be Nixon and Watergate. Here, there apparently *was* some uncertainty and hesitation in the higher circles, some anxiety about whether the reins of government were in responsible hands, and a widespread suspicion that the president himself had conspired in illegal, indeed felonious, acts. As discussed in the first chapter, however, it would take a rather imaginative set of assumptions to find cause in any of this in the political alienation of the mass. Besides, despite the potential for instability, a transition out of the Nixon presidency *was* eventually accomplished. The result of this transition, to make one final point, was the spectacle of a sitting president who had never been elected to anything beyond U.S. Representative from Grand Rapids. Here, some serious question might well have been raised about the legitimacy of the entire transaction and some "corrective" insurgency subsequently undertaken, but nothing of the sort transpired, not even distant rumblings. So, despite the sharp increases in alienation and political discontent over the last decade, despite the recurrent potential for instability, we conclude that the American democratic system is keeping an even keel.

This brings us to the second major element in our critique of political alienation theory: that the character of political alienation in the mass is seriously distorted in the available accounts. This distortion proceeds along a number of lines. First, there is an assumption that alienation is rooted in the "dislocations" of the modern society. Secondly, there is a recurrent (although often implicit) suggestion that political alienation is somehow an irrational and quasi-pathological dimension of political consciousness. Third, there is the common depiction of alienation as a "loss" or "disconfirmation" of some previous, more desirable state. Finally, there is the assumption that political alienation is a unitary phenomenon, that it makes some sense to speak about "the alienated" as a distinct political group. Most of the hypotheses that link alienation to disruptive political behavior are based on one or more of the assumptions just listed, but none of them is sustained by the evidence reported in previous chapters.

First, political alienation is almost certainly *not* rooted in the "disruptions" and "dislocations" of the modern mass society. Virtually all available evidence contradicts this thesis. Instead, the evidence points to class political cultures and the mechanisms by which those cultures are transmitted, as the origin of alienation. The themes of powerlessness and distrust are part of the content of political socialization in the working and lower classes, just as the opposite themes form the basis for political socialization in the upper middle and upper classes. In neither case, incidentally, is there any implication or persuasive evidence that the socialization process is perfectly successful. On the contrary, as evidence presented in this book makes clear, there are many "integrated" workers and many "alienated" executives. The general effects of the process, however, are in the indicated direction. Political alienation originates, then, *not* in "urbanization," "rationalization," or "dislocation," but, speaking epigrammatically, in supper-time conversation, as one of the informal political "lessons" transmitted across generations in the lower and working classes.

One implication of the "class cultures" thesis is that efficacy and trust, or their opposites, are not isolated political attitudes, but rather elements in entire belief configurations that characterize the various social classes. To date, relatively little evidence exists, one way or the other, on this point. The most suggestive research produced so far is that reported by Rytina and associates (especially Huber [Rytina] and Form 1972). According to this source, the political culture of the upper middle class includes, not only confidence in their ability to influence political decisions and confidence in the political leadership, but also beliefs, such as "no one group really runs the country. Instead, important decisions about national policy are made by lots of different groups," that "there is plenty of opportunity in America and anyone who works hard can go as far as he wants," that "all young people of high ability have a fairly equal opportunity to go to college," and that "in America, everyone gets fair and equal treatment under the law (Form and Rytina 1969; Rytina *et al.* 1970)." In the poor and working classes, the opposite beliefs were primarily found. This is not to say that *everyone* in the upper middle class accepts these beliefs, or that everyone outside the class rejects them. Rather, these are the tendencies revealed by the evidence, and these tendencies are consistent with the depiction of the political consciousness of the upper middle class offered in earlier chapters. For the most part, the higher strata *are* "socialized to the value of equality," and to the belief that equality is an operant fact. Therefore, one might expect the later "disconfirmations" encountered in adult political life to have their greatest impact here. We return to this point later in our discussion.

Although apparently rooted in class political cultures, the attitudes of efficacy and trust, or their opposites, are not firmly fixed by early training or indoctrination, in contrast to a direct implication of consensus theory. Rather, these attitudes are periodically re-evaluated to take into account changing circumstances, usually when there is some objective change in the responsiveness or quality of political leadership. This selective offering and withdrawal of support, depending on the quality of outputs produced, more closely resembles the "eternal vigilance" of classical theory than the "rather unstable basis of loyalty" depicted in modern texts. This is perhaps the *least* realistic assertion in the modern theory, that citizen support must, or even could, be independent of the effects of day-to-day outputs.

The evidence just discussed bears directly on the second and third "distortions" listed earlier: It strongly suggests that political alienation is rooted in the conditions of social and political life, not in something "irrational" or "pathological," and certainly not in anything that is experienced as a "loss." Many of the politically alienated in the adult population have borne their alienation since very early in their lives. As such, their alienation is an attitude that would normally fall prey to the "acclimatization" process mentioned earlier. It is simply not reasonable to expect that people will walk around from age eight until death angry and frustrated by their sensed inability to influence political decisions, constantly on the look for some Herculean movement that will correct the sensed injustice. Rather, one would develop other attitudes and orientations that would make one's alienation tolerable. This is another issue for which no well-developed research literature exists, so the content and character of those "other attitudes" can only be guessed at. They might include some correlative belief that things could scarcely be otherwise, that powerlessness and distrust are the normal and natural state of affairs. There might also be some feeling that, bad as it is, the on-going system is no worse than any available alternative. After all, if all politicians are corrupt and cannot be trusted, there is little reason to replace one set of politicians with another. A third possibility is that these alienated attitudes eventually come to serve as "rationalizing" beliefs. If "people like me" really do not have a say in governmental decisions, there is no need to go through the motions of political participation. Since, as we discuss later, most people are not all that interested in politics anyway, alienation, in many cases, might well be experienced as a "relief," as an attitude that relieves one of democratic responsibilities.

It should be emphasized that the preceding paragraph describes the central tendencies suggested by the evidence; it says nothing about outlying cases. Obviously, there will be instances in which alienation *is* experienced as a loss or disconfirmation, instances in which one's early socialization has provided an inadequate preparation for the political frustrations encountered as an adult. The trends in political alienation even imply that the phenomenon of experiencing alienation in this manner has probably increased. This signals another problem in the alienation literature, the failure to distinguish empirically between the "recently alienated" and the "always alienated." Any typical study of "the alienated" mixes these two vastly different experiences together, and this, we presume, has contributed to the confused and contradictory findings. Most hypotheses linking alienation to disruptive behavior assume that alienation *is* experienced as a loss; evidence reviewed here suggests that persons experiencing their alienation in this way are probably far outnumbered by those whose alienation has long been a part of their political thinking. Without some empirical procedure for separating the two groups, the disruptive potential of political alienation can never be definitively assessed.

Some indication of the importance of this distinction is afforded by data presented earlier, although, in the available surveys, the "recently" and "always" alienated can only be distinguished through remote inference. In our case, the inference has been based on the Easton–Dennis findings that socialization into "regime norms" is most characteristic of the high status, upper middle class groups. One implication of this finding is that relatively more upper middle class persons *do* enter adult political life imbued with positive feelings of support for the regime, and, correlatively, that proportionately more of them experience their adult alienation as a "disconfirmation" of previous beliefs. Consistent with these implications, the relatively few "disruptive" consequences that we have been able to isolate have been concentrated primarily among the politically alienated in the upper middle class. This evidence is drawn essentially from the Goldwater experience of 1964, when the college-educated were apparently mobilized by Goldwater and picked him by a two-to-one majority. Given the many inferences that are necessary to link these behaviors to the "recency" of alienation within the group, no firm conclusions can be drawn from these results. The only suggestion is that the distinction between "recently" and "always" alienated should be pursued in subsequent research, and that the search for disruptive consequences should focus on the former.

The final, and potentially most misleading, distortion of the character of political alienation is the assumption that it is a unitary phenomenon, that "the alienated" actually exist, and can be refered to, as a group. Once again, the evidence does not support this depiction. This point has been made so many times in the course of our presentation that it serves little purpose to review all the evidence here. "The alienated" in contemporary American society contains blacks and southern whites, liberals and conservatives, Democrats and Republicans, Protestant and Catholics—all in approximately equal proportions. The "group" is composed primarily of persons from the working and lower middle classes but contains sizable numbers of professionals and businessmen as well. It contains some "authoritarian" young workers and many aging widows and grandparents. It is, in the contemporary argot, a very mixed bag. The "mix," in turn, imposes some formidable limits on any "insurgencies" that might ensue. Policies that excite or appease one faction would normally be received with some hostility by another faction. Their unanimous joint response to a single political stimulus is consequently improbable. As a group, they are divided on all the major issues of the day. The alienated share little beyond their discontent that would bind them together as a cohesive social or political force.

On the basis of what must now be regarded as empirically dubious assumptions, political alienation is often linked to attitudinal and behavioral dispositions that are said to threaten the stability of democratic regimes. This leads to the third and final major element of our critique, that the presumed linkage to potentially disruptive behavior has not yet been convincingly demonstrated. Since the plausibility of the theory depends primarily on these linkages, this is by far the most serious of the theory's shortcomings.

First, there is very little evidence to suggest that political alienation is accompanied by uniquely regressive ideologies. Most researchers who have attempted to address this issue have remarked on the relative absence of any persuasive evidence: It is "one of the more popular (and untested) themes in modern social science," "more speculative than empirical," and so on (see our review in Chapter 3). The lack of empirical support is not difficult to understand, since the hypothesis is based on the erroneous assumption that the alienated pine for their "prior," unalienated existence. Accordingly, the evidence presented here also uncovered little support. There were, to be sure, modest correlations in the general direction indicated by the hypothesis, on the order of .2. These correlations, however, mask what is, to us, the most salient feature of the data, that the alienated are deeply split among themselves on most major components of political ideology. This makes it seem unlikely that alienation, in and of itself, leads to "backward" or "unenlightened" political preferences. A more plausible hypothesis, suggested by the analysis of Chapter 7, is that alienation is really the *dependent* variable in the "alienation–ideology" relationship. When one's preferences are not being adequately reflected in the policy process, there is a tendency to become alienated. The relationship between alienation and ideology, in short, probably varies according to the specific policies being pursued by the elite.

A second hypothesis is that the alienated harbor a diffuse negativism directed toward all things political, but, here too, little persuasive evidence exists. For the most part, this particular "linkage" has been established almost exclusively by assertion. In contrast, evidence presented here shows that the politically alienated are not especially likely to "vote against" or to cast a protest vote, are not hostile to all politicians, and are no less able than the rest of the population to discern important differences between the major parties. When they do bother to vote (somewhat less frequently than the nonalienated, to be sure), the factors that "constrain" their votes are pretty much the same as that predominate among the rest of the population; like almost everybody else, they vote along class, party, regional and ideological lines.

Lacking the regressive ideologies and diffuse negativism that might otherwise facilitate "demagogic" appeals, it is not reasonable to expect that the politically alienated would have been mobilized by either Goldwater or Wallace, and the evidence presented here suggests they were not. Even in the white South or among political conservatives, there was no sharp rise in participation among the "previously apathetic and alienated" masses or, more accurately, none that clearly benefited the extremist candidates. There was, among the politically alienated, a very slight *preference* for such candidates, but this minor tendency must be assessed in light of their strong proclivity to participate less. Again, the modest correlations mask an even more important aspect of the data, namely, that large majorities of the politically alienated in fact *rejected* the demagogic appeals. Here it is worth recalling that some three-fifths of the highly alienated, working-class southern whites did *not* vote for Wallace in 1968, despite the common assumption that this group, if no other, should have been enthusiastic about the prospects of a Wallace victory. There is always the possibility that some future demagogue, cleverer and more charismatic, will succeed where the others have failed, but, given what is now known about the character of political alienation, this possibility can only be regarded as remote.

Of the many "linkages" asserted in political alienation theory, the only one that is clearly documented is that the alienated participate less. Several dozen prior studies, as well as the evidence presented in this book, confirm this conclusion. If this is the sole political consequence, then in what conceivable way does alienation pose a threat to democratic government? By depressing participation, alienation lessens "demands" on the system, reduces "strain," and contributes to the "mainly passive electorate." If political alienation *does* pose a threat to the stability of democratic regimes, compelling evidence on the point has yet to be encountered, either in the prior literature or in the surveys analyzed here.

THE CHARACTER OF "SUPPORT" IN DEMOCRATIC SOCIETIES

As mentioned earlier, much of consensus theory is based on a presumed and largely metaphorical "system need" for the "consent of the governed." Although the phrase itself is seldom encountered, concepts, such as "the reservoir of diffuse support," "the democratic political culture," or "the vast store of political good will," might easily have come from Locke or Rousseau. Whatever else might be said on their behalf, they apparently do not capture the complexities of the evidence reported in this volume.

One alternative to consent is dissent, and, in recent years at least, this alternative has received a fair amount of academic attention. There is much research literature on the dissent of blacks, students, Vietnam protestors, the New Left, and the "radical right." Despite the title of this volume, it would not be wise to equate dissent with political alienation, at least not as it has been conceptualized and measured here. At best, one might conclude that alienation is a necessary, but not sufficient, condition. The politically alienated *in the mass public* have played little significant role in the various disruptions of the last decade.

This suggests the need for a third alternative, one that falls somewhere between unreasoning diffuse support and open hostility or active opposition to the on-going system. For convenience, we will call this *assent* or, in Michael Mann's phrase, "pragmatic acquiescence." The chief distinguishing trait of assenters is that they "go along" with the system, not because they are "deeply attached to the regime as such," but because the system is pretty much beside the point of their lives and felt concerns. Most of the political alienation discussed here seems to fit this third description.

All democratic regimes are probably characterized at all times by some mix of consent, assent, and dissent. The stability of the regime, in turn, will depend on the make-up of the mix, the politics involved, the interactions that take place between the elements, the extant mechanisms of "control," and so on. It is not a simple matter of regimes requiring immense quantities of consent or making every conceivable effort to contain dissent. The character of "support" in democratic societies is far more complicated. In the following pages, we discuss some of the complexities involved, the nature of the mix in contemporary American society, and the way in which the mix apparently provides for stable democratic government.

Consent

Consenters provide the bedrock of popular support for the regime, the unwavering loyalists who can be counted on to defend the regime in its time of crisis. They are enthusiasts for the current arrangements. In democratic societies, they hold firm to the "democratic myths." They are confident in their political abilities, trust the political leadership, and believe sincerely in the "democratic way." In terms of the measures employed in this research, they are the politically nonalienated. They exhibit the traits which, in the consensus texts, are identified with diffuse support.

The first thing to note about consent is that no democratic society can do without it. On this score, consensus theory makes an important (even if rather obvious) point. The second thing to note, however, is that democratic societies get by with far less consent than is implied in consensus theory. The evidence discussed in this volume suggests that democracies function reasonably well with the consent of no more than half their population. How far below the 50% mark consent can "safely" fall remains an open empirical question. As we discuss later, if the nonconsenters fall into the ranks of assenters, then there is little reason to think that pure consent would be required of more than, say, 10% or 15% (enough, for example, to "cover" the military, business, industrial, and financial establishments). These, however, are arbitrary guesses. The only firm conclusion that can be drawn from the evidence is that the consent of half the population is sufficient.

The political importance of the "consenting half," however, is far disproportionate to their numbers. Judging from the evidence of Table 9.1, this half contributes 75% or 80% of those who characteristically vote in national elections. On other matters of political participation, such as working actively on behalf of favored candidates, the bias is even more pronounced. Virtually everyone who ever engages in that sort of activity is drawn from the consenting half. One major source of democratic stability, then, is that the largest share of input into the system comes from those who consent. This assures a modicum of restraint and moderation but, more importantly, assures that the "inputs" themselves will seldom directly challenge the legitimacy of the regime. In Easton and Dennis's phrase, the consenting half contains the large majority of "politically relevant members."

In contemporary American society, the social composition of the consenting half is predominantly upper middle class—or, more precisely, the white, non-South, non-Jewish, middle-aged, upper middle class, which is the central element in the group and, in modern theory, the responsible managers of the democratic society. It seems quite probable that the consent of this group is critical for the persistence of the regime. These persons staff the "second echelon" in all the major social institutions—government, business, finance, industry, commerce, and so on. (The "first echelon," of course, is staffed primarily by the upper class, which can itself be safely included in the consenting half.) The system could quite easily grind to a halt if their consent was withheld. Moreover, this group has the political resources that would be necessary to mount a serious opposition, assuming that, through some unlikely historical accident, they became inclined to do so. They are located in occupational contexts in which leaves of absence can be readily obtained. They have the financial resources to sustain them through periods of political activism. They are skilled in the manipulation of people and bureaucracies. They are well-educated and competent in the arts of politics. In short, they are in a position to mete out some punishment to the regime when things are not going their way. Therefore, it is unlikely that the regime could persist without their active support.

What keeps the upper middle class in the consenting half? First, the hypothesized mechanisms of consensus, namely, early socialization into regime norms, seem to work best for this class. They are instructed from an early age on their rights and responsibilities as democratic citizens, and, according to our evidence, they cling to those early lessons even in the face of what appear elsewhere to be contradicting experiences. They also believe, as discussed earlier, that the ideals of freedom, equality, and justice find true expression in the operation of American democracy. So, in large measure, the group consents because it has been trained to consent and because it genuinely believes that the system is the best possible means to attain socially desirable ends.

A second important factor, of course, is that the upper middle class benefits most from the continuation of on-going arrangements. They enjoy, in a far disproportionate amount to their numbers, all the amenities that the advanced industrial society can provide—gracious suburban dwellings, university education, quality health care, the niceties of culture, in sum, all the pleasantries of the affluent life. Not to consent under these circumstances would be a very irrational act. There is no reason for them to issue excessive demands to the regime; their every reasonable appetite has long since been satiated.

Although the upper middle class predominates in the consenting half, every other significant social grouping in the society has some representation there. For example, even at the height of black political alienation in 1970, about a third of the blacks were, nonetheless, included in the consenting half (see Table 7.2). The "reservoir of consent" also contains approximately half of the white South, half of the working class and lower middle class outside the South, and so on. This is a mere consequence of the fact that political alienation is pretty weakly correlated with most sociodemographic variables.

The fact that there is some consent virtually everywhere in the society has many important political implications. In every significant social group, there are representatives from the consenting half who serve as a source of moderation and restraint, as role models for political virtue. In most cases, the opinion leadership of any group is drawn from the consenting half, as are most of the members who are active and interested in politics. Any political leadership that emerges within the group is itself probably drawn from the consenting half. As such, the influence of the consenters on mass politics reaches far beyond the boundaries of consent itself. The consenters probably aid immeasurably in keeping assenters from becoming dissenters.

Thus, consenters occupy a key role in the "two-step flow" of political influence and information, not only in the upper middle class, but nearly everywhere in the society. The consenting members of any social group are directly "plugged in" to the flow: They follow the media for political news, engage in political conversation and discussion, are active and involved in politics. Most of the political information that passes through the social group, therefore, sooner or later has to "filter" through them. Because of the leadership position that they occupy, they are able to "interpret" this information on behalf of the group. This, in turn, allows them (more or less) to set the boundaries of the group "response." There is, to be sure, nothing conspiratorial or Machiavellian in this; on the contrary, it is a natural consequence of the uneven distribution of political interest in the democratic population. The consenters speak "for" their respective social groups mainly because they are the only ones who have anything to say.

Outside the upper middle class, the mechanisms of consent are initially somewhat more problematic. Again, it is probable that early socialization plays a role. In all social groups, that is, there will be at least some members who "buy" the regime norms. In the Jaros *et al.* study of political socialization among poor Appalachian whites, for example, about a fifth scored high on political trust (1968:570), despite the generally high level of political alienation that predominated in their sample. Similar results could be gleaned from virtually all studies of early socialization. Thus, while the evidence discussed in this book casts some doubt on socialization as an account of political attitudes in "*the* democratic citizenry," the account is probably accurate for one important part of the citizenry, those who eventually constitute the consenting half.

A second possible source of consent outside the upper middle class may be differential standards of reference or comparison, or what, in modern theory, would be known as the *inverse* of relative deprivation. Since, as is often said, there is comparatively little objective oppression in modern American society, much is commonly made of *relative* deprivation as a source of strain and, potentially, of dissent. Now, it is true that, relative to *somebody*, virtually everybody is deprived (the Kennedys, for example, are deprived relative to the Rockefellers); thus, as long as there is anything less than absolute equality in the distribution of scarce resources, the possibility for relative deprivation exists. At the same time, everybody is also pretty well off, relative to somebody *else*. Thus, the critical issue is the standard of comparison, the point of salient reference. The upper middle class fares rather well against any reasonable standard (although many of them probably aspire to even higher strata), and this, one presumes, must contribute to their allegiance to the regime. In social strata in which the objective circumstances of life are less pleasant, allegiance may be a function of the referent against which comparisons are being made. The young factory worker in the crowded city flat who compares his existence to that of the young junior executive on his way up in the world might not be especially enthusiastic about or allegiant to the regime. On the other hand, if that same factory worker was to compare his standard of living to that of his father at an equivalent point in the father's career, he might conclude that he was rather well off and be grateful for the benefits which the system has bestowed upon him. Little evidence exists on these points; that consent outside the higher strata is a function of differential reference groups can only be taken as one plausible hypothesis to be pursued in later research.

Dissent

The inverse of consent is dissent, and this too is, no doubt, present in every democratic society. In all such societies, there are periodic outcroppings of radical protest and revolt, usually at the hands of those who are hostile and punitive toward the incumbent regime. Threats to democratic stability, where they exist, originate among the dissenters and are, in most circumstances, confined to the dissenting group. Because, in contemporary American society, the dissenters constitute a numerically (if not politically) insignificant fraction of the population, we have had little to say about them in this book. It is not the kind of group that is profitably studied in mass population surveys. There is, however, one important conclusion to be drawn already, which is that any insurgencies that arise from this group should probably not be analyzed as *mass* political phenomena.

The presence of dissent in a democratic society can often be attributed to specific policies pursued by the regime, not to personal pathologies or "outside agitation." In the United States in the last decade, the major prominent instances of overt dissent were occasioned by elite decisions that led to institutionalized discrimination against blacks and to American involvement in Vietnam. Foreign policy disasters, historically, have been especially important sources of active dissent. The defeat of Germany in World War I and the humiliation of Versailles created a permanent group of unrepentant dissidents who eventually formed the cadres and street fighters of Hitler's insurgency. Likewise, the failure of French policy in Algeria promoted considerable dissent, especially within the military, which, in turn, led to the collapse of the Fourth Republic. One important conclusion, then, is that the safest protection against the hazards of dissent is to avoid the pursuit of policies that might create it. Although this is an obvious point, it is, nonetheless, frequently overlooked in "systemic" accounts.

How do democratic regimes survive in the face of active dissent? The critical variable here has very little to do with "democratic political cultures," "regimes norms," or "diffuse support." When the regime is able to defeat the insurgency militarily, it survives. When it cannot, it does not survive. Since, as Engels himself put it, "An unarmed people is a negligible force against the modern army of today (1968:23)," one implication of this fact is that there are very few successful insurgencies in modern democracies. Without the active support of the military, or at least the police, insurgencies stand very little chance of success. The corollary is that, once they have won the support of the military, they stand very little chance of failure. A further implication, mentioned in an earlier context, is that one would learn far more about the "sources of democratic stability" by studying military academies or the Joint Chiefs of Staff than by analyzing political alienation in the mass.

Deployment of a nation's military arsenal to assure domestic tranquillity is a relatively infrequent occurrence and is obviously something that the regime would prefer not to do. It creates a nasty image, if nothing else, and there is always the possibility—usually remote, but sometimes not so remote—that the military would refuse to obey or would side with the insurgents in the streets, although not many democratic regimes would demur very long once they had been threatened. When the American regime was faced with black insurgency in Watts and Detroit or New Left insurrection on the campus, there was little hestitation before calling out the army or the national guard. In many cases, of course, these measures only increased the magnitude and ferocity of dissent, but, at the same time, they also placed some strict outer limits on what that dissent was able to accomplish.

The most difficult problem faced by a democratic regime occurs when the dissidents have managed to attract a significant mass following. For one thing, this makes the "military solution" much more difficult. It is simply not in the nature of things for democratic regimes to customarily annihilate significant segments of the population. At the same time, dissident movements with sizable mass support are rather uncommon, owing, in large measure, to the characteristics of the insurgents themselves, who tend to be zealous true believers who resist the ideological contamination of mass appeals. Likewise, there is often nothing in the programs or demands of the insurgents that the "mass" would find very appealing. The history of New Left insurgency in the United States illustrates these points. From the beginning, the issue on the New Left was the war in Vietnam, and here the potential for a mass base was enormous, especially in the working class. As Hamilton (1968) has shown, working class disfavor with the war dates back to 1964—the earliest available evidence. It can be assumed that this opposition had a very pragmatic character to it; people were objecting to the war-related deterioration of standards of living and, especially, to the needless slaughter of sons, husbands, and fathers (Schuman 1972). The New Left, however, was never content to contest the war on these grounds. They were not about the business of just ending the war; they were concerned with "ending American imperialism" and "smashing the capitalist state." On these issues, any hope for mass support was lost. So, when "push came to shove" at Wisconsin or in the streets of Chicago, it was a relatively simple matter for the regime to deploy its armed might. The available evidence suggests that many in the mass welcomed this "solution" (Robinson 1970).

A second point, which is an implication of the first, is that once a dissident movement seeks to attract a mass base, it is usually forced to moderate and restrain its demands. The masses in modern democratic societies do not, for the most part, show much attraction to bizarre, far-out policies. They are "available" to insurgent movements only on the condition that those movements maintain some touch with reality, that they avoid the crazy and the inane. In this respect, contrary to much modern theory, the masses play an important moderating role. (We return to this point later.) One example of this would be the May Revolt in France in 1968, the most recent serious disturbance in what is commonly referred to as the least stable of the major Western democracies. By any standard, the May Revolt would qualify as a mass political movement. A national survey conducted the following August found 45% of the French population ($n = 1667$) to be "very" or "somewhat" favorable to the "events of May," 20% who had gone on strike during the Revolt, and 10% who had participated in the demonstrations supporting the students and workers. In this case, then, the French masses were in the streets, or, if not in the streets themselves, at least supportive of those who were. The question is *why* were they in the streets. Respondents who had indicated some participation in the Revolt were asked a simple follow-up question, "What did you expect to obtain?" Of the 439 respondents who answered the question, 33% said they were there for "job security," and another 26% said "increased salaries." These were far and away the most common responses. A series of similar "pragmatic" goals—for example, lowering the retirement age, freedom to unionize, increased autonomy in work, and so on—were the responses of an additional 24%. All told, the proportion of May Revolt participants who sought mainly bread-and-butter goals amounted to 83% of the total. This left 5% who were there to "support the students and the workers," 6% who wanted a "change in government and policy," 3% who wanted "other changes in the society and economy of France," and a meager 2% who hoped to hasten the "end of capitalism." The *mass* base of the May Revolt, in short, depended heavily on very pragmatic and attainable social, economic, and political goals. The final outcome of the Revolt is also instructive. After a month of chaos and near civil war, the Assembly was dissolved and new elections called, and, in the ensuing election, the Gaullists swept 358 of the 485 seats. (Some re-definition of district boundaries, to be sure, contributed to the victory.) Once returned to power, the de Gaulle government initiated educational reforms to placate the students and modest work reforms to appease the workers and unions. Having corrected, or at least attended to, the policies that occasioned the Revolt, there followed a rapid return to normal, and, in two subsequent elections, the Fifth Republic has shown little instability or decay.

One additional problem faced by insurgent movements in seeking a mass base is that the potential clientele is very hard to come by. Following the distinctions made earlier, the dissenters can either draw from consenters or assenters. Consenters, obviously, can be left out of the picture altogether; it is here that any insurgency will face its most serious opposition. This leaves the assenters to provide the mass base. The assenters, however, as we discuss momentarily, contain the politically least active and least involved elements of the population. They are preoccupied with matters considered to be far more important than even normal democratic participation, much less rising up to overthrow the regime. In addition, of course, they have serious doubts about the utility of political activity and are naturally suspicious of political leaders. As discussed earlier, they might be "mobilized" by a sure winner, or even a possible winner, but insurgent movements seldom fit this description. So, for the most part, the assenters are also "out of the picture" as a source of mass support. This is not to argue that "it" would never and could never happen, only that the common depiction of a mass public ever available for service in dissident movements is, by and large, not supported by any persuasive evidence.

Two final points can be made about the character of dissent. First, dissenters frequently have ties to the consenting half. The New Left in the United States, for example, was primarily composed of children from the upper middle class, and much the same could be said, obviously, about dissident students everywhere in the industrialized world. Likewise, the "radical right," at least in the United States, has drawn the bulk of its active support from the higher strata (e.g., Wolfinger et al. 1964). When this is the case, the dissidents normally face some recurring pressure in their families, neighborhood, work place, and elsewhere to moderate demands, purge extremist elements, and bring themselves "into line" with the comfortable politics and outlooks of the familiar milieu. The true zealot, to be sure, is not likely to succumb to these influences, but there might well be an impact on the wavering and the uncertain. This brings us to the final point, that dissident movements are often seriously fractionated among themselves. For example, at the height of student insurgency at Wisconsin (and at most other major universities), there were perhaps 20 or more distinct organizations supporting the politics of the New Left. (This figure counts everything from the Young Democrats to the Mother Jones Revolutionary League.) These organizations engaged in continuous ideological debate and internal "purification." Internecine conflicts were common; the groups came and went with astonishing frequency. The result of this fractionation was that joint political actions were seldom undertaken, the major exceptions being rowdy romps through the campus and the surrounding community, which attracted most of the dissidents and managed to alienate almost everybody else. The impact of student dissent was greatly diminished, largely by their own doing.

Assent

For obvious reasons, consenters are seldom a threat to democratic government. Because of their usual numerical insignificance, the difficulties faced in attracting a mass base, and their inferior military prowess, the dissenters are, in all but the rarest of circumstances, less a threat to stability than a permanent thorn in the flesh of the regime. All this suggests that the key to stable democratic government resides among the assenters—the other half of the society whose outlooks and attitudes are not adequately depicted in either of the two preceding accounts.

Almost everything that has been said about political alienation in this book applies essentially to the "assenting half." Indeed, for our purposes, their political powerlessness and distrust are the defining characteristics. The major salient features of the group are, therefore, as follows: First, they are *not* active supporters of the regime; rather, they "go along," probably because no other sort of behavior ever occurs to them. They do not, usually, "fight City Hall" primarily because they believe "you can't fight City Hall." This does not mean they believe that City Hall might not be worth fighting, only that little would be gained in the attempt. Thus, as mentioned earlier, they are not "deeply attached to the regime as such." Rather, they have only a remote attachment to anything political. Second, an implication of the first, the assenting half is politically inactive—not through some sublimated pathology, but because to do otherwise would, in their eyes, be a futile, pointless act. To be sure, the evidence indicates that many of them do vote, and many of them follow politics in the media. The evidence also indicates, however, that they doubt whether much is accomplished through these activities. So the first important point to note about assent is that relatively little of it ever enters in the normal democratic process. The assenting half are spectators to somebody else's game.

One direct implication of this point is that it would not usually matter very much how mean or vicious the politics of the group might be. The assenting half could harbor the most authoritarian and despicable preferences imaginable, but as long as they never voted, never engaged in political activity, never did anything on behalf of their beliefs, their preferences would have little impact. There is, after all, no "National Association for the Advancement of Alienated People" to lobby for group goals, no "League of Alienated Voters" to win the President's ear, no "Vietnam Veterans Against Alienation" to command attention in the press. Virtually by definition, the alienated are the unorganized and the unrepresented. In normal circumstances, then, it is not to be expected that they will pose much of a hazard to the democratic regime.

Yes, but . . . but what about the nonnormal circumstance, the unusual occasion, the forces that transform assent into dissent and, thereby, transform inactive to active opposition? The barriers to this transformation have already been discussed elsewhere. The assenting half is a very heterogeneous group. Opinion leadership, and, therefore, political direction, tends to be supplied from "outside." As a whole, the assenting half are disproportionate nonpossessors of the resources and skills of insurgency. For these and other reasons—mainly, their lack of ideological purity and fervor—they are typically avoided by dissident groups. To emphasize this point, this is not to say that they could never be mobilized into active opposition. All that is being said here is that there are some formidable obstacles that would have to be overcome.

One of the most serious barriers to mobilization of the assenting half is that its members are preoccupied with the day-to-day humdrum of life. (Evidence on this point is discussed later.) The major pressing concerns involve the care and feeding of self and family and otherwise "making do" and "getting by." This, obviously, does not mean that they are consumed by abject misery. It simply means that providing the basic necessities is, in itself, a full-time activity. Any free time would normally go to leisure and relaxation, probably not for insurrectionary or even normal democratic politicking. Little direct gratification woud be derived from such activity, and there is, again, that key element of their beliefs that must be taken into account—that it would all be fruitless anyway.

This bears directly on the cornerstone assumption of the modern theory of democracy, what we earlier called the assumption of "mass insatiability," that the masses in modern democratic societies recurrently demand more than the system can supply, and that the attendant disappointment is a constant source of stress for the regime. In truth, none of the evidence points to such a conclusion. As shown in the *Civic Culture*, for example, "The proportion of individuals for whom civic activity is highly salient tends to be small (1965:210)." When asked, "What are the activities that interest you most, that you prefer to spend your free time on?" a mere 2% of the U.S. respondents in the *Civic Culture* sample said "civic-political activities," and even this counts multiple responses. Evidence discussed in an earlier chapter suggests the same point: Except for voting and, perhaps, following politics in the media, the immense majority, especially in the assenting half, engages in no other recognizably political activity. The evidence presented by Verba and Nie (1972) follows along similar lines. Their Table 2-1, for example, finds 72% of the population who report regularly voting in presidential elections. On voting in local elections, however, the proportion drops to under half. Then, there is a series of items that elicits positive responses from about a third—"have worked with others in trying to solve some community problems," and so on. Once items, such as "have attended at least one political rally or meeting in the last three years," are encountered, the participating fraction drops below a fifth. Later, some summary judgments on the meaning of this evidence are undertaken (1972:79–81). One group isolated in the analysis is "the inactives." The defining trait is that they simply do not participate. By the authors' reckoning, this describes a fifth of the population; almost all of them, one assumes, are located in the assenting half. Another fifth is made up of the "voting specialists," who "in many ways are like the inactives." In simple terms they vote and do nothing else. Again, most of this group would be located in the assenting half. The two together constitute 43% of the total population, and on the assumption made earlier, perhaps 80–90% of the assenting half. This picture is fully consistent with the evidence presented in Table 9.1—that evidence is drawn not from 1 survey but from 4, spanning the period from 1956 to 1968 and encompassing 10 separate measures of participation. From these and similar data which are widely available, one does not get an image of an insatiable mass constantly issuing demands. Rather, the picture is one of a mass public for whom politics is simply not a salient concern.

How is the widespread inactivity and withdrawal to be explained? The answer seems to be that, especially in the assenting half, politics and government is simply seen as outside the realm of life's major troubles. Hamilton (1972:83–151) has reviewed poll evidence on the basic fears and worries and reports that, for the large majority, bread-and-butter concerns predominate. A more recent poll confirms this same point: "The American people continue to be pre-occupied with two matters—their health and standard of living (Cantril and Roll 1971:15)"—both of these are tied rather directly to one's immediate financial circumstances. Thus, in terms of the things people really worry about, politics would matter if the outcome of the process were thought to have an impact on one's economic well-being. In this light, one question asked by the SRC in all of its surveys assumes special significance: "Do you think it will make any difference in how you and your family get along financially whether the Democrats or the Republicans win the election?" In the total population since 1956, the proportion saying "no" has *always* been two-thirds or more, and, in the off-year election of 1970, the proportion rose to 87%. Again, it can be assumed that there is relatively less of this sentiment in the consenting half and relatively more in the assenting half. In the latter group, in short, nearly everyone must believe that politics is irrelevant to the things that concern them most.

One final item bearing on the "insatiability" of the mass concerns responses to the question, "What do you personally feel are the most important problems the government in Washington should try to take care of?" In years when the nation is at war, convergence of opinion is on that issue. Thus, in 1968, more than two-thirds of the respondents mentioned Vietnam as the first, second, or third most important problem. In years when the nation is not at war, a different pattern obtains. The 1964 survey provides a case in point. Slightly more than a fifth of the 1964 respondents could think of *no single problem* that the government in Washington should try to take care of. This was the modal response. In the assenting half, presumably, the proportion would be considerably higher. On the other hand, about 80% could name at least one important problem. In the follow-up question asking about the second most important problem, however, the nonresponse climbed to 42%, and, for the third most important probem, it reached 72%. This would suggest that about three-quarters of the population can think of no more than one or two important problems that the government should be trying to deal with, except in times of war. In the assenting half, this would probably describe almost everybody. This brings us back to a point made earlier: If the regime can avoid unpopular foreign policy ventures and prevent erosions in the standard of living, this will normally be sufficient to "satiate" and contain the masses.

There is, in sum, little persuasive evidence that the mass is insatiable and, therefore, little evidence that the assenting half—the politically discontented in the modern society—constitutes a threat to democratic *stability*. The evidence that seemingly "should" be there, in survey after survey, context after context, simply is not there. A far more plausible case can thus be made that the existence of an assenting half—a "go-along, why-bother" orientation characterizing every second citizen—constitutes a real and immediate threat to the *responsiveness* of the regime. By depressing interest in political affairs, a large body of opinion is simply subtracted from the on-going democratic process. It might be that this body of opinion is thoroughly reactionary, modestly liberal, or downright progressive, or, most likely of all, some combination of all these elements. How it stacks up in these regards is obviously an empirical question. On one point, however, there can be little doubt: Whatever its character, that opinion is not in there, is not contributing to the "continuous political process" of the regime. Now, one could say that, under some circumstances, this would be for the better. It is one of the problems of democracy that a fool's vote and a wise man's vote all count the same. When the "missing opinion" is the opinion of half the society, however, it suggests, at least to all appearances, that something fundamental has gone wrong in the operation of the democratic system.

This, however, would not be the conclusion drawn in the modern theory of democracy. In this view, a mainly passive electorate is seen to be quite functional for the regime. The masses are said to be incompetent in the tasks of democratic government, hostile to the rules of democratic procedure, and somewhat dangerous once admitted to the democratic arena. Democracy, then, really *is* best served when these groups are eliminated from the political process. Since we can go no further in our argument until these views are examined, let us next consider the assumption of mass incompetence.

THE POLITICAL COMPETENCE OF THE MASS

Monsma has conveniently summarized the issues that currently concern us:

> Numerous surveys have demonstrated that the average citizen does not have the qualities the rational-activist model demands of him. Instead, he has very limited political interest and knowledge; possesses little, if any political ideology; and actually espouses many anti-democratic, anti-libertarian ideas. Yet surprisingly enough, democracy continues to exist in the United States—even with a considerable degree of vigor [1971:350].

Of the "numerous surveys" that could allegedly be cited on behalf of these claims, four are specifically mentioned in the accompanying footnote: *Voting* (1954), *The American Voter* (1964), the Prothro and Grigg study of "Fundamental principles of democracy" (1960), and McCloskey's "Consensus and ideology in American politics" (1964). We assume that these four were chosen for citation because they make the best possible case on behalf of the argument; certainly, they are among the most common references in the literature of democratic elitism. What lessons, then, do they contain?

The first point to note is that, taken as a whole, these four sources are dated. *Voting* deals with the 1948 election; *The American Voter* deals with the 1956 election. Likewise, data for the Prothro–Grigg study were collected in some unspecified year prior to 1960, and the McCloskey data were collected in 1957–1958. On their own, there is nothing objectionable about aging data; in a field that all too frequently indulges in unrestrained speculation, any evidence at all is to be gratefully appreciated. The continued citation of these studies, however, carries an implication that nothing has changed in the intervening decades, that no improvement or adjustment in the character of things is possible, that circumstances and situations, once noted, persist into the indefinite future. As we discuss later in the chapter, such assumptions can sometimes lead to serious and egregious distortions. Surely, findings that the masses are incapable of managing their own political affairs should be continually re-assessed. Resolute pessimism should not be forever based on the research findings of 20 years past.

We begin our review with the earliest of the four studies, *Voting*. In this volume, the most relevant chapter is the concluding one, "Democratic theory and democratic practice," in which the implications of the results for the theory of democracy are discussed. The data, in the authors' words, "reveal that certain requirements commonly assumed for the successful operation of democracy are not met by the behavior of the 'average' citizen (1954:307)." There are four items, in particular, in which the "average voter" falls short: political interest and discussion, political knowledge, voting on political principles, and rationality.

First, the authors lament the finding that most citizens engaged in little genuine discussion about the issues or candidates; this is in contrast to the "theoretical requirement" of "the capacity for and the practice of discussion (1954:307)." Yet they also note that, in this particular election, "there was little true discussion between the candidates, little in the newspaper commentary, little between the voters and the official party representatives, some within the electorate (1954:308)." This particular study was conducted in a heavily Republican community in upstate New York. The character of political discussion in such a community would normally reflect the nature of the Republican campaign, and it was Dewey specifically, reserved and aloof, who was not discussing issues or stating policy positions. Truman, on the other hand, was very active in this regard, and the evidence reflected this difference: Respondents were "ignorant" and "uninformed" about Dewey's positions; where Truman was concerned, they had a clearer picture (1954:219). This suggests that any "deficiencies" revealed in the data be initially attributed to the candidates and the media who had abnegated their "information" responsibilities. A second implication is that, when candidates *do* discuss the issues, and when these discussions *are* reported in the press, the quality of discussion in the mass public increases. It is very difficult to discuss candidate positions that are not being made available.

The second desideratum where the "voter falls short" is that "the democratic citizen is expected to be well-informed about political affairs (1954: 308)." But how does one become well-informed when the necessary information is not being made available? In 1948, it would have been very difficult for anyone to become "well-informed" about Dewey's positions, simply because Dewey was not spelling them out. A second point to note in this context is that the questions about knowedge of the issues were asked in August, a month before the beginning of the campaign. "Similar data for October, at the end of the campaign, would almost certainly raise these estimates (1954:228, Footnote 6)."

Third, "The democratic citizen is supposed to cast his vote on the basis of principle—not fortuitously or frivolously or impulsively or habitually, but with reference to standards not only of his own interest but of the common good (1954:308–309)." This again, is "an impossible demand on the democratic electorate." This conclusion, however, is based on their finding that "many voters vote not for principle in the usual sense of the term but 'for' a group to which they are attached—their group (1954:309)." Now what is the "principle in the usual sense of the term" that would suggest that voting on the basis of group ties is "unprincipled," or "fortuitous," or "impulsive," or "habitual"? Indeed, as Almond and Verba have pointed out, completely individualistic influence attempts are normally dysfunctional; interests are best served when influence is aggregated. The person who votes for "his group" is merely asserting the political principle that what is best for my group is best for me; given the nature of political influence, there can be little doubt that this is an accurate and highly rational judgment.

Finally, "The democratic citizen is expected to exercise rational judgment in coming to his vote decision (1954:309)." Again, the voter is seen to fall short. It would be difficult, however, to come to an entirely rational decision unless the necessary information were being made available. Lacking such information, the voter merely acts as rationally as possible under conditions of severely limited knowledge: He or she votes for the party that has served well in the past (call this "trial and error" rationality) or for the party that best serves group interests (call this the rationality of aggregate action).

Concerning the "rationality" of the vote, Verba and Nie have made the following observations:

> [The voter] does not choose the occasion to vote, nor does he choose the agenda; he doesn't choose the issues that divide the candidates; nor does he usually have much voice in choosing the candidates themselves. And given the fact that his own agenda is quite individual and may contain many and varied issues, it is unreasonable to expect that there will be a voting choice

tailored to his own particular policy preferences at the moment. . . . His vote can only be a rather blunt instrument under these circumstances; it cannot have . . . sharpness and precision [1972:106].

The second source cited by Monsma is *The American Voter*. We direct attention particularly to Chapter 8, "Attitude structure and the problem of ideology." In this chapter, the charge is that the mass is politically incompetent because it is unable to think in ideological terms. Phrases, such as "liberal" and "conservative," go largely unrecognized, and, where recognized, they are poorly defined. Even the ideological leanings of the parties are only dimly perceived. Thus, public attitudes on major political issues have no discernible internal "structure," do not cohere among themselves in any meaningful way. This, it is said, rules out even the possibility of voting on the basis of one's best political interests. The interests themselves are ill-understood and inconsistent with one another.

Suspending judgment on the evidence itself, this is a peculiar charge. On the assumption that ideologues tend toward political extremism, the non-ideology of the mass should be well-suited to the compromise and conciliation that successful democracy requires. More importantly, the *American Voter* authors are explicitly dubious of their own empirical procedures:

> It is important to recognize the degree to which our "normal" or *a priori* expectations in these matters are conditioned by sophisticated views of the parts that make up a coherent political ideology. . . .
> The fact that an issue reaction [that is, an opinion] fails to fit into a larger organization of attitude that seems appropriate for it does not mean that the response is random or in any other sense "uncaused." *The problem is rather that the structure imposed on the situation by the analyst turns out in such instances to be inadequate.* It may be that the sources of responses to an issue are so diverse from individual to individual that all sense of patterning across an aggregate is lost. More often, clear roots may exist, but the analyst ignores them because they have no place in his preconception concerning "logical" or traditional ideological positions. His organizing dimensions simply depart from the modes of organization abroad in the general population [1964:112–113, italics added].

What is being said here, in short, is that the failure of mass attitudes to cohere in "ideological" ways may reflect nothing more than the inability of the analyst to deal with the complexities of attitudinal organization "abroad in the total population." Here, it is useful to mention Luttberg's recent research on "The Structure of Beliefs among Leaders and the Mass Public," which suggested that belief systems in the mass were just as "constrained" as belief systems among political leaders. What differed, according to Luttberg, were the *organizing principles* that constrained the beliefs (1968:401–414).

A related problem is that the 1956 election was not an ideologically salient one. It was probably *the* consensus election of recent decades. There were no looming foreign policy issues. Korea was ended. Domestic agitation over race was four years in the future. The economy was reasonably strong and healthy. Stevenson was not pushing the traditional Democratic welfare-state issues. There would have been little reason to develop a "coherent" political ideology to be employed in 1956. Ideological issues formed no important part of the campaign.

One implication is that, in more ideologically charged elections, mass political ideologies should become more apparent, belief elements should "straighten out" along recognizable dimensions, and the organizing principles should rise closer to the surface. A direct comparison between the 1956 and 1964 election surveys showed some support for this implication (Field and Anderson 1969). A similar replication on the 1972 survey, we expect, would produce equivalent results.

Finally, despite the stylized representation of the *American Voter* that is frequently encountered in secondary accounts, the major finding in fact *opposes* the view that the public is incapable of thinking in traditional "left-right" terms:

> We have isolated an attitude structure capturing the core ideological controversies of our epoch [that is, the liberal–conservative continuum]. The structure exists empirically, and, moreover, it shows relationships of substantial magnitude with partisan preference in the direction that would be predicted by notions of ideology. That is, people sort themselves into patterns of responses that are coherent in terms of a liberal-conservative dimension; and people who choose liberal alternatives tend to identify with the more liberal, or "leftist," Democratic Party, whereas people choosing conservative alternatives tend more often to express loyalty to the conservative, "rightist," Republican Party [1964:115–116].

The remainder of the discussion considers extensions, exceptions, and interpretations of the broad general outlines revealed in the passage; the main message, apart from the interpretations, exceptions, and extensions, is that most people do arrange themselves from left to right, choose the party that best reflects this arrangement, and, thus, vote in a manner consistent with their ideological beliefs.

The third source cited is Prothro and Grigg's study of the "fundamental principles of democracy." This study assays subscription to key democratic values, such as majority rule, minority rights, and their specific applications; the charge is that the mass rejects democratic values when they are applied to specific situations, such as allowing communists or Negroes to run for office, and so on. Following the tenets of democratic elitism, the study closes with a discussion of the "functional nature of apathy for the democratic system."

What confidence can be placed in these conclusions? First, the study is based on a very limited sample: 144 residents of Ann Arbor, Michigan and

100 residents of Tallahassee, Florida. Second, the 10 items used to measure antidemocratic sentiments are written in agree–disagree format; of the 10, the "agree" response is also the antidemocratic response in 6 cases. Thus, the results are confounded with an uncontrolled acquiescent response set bias (see Chapter 4). Despite this, a democratic majority emerged on 6 of the items, with democratic minorities of 45% or greater on 3 more items. The most overwhelming *rejection* of democratic values comes on the item stating, "In a city referendum deciding on tax-supported undertakings, only taxpayers should be allowed to vote." About 79% of the total sample agreed with this sentiment. By way of contrast, we should note that another 79% of the sample also *agreed* that "if a person wanted to make a speech in this city favoring government ownership of all the railroads and big industries, he should be allowed to speak." Averaged across the 10 items, the proportion giving prodemocratic responses was 54.6%. All told, there is little that is starkly ominous in these results. The most sizable rejections of democratic values come on what appear to be rather trivial matters, and, on what are manifestly nontrivial matters, such as the right to free speech, the majority was solidly prodemocratic. (In the late 1950s, to be sure, there would have been little zealous protection of the rights of Communists, but, as we discuss later, this pattern has changed considerably in the years since.) Here, we should mention that majority support for the right of a Socialist to make a speech was found in every cell of their Table One: in Tallahassee and in Ann Arbor, among high- and low-income respondents, among the educated and the uneducated alike. The smallest prodemocratic majority is registered by the less-educated respondents; here the majority was "only" 66%. Finally, there is some question as to whether the antidemocratic opinions expressed in this survey really would constitute a behavioral threat. The authors note:

> [a] sizable number (42.0%) of our Southern respondents said, for example, that "a Negro should not be allowed to run for Mayor of this city," but a few months before the survey a Negro actually did conduct an active campaign for that office without any efforts being made by the "white" people to obstruct his candidacy. In this case, the behavior was more democratic than the verbal expressions (1960:294).

Monsma's final source is McCloskey's study of "Consensus and ideology in American politics." Like Prothro and Grigg, this study also deals with support for basic democratic principles, but, unlike the earlier study, it is based on a large, nationally representative sample ($n = 1484$). As such, the results are to be taken rather more seriously. What, then, *were* the results?

Rules of the Game

On 12 items expressing support for the rules of democratic procedure, an antidemocratic majority emerged on only one item. A 52% majority had some doubts as to whether or not a person "who can't do so intelligently" should be allowed to vote. (In a footnote, McCloskey notes that nonresponse to all items discussed here amounted to less than 1%, so the prodemocratic minority on this item would have been about 48%.) One might mention, on this score, that, at the time of this survey, literacy tests were still very much a part of the "rules of the democratic game," so it is not clear whether this 52% majority was supporting or opposing "the rules." It matters little, however, since, on the remaining 11 items, the majority was decisively, often overwhelmingly, prodemocratic. One item, for example, read: "There are times when it almost seems better for the people to take the law into their own hands rather than wait for the machinery of the government to act." Three-fourths of the respondents *disagreed* with the statement. There were some genuinely Fascist items also included: "The majority has the right to abolish minorities if it wants to" (rejected by 72%), "almost any unfairness or brutality may have to be justified when some great purpose is being carried out" (rejected by 67%), and "to bring about great changes for the benefit of mankind often requires cruelty and even ruthessness" (rejected by 69%). A summary judgment based on these 12 items is that some two-thirds to three-fourths of the population did *not* reject the abstract principles upon which democratic government is erected. (In all cases, of course, there are sizable minorities who do make these rejections.)

Free Speech and Opinion

On eight questions dealing with support for free speech and expression of opinion, an antidemocratic majority emerged on none of these items. The largest antidemocratic minority comes on the question, "I would not trust any person or group to decide what opinions can be freely expressed and what must be silenced." "Only" two-thirds of the respondents agreed with this statement. In all other cases, the prodemocratic majority amounted to 80–90%. The most sizable agreement came on the following item: "No matter what a person's political beliefs are, he is entitled to the same legal rights and protection as anyone else." Here, the prodemocratic majority amounted to 94.3%.

Specific Applications

On nine questions "expressing support for specific applications of free speech and procedural rights," a democratic majority emerged on five. The largest *anti*democratic majority comes on the question, "Any person who hides behind the laws when he is questioned about his activities doesn't deserve much consideration." Three-fourths of the respondents agreed with this. It might be asked, however, just what they were agreeing to, what that phrase, "doesn't deserve much consideration," means for the operation of democracy. A more specific and straightforward item read, "In dealing with dangerous enemies like the Communists, we can't afford to depend on the courts, the laws, and their slow and unreliable methods." Here, the three-fourths majority *rejected* the statement. The other three items showing an antidemocratic majority also do not seem very ominous or threatening. Two-thirds, for example, agreed that "if someone is suspected of treason or other serious crimes, he shouldn't be entitled to be let out on bail." Similarly, three-fifths agreed that "freedom does not give anyone the right to teach foreign ideas in our schools." Finally, just half (50.3%) agreed that "A book that contains wrong political views cannot be a good book and does not deserve to be published." Some of the things that respondents are *not* agreeing to when they agree with these statements should be mentioned. They are *not* agreeing, for example, that people suspected of treason should be taken out to the nearest oak and hung, only that they "shouldn't be entitled" to bail. Likewise, they are *not* agreeing that a book with "wrong" political views *should not* be published, or that steps should be taken to assure that such books are not published, only that they do not *deserve* to be published. The antidemocratic sentiments being expressed are rather mild, and, besides, there was a *pro*democratic response to the majority of these specific applications.

Belief in Mass Competence

The McCloskey survey contained five questions asking about matters that go to the heart of the modern critique of classical democratic theory; interestingly enough, four of the five items found majority support for elements of the critique. About three-fifths of the respondents, for example, agreed that "the main trouble with democracy is that most people don't really know what's best for them," that "few people really know what is in their own best interests in the long run," that " 'issues' and 'arguments' are beyond the understanding of most voters," and that "it will always be necessary to have a few strong, able people actually running everything." Again, it is hard to see what threat beliefs such as these pose to democratic stability; for the most part, these seem only to be generalizations from one's own political experience. Here it is worth quoting McCloskey at some length: "Many feel themselves hopelessly ineffectual politically. Approximately half perceive government and politicans as remote, inaccessible, and largely unresponsive to the electorate's needs or opinions. About the same proportion regard politics as squalid and seamy, as an activity in which the participants habitually practice deception, expediency, and self-aggrandizement (1964:[1969:280])." This, in our terms, accurately describes the sentiments of the assenting half. Despite all the distrust and felt powerlessness, however, the basic thrust of the rest of McCloskey's evidence is that the majority—usually the *large* majority—is tolerant and protective of democratic rights and traditions. The majority, for the most part, does *not* reject the principles upon which democratic government is erected; what they *do* reject is any suggestion that the people themselves have the power or ability to rectify this situation. This brings us back, finally, to the point made earlier, that the assenting half probably threatens democratic responsiveness more than democratic stability.

In sum, the four surveys cited by Monsma on behalf of the "hypothesis of mass incompetence" turn out, on closer inspection, not to show this at all. In some cases, the opposite conclusion would be more appropriate, that, despite some imposing barriers (for example, the perceived absence of "role models" among the political elite), most people are committed to basic democratic rights. In virtually all cases, one can readily question whether the mass itself is directly responsible for any "deficiencies" that it exhibits. Certainly, the evidence presented by these four studies would not be sufficient, on its own, to justify the conclusion that democracy would be seriously threatened by some increase in the interest and activity of the mass.

Now, it must be admitted that the literature on mass incompetence is far more extensive than the four studies reviewed here show (see Chapter 1, Footnote 2). Likewise, one should *not* conclude from this review that antidemocratic sentiment is absent in the mass. The review, however, does raise the possibility that such sentiment is far less extensive than is commonly thought, that the easy dismissal of the mass as a potential source of decency, generosity, or worthwhile "political input" is more a pointless and gratuitous insult than a persuasively documented empirical point. Indeed, one might note here that the hypothesized "deficiencies" are more readily located in the theory itself than in the evidence on mass political opinions. First, there is the theory's overt authoritarianism. Following closely the depiction of *The Authoritarian Personality*, the theory exhibits "a submissive, uncritical attitude towards idealized moral authorities," namely, the political elite, and, likewise, has "a tendency to be on the lookout for, and to condemn, reject, and punish people who violate conventional values," in this case, the values embodied in the theory itself (Adorno *et al.* 1950:228). Second, the theory is antidemocratic in the classical sense of the word. It is neo-aristocratic; it argues that a relatively small group of "competent" and "sophisticated" elites should be "insulated," the better to ride herd over unruly masses. Third, the theory is "negativistic." It has a tendency to describe people and events in negative terms, as "volatile" and "potentially explosive," "profoundly and fanatically alienated," and so on. Finally, the theory is deeply convinced of the superiority of its own values and culture against all others. It defines the political elite (and people like them, including, to be sure, the theorists themselves) as the decent and humane element in a society that is otherwise corrupt and dangerous.

The paramount lesson of modern democratic theory is, thus, that government should limit its pursuits to the modest and incremental, so as not to disturb the frail peace upon which democracy is erected. What is or is not possible at any given historical instant, however, is something that can only be determined by evidence, and the evidence reviewed and presented here raises a serious question as to whether participatory democracy is quite as hazardous or unstable as modern theory suggests. There is little doubt that democratic elitism, from Michels onward, has provided a useful corrective to the starry-eyed optimism of classical democratic theorists, but there is now a considerable suspicion that, in its haste to "correct," the modern theory has erred in the opposite direction. In detailing the hazards of mass partici- pation, the theory has overlooked or minimized the potential and possibili- ties. This raises the final issue to be addressed in this volume, the prospects of participatory democracy in the modern age.

THE PROSPECTS OF PARTICIPATORY DEMOCRACY

The final argument proceeds along five lines: (1) How is "participatory democracy" in the United States working now? What are the major features of the mass political inputs as they currently exist? (2) How could the cur- rent system be changed? More specifically, how could it be changed to alter the nature of mass political inputs? (3) Is there any evidence that the possible changes would have the intended effect, that is, would increase the overall responsiveness of the system? (4) Would these changes significantly increase the danger of mass political insurgencies? (5) Would the changes result in a more just or humane society?

The first point to note about the character of mass participation as it now exists is that it is essentially confined to the consenting half. This is some- what less true for voting itself, but then, on the other hand, voting is proba- bly the least effective form of political participation. All other forms of participation are heavily concentrated in the consenting half. The most com- plete accounting of what this implies has been provided by Verba and Nie (1972), and here we borrow heavily from their analysis.

One direct implication is that "participation helps those who are already better off (1972:228)." The consenting half is disproportionately (although not exclusively) upper middle class. The participants, then, are those who have already benefited greatly from the "outputs" of the system; conversely, the nonparticipants are those whose objective circumstances would warrant the greatest improvement. Thus, one salient feature of the "participation bias" is that it aids in perpetuating the unequal distribution of scarce social and economic resources. A related implication is that the results of the par- ticipation process are inherently misleading. Those results represent, gen- erally, the policy preferences of the consenting half, not of the whole society. If nothing else, this provides the leadership with a very distorted mandate.

The net effect of the participation bias is to push popular input in a con- servation direction. The data analyzed by Verba and Nie show that "partici- pants are less aware of serious welfare problems than the population as a whole, less concerned about the income gap between rich and poor, less interested in government support for welfare programs, and less concerned with equal opportunities for black Americans (1972:298)." This is not to say that there are *no* lower status activists working for more progressive change. Any daily newspaper would belie such a conclusion; indeed, as Verba and Nie mention, they are a "highly assertive group." "But though quite visible, they remain a small group—only 2 per cent of the population, and they are counter-poised against the almost glacial pressure of a much larger number of conservative activists. The latter group may not speak as dramatically, but as our data [make clear], they speak very effectively (1972:339)."

In answer to the first question, "How is participatory democracy working now?" we conclude that it is working to benefit those who are already well-off, and, by implication, that it contributes to the continued deprivation of those who are not. This is not to assert that *no* progressive outcomes are ever accomplished, or that the assenting half *never* benefits from the political process. It is just that the tendencies revealed in the data are in these directions. How, then, might those tendencies be reversed?

The most obvious technique of democratizing the benefits of participation would seem to be democratizing participation itself, and, here again, Verba and Nie have reached an eminently reasonable conclusion: "If there were more class-based ideologies, more class-based organizations, more explicit class-based appeal by political parties, the participation disparity between upper- and lower-status citizens would very likely be less (1972:340)." Comparative evidence from countries where this is generally the case support the conclusion: The correlation between social status and participation is stronger in the United States than in England, Italy, Mexico, Germany, Nigeria, the Netherlands, Austria, and Japan (1972:340). Short of organizing a working class Socialist party (the main distinguishing feature of the societies just enumerated), there are many other plausible mechanisms that might facilitate participation in the assenting half. One of these would be to provide some effective demonstration that the outcome of the political process has a direct bearing on major pressing concerns. Obviously, it does, so it should not be very difficult to convince people of this. Some of the structural impediments to participation could also be removed, for example, through national standardization of registration laws and practices, some system of "post card" registration, or federally subsidized voter registration. In the last years, the government has become heavily involved in the subsidization of presidential election campaigns; there are, thus, very few compelling reasons why they should not also subsidize participation in those campaigns, for example, by providing citizens with a receipt on the occasion of their voting, good for $1 against the following year's taxes. It is not necessary to wax enthusiastic over several pages about possible mechanisms of facilitation. Anyone who was of a mind to do so could quite easily suggest a handful of feasible, workable possibilities. A more serious issue here is, first, whether or not such mechanisms would have the intended effect of incrementing the responsiveness of the regime, and, second, whether increased "responsiveness" would, in the long run, be to the good or to the bad.

The first of these issues is not entirely clear-cut. The mechanisms of accountability may already be beyond the point of salvation, and the people who tend to rise to positions of political power may be so corrupt and greedy that nothing is able to bring them under control. Relatively little evidence exists on these points, one way or the other. What evidence there is, however, points to an opposite conclusion, that participation does have some important effects. In the series of studies by Aiken and Alford, for example, it was found that community innovations (Model Cities programs, public housing projects, and so on) were more common among cities with decentralized power structures and high participation than among those controlled by elites (1970a,b,c). Such programs, of course, do not always add to the quality of urban life, but they take clear steps in this direction. The worst that could be concluded on the basis of these studies is that popular participation brings public concerns and problems to the surface and compels elites to respond to them. Whether or not they respond effectively or efficiently is quite another matter, but at least they are compelled to respond.

More direct evidence bearing on these points has been presented by Verba and Nie. These researchers interviewed political leaders and ordinary citizens in a sample of 64 communities sized 50,000 and less. Both groups were asked about the most important issues facing the local community. In this manner, a measure of "concurrence" between elite and mass political agendas was developed. The assumption here, of course, is that responsiveness will increase if elites and masses agree on what the most important issues are; certainly, this would be a necessary, if insufficient, condition. Consistent with the Aiken and Alford results, elite–mass concurrence was indeed highest in communities in which participation was greatest. This relationship was not perfectly regular, particularly among communities in which participation was especially low. Outside this bottom quartile, however, the relationship between participation and concurrence was strong and positive (1972:331). These data, in conjunction with the Aiken–Alford studies, support the viewpoint that democratic participation does indeed have some effect.

It is not difficult to imagine why this might be the case. The more people participate, the greater is the probability that those who are elected will reflect, however crudely, the majority preferences. Likewise, where the population is more active and informed, it becomes more costly for elites to ignore those preferences. We are aware of Alford and Friedland's (1975) conclusion that the level of industrialization or economic development is a far stronger determinant of public expenditures and policy than voting turnout or popular participation, but this does not dissuade us from the view. The level of industrialization in a community is something about which very little can be done; the level of popular participation is another matter altogether. Participation, whether mere voting or other, more direct modes, adds to the amount of information that flows through the system and upon which subsequent decisions can be made. Even unanimous participation, of course, would not *compel* elite responsiveness, but it is probably not possible to compel responsiveness through *any* set of mechanisms or structures. All that increased participation would do is raise the probability that elite decisions will take popular preferences into account. The net result, then, would not be "democracy," in the naive and impossible sense, but some closer approximation of democracy, in the realistic and fully attainable sense: a participant political system based upon "the expressed will of the whole society."

Would such a system, over the long run, be better or worse than the existing alternative? Historically, the major source of hesitance here would be the assumption that the masses, once freed of "systemic constraints," are readily available to demagogues "bent on the transformation of the world." Empirically, these fears are not well-founded. In the United States at least, extremists of this sort have not been very popular. In fact, they have been regularly trounced in national elections. As we have taken pains to show everywhere in this book, it is certainly *possible* that some future demagogue might be swept to power by rampaging masses, but the present conditions on the current American political scene suggest that this is, at best, a remote possibility.

Consider first the "disgrace" and "defeat" of American policy in Vietnam. From one perspective, this would be a "haunting similarity" to Weimar Germany, but, actually, the comparison is rather difficult to draw with any precision. There is relatively little fanatic nationalism in the United States that would compare with the attitudes, for example, of the German upper classes in the Weimar regime. Vietnam was not a "grand national effort"; it was a dirty and unpopular escapade with enormously deleterious domestic consequences. The large majority of the mass public, by 1970, considered that it had been a mistake to get into Vietnam in the first place. Nixon's "peace with honor" and, finally, the collapse of the corrupt Thieu regime must have been met more with relief or resignation than despair. This is far removed from the foreign policy disasters of Weimar, which were truly "national humiliations."

Another circumstance historically associated with mass demagoguery is the deterioration of the "responsible" center parties. There is some evidence that points to a similar decay in the United States, such as identification with the two major parties has been in continuous decline since 1964. After every presidential landslide, however, there is a burst of speculation on the "decay of the two-party system," and, despite this, the defeated parties have always come back, often with notable vigor. The Republicans, after all, came back strongly after 16 years of the New Deal, then came back again, just as strongly, after the Goldwater debacle of 1964. Likewise, the Democrats recovered from Eisenhower's 1956 landslide and will no doubt recover from

McGovern as well. This is not to say that the dissolution of one of the major parties is impossible, only that, at the present time, it seems rather unlikely. The simultaneous collapse of both center parties, of course, is even less likely.

A third "dissimilarity" is that, historically at least, mass demagoguery has been most apparent where the decay of the center parties is accompanied by active insurgent parties at one or both extremes. Again, there is little evidence of any such development in the contemporary United States. The left parties that do exist are hopelessly weak and fractionated; much the same could be said for the insurgent parties on the right. The Communist Party of the United States of America, the American Nazi party, and the several dozen other "parties of dissent" are more a source of annoyance, if not of humor, than a real threat to the democratic regime. There is, of course, Wallace's American Independent party, the closest approximation to an active insurgent party currently present on the scene. Here the potential for disruption may be greater. On the other hand, however, no one has yet produced any persuasive evidence that Wallace's fate in the immediate future will be any different than his fate in 1968. Perhaps his chances would be better now than they were then, but no one has yet made a convincing case for this. A recent Harris poll, in fact, gives the contrary indication. The poll, released June 19, 1975, shows that a "53–31 percent majority now feels that Wallace is an 'extremist,' " up somewhat from the 48% plurality who felt that in June, 1974. Running as the nominee of the national Democratic party, the same poll has Wallace losing to Ford by a 60-31% majority, with a 46–47 split even in the south. It is very unlikely that he would do any better running as an Independent; in fact, it is quite likely that he would do much worse. The press release concludes that Wallace's reputation as an extremist "has plagued him in the past, and although he seemed close to overcoming it a year ago, it is now likely to ruin his chances in 1976."

One of the problems faced by insurgencies in the United States is that national parties do not really exist in the strict organizational sense. The national parties are really loose federations of 50 separate state organizations. This has two important implications. First, it means that insurgent movements will have difficulties in "capturing the party," since they have to capture not one but 50 parties. Second, it means that to build a third or a fourth party really implies building 50 such parties, putting together an effective organization not once but 50 consecutive times (Hamilton 1972). This will obviously be a formidable task, not that it cannot be done. Wallace showed that it is possible. But it cannot be done easily. In addition, as Wallace has also shown, the chances for success, once the energies and resources have been spent, are dim. This alone should be somewhat discouraging to other dissidents planning a similar strategy.

In terms of potential mass insurrection, probably the most serious development in this and most other advanced industrial democracies is the collapse of the world economic situation. Already, this has posed some problems for the stability of the British democratic regime and may have contributed to the recent Communist gains in Italy. Since the rate of unemployment in the United States is more than double that of any industrialized European democracy, it might initially be thought that the prospects for mass disruption would be even greater here. As we mentioned earlier, however, there is a recurrent perception in the United States that the political process is somewhat irrelevant to one's financial situation and standard of living, and this would normally be expected to dampen any disruptive potential. Likewise, without strong insurgent parties or working class organizations to capitalize on the situation, it is difficult to imagine that any ultimate instability will result. Where is the party or leader who seems capable of mobilizing economic discontent? The Democratic party might play such a role, but this would clearly not threaten the on-going political system. Conceivably, the American unions might lead a revolt of the working class, but this does not seem very probable. The major unions found themselves unable to endorse the McGovern "insurgency" in 1972; their active support of an even more radical movement, no matter what the economic situation, is unlikely. Wallace would no doubt be willing to lead a "little man's" revolt; indeed he probably sees this as his unique historical role. He has not, however, performed well in this role in the past, and he is not likely to do so in the future. As before, one can readily admit that there might well be some potential leader waiting in the wings to channel the discontent and to exploit it as a basis for mass political action. Obviously, if the economy continues to deteriorate, the chances for such insurgency increase accordingly. Even if the recession seriously worsens, for example, to the point where unemployment reaches the levels of the 1930s, the chances would still not be very great, to which the political history of that earlier depression attests. The 1930 depression, for all practical purposes, *ended* the various political insurgencies of the 1920s; a 1970s depression might well do the same for the insurgencies of the 1960s. Even this takes the argument farther than it needs to be taken. Already, the economic signs are growing brighter, and, as of this writing, the Republican incumbent is pulling ahead of the most popular Democratic contender. Is it possible that the final outcome of recent economic decay in the United States will be the return of a Republican administration to power? Presently, even this would have to be taken as an even-money bet.

There is one final condition present on the current American scene that makes mass extremism or demagoguery unlikely: On most significant issues of public policy, the majority (and often the *large* majority) *rejects* the "backward" or "unenlightened" option in favor of more moderate and progressive policy directives. This brings us to the final element in the argument, the possibility of worthwhile policy inputs from the masses. Suppose that there did occur some sharp increase in participation in the assenting half, such that the outcome of the political process roughly represented the "will of the whole society." Suppose, moreover, that the system was accustomed to pursuing the policy preferences expressed through the participation input. To what policies would we thereby be committed? How would they differ from what we have been committed to in the past?

First, American involvement in Vietnam would have been more quickly terminated. Elite policy from 1964 to 1970 was toward continued escalation; popular opinion in the same period abandoned the escalation option in sizable proportions. In 1970, the Republican president was asserting that Vietnam had been the nation's "finest hour." In that same year, 62% of the population believed that we "should have stayed out" of Vietnam in the first place, and about three-fourths *rejected* the escalation option. The 1970 SRC survey asked respondents to rate themselves on a 7 point "hawk–dove" scale. About two-fifths placed themselves on the side of "immediate withdrawal"; about a quarter placed themselves in the middle; and less than a third chose "complete military victory." Public opinion in the entire period of American involvement was consistently more dovish than official policy.

In the case of Vietnam, then, greater responsiveness on the part of elites would have had some major positive effects. There would have been less death and destruction. There would have been less domestic agitation. The tragedy of Kent State might have been avoided. The deterioration of the economy due to Vietnam might have been forestalled. The flow of world respect away from the United States might have been stanched. Johnson might have been re-elected to a second term; thus, Nixon and all that he has come to represent might have been avoided. The current situation of the United States in the world economy would almost certainly be brighter. Additional benefits flowing from any of these can only be imagined.

Likewise, the mass public was ready for *detente* long before elite policy moved clearly in this direction. One question along these lines asks whether "our government should sit down and talk to the leaders of the Communist countries and try to settle our differences" or whether "we should refuse to have anything to do with them." In 1964, the proportion favoring the flexible and conciliatory approach amounted to 88% of those with an opinion ($n = 1277$); the comparable figure for 1968 was 91% ($n = 1339$). A related question asks whether or not our farmers and businessmen should be allowed "to do business with communist countries as long as the goods are not used for military purposes." In 1968, a sizable minority (45%) favored this policy, by 1972, the proportion in favor rose to 65%. Large majorities in all years agreed that "we should give aid to foreign countries if they need help." In 1972, 77% ($n = 1066$) thought that "mainland China should be a member of the United Nations." What is absent from all these responses is the tough and punitive orientation that characterized elite opinion throughout the cold war era.

One area in which mass opinion is said to be particularly deficient concerns minority rights, tolerance of diversity, and related "civil liberties" issues.

The SRC surveys have asked respondents whether they "are primarily concerned with doing everything possible to protect the legal rights of those accused of commiting crimes" or whether "it is more important to stop criminal activity even at the risk of reducing the rights of the accused." Majorities in both 1970 and 1972 rejected the antilibertarian option. Of those with opinions, 49% in 1970 ($n = 1293$) and 46% in 1972 ($n = 1940$) thought it was more important to stop criminal activity. The remainder fell either midway between the options (17% and 19%, respectively) or were more concerned with protecting the rights of the accused (34% and 35%, respectively). A related set of items is included in the 1973 NORC General Social Survey ($n = 1504$). One item concerns allowing "a person to make a speech against churches and religion." About two-thirds (65%) said that this person should be allowed to speak. A similar proportion (61%) did *not* favor removing such a person's book from the libraries. A large minority (41%) favored allowing this person to teach in colleges and universities. (To be sure, 56% opposed this latter freedom.) A person who "favored government ownership of all the railroads and all big industries" fared even better. Large majorities supported his right to speak (77%), his right to teach (57%), and his right to have his book in the public library (71%). An "admitted Communist" enjoyed 60% support for his right to speak, 58% support for his right to publish, and 39% support for his right to teach. As "admitted homosexual" would have found 61% supporting his right to speak, 53% his right to publish, and 48% his right to teach (versus 47% opposing that right, with the remainder undecided.) There are, of course, "backward" minorities (and occasionally majorities) on all items mentioned here, and no purpose is served by denying their existence or ignoring their possible effects. But at the same time, it should be clear that these regressive measures are supported by *minorities*, not by the entire U.S. population.

The NORC items, of course, replicate the now classic Stouffer study of "Communism, Conformity, and Civil Liberties," a central text in the democratic elitism tradition. Data for Stouffer's study were collected in 1954, during the McCarthy period and at the height of the postwar "red scare." A direct comparison of the findings from that study with the NORC data collected two decades later shows an average increase in tolerant response of about 30 percentage points (Davis 1974). This has a number of implications. First, it indicates that mean and intolerant preferences are not necessarily social constants. The mass public is apparently "educable" in matters such as this. Second, judging from the Nixon–Mitchell "law and order" policies (for example, the Omnibus Crime Control Act of 1969, or their response to protestors and dissenters of all sorts) mass opinion on these issues is probably somewhat more enlightened than that of the political leadership. Finally, bleak references to the Stouffer study should now be suspended, since its findings no longer describe the opinions of the population.

On matters concerning the "welfare state," mass opinion again outstrips that of the political elite. The SRC has asked a question about federalized health care in every study since 1956 and has consistently found majority preference to lie in this direction. In 1968, the proportion feeling that the government "should help people get doctors and hospital care at low cost" amounted to 66% of those with an opinion on the issue ($n = 1220$). The comparable figure in 1956 was 67% ($n = 1407$). A somewhat different question in 1972 asks whether there should be "a government insurance plan which would cover all medical and hospital expenses." A 7-point self-rating found 46% of those with an opinion in favor of this, and 40% opposed, with the remaining 14% falling midway between the two positions ($n = 1112$). A comprehensive national health insurance program, of course, has been debated in every session of Congress since 1948 and has yet to become law. In this, elite policy has lagged far behind mass preference.

The potential contribution of federalized health care to the well-being of the American population is enormous. According to the latest United Nations figures, infant mortality is higher in the United States than in 25 other nations. Of these 25 nations, 20 have some form of national health care. Elite reticence on this means that more babies die each year than need to, and this situation is obviously something a decent and humane society should rectify.

On the matter of unnecessary death, public opinion concerning gun control might also be mentioned. Numerous surveys have documented public support for gun control legislation. The 1973 NORC survey contains one item that asks if respondents "would favor or oppose a law which would require a person to obtain a permit before he or she could buy a gun." About three-fourths of the population (73%) favor such legislation.

Finally, race is an issue upon which the mass public is said to be especially backward. At the best, the mass is thought to prefer that blacks be left to "pull themselves up by the bootstraps," and, at worst, that black advances be thwarted by whatever action is necessary. Along these latter lines, a particularly instructive question from the 1972 SRC survey reads:

> There is much discussion about the best way to deal with the problem of urban unrest and rioting. Some say it is more important to use all available force to maintain law and order—no matter what results. Others say it is more important to correct the problems of poverty and unemployment that give rise to these disturbances. Where would you place yourself on this scale?

This question contrasts a reasonable, humane, and intelligent option with a hard-line, militaristic option. Given the presumed "hysterical reactions" to racial unrest, however, it comes as something of a surprise to find the clear majority aligning itself with the more intelligent option. Respondents were again asked to rank themselves on a 7-point scale. The largest single group rated themselves as "1"—most in favor of solving the problems of poverty and unemployment. These decent and humane citizens constituted 30% of the total, in contrast to the 13% who gave themselves a "7"—most in favor of using all available force. Taking the "1s" through "3s" together, those favoring, at some level, "solving the problems" over "all available force" amounted to 53% of the population. An additional 14% ranked themselves at the midpoint of the scale, and yet another 13% had not given the problem sufficient thought to answer the question. This leaves a constituency of 20% supporting the option of all available force.

The 1972 SRC survey also contains a series of questions concerning why "on the average, white people get more of the 'good things in life' in America than black people." Respondents were asked what they thought was "the most important reason"; in this, they were to choose among several options. One explanation (following the Jensen–Herrnstein thesis) was that "blacks come from a less able race." This thesis was supported by 4%. Approximately 5% bought the "culture of poverty" argument that "black Americans teach their children" values and skills that do not prepare them for success. Another 5% suggested that "these differences are brought about by God." About a tenth blamed "a small group of powerful and wealthy white people who control things and act to keep blacks down." The two most common responses were, first, that "it's really a matter of some people not trying hard enough" (38%), and, second, that "generations of slavery and discrimination have created conditions that make it difficult for blacks to work their way out of the lower class" (37%). All figures are for white respondents only. Taking the three "liberal" options (differential values, small group of powerful people, slavery and discrimination), one finds a liberal majority of 51%.

Integration of public schools is perhaps the most hotly contested of all issues related to race. Public opposition to busing is often cited as the most visible symbol of white hostility on the racial issue. The 1972 SRC survey indeed confirms that public opposition to busing is widespread: A mere 9% thought integration was so important that busing was acceptable; 5% were ambivalent; 2% had given it no thought; and the remaining 84% were opposed to it, 74% registering the strongest opposition that the question would allow them.

It would be a mistake, however, to read this as overwhelming opposition to the *principle* of integrated schools. An earlier question in the same survey asked, "Do you think the government in Washington should see to it that white and black children go to the same schools or stay out of this area as it is not its business?" Again, the majority of those with an opinion registered some opposition (55%), but 45%—certainly a large minority—were, in principle, not opposed. Even this is a spurious "majority," since part of it is constituted of those who oppose integration per se and another part constituted by those who favor integration but oppose government intervention. A later question asks, "What about you, are you in favor of desegregation, strict segregation, or something in between?" The "strict segregationists" constituted 13% of the sample, with the remainder split between desegregation (42%) and "something in between" (46%).

Additional evidence is supplied by a Gallup poll released in October, 1973 (discussed in Greeley 1975). Gallup presented respondents with a series of alternatives to busing and then asked, "Which, if any, of these ways do you think would be best to achieve integration in public schools in terms of different economic and racial groups?" Among whites only, 19% said they were opposed to the integration of schools, and another 16% had no opinion on the issue. The most frequent response was "change school boundaries to allow more persons from different racial and economic groups to attend the same schools." This rather sensible and pragmatic option was chosen by 27%. There was an additional 21% who thought the best solution would be to "create more housing for low-income people in middle-income neighborhoods," another obviously sensible solution. Finally, there were 4% who favored busing and about 20% who favored some other technique. The intense hostility generated by the busing issue, in short, should not be interpreted as the manifestation of some underlying "racist" syndrome (see also Kelley 1974).

Schools are touchy subjects; they arouse concerns and anxieties that may or may not extend into other areas. As far as racial integration of schools is concerned, the worst one could conclude is a rough stand-off between liberal and illiberal forces on the principle and overwhelming opposition to busing as the means of implementation. On other racial matters, the liberal element constitutes nothing less than the overwhelming majority. One question asks, "Should the government support the right of black people to go to any hotel or restaurant they can afford, or should it stay out of this matter?" On this item, the liberal majority amounted to 72%. Another item gave people the option of either agreeing that "white people have a right to keep black people out of their neighborhoods if they want to" or that "black people have a right to live wherever they can afford, just like anybody else." Here the liberal majority amounted to 83%. A question asking whether the government in Washington "should make every possible effort to improve the social and economic position of blacks and other minority groups" or "not make any special effort because they should help themselves" found 34% in favor of every possible effort, 42% opposed to such effort, with the remaining 23% falling somewhere in between these two positions. The 1973 NORC study uncovers some similar patterns. Approximately 62% of the *whites only* said they would *not* favor laws prohibiting marriage between Negroes and whites; 65% of the whites would "not object at all" if a member of the family wanted to bring a black friend home for dinner.

Of course, one would be remiss not to mention the mean and petty responses that can also be found in survey materials such as this. Majority support for capital punishment still exists. In the 1973 NORC survey, 63% favored the death penalty for persons convicted of murder. Likewise, 73% felt that the courts do not deal "harshly enough" with criminals. Relatively few people embrace a progressive position when it comes to crime; most want it ended as quickly as possible, by whatever method seems necessary. On the other hand, if many of the other popular preferences discussed earlier were followed, there would very likely be a sharp reduction in criminal activity, and then it would matter less what the popular reactions to crime were. And at the same time, few progressive solutions to the crime problem have emanated so far from elite circles either. The Omnibus Crime Control Act mentioned earlier, with its famous "no-knock" provision, or the Law Enforcement Assistance Agency, dispenser of federal funds for the expansion of local police arsenals would be two examples of manifestly nonprogressive programs formulated and pursued by the elites.

It is not a matter, then, of flatly denying that backward preferences, even vicious and authoritarian preferences, exist among the mass. There is little question that they do. These preferences, however, coexist with many enlightened and progressive preferences as well. Moreover, the less than noble sentiment that is present must be evaluated against the background of the policies to which the political leadership has committed us. These policies indicate a certain residual "backwardness" in the latter circles as well. In short, there is no guarantee that elite preferences will necessarily and invariably be more enlightened than the policy preferences of the mass, and, in many cases, as the data discussed here suggest, quite the reverse may well be true. Likewise, there is no guarantee that greater popular participation and any attendant increase in the responsiveness of the regime would *necessarily* result in a more just and humane society, but neither can one be certain that it would not. All that can be concluded with any confidence is that a social, economic, and political system built upon the expressed preferences of the democratic majority would probably not be any worse, and could conceivably be much better, than the present system.

Persons or groups planning to embark upon some program of social or political change would, thus, do well to consider the following questions. First, are the desired changes, or the means by which they are to be accomplished, likely to result in some antidemocratic or extremist insurgency in the mass? For most purposes, anxiety on this score can apparently be dismissed. Certainly, the presence of the assenting half—the politically discontented mass in American society—in itself should impose no serious restrictions on what can or cannot be done. At the present, this half of the society amounts primarily to an immense untapped resource. Whether or not it could *ever* be tapped is quite another question. Once tapped, however, it is doubtful that the result would be some overt deterioration in the stability of liberal democratic institutions. Second, are the desired changes things that the mass needs or wants, things that are not needed or wanted but which the mass might tolerate, or things that would probably not be tolerated under any circumstances? By these criteria, programs for change fall into one of three categories: the easy, the possible, and the difficult.

The latter category probably contains far fewer progressive policies than is normally thought to be the case. Judging from the evidence, it would be difficult to erect a popular political movement based on the abolition of capital punishment, but it would probably not be so difficult to embark on policies that would reduce the need for capital punishment. Likewise, it would be very difficult to "mobilize the masses" on behalf of an expanded program of busing to achieve racial integration, but it would be considerably less difficult to embark on policies that, in the long run, would have the same effect. In these cases, the tactical problem is to avoid phrasing one's issues and solutions in terms that would provoke opposition that might otherwise lie dormant. To retreat from progressive change because of opposition that is largely illusory or that has been created on one's own is needlessly immobilizing.

Many of the changes that are normally thought to be difficult, if not impossible, actually fall into the category of things that the mass neither needs nor wants but would easily tolerate. Amnesty is one notable example. Prior to the announcement of Ford's limited amnesty program, all the available survey and poll evidence found large majorities opposed to the concept. In the 1972 SRC survey, for example, opposition on the issue ran to 72% of those who answered the question. Yet polls conducted in the weeks immediately following Ford's announcement found large majorities in *support* of the amnesty program. In the case of amnesty, what appeared to be overwhelming opposition turned out to be relatively "soft," not something that prevented the desired changes from occurring. It is doubtful that opposition to busing would have this same "soft" character, but the opposition to decriminalizing marijuana might. In such cases, it would obviously be unreasonable to expect the impetus for progressive change to arise among the mass, but, at the same time, it would be unwise to misread the character of any opposition that does exist. To do so is to forgo by default progressive change that might otherwise be possible.

The category of "easy" changes includes those issues where the potential for a sizable mass following exists. Among the progressive possibilities here would be federalized health care, stricter gun controls, and many of the other topics discussed earlier. That these changes have yet to occur is certainly not because mass opinion is somehow "deficient." These, too, are the kinds of changes most likely to result from democratizing the participation input.

In sum: Survey materials, such as those being discussed here, only indicate the raw materials available for the democratic political process. On their own, they guarantee nothing and rule nothing out. It is left to the politically active, to the organizers, to fashion this raw material into a finished political product. One possible approach would be to ignore the material altogether, in the hope that any latent undemocratic potential would thereby remain unprovoked. Given the evidence assembled here, however, this does not seem to be the wisest action to pursue. The alienated and discontented masses in modern American society do not appear to be lying in wait, nervous and anxious, ready to thwart any responsible policy initiative. For all intents and purposes, they are currently irrelevant to the on-going process. Whether their irrelevance could be reversed or their suspicions and hostilities overcome is not something that can be decided with the evidence at hand, although there are some clear indications as to how this *might* be accomplished. Assuming it were accomplished, however, the data speak more clearly: There is little reason to expect that any monumentally disruptive consequences would result. Obviously, it would be a serious tactical mistake to *over*estimate the political intelligence or capability of the mass. To do so would only lead to frustrating and immobilizing failures. To deny, however, that the "alienated masses" even have any intelligence, to hesitate in the face of an imaginary foe, and, thereby, simply to surrender the initiative for needed social and political changes is far more than a tactical mistake. It is an unnecessary and counter-productive insult to the common, ordinary people upon whom any democratic society must ultimately be erected.

References

Abcarian, G., and S. M. Stanage
    1965   "Alienation and the radical right." *Journal of Politics* 27 (November): 776–796.
Aberbach, J. D.
    1967   *Alienation and Race.* Unpublished doctoral dissertation. New Haven, Connecticut: Yale University.
    1969   "Alienation and political behavior." *American Political Science Review* 62 (March): 86–99.
Aberbach, J. D., and J. L. Walker
    1970   "Political trust and racial ideology." *American Political Science Review* 64 (December): 1199–1219.
Abramson, H. J.
    1973   *Ethnic Diversity in Catholic America.* New York: Wiley.
Adorno, T. W., E. Frenkel-Brunswik, D. J. Levison, and R. M. Sanford
    1950   *The Authoritarian Personality.* New York: W. W. Norton.
Agger, R. E., M. N. Goldstein, and S. Pearl
    1961   "Political cynicism: Measurement and meaning." *Journal of Politics* 23 (August): 477–506.
Agger, R. E., and V. Ostrom
    1956   "Political participation in a small community." Pp. 138–149 in Eulau, Eldersveld, and Janowitz (eds.), *Political Behavior.* New York: The Free Press.
Agnello, T. J.
    1973   "Aging and the sense of political powerlessness." *Public Opinion Quarterly* 37 (Summer): 251–259.
Aiken, M.
    1970   "The distribution of community power." Pp. 487–525 in M. Aiken and P. Mott (eds.), *The Structure of Community Power.* New York: Random House.
Aiken, M., and R. R. Alford
    1970a   "Community structure and innovation: The case of urban renewal." *American Sociological Review* 35 (August): 650–665.
    1970b   "Community structure and innovation: The case of public housing." *American Political Science Review* 64 (September): 843–864.
    1970c   "Community structure and the war on poverty." in Mattei Dogan (ed.), *Studies in Political Ecology.* Paris.
Aiken, M., L. A. Ferman, and H. L. Sheppard
    1968   *Economic Failure, Alienation and Extremism.* Ann Arbor: University of Michigan Press.
Aiken, M., and P. E. Mott, Eds.
    1970   *The Structure of Community Power.* New York: Random House.

Alford, R. R., and R. Friedland
1975   "Political participation." forthcoming in the *Annual Review of Sociology*, 1975.
Alford, R. R., and H. M. Scoble
1968   "Sources of local political involvement." *American Political Science Review* 62 (December): 1192–1206.
Almond, G., and S. Verba
1965   *The Civic Culture*. Boston, Massachusetts: Little, Brown.
Apter, D. E., Ed.
1964   *Ideology and Discontent*. New York: The Free Press.
Arcus, R., R. Tessler, and J. D. Wright
1975   "Misinformation as a source of opposition to fluoridation referenda: Testing an alternative to the 'alienated voter' hypothesis." Unpublished manuscript. Amherst, Massachusetts: University of Massachusetts.
Arendt, Hannah
1951   *The Origins of Totalitarianism*. Cleveland, Ohio: World Publishing Co.
Aronowitz, S.
1971   "Does the United States have a new working class?" Pp. 188–216 in G. Fischer (ed.), *The Revival of American Socialism*. New York: Oxford University Press.
1973   *False Promises: The Shaping of American Working Class Consciousness*. New York: McGraw-Hill.
Asher, H.
1974   "The reliability of the political efficacy items." *Political Methodology* 1 (Spring): 45–72.
Bachrach, P.
1967   *The Theory of Democratic Elitism*. Boston, Mass.: Little, Brown.
Balch, G. I.
1974   "Multiple indicators in survey research: The concept 'sense of political efficacy'." *Political Methodology* 1 (Spring): 1–43.
Bell, D.
1959   "The rediscovery of alienation: Some notes along the quest for the historical Marx." *Journal of Philosophy* 56 (November): 933–952.
Bell, D., Ed.
1964   *The Radical Right: The New American Right*. Garden City, New York: Doubleday.
Bendix, R.
1953   "Social stratification and political power." Pp. 596–609 in R. Bendix and S. M. Lipset (eds.), *Class, Status and Power*, 1st ed. New York: The Free Press.
Bendix, R., and S. M. Lipset, Eds.
1953   *Class, Status, and Power: A Reader in Social Stratification*, 1st ed. New York: The Free Press.
1959   "On the social structure of western societies: Some reflections on comparative analysis." *Berkeley Journal of Sociology* 5 (Fall): 1–15.
Berelson, B. R., P. F. Lazarsfeld, and W. N. McPhee
1954   *Voting: A Study of Opinion Formation in a Presidential Campaign*. Chicago, Illinois: University of Chicago Press.
Blau, P. M., and O. D. Duncan
1967   *The American Occupational Structure*. New York: Wiley.
Bohrnstedt, G. W.
1970   "Reliability and validity assessment in attitude measurement," Pp. 80–100

in G. Summers (ed.), *Attitude Measurement*. Chicago, Illinois: Rand Mcnally.

Bonjean, C., R. J. Hill, and S. McLemore
1967   *Sociological Measurement*. San Francisco, California: Chandler.

Booker, S.
1973   "Blacks remember the civil rights role of Lyndon B. Johnson." *Jet* (February 8): 14ff.

Boskoff, A., and H. L. Zeigler
1964   *Voting Patterns in a Local Election*. Philadelphia, Pennsylvania: Lippincott.

Boynton, G. R., S. C. Patterson, and R. D. Hedlund
1968   "The structure of public support for legislative institutions." *Midwest Journal of Political Science* 12 (May): 163–180.

Braungart, R. G.
1971   "Family status, socialization, and student politics: A multivariate analysis." *American Journal of Sociology* 77 (July): 108–130.

Brinton, Crane
1965   *The Anatomy of Revolution: Revised and Expanded Edition*. New York: Vintage Books.

Burdick, E., and A. J. Brodbeck, Eds.
1959   *American Voting Behavior*. New York: The Free Press.

Burnham, W. D.
1969   "The end of American party politics." *Transaction* 7 (December): 12–22.

Campbell, A.
1962   "The passive citizen." *Acta Sociologica* 6 (Spring): 9–21.
1971   *White Attitudes towards Black People*. Ann Arbor, Michigan: Institute for Social Research.

Campbell, A., and P. E. Converse, Eds.
1972   *The Human Meaning of Social Change*. New York: Russell Sage Foundation.

Campbell, A., P. W. Converse, W. E. Miller, and D. E. Stokes
1960   *The American Voter*. New York: Wiley.

Campbell, D., and D. Fiske
1970   "Convergent and discriminant validation by the multi-traitmultimethod matrix." Pp. 100–122 in G. Summers (ed.), *Attitude Measurement*. Chicago: Rand Mcnally.

Cantril, A. H., and C. W. Roll, Jr.
1971   *Hopes and Fears of the American People*. New York: Universe.

Carr, L.
1971   "The Srole items and acquiescence." *American Sociological Review* 36 (April): 287–293.

Christie, R., and M. Jahoda, Eds.
1954   *Studies in the Scope and Method of the Authoritarian Personality*. Glencoe, Illinois: The Free Press.

Citrin, J.
1974   "Comment: The political relevance of trust in government." *American Political Science Review* 68 (September): 973–988.

Cnudde, C. F., and D. E. Neubauer, Eds.
1969   *Empirical Democratic Theory*. Chicago, Illinois: Markham.

Coleman, J. S.
1963   "Comment on 'On the concept of influence'." *Public Opinion Quarterly* 27 (Spring): 63–82.

Converse, P. E.
1964   "The nature of belief systems in mass publics." Pp. 206–261 in D. Apter (ed.), *Ideology and Discontent*. New York: The Free Press.
1972   "Change in the American electorate." Pp. 263–337 in A. Campbell and

P. E. Converse (eds.), *The Human Meaning of Social Change*. New York: Russell Sage Foundation.

Converse, P. E., A. R. Clausen, and W. E. Miller
1965   "Electoral myth and reality: The 1964 election." *American Political Science Review* 59 (June): 321–336.

Converse, P. E., W. E. Miller, J. G. Rusk, and A. C. Wolfe
1969   "Continuity and change in American politics: Parties and issues in the 1968 election." *American Political Science Review* 63 (December): 1083–1105

Conway, M.
1968   "The white backlash reexamined: Wallace and the 1964 primaries." *Social Science Quarterly* 49 (December): 710–719.

Cummings, M. J., Jr., Ed.
1966   *The National Election of 1964*. Washington, DC: The Brookings Institution.

Curtis, J.
1971   "Voluntary association joining: A cross-national comparative note." *American Sociological Review* 36 (October): 872–880.

Cutler, N. E., and V. L. Bengston
1974   "Age and political alienation: Maturation, generation, and period effects." *The Annals* 415 (September): 160–175.

Dahrendorf, R.
1967   *Society and Democracy in Germany*. Garden City, New York: Doubleday.

Davis, J.
1974   "Tolerance of atheists and communists in 1954 and 1972–73." Mimeographed paper. National Opinion Research Center, University of Chicago.

Dean, D. G.
1960   "Alienation and political apathy." *Social Forces* 38 (March): 185–189.
1961   "Alienation: Its meaning and measurement." *American Sociological Review* 26 (October): 753–758.

Dempsey, J.
1975   *The Independent Voter*. Unpublished doctoral dissertation. Amherst, Massachusetts: University of Massachusetts, Department of Political Science.

Dizard, J. E.
1974   "Review of David Schwartz', *Political Alienation and Political Behavior.*" *American Journal of Sociology* 80 (November): 794–795.

Dodder, R. A.
1969   "A factor analysis of Dean's alienation scale." *Social Forces* 48 (December): 252–255.

Dogan, M., and S. Rokkan
1969   *Quantitative Ecological Analysis in the Social Sciences*. Cambridge, Massachusetts: MIT Press.

Donovan, B.
1971   "Press was caught off guard in massacre story." *Madison Capital Times* (September 18): 20.

Douvan, E., and A. Walker
1956   "The sense of effectiveness in political affairs." *Psychological Monographs* 70 (whole # 429): 1–19.

Draper, T.
1972   "The specter of Weimar." *Social Research* 39 (Summer): 322–340.

Duncan, O. D., and B. Davis (Duncan)
1953   "An alternative to ecological correlation." *American Sociological Review* 15 (June): 351–358.

Duncan, O. D., H. Schuman, and B. D. Duncan
1973   *Social Change in a Metropolitan Community*. New York: Russell Sage Foundation.

Dye, T. R., and L. H. Zeigler
1972   *The Irony of Democracy: An Uncommon Introduction to American Politics.* New York: Duxbury Press.

Easton, D.
1965   *A Systems Analysis of Political Life.* New York: Wiley.

Easton, D., and J. Dennis
1967   "The child's acquisition of regime norms: Political efficacy." *American Political Science Review* **61** (March): 25–38.
1969   *Children in the Political System.* New York: McGraw-Hill.

Eckhardt, K. W., and G. Hendershot
1967   "Transformation of alienation into public opinion." *Sociological Quarterly* **8** (Autumn): 459–467.

Edelman, M.
1971   *Politics as Symbolic Action: Mass Arousal and Quiescence.* Chicago: Markham.

Engels, F.
1968   *The Role of Force in History.* New York: International Publishers.

Erbe, W.
1964   "Social involvement and political activity." *American Sociological Review* **29** (February): 198–215.

Faris, R. E. L.
1967   *Chicago Sociology: 1920–1932.* Chicago, Illinois: University of Chicago Press.

Farris, C. D.
1960   "Selected attitudes on foreign affairs as correlates of authoritarianism and political anomie." *Journal of Politics* **22** (February): 50–67.

Fendrich, J. M., and L. J. Axelson
1971   "Marital status and political alienation among black veterans." *American Journal of Sociology* **77** (September): 245–261.

Field, J. O., and R. E. Anderson
1969   "Ideology in the public's conception of the 1964 election." *Public Opinion Quarterly* **33** (Fall): 380–398.

Finifter, A. W.
1970   "Dimensions of political alienation." *American Political Science Review* **64** (June): 389–410.

Finney, H. C.
1971   "Political libertarianism at Berkeley: An application of perspectives from the new student left." *Journal of Social Issues* **27** (Spring): 35–61.

Fischer, C. S.
1973a   "On urban alienations and anomie: Powerlessness and social isolation." *American Sociological Review* **38** (June): 311–326.
1973b   "Urban malaise." *Social Forces* **52** (December): 221–235.

Fischer, S. (ed.)
1971   *The Revival of American Socialism.* New York: Oxford University Press.

Flacks, R.
1967   "The liberated generation: An explanation of the roots of student protest." *Journal of Social Issues* **23** (Fall): 52–75.
1971   *Youth and Social Change.* Chicago: Markham.

Form, W. H., and J. Huber Rytina
1969   "Ideological beliefs on the distribution of power in the United States." *American Sociological Review* **34** (February): 19–31.
1971   "Income, race, and the ideology of political efficacy." *Journal of Politics* **33** (August): 659–688.

Fraser, J.
1970   "The mistrustful-efficacious hypothesis and political participation." *Journal of Politics* **33** (May): 444–449.
1971   "Personal and political meaning correlates of political cynicism." *Midwest Journal of Political Science* **15** (May): 347–364.
Fromm, E.
1941   *Escape from Freedom.* New York: Holt.
1955   *The Sane Society.* New York: Holt.
Galtung, J.
1964   "Foreign policy opinion as a function of social position." *Journal of Peace Research* **1**:3–4 (Winter): 206–231.
Gamson, W. A.
1968   *Power and Discontent.* Homewood, Illinois: The Dorsey Press.
Geiger, T.
1930   "Panik im Mittelstand." *Die Arbeit* **7**: 637–654.
Gerson, W. M.
1965   "Alienation in mass society: Some causes and consequences." *Sociology and Social Research* **49** (January): 143–152.
Glazer, N., and D. P. Moynihan
1970   *Beyond the Melting Pot,* 2nd ed. Cambridge, Massachusetts: MIT Press.
Glenn, N. D.
1967   "Massification vs. differentiation: Some trend data from national surveys." *Social Forces* **47** (December): 172–179.
1972   "Sources of the shift to political independence: Some evidence from a cohort analysis." *Social Science Quarterly* **53** (December): 494–519.
Gooding, J.
1972   "White collar woes and blue collar blues." Pp. 255–261 in R. C. Edwards, M. Reich, and T. E. Weisskopf (eds.), *The Capitalist System.* Englewood Cliffs, New Jersey: Prentice-Hall.
Goodman, L.
1959   "Some alternatives to ecological correlation." *American Journal of Sociology* **64** (May): 610–625.
Goudsblom, J.
1967   *Dutch Society.* New York: Random House.
Greeley, A. M.
1972a   "New ethnicity and blue collars." *Dissent* **19** (Winter): 270–277.
1972b   *The Denominational Society.* Glenview, Illinois: Scott, Foresman, and Company.
1972c   "Political attitudes among American white ethnics." *Public Opinion Quarterly* **36** (Summer): 213–220.
1974   *Ethnicity in the United States: A Preliminary Reconnaissance.* New York: Wiley.
1975   "A semi-'pelagian' view of the American people." Unpublished paper. National Opinion Research Center. Chicago, Illinois.
Greenberg, E. S.
1970   "Black children and the political system." *Public Opinion Quarterly* **34** (Fall): 333–345.
Gusfield, J. R.
1962   "Mass society and extremist politics." *American Sociological Review* **27** (February): 19–30.
Hamilton, H. D.
1971   "The municipal voter: Voting and non-voting in city elections." *American Political Science Review* **65** (December): 1135–1140.

Hamilton, R. F.
  1966   "The marginal middle class: A reconsideration." *American Sociological Review* **31** (April): 192–199.
  1968   "A research note on the mass support for 'tough' military initiatives." *American Sociological Review* **33** (June): 439–445.
  1971   "The 1968 election: Wallace and the working class." Unpublished manuscript. Montreal, Canada: McGill University, Department of Sociology.
  1972   *Class and Politics in the United States.* New York: Wiley.
  1975   *Restraining Myths.* Beverly Hills, California: Sage Publications.
  forthcoming *The Support for the National Socialists.*
Hamilton, R. F., and J. D. Wright
  1975a   *New Directions in Political Sociology.* Indianapolis, Indiana: Bobbs-Merrill.
  1975b   "The support for hardline foreign policy." Pp. 183–218 in R. F. Hamilton, *Restraining Myths.* Beverly Hills, California: Sage Publications.
Harwood, R.
  1971   "Press must wash its own face." *Madison Capital Times* (July 24).
Hawkins, B. W., V. L. Marando, and G. A. Taylor
  1971   "Efficacy, mistrust, and political participation: Findings from additional data and indicators." *Journal of Politics* **33** (November): 1130–1136.
Hawley, A.
  1963   "Community power and urban renewal success." *American Journal of Sociology* **68** (January): 422–431.
Hofstadter, R.
  1955   *The Age of Reform.* New York: Alfred A. Knopf.
Horan, P. M.
  1971   "Social positions and political cross-pressures: A re-examination." *American Sociological Review* **36** (August): 650–660.
Horowitz, I. L.
  1972   *Foundations of Political Sociology.* New York: Harper.
Horton, J. E., and W. E. Thompson
  1962   "Powerlessness and political negativism: A study of defeated local referendums." *American Journal of Sociology* **67** (March): 485–493.
House, J. S., and W. M. Mason
  1975   "Political alienation in America: 1952–1968." *American Sociological Review* **40** (April): 123–147.
Huber, J., and W. H. Form
  1972   *Income and Ideology.* New York: The Free Press.
Hughes, A.
  1967   "Authoritarian orientation, alienation, and political attitudes in a sample of Melbourne voters." *Australian and New Zealand Journal of Sociology* **3** (October): 134–149.
Hyman, H. H., and C. R. Wright
  1971   "Trends in voluntary association memberhips of American adults: Replication based on secondary analysis of national sample surveys." *American Sociological Review* **36** (April): 191–206.
Jackman, M.
  1972   "Social mobility and attitude toward the political system." *Social Forces* **50** (June): 462–472.
  1973   "Education and prejudice or education and response set?" *American Sociological Review* **38** (June): 327–339.
Janda, K.
  1965   "A comparative study of political alienation and voting behavior in three suburban communities." *Studies in History and the Social Sciences,* Normal,

REFERENCES **309**

Illinois: Illinois State University, Department of Social Sciences, Pp. 53–
67.
Jaros, D., H. Hirsch, and F. J. Fleron, Jr.
1968   "The malevolent leader: Political socialization in an American subculture."
American Political Science Review **62** (June): 564–575.
Jaros, D., and G. L. Mason
1969   "Party choice and support for demagogues: An experimental examination."
American Political Science Review **63** (March): 100–110.
Kelley, J.
1974   "The politics of school bussing." *Public Opinion Quarterly* **38** (Spring):
23–39.
Kelley, S., Jr.
1966   "The presidential campaign." Pp. 42–81 in M. J. Cummings (ed.), *The
National Election of 1964*. Washington, DC: The Brookings Institution.
Kelley, S., R. E. Ayres, and W. G. Bowen
1967   "Registration and voting: Putting first things first." *American Political
Science Review* **61** (June): 359–377.
Kelly, K. D., and W. J. Chambliss
1966   "Status consistency and political attitudes." *American Sociological Review*
31 (June): 375–382.
Keniston, K.
1965   *The Uncommitted*. New York: Harcourt.
1967   "The sources of student dissent." *Journal of Social Issues* **23** (Fall): 108–
137.
Key, V. O.
1961   *Public Opinion and American Democracy*. New York: Alfred A. Knopf.
Killian, L. M.
1968   *The Impossible Revolution? Black Power and the American Dream*. New
York: Random House.
1975   *The Impossible Revolution*, 2nd ed. New York: Random House.
Kish, L.
1965   *Survey Sampling*. New York: Wiley.
Komarovsky, M.
1946   "The voluntary association of urban dwellers." *American Sociological Review*
11 (December): 686–698.
Kornhauser, W.
1959   *The Politics of Mass Society*. New York: The Free Press.
Krickus, R. J.
1971   "White working class youth." *Dissent* **18** (October): 503ff.
Kritz, M.
1970   "The Wallace vote: The organizational factor." Unpublished Master's
thesis. Madison, Wisconsin: University of Wisconsin, Department of
Sociology.
Ladd, E. C.
1969   *Ideology in America: Change and Responses in a City, a Suburb, and a
Small Town*. New York: W. W. Norton.
Lane, R. E.
1965   "The politics of consensus in an age of affluence." *American Political
Science Review* **59** (December): 874–895.
Langton, K. P.
1969   *Political Socialization*. New York: Oxford University Press.
Lazarsfeld, P. F., B. Berelson, and H. Gaudet (Erskine)
1948   *The People's Choice*. New York: Columbia University Press.

LeBon, G.
1960   *The Crowd.* New York: Viking.
Lederer, E.
1967   *The State of the Masses: The Threat of a Classless Society.* New York: Howard Fertig.
Lenski, G.
1961   *The Religious Factor: A Sociologist's Inquiry.* Garden City, New York: Doubleday.
Levin, M. B.
1960   *The Alienated Voter: Politics in Boston.* New York: Holt.
Levin, M. B., and M. Eden
1962   "Political strategy for the alienated voter." *Public Opinion Quarterrly* 26 (Spring): 47–63.
Levine, H.
1974   "The culture of Fascism." *The Nation* 219 (August 17): 103–107.
Levine, R. A.
1971–72   "The Silent Majority: Neither simple nor simple-minded." *Public Opinion Quarterly* 35 (Winter): 571–577.
Levison, A.
1974   *The Working Class Majority.* New York: Coward, McCann, and Geohegan.
Levitan, S. A., Ed.
1971   *Blue Collar Workers: A Symposium on Middle America.* New York: McGraw-Hill.
Lippman, W.
1922   *Public Opinion.* New York: Macmillan.
Lipset, S. M.
1962   Introduction to R. Michels, pp. 15–39. *Political Parties.* New York: The Free Press.
1963a   *Political Man.* Garden City, New York: Doubleday.
1963b   "The sources of the 'radical right'." Pp. 307–371 in D. Bell (ed.), *The Radical Right: The New American Right.* Garden City, New York: Doubleday.
1967   "Political sociology," Pp. 438–499 in N. Smelser (ed.), *Sociology: An Introduction.* New York: Wiley.
1968   "Social class." *International Encyclopedia of the Social Sciences,* Volume 15. New York: Macmillan, pp. 296–316.
1970   *Revolution and Counter-Revolution.* Garden City, New York: Doubleday.
Lipset, S. M., and P. Altbach
1966   "US campus alienation." *New Society* 1 (September): 361–364.
Lipset, S. M., P. F. Lazarsfeld, A. H. Barton, and J. Linz
1954   "The psychology of voting: An analysis of political behavior." Chap. 30 in G. Lindzey (ed.), *Handbook of Social Psychology.* Reading, Massachusetts: Addison-Wesley,
Lipset, S. M., and E. Raab
1969   "The Wallace whitelash." *Transaction* 7 (December): 23–35.
1970   *The Politics of Unreason.* New York: Harper.
Lipset, S. M., M. Trow, and J. Coleman
1956   *Union Democracy: The Internal Politics of the International Typographers Union.* (Glencoe: The Free Press).
Lipsitz, L.
1965   "Working class authoritarianism: A re-evaluation." *American Sociological Review* 30 (February): 103–109.

Litt, E.
  1963a   "Civic education, community norms, and political indoctrination." *American Sociological Review* **28** (February): 69–75.
  1963b   "Political cynicism and political futility." *Journal of Politics* **25** (May): 312–323.
Litwak, E., N. Hooyman, and D. Warren
  1973   "Ideological complexity and middle-American rationality." *Public Opinion Quarterly* **37** (Fall): 317–332.
Luttbeg, N. R.
  1968   "The structure of beliefs among leaders and the public." *Public Opinion Quarterly* **32** (Fall): 398–409.
Lyons, S. R.
  1970   "The political socialization of ghetto children: Efficacy and cynicism." *Journal of Politics* **32** (May): 288–304.
Lystad, M. H.
  1969   *Social Aspects of Alienation: An Annotated Bibliography.* Washington, DC: US Government Printing Office.
  1972   "Social alienation: A review of current literature." *The Sociological Quarterly* **13** (Winter): 90–113.
Maccobby, M.
  1972   "Emotional attitudes and political choices." *Politics and Society* **2** (Winter): 209–239.
Mann, M.
  1970   "The social cohesion of liberal democracy." *American Sociological Review* **35** (June): 423–439.
Mannheim, K.
  1940   *Man and Society in an Age of Reconstruction.* London: Kegan, Paul, Trench, and Trubner.
Marcuse, H.
  1964   *One-Dimensional Man.* Boston, Massachusetts: Beacon Press.
Mason, G. L., and D. Jaros
  1969   "Alienation and support for demagogues." *Polity* **1** (Summer): 477–498.
Masotti, L., and D. Bowen, Eds.
  1968   *Riots and Rebellion: Civil Violence in the Urban Community.* Beverly Hills, California: Sage Publications.
Matthews, D. R.
  1954   *The Social Background of Political Decision Makers.* New York: Random House.
McCloskey, H.
  1964   "Consensus and ideology in American politics." *American Political Science Review* **58** (June): 361–382. References in the text are as reprinted in Cnudde and Neubauer (eds.) *Empirical Democratic Theory.* Chicago, Illinois: Markham, 268–302.
McDill, E. L.
  1961   "Anomie, authoritarianism, prejudice, and socioeconomic status." *Social Forces* **39** (March): 239–245.
McDill, E., and J. C. Ridley
  1962   "Status, anomia, political alienation, and political participation." *American Journal of Sociology* **68** (September): 205–213.
McKinney, J. C., and L. B. Bourque
  1971   "The changing south: National incorporation of a region." *American Sociological Review* **36** (June): 399–412.

McLeod, J., S. Ward, and K. Tancill
1965–66   "Alienation and the uses of the mass media." *Public Opinion Quarterly* 29 (Winter): 583–594.
Merriam, C. F., and H. F. Gosnell
1924   *Non-Voting.* Chicago, Illinois: University of Chicago Press.
Michels, R.
1962   *Political Parties.* New York: The Free Press.
Middleton, R. L.
1963   "Alienation, race, and education." *American Sociological Review* 28 (December): 973–977.
Milbrath, L. W.
1965   *Political Participation.* Chicago: Rand Mcnally.
Miller, A. H.
1974   "Political issues and trust in government: 1964–1970." *American Political Science Review* 68 (September): 951–972.
Miller, S. M., and F. Reissman
1961   "Working class authoritarianism: A critique of Lipset." *British Journal of Sociology* 12 (September): 267–268.
Mills, C. W.
1943   "The professional ideology of social pathologists." *American Journal of Sociology* 49 (September): 165–180.
1951   *White Collar.* New York: Oxford University Press.
1955   "The conservative mood." *Dissent* 1 (December): 22–31.
1956   *The Power Elite.* New York: Oxford University Press.
Mokken, R.
1971   *A Theory and Procedure of Scale Analysis.* The Hague: Mouton.
Monsma, S. V.
1971   "Potential leaders and democratic values." *Public Opinion Quarterly* 35 (Fall): 350–357.
Moore, B.
1958   *Political Power and Social Theory.* New York: Harper.
Mueller, J. N.
1971   "Trends in popular support for the wars in Korea and Vietnam." *American Political Science Review* 65 (June): 358–375.
Muller, E. N.
1970   "Correlates and consequences of beliefs in the legitimacy of regime structures." *Midwest Journal of Political Science* 14 (August): 392–412.
Natanson, M.
1967   "Alienation and social role." Pp. 255–268 in James Edie (ed.), *Phenomenology in America.* Chicago, Illinois: Quadrangle Paperbacks.
National Advisory Commission on Civil Disorders
1968   *Report.* New York: Bantam Books.
Neal, A. and M. Seeman
1964   "Organizations and powerlessness: A test of the mediation hypothesis." *American Sociological Review* 29 (February): 216–226.
Nelson, J. I.
1968   "Anomie: Comparisons between the old and new middle class." *American Journal of Sociology* 74 (September): 184–192.
Nettler, G.
1957   "A measure of alienation." *American Sociological Review* 22 (December): 670–677.

Nisbet, R. A.
1953   *The Quest for Community.* New York: Oxford University Press.
1966   *The Sociological Tradition.* New York: Basic Books.
Novak, M.
1971   *The Rise of the Unmeltable Ethnics.* New York: Macmillan.
O'Lessker, K.
1968   "Who voted for Hitler? A new look at the class basis of Naziism," *American Journal of Sociology* **74** (July): 63–69.
Olsen, M. E.
1965   "Alienation and political opinions." *Public Opinion Quarterly* **29** (Winter): 200–212.
1969   "Two categories of political alienation." *Social Forces* **47** (March): 288–299.
1970   "Social and political participation of blacks." *American Sociological Review* **35** (August): 682–697.
Oppenheimer, M.
1970   "White collar revisited: The making of a new working class." *Social Policy* 1 (July–August): 27–32.
1975   "The unionization of the professional." *Social Policy* **5** (January–February): 34–40.
Ortega y Gassett, J.
1957   *The Revolt of the Masses.* New York: W. W. Norton.
O'Toole, J., et alia
1973   *Work in America: Report of a Special Task Force to the Secretary of HEW.* Cambridge, Massachusetts: The MIT Press.
Padover, S. K., Ed.
1939   *Thomas Jefferson on Democracy.* New York: New American Library.
Paige, J. M.
1971   "Political orientation and riot participation." *American Sociological Review* **36** (October): 810–820.
Paletz, D. L., P. Reichert, and B. McIntyre
1971   "How the media support local government authority." *Public Opinion Quarterly* **35** (Spring): 80–92.
Parenti, M.
1967   "Ethnic politics and the persistence of ethnic identification." *American Political Science Review* **61** (September): 717–726.
Parker, R.
1972   "Those blue-collar worker blues." *The New Republic* (September): 16–21.
Parsons, T.
1951   *The Social System.* New York: The Free Press.
1964   "Social strains in America." Pp. 209–238 in Bell (ed.), *The Radical Right.* Garden City, New York: Doubleday.
1967   *Sociological Theory and Modern Society.* New York: The Free Press.
1970   "Equality and inequality in modern society, or social stratification revisited." *Sociological Inquiry* **40** (Spring): 13–72.
Parsons, T., E. Shils, K. D. Naegele, and J. R. Pitts
1961   *Theories of Society.* New York: The Free Press.
Peabody, D.
1961   "Attitude content and agreement set in scales of authoritarianism, dogmatism, anti-Semitism, and economic conservatism." *Journal of Abnormal and Social Psychology* **63** (July): 1–11.

Pettigrew, T. F., R. T. Riley, and R. D. Vanneman
    1972   "George Wallace's constituents." *Psychology Today* (February): 47ff.
Phillips, W. R.
    1970   *Joining Organizations and Feeling Politically Powerful*. Unpublished doctoral dissertation. Madison, Wisconsin: University of Wisconsin.
Pierce, J. C., and D. D. Rose
    1974   "Nonattitudes and American public opinion: The examination of a thesis." *American Political Science Review* 68 (June): 626–649.
Pinard, M.
    1968   "Mass society and political movements: A new formulation." *American Journal of Sociology* 73 (May): 682–690.
Polsby, N.
    1960   "Towards an explanation of McCarthyism." *Political Studies* 8 (October): 250–271.
    1966   "Strategic considerations." Pp. 82–110 in Cummings (ed.), *The National Election of 1964*. Washington: The Brookings Institution.
Pool, I., R. P., Abelson, and S. Popkin
    1965   *Candidates, Issues, and Strategies*. Cambridge, Massachusetts: MIT Press.
Prothro, J. W., and C. M. Grigg
    1960   "Fundamental principles of democracy: Bases of agreement and disagreement." *Journal of Politics* 22 (May): 276–294.
Quinney, R.
    1964   "Political conservatism, alienation and fatalism: Contingencies of social status and religious fundamentalism." *Sociometry* 27 (September): 372–381.
Rallings, C. S.
    1974   "'Two types of middle-class Labour voter?" *British Journal of Political Science* 5 (April): 107–112.
Ransford, H. E.
    1967–68   "Isolation, powerlessness, and violence: A study of attitudes and participation in the Watts riot." *American Journal of Sociology* 73 (January): 581–591.
Reagan, M.
    1956   "America as a 'mass society'." *Dissent* 3 (Fall): 346–356.
Reissman, F.
    1972   "The backward vanguard." *Society* 10 (November–December): 104–106.
Reiter, H. L.
    1971   "Blue collar workers and the future of American politics." Pp. 101–129 in Levitan (ed.), *Blue Collar Workers*. New York: McGraw-Hill.
Robinson, J. P.
    1970   "Public reaction to political protest: Chicago 1968." *Public Opinion Quarterly* 34 (Spring): 1–9.
Robinson, J. P., J. G. Rusk, and K. B. Head
    1968   *Measures of Political Attitudes*. Ann Arbor, Michigan: Institute for Social Research.
Robinson, P. A.
    1969   *The Freudian Left: Wilhelm Reich, Geza Roheim, Herbert Marcuse*. New York: Harper.
Robinson, W. S.
    1950   "Ecological correlations and behavior of individuals." *American Sociological Review* 15 (June): 351–358.
Rogin, M.
    1966   "Wallace and the middle class: The white backlash in Wisconsin." *Public Opinion Quarterly* 30 (Spring): 98–108.

1967   *The Intellectuals and McCarthy: The Radical Specter.* Cambridge, Massachusetts: The MIT Press.

1969   "Politics, emotion and the Wallace vote." *British Journal of Sociology* 20 (March): 27–49.

Rohter, I. S.
1969   "Social and psychological determinants of radical rightism." Pp. 193–237 in Schoenberger (ed.), *The American Right Wing.* New York: Holt.

Rokkan, S.
1964   "Review of *The Civic Culture,*" *American Political Science Review* 57:3 (September), 676–679.

Rose, A. M.
1968   *The Power Structure.* New York: Oxford University Press.

Rosenberg, M.
1954   "Some determinants of political apathy." *Public Opinion Quarterly* 18 (Winter): 349–366.

1956   "Misanthropy and political ideology." *American Sociological Review* 21 (December): 690–695.

Roszak, T.
1968   *The Making of a Counter-Culture.* Garden City, New York: Doubleday.

Rotter, J. B.
1966   "'Generalized expectancies for internal vs. external control of reinforcements." *Psychological Monograph* 80 (Whole # 609): 1–28.

Rowan, C. T.
1960   "Who will get the Negro vote?" *Ebony* (November): 40–49.

Rytina, J. H., W. H. Form, and J. Pease
1970   "Income and stratification ideology: Beliefs about the American opportunity structure." *American Journal of Sociology* 75 (Part Two): 703–716.

Sapolsky, H. M.
1969   "The flouridation controversy: An alternative explanation." *Public Opinion Quarterly* 33 (Summer): 240–248.

Schnaiberg, A.
1969   "A critique of Karl O'Lessker's 'Who voted for Hitler?'" *American Journal of Sociology* 74 (May): 732–735.

Schoenberger, R. A., Ed.
1969   *The American Right Wing.* New York: Holt.

Schooler, C.
1968   "A note of extreme caution on the use of Guttman scales." *American Journal of Sociology* 74 (November): 296–301.

Schuler, E. A., T. F. Hoult, D. L. Gibson, M.L. Fiero, and W. B. Brookover, Eds.
1960   *Readings in Sociology: Second Edition.* New York: Crowell-Collier.

Schulman, J.
1968   "Ghetto area residence, political alienation, and riot participation," Pp. 261–284 in L. Masotti and D. Bowen (eds.), *Riots and Rebellion.* Beverly Hills, California: Sage Publications.

Schuman, H.
1972   "Two sources of anti-war sentiment in America." *American Journal of Sociology* 78 (November): 513–535.

Schwartz, D. C.
1973   *Political Alienation and Political Behavior.* Chicago: Aldine.

Searing, D. D., J. J. Schwartz, and A. E. Lind
1973   "The structuring principle: Political socialization and belief systems." *American Political Science Review* 67 (June): 415–432.

Seeman, M.
1959   "On the meaning of alienation." *American Sociological Review* 24 (December): 783–791.
1972   "The signals of '68: Alienation in pre-crisis France." *American Sociological Review* 37 (August): 385–402.

Segal, D. R.
1969   "Status inconsistency, cross-pressures, and American political behavior." *American Sociological Review* 34 (June): 352–359.

Selznick, G. J., and S. Steinberg
1969   *The Tenacity of Prejudice: Anti-Semitism in Contemporary America.* New York: Harper.

Selznick, P. M.
1949   *The Organizational Weapon.* Glencoe, Illinois: The Free Press.
1951   "Institutional vulnerability in mass society." *American Journal of Sociology* 56 (January): 320–331.

Sherrill, R.
1968   *Gothic Politics in the Deep South.* New York: Ballantine Books.

Shively, W. P.
1972   "Party identification, party choice, and voting stability: The Weimar case." *American Political Science Review* 66 (December): 1203–1225.

Simmons, J. L.
1966   "Some inter-correlations among 'alienation' measures." *Social Forces* 44 (March): 370–372.

Simon, W., and J. Gagnon
1970   "Working class youth: Alienation without an image." Pp. 45–59 in L. K. Howe (ed.), *The White Majority: Between Poverty and Affluence.* New York: Random House.

Simpson, M. E.
1970   "Social mobility, normlessness, and powerlessness in two cultural contexts." *American Sociological Review* 35 (December): 1002–1013.

Smelser, N. J., Ed.
1967   *Sociology: An Introduction.* New York: Wiley.

Smith, C., and F. Freedman
1972   *Voluntary Associations: Perspectives on the Literature.* Cambridge, Massachusetts: Harvard University Press.

Sokol, R.
1968   "Power orientation and McCarthyism." *American Journal of Sociology* 73 (January): 443–452.

St. Angelo, D., and J. W. Dyson
1968   "Personality and political orientation." *Midwest Journal of Political Science* 12 (May): 202–223.

Stodder, J.
1973   "Old and new working class." *Socialist Revolution* 3 (September–October): 99–110.

Stokes, D. E.
1962   "Popular evaluations of government." in H. Cleveland and H. Lasswell (eds.), *Ethics and Bigness.* New York: Harper.

Stone, C. N.
1965   "Local referendums: An alternative to the alienated voter model." *Public Opinion Quarterly* 29 (Summer): 213–222.

Stouffer, S.
1954   *Communism, Conformity, and Civil Liberties.* Garden City, New York: Doubleday.

Summers, G., Ed.
1970   *Attitude Measurement*. Chicago: Rand Mcnally.
Szymanski, A.
1972   "Trends in the American class structure." *Socialist Revolution* 2 (July–August): 101–122.
Templeton, F.
1966   "Alienation and political participation: Some research findings." *Public Opinion Quarterly* 30 (Summer): 249–261.
Thompson, W. E., and J. E. Horton
1960   "Political alienation as a force in political action." *Social Forces* 38 (March): 190–195.
Thomson, C. A. H.
1966   "Mass media performance." Pp. 111–157 in Cummings (ed.), *The National Election of 1964*. Washington, DC: The Brookings Institution.
Treiman, D. J.
1970   "Industrialization and social stratification." *Sociological Inquiry* 40 (Spring): 207–234.
Trow, M.
1958   "Small businessmen, political tolerance, and support for McCarthy." *American Journal of Sociology* 64 (November): 270–281.
Verba, S.
1965   "Organizational membership and democratic consensus." *Journal of Politics* 27 (August): 467–497.
Verba, S., R. Brody, E. Parker, N. Nie, N. Polsby, P. Eckman, and G. Black
1967   "Public opinion and the war in Vietnam." *American Political Science Review* 61 (June): 317–333.
Verba, S., and N. H. Nie
1972   *Participation in America: Political Democracy and Social Equality*. New York: Harper.
Viereck, P.
1941   *Meta-Politics: The Roots of the Nazi Mind*. New York: Alfred A. Knopf.
1962   *The Unadjusted Man*. New York: Putnam.
Watson, B., and W. Tarr
1964   *The Social Sciences and American Civilization*. New York: Wiley.
Watts, M. W.
1973   "Efficacy, trust, and commitment to the political process." *Social Science Quarterly* 54 (December): 623–631.
Westby, D. L., and R. G. Braungart
1966   "Class and politics in the family backgrounds of student political activists." *American Sociological Review* 31 (October): 690–692.
Widich, B. J.
1972   "The men won't toe the Vega line." *The Nation* (March 27): 403–404.
Williams, W. A.
1966   *The Contours of American History*. Chicago, Illinois: Quadrangle Paperbacks.
Wittman, D. A.
1973   "Parties as utility maximizers." *American Political Science Review* 67 (June): 490–498.
Wolfinger, R. E., B. K. Wolfinger, K. Prewitt, and S. Rosenhack
1964   "America's radical right: Politics and ideology." Pp. 262–293 in D. Apter (ed.), *Ideology and Discontent*. New York: The Free Press.
Wright, C. R., and H. H. Hyman
1958   "Association memberships of American adults: Evidence from national

sample surveys." *American Sociological Review* **23** (June): 284–294.
Wright, J. D.
1972a   "Life, time, and the fortunes of war." *Transaction* **9** (January): 42–52.
1972b   "The working class, authoritarianism, and the war in Vietnam." *Social Problems* **20** (Fall): 133–150.
1972c   "Popular misconceptions, public opinion, and the war in Vietnam: Age, class, and trends in support, 1964–1970." Paper read at the annual meetings of the Society for the Study of Social Problems, New Orleans, Louisiana (August, 1972).
1973a   "On the mobilizability of the politically alienated." Paper read at the annual meetings of the Midwestern Sociological Society, Milwaukee, Wisconsin (April, 1973).
1973b   *Political Alienation in the United States: 1956–1970.* Doctoral dissertation. Madison, Wisconsin: University of Wisconsin.
1975a   "Political socialization research: The 'primacy' principle." *Social Forces* **54** (September): 243–255.
1975b   "The socio-political attitudes of white, college educated youth." *Youth and Society* **6** (March): 251–296.
1975c   "Does acquiescence bias the 'Index of Political Effcacy?" *Public Opinion Quarterly* **39** (Summer): 219–226.
1976   "Alienation and political negativism: New evidence from national surveys," *Sociology and Social Research* **60** (January): in press.
Wright, J. D., and N. Danigelis
1974   "Social trends and sociological research." Paper read at the annual meetings of the American Sociological Association, Montreal, Quebec (August).
Wrong, D.
1954   "Theories of McCarthyism—A survey." *Dissent* **1** (Autumn): 385–392.
Yankelovich, D.
1974   *The New Morality: A Profile of American Youth in the '70's* New York: McGraw-Hill.

Author Index

Subject Index

QUANTITATIVE STUDIES IN SOCIAL RELATIONS

Consulting Editor: Peter H. Rossi

UNIVERSITY OF MASSACHUSETTS
AMHERST, MASSACHUSETTS

A 6
B 7
C 8
D 9
E 0
F 1
G 2
H 3
I 4
J 5